D1525423

The Queen of
American Agriculture

The Founders Series

The Queen of American Agriculture

A Biography of
Virginia Claypool Meredith

FREDERICK WHITFORD
ANDREW G. MARTIN
PHYLLIS MATTHEIS

Purdue University Press
West Lafayette, Indiana

Printed in the United States of America.

ISBN 978-1-55753-512-2 (special edition leather)
ISBN 978-1-55753-518-4 (hardcover with dust jacket)

Design by Dawn L. Minns

Library of Congress Cataloging-in-Publication Data

Whitford, Fred, 1955-
The queen of American agriculture : a biography of Virginia Claypool Meredith /
Frederick Whitford, Andrew G. Martin, and Phyllis B. Mattheis.
    p. cm. ~ (Founders series)
  Includes bibliographical references.
  ISBN 978-1-55753-512-2
  1. Meredith, Virginia Claypool, 1848-1936. 2. Women in agriculture~Indiana~Biogra-
phy. I. Martin, Andrew G. II. Mattheis, Phyllis B. III. Title. IV. Series.
  S417.M43W47 2008
  630.92~dc22   2008005594

DEDICATION

*This biography is dedicated to Purdue University Extension
educators, campus Extension specialists, paraprofessionals, and
volunteers who help others realize their potential, turn dreams
into realities, and make the seemingly impossible possible.
It is this extended Extension family who truly believes that
education has no bounds in what it can do to improve the
lives of Indiana's citizens and their communities.*

In honor of the memory of
Steve Salomon
*May 18, 1957–August 13, 2007
We'll never forget your love for Indiana agriculture.*

CONTENTS

ACKNOWLEDGMENTS

THE AUTHORS WOULD LIKE TO GIVE SPECIAL THANKS to Robert Miller, the great-nephew of Virginia Meredith, and his daughter, Virginia Nilles, who allowed us to visit with them and see their memorabilia from the Meredith family.

We would be remiss if the editor of our book, Carolyn McGrew, was not mentioned. Her professional editing and her willingness to go beyond just the words helped to make the life of Virginia Meredith a more cohesive and easier-to-read biography.

Special recognition goes to Dawn L. Minns for her artistic talents in designing the dust jacket and the layout of the book. Thank you also to Marilyn Augst of Prairie Moon Indexing for preparing the index.

The following individuals provided important contributions and assistance in the development of this biography on Virginia Meredith:

Anne Marie Chase, Chicago History Museum
Christine Chouccoli, Warren County–Vicksburg Public Library
Joanne Goode, Glendale Historic Preservation, Glendale, Ohio
Constance Gordon, Special Collections and Preservation Division,
    Harold Washington Library Center, Chicago, Illinois
Lori Griffin, Cambridge City (Ind.) Library, History Room volunteer
Lois Hendrickson, University Archives, University of Minnesota
Patty Hersberger, Cambridge City (Ind.) Library, History Room volunteer
Sue King, Archivist, Morrisson-Reeves Library, Richmond, Indiana
Roberta Lemley, Cambridge City (Ind.) Library, History Room volunteer
Lesley A. Martin, Chicago History Museum
Sammie Morris, Archivist, Purdue University Special Collections
Debbie Vaughan, Chicago History Museum
Phyllis Webster, Mason, Michigan
Elizabeth Wilkinson, Manuscript Librarian, Indiana State Library
Ashley Woodward, Purdue University

INTRODUCTION

Yes, I am a farmer, and proud of it.
—Virginia Meredith, *Dignam's Magazine,* September 1905

V IRGINIA CLAYPOOL MEREDITH'S life in 1882 was turned upside down when her husband, Henry, who had been ill for nearly two weeks, died at their farm. Leaning on a fence, she pondered her future as much of the nationally acclaimed Oakland Farm—now hers by inheritance—spread out before her view. At the age of thirty-three, Virginia Meredith had come to a crossroads. She looked back toward the beautiful Federal-style home that her father-in-law, General Solomon Meredith, had purchased years before and thought of all the important guests—politicians, livestock breeders, and farmers—who had been entertained there. If she kept the home and farm, she would be solely responsible for the upkeep of a significant property.

There were 115 acres in pasture where prize Shorthorns and Southdown sheep lazily grazed across the fields. Virginia wondered and worried whether she could continue to improve upon the livestock breeding program that her father-in-law and husband had so diligently undertaken to make Oakland Farm a place that breeders from around the country visited to seek advice and purchase livestock.

If she kept the farm, she would undoubtedly hear from those around her that a woman's role was to manage the home, not the fields and livestock. But Virginia took strength in the advice that her father, Austin Claypool, had continuously stressed to her early in life: a woman could do anything that she put her mind to. Claypool, a successful grain farmer in his own right, had taught her all that he knew about farming, politics, and the value of education.

It came to her after much deliberation that she would accept the challenge of keeping and maintaining the farm herself. This single decision to run Oakland Farm would change her life forever. It would take some time, but Virginia Claypool Meredith would eventually emerge from the shadows of her husband and father-in-law. She would become something of a celebrity in her own right as she crisscrossed the country speaking on agricultural production and the farm home.

Her role in directly managing the affairs of a large and prosperous farm in east-central Indiana opened doors that were too often closed to women of her time. As her fame spread across the Midwest, her presentations began to focus more on the need for education of women, in general, and rural women, in particular. While striving to change society's expectations for women, she also gave a voice to the important role of women in the home. It would take a lifetime of work, but Virginia Meredith would become known as "the most remarkable woman in Indiana" and be called the "Queen of American Agriculture."[1]

Mention her name today and her achievements are also remembered because of her association with Purdue University: the first woman appointed to serve on the university's board of trustees, a residence hall named in her honor, and the collaborative work with her adopted daughter, Mary L. Matthews, in creating the School of Home Economics, the predecessor of today's College of Consumer and Family Sciences.

Unfortunately, Meredith's personal papers and letters were destroyed by fire, so the details of her life can only be reconstructed using widely scattered old manuscripts, newspaper clippings, and magazine articles. Pieced together, these writings bring life to this noteworthy woman, showing us how, by all accounts, she unlocked doors for women of the next generation. By force of her personality, her extensive knowledge of agriculture, and her dogged determination, she became a voice for rural people.

In those days following her husband's death, Virginia Claypool Meredith was surely unaware of the journey upon which she was about to embark. This biography attempts to chronicle her journey and her remarkable life.

Farm and Family

A Hoosier Family's Rise to Prominence

CHAPTER 1

*Mrs. Meredith firmly believes that farming
is a vocation peculiarly adapted to women, first,
because their "work is not discounted on account of sex.
A bushel of wheat brings market price; a cow makes as many—
or more—pounds of butter when owned by a woman,
as when owned by a man."*

—Interview with Virginia Meredith, *Indianapolis News,* 3 January 1900

VIRGINIA CLAYPOOL'S ANCESTORS were early pioneers in east-central Indiana at the turn of the nineteenth century. Successful, wealthy, powerful, and influential describe the early Claypool family, who established themselves and generations to follow as accomplished business owners, esteemed farmers and stock breeders, and effective politicians. The Claypools were heavily invested in railroads, banks, sawmills, taverns, and farm property. As their farms and businesses prospered, their prominence and visibility soon led to them being elected to political office at all levels of government. Virginia Claypool Meredith's birth to this prominent family with historic roots in Indiana had a tremendous impact on her views and outlook on life.

Virginia's grandfather, Newton Claypool (1795–1864), was born in Randolph County in western Virginia, and in 1799, at the age of four, moved with his father to Ohio.[1] Little is known about Newton's childhood, but records show that, as a young adult, he purchased a tract of land in Fayette County just months prior to Indiana's admission into the Union on December 11, 1816.[2]

In order to bring his bride-to-be from her home in Ohio, Newton needed to build a cabin for her on the Indiana frontier. He rose early in the morning and worked into the evening to cut enough trees for the cabin, and early on, he encountered a difficult problem: the only sawmill around his property was backlogged with orders. He knew that to wait his turn for his logs to be sawed at the mill would delay his dream of starting a new life in Indiana.

The imaginative Newton Claypool would not be deterred. He struck a rather simple deal with the owner of the sawmill. Newton rented the sawmill, where he "sawed at night the lumber of the house he planned to build." [3]

In 1818, the twenty-three-year-old Newton returned east to marry his Ohio sweetheart, Mary Kerns, on January 8. Husband and wife loaded their possessions onto their horses and set out on the journey to their new home.[4] Together they traveled 200 miles on horseback to reach their cabin in the sparsely populated backwoods near a "little village of a few houses, called Connersville." [5]

Life in general was difficult for the pioneers as they tried making a living growing crops and raising livestock on land that just a few years back had been prairies, sloughs, and woodlands. Neighbors often were isolated by miles. Few physicians were available to treat sick patients, and sadly, children often failed to live through infancy. For many, going to town to purchase store-bought products required a wagon with a team of horses, leaving early in the morning and sometimes returning late at night on nearly impassable roads. But people like Newton Claypool and his wife had the grit, determination, and fortitude to overcome the countless obstacles they faced every day.

Newton quickly established himself as a successful livestock farmer and hog dealer in the region. He also worked alongside his brother, Solomon Claypool, managing a dry goods store in Connersville until 1836, where they traded with local people, including Native Americans.[6] Newton's hard work soon made him a prominent and highly respected man in and around Connersville.

Success in business soon led Newton to try his hand at politics. In 1819, the young Newton campaigned and was elected the first county treasurer of Fayette County, a position he held for five years. He went on to become a member of the Indiana House of Representatives, where he served from 1825 to 1828 and again from 1842 to 1845. He also served three terms in the Indiana Senate from 1828 to 1831 and another from 1836 to 1837, when he was elected to fill the seat of a state senator who had resigned his position in the legislature.[7]

And while his political stature grew, his wealth also continued to grow. His disposable income allowed him to purchase a home in Indianapolis, the "historic house where Lincoln stayed when he spoke in the city." [8] He resided there during his work in the statehouse, rather than commuting back home to his farm. In 1836, at the end of his senate term, Newton purchased a farm just north of Connersville, where he would build Maplewood, a home that would eventually be passed down to his son, Austin, and granddaughter, Elizabeth Claypool Earl.

Throughout his career, Newton stayed involved with local agricultural issues that impacted the farming community in the Fayette County area, and following his time at the statehouse, he was elected president of the Fayette County Agricultural Society in 1854.[9] During the mid-1800s and well into the early 1900s, a person's political prominence in agriculture was linked to membership and involvement in county agricultural associations such as this, and those who rose within the ranks of the local societies often became elected delegates to the politically powerful and influential Indiana State Board of Agriculture. For a brief period in 1852, Newton Claypool became a delegate to this board, which was composed of leading farmers from around the state. Board members worked with politicians to advance the cause of farming within the state through conferences and meetings designed to address the concerns of the farming community.

Newton "was reasonably successful, leaving at his death, which occurred May 14, 1864, a very considerable estate."[10] By all indications, Newton Claypool had become rather wealthy through shrewd investments in taverns, stores, and the turnpike from Connersville to Milton, and as the founder of the First National Bank of Connersville.[11]

Newton Claypool, in many ways, linked the past to the future. Newton, like his father, Abraham Claypool (1762–1845), set the benchmark for future generations of Claypools by becoming politically involved and seeking public office. However, Newton paved the way for his family to become business owners as well as politicians. Newton's wealth propelled the Claypool family, including granddaughter Virginia, into the upper social echelons of important families.

Austin Claypool (1823–1906), Virginia Meredith's father, was one of ten children born to Newton and Mary Claypool. By the time of Austin's birth, Newton had already established himself as a success in the Connersville community and in politics. Growing up, Austin benefited greatly from his father's wealth and influence as well as from his accomplishments.

> Growing up in a home of culture and refinement, . . . Mr. [Austin] Claypool
> was not only a well educated man for his day but he was rich in the experi-
> ences with intimate contacts with men of important affairs throughout a
> long and busy life had brought him.[12]

It was only natural that Austin would follow in his father's footsteps. As a young
man, Austin soon became responsible for buying cattle and selling them for
profit in the markets in and around Cincinnati, Ohio.[13]

On May 20, 1846, Austin married Hannah Ann Petty, the daughter of a
well-known pork trader and packer, Williams Petty, and his wife, Elizabeth.
Eight children were born to Hannah and Austin Claypool, but only four—two
boys and two girls—survived to adulthood: Virginia, Frank, Elizabeth, and
Marcus.

Austin's business accomplishments grew along with his family. By all
accounts, he greatly profited from buying and selling farmland. Records show
he seldom made a bad investment or lost money in a business transaction.
Indeed, Austin had learned well from his father.

> The greater portion of the decade succeeding his marriage Mr. Claypool
> resided in Wayne County, Ind., and up to its close he had speculated quite
> extensively in land, having in 1845 purchased 240 acres in Fayette County,
> which were not held long. Subsequently he made a purchase of 560 acres
> in Wayne County at $30 per acre, which he disposed of at $70 per acre.
> . . . During the [Civil] war his business life was again marked by another
> extensive land purchase and sale which involved considerable money and
> none the less business judgment and foresight, yet he was not wanting
> in the latter nor in nerve for so great an investment, for time proved the
> success of the speculation, which was the purchase of 900 acres of land in
> Fayette County for $52,000 and its disposal for $72,000.[14]

His financial success in farming provided the capital to invest in banks and
other ventures such as paper mills, railroads, and turnpikes.[15] Austin and Hannah provided a very comfortable lifestyle for their children. In fact, all of
Austin's children "graduated from good institutions of learning."[16]

Austin achieved local renown as a grain farmer, eventually acquiring
several "large farm operations in Wayne and Fayette counties."[17] As his operation grew, so did his reputation. At the age of 35, he won the Best Ten Acres
of Oats at the 1858 Indiana State Fair, a prestigious and much coveted award
from his peers.[18] His involvement with the state fair continued when he was

invited to be a judge in 1866. Judging a state fair—then, as today—signified one's prominence and expertise in agriculture. He was responsible for choosing the farmer who had grown the best field crops for that year's competition.[19] In 1871, he was the "'attending member' of the Board at the Breeding Cattle competition," which meant he was responsible for ensuring that the cattle judging at the Indiana State Fair was conducted honestly.[20]

Austin Claypool did not hold any local, state, or national political office. Nevertheless, he was active in political campaigns, becoming an outspoken supporter of Abraham Lincoln when he campaigned in Indiana for the presidency.[21] Austin's political influence came through his affiliation with the county agricultural society and the Indiana State Board of Agriculture. Like his father before him, Austin was an energetic supporter of his county's agricultural society, then called the Fayette County Joint Stock Agricultural and Mechanical Society. In 1866 and 1867, he was elected president of the society, just as his father had been years before.[22] He would serve brief stints as secretary as well.[23]

His rise within statewide agricultural circles began in 1869, when he was elected as the Fayette County delegate to the Indiana State Board of Agriculture. This brought him into contact with the most influential farmers and politicians of the day. In 1871, forty-eight-year-old Austin Claypool became a member of the board as an elected representative from the board's tenth district, which included Fayette, Union, Wayne, and Henry Counties.[24] A total of sixteen districts comprised the main decision-making body of the board.[25] In 1877, Claypool served on the executive committee of the Indiana State Board of Agriculture.[26]

Austin's popularity among the delegates earned him a choice position when he was appointed by the Indiana State Board of Agriculture to serve as its delegate to the National Agricultural Congress, which opened its convention in Chicago, Illinois, on September 25, 1877. [27] He remained a district representative until 1879, when Henry C. Meredith—his son-in-law and Virginia's husband—replaced him as the representative for the tenth district.[28]

Governor Thomas Hendricks appointed fifty-year-old Austin Claypool to the
Purdue University Board of Trustees in March 1874. His fifteen-month tenure
happened during a critical juncture for the institution. At that time, Purdue was
a university in name only. While the land had been acquired by 1869, no classes
had been held yet. Policies had to be written and professors hired as the first
steps toward getting the school up and running.

Austin listened attentively as the board discussed which courses would
be offered to the first students, what criteria and admission requirements the
students would have to meet, how the trustees would manage the financial
affairs of the school, and other matters related to the operation of the Purdue
University farm. He participated in hiring the second university president,
hiring the first faculty members, and designing degree programs. As a trustee,
he would help decide what campus buildings were needed, manage the design
and construction of the university barns, and determine where to sink wells. It
must have been exciting for the trustees to see their efforts establish the campus infrastructure.

By necessity, the first trustees would micromanage the affairs of the university. Not only did they have to agree among themselves on which breeds of
cows, horses, and hogs to stock on the Purdue farm and which crops the farm
manager should grow, as this June 1874 record shows, they even had to approve
the livestock purchase: "On motion Superintendent was authorized to buy four
cows for the use of the Boardinghouse, the same to be paid by the Treasurer,
upon bills approved by the Secretary."[29]

Austin was in attendance when the board of trustees agreed to accept the
resignation of Richard Owen, who was the first president of Purdue (1872–
74).[30] Owen elected to step down as a result of negative press criticizing him
for developing a lengthy plan to build the physical structures at Purdue while
ignoring other facets of operating a school, such as plans for classes, courses,
and teaching. He returned to Indiana University, where he resumed work as a
geology professor, a position that he had formerly held there.

On June 12, 1874, the board voted to replace Owen with Abraham
Shortridge, an Indiana native born in Richmond.[31] His professional association
with colleges included teaching positions at Milton College, Dublin College,
and Whitewater College. At the time of his hiring at Purdue University, he had
been working as the first superintendent of the schools in Indianapolis.[32]

Just a few months later—on September 16, 1874—Purdue University held
its first official class, with six faculty members teaching thirty-nine students.

Indiana's land-grant school was now operational. Austin Claypool was still a trustee when the first Purdue University degree was awarded in May 1875 to John B. Harper in chemistry.

Austin Claypool's tenure as a trustee totaled just a little more than one year, lasting from March 10, 1874, to July 1, 1875. On March 9, 1875, a state law reorganized the board of trustees, slimming it down to six members, two of which would come from the Indiana State Board of Agriculture and one from the Indiana State Board of Horticulture. Governor Thomas A. Hendricks's picks were reduced to three members of his choosing. Austin lost his seat when the governor failed to reappoint him to the board. Nearly fifty years later, his daughter, Virginia, would make history when she was appointed to the very same board.

Austin and Hannah Claypool's first child arrived on November 5, 1848, at their home on Maplewood Farm near Connersville, Indiana. She was named Virginia to honor the birthplace of her grandfather, Newton Claypool.[33]

Virginia was born to progressive and prosperous parents. Her twenty-five-year-old father took a much different view than other men of the time when it came to raising his girls. His daughters would be afforded all of the advantages and training given to his boys.

> ...Austin B. Claypool...believed in educating his girls just as he educated his boys, and in giving both the best to be had. He made companions of his children, and little Virginia he took with him on countless drives to pastures and fields, talking with her meanwhile on farm subjects.[34]

She obtained her education as a young girl in Fayette County, Indiana, while she was taught the principles of successful farming and business management by a father who excelled in these professions.[35] In addition, the active and boisterous involvement of Virginia's grandfather and father would bring men of importance and power to her childhood home. Virginia learned to be comfortable around such guests—political leaders, businessmen, and agriculturists—while helping her mother entertain them when they came to do business with the Claypool men.

The Civil War broke out when Virginia was twelve years old. Years later, she recalled three memories from those days:

> • My father always talked of public affairs to us children. He was a supporter of Lincoln, and was active in the Wide Awakes, a political organization

with a military flavor. There was no way to transport men except by farm wagons drawn by horses. We lived in a neighborhood of Quakers, whose religion made them conscientious objectors. One day father asked Aaron White, a prominent Quaker, if he could lend his horses to draw the men to a meeting. "Austin," he answered, "Thee knows I am opposed to war. But my horses are in the stable and the harness hangs beside them."[36]

• I recall clearly that day when the news came that Fort Sumter had been fired on; I recall how hearts were heavy, and the world looked black. And wherever there were young men—in college, in factory or on farm—patriotic fervor mounted high. It has been said that all wars are fought by boys and that the sorrows of war are borne by women; always, however, there are groups of mature men—patriots—who do the hard thinking and planning that belong to the actualities of war....

At the time of the War of the Rebellion organization was lacking, pitifully lacking, in the care of our soldiers at the front, and upon home folk fell a heavy burden; there was work for all. I myself, a young girl [at twelve years old], rose to heights of heroism—at least I felt that I was rising to such heights. At the time when Morgan's army invaded our state, I loaned my own riding horse to one who was going with the mounted company to repel the invasion. Well, my horse came back safely, as did the gallant volunteer who rode him![37]

In 1863, when Virginia was nearly fifteen, her father sent her to Glendale Female College in Glendale, Ohio.[38] This religious-based institution was twelve miles north of Cincinnati. The college opened its doors to the first class in 1854 as American Female College and was renamed as Glendale Female College soon after. It continued under that name until it ceased operations in 1929. During its seventy-five years, Glendale would be known as one of the premier colleges of higher education for women in the Midwest.

Glendale College was situated on approximately two acres. The main building was a three-story structure of fifty rooms, including a dining room, six recitation rooms, nine music rooms, a main hall, and a chapel. The library contained two thousand volumes, which students could access "without extra charge," and the college prided itself on its well-equipped science department.[39]

Glendale was an expensive private school that attracted students from families of wealth. Virginia's family would have been required to pay the following costs in advance:

Expenses.

Board in the Institution, room furnished, tuition in all the branches
  of the regular course, fuel, light, and washing (one doz. pieces weekly),
  per session $150

Tuition for day scholars in the collegiate department, per session $25

Tuition for day scholars in the preparatory department, per session $20

The highest branches pursued will ordinarily determine the price of tuition.

Extra Studies and Charges.

Music on the piano, melodeon, or guitar, per session $30

Use of instruments for the two former, per session $5

Drawing and Painting, per session .... $15 and 25

French and German, each, per session $10

Classes were demanding, and students were examined on many subjects.
Virginia's school year lasted forty weeks and was divided into two sessions. [40]
Her four-year program consisted of the following classes:

Freshman Class.

First Term.

Arithmetic, finished.
Latin Grammar.
Watts on the Mind.
Universal History.

Second Term.

Elementary Algebra.
English Grammar.
Latin Reader.
History of England.

Sophomore Class.

First Term.

University Algebra.
Natural Philosophy.
Geology.
History of Greece.
Latin.

Second Term.

Algebra, finished.
Physiology.
Astronomy.
Physical Geography.
History of Rome.

Junior Class.

First Term.

Geometry.
Rhetoric.
History of France.
Greek Grammar.
Chemistry.

Second Term.

Geometry, finished.
Botany.
Evidences of Christianity.
Greek Reader.
Caesar.

Senior Class.

First Term.	*Second Term.*
Natural Theology.	Butler's Analogy.
Trigonometry.	Story on the Constitution.
Logic.	Virgil, continued.
Virgil.	Mental Philosophy.
Greek Reader.	Greek Testament.
Moral Science.	English Literature.[41]

In addition, students attending Glendale were required to uphold the strict standards set forth by the college: "... the regulations involving such restrictions only as are necessary to secure correct deportment, the formation of good habits and manners, a just appropriation of the hours of each day, and the attainment of high moral and virtuous principles."[42]

The college stipulated who could visit students and when students could leave the premises:

> Pupils, in coming to the Institution, should be provided with a sufficient wardrobe and other necessaries, or supplied from home. They will not be permitted to spend money, or leave the College, except under the guidance of teachers or parents.[43]

First and foremost, students were not allowed to receive visitors on Sunday, nor could they leave or return on that day. The young women were expected to attend religious services that day and prepare a lesson plan for what was being studied in Bible class.

The college staff was very proud of the institution's strict moral code and reassured worried parents of their daughters' safety, noting, "[N]o death having occurred among the inmates of the Institution since its establishment."[44] Families were told that their daughters would be living in an area absent "of the various excitements and temptations that attend female institutions located in cities, or in the immediate vicinity of institutions for young men. . . ."[45]

Virginia proved to be a dedicated student who excelled in her studies both in and outside of class. While at Glendale, she developed a keen interest in public affairs at the urging of her father.

> Father's chief demand was that we should be public-spirited. He insisted that I should read the Cincinnati Gazette and other daily papers. So I spent my time in the college reading room, devouring the editorials and dispatches of three or four papers a day. In this way I formed a taste of keeping up with current news which has stayed with me.[46]

In 1866, Virginia graduated with honors from Glendale Female College, having earned a bachelor of arts degree.[47] Her graduating class totaled five students, with fellow graduates representing Illinois, Indiana, Kentucky, and Minnesota. After graduation, Virginia returned to her parent's home to help with the farm and entertain guests.

Four years later, on April 28, 1870, she married Henry Clay Meredith, the only living son of Civil War General Solomon Meredith. Through her upbringing and education, Virginia Claypool Meredith was well groomed to begin her new role as a wife and daughter-in-law to this very influential family.

The Claypool Family Tree

Abraham Claypool (1762–1845) m. **Ann Elizabeth Wilson** (1766–1849)
Children
Solomon, Jacob, Ann, Wilson, Abel, Isaac, Sarah, Maria,
and
Newton Claypool (1795–1866) m. **Mary Kerns** (1798–1864)
Children
Benjamin, Abraham, Edward, Jefferson, Sara, Elizabeth, Mary, Maria, Newton,
and
Austin Bingley Claypool (1823–1906) m. **Hannah Ann Petty** (1828–1923)
Children
Frank, Elizabeth, Marcus,
and
Virginia Claypool (1848–1936) m. **Henry Clay Meredith** (1843–1882)
Children
Adopted **Mary Lockwood Matthews** (1882–1968) and
Meredith Matthews (1887–1962)

An Independent Woman Emerges

CHAPTER 2

If a woman can make bread and direct some one else how to make bread, she can do the infinitely simpler thing—make hay. If she can make butter or teach another the delicate process that involves painstaking care and sound judgment, she can certainly accomplish the comparatively simple process of growing corn. If she can take care of boys and girls, how easy is it in comparison to maintain the health and promote the growth of cattle, horses and sheep.

—Virginia Meredith, *Indianapolis News,* 3 January 1900

THE MEREDITH FAMILY'S famous Oakland Farm and its prized Shorthorns provided the backdrop against which Virginia Claypool Meredith would excel in life. Oakland Farm belonged to Virginia's father-in-law, Civil War General Solomon Meredith, who was well known throughout eastern Indiana and beyond. Virginia's connection to the general and his farm elevated her status in and around Cambridge City, provided her with important social and political connections, and equipped her with a practical education on managing a livestock farm. Solomon Meredith and Oakland Farm were the conduits that would propel Virginia Meredith to the national stage as an agriculturalist and home economist.

General Solomon Meredith (1810–75) originally hailed from Guilford County, North Carolina. As a young man of nineteen and standing six feet seven inches, Solomon and a friend, Richard J. Hubbard, decided to seek their fortunes in the West.[1] They set off and arrived in Indiana from North Carolina on May 5, 1829, after walking the entire distance.

Solomon Meredith's first job was cutting cords of wood, which earned him six dollars a month, a sizable amount considering he only had "cash capital of twelve and a half cents" when he arrived in Indiana.[2] During the 1830s and 1840s, Solomon bought and sold plotted lots in Cambridge City. He was frugal with his earnings, and "with the money thus accumulated, he possessed a capital sufficient to engage in other pursuits where little capital was required."[3]

Soon thereafter, Solomon began a journey into politics that occupied much of his time from 1834 to 1859. He was elected sheriff of Wayne County in 1834 at the age of twenty-four and reelected in 1836. It was during his first term that he married Anna Hannah from Centerville, Indiana, on March 17, 1836. Anna was born in Brownsville, Pennsylvania, on April 12, 1812. She was the daughter of Samuel Hannah, who was, at the time of the marriage, the clerk of the Wayne Circuit Court in Richmond, Indiana, and would later become Indiana's secretary of state.[4] Solomon and Anna Meredith would have four children: one daughter who died in infancy and three sons.[5]

At the end of his second term as county sheriff, Solomon opened up a mercantile store in 1838 in the local community of Milton. This successful dry goods business was later located in Cambridge City in 1839. He managed the store until its sale in 1843.[6] He also served as director and financial agent of the Indiana Central Railroad and would later become the president of the Cincinnati and Chicago Railroad Company.

Solomon Meredith was a staunch Republican. He was a delegate at the nominating convention for the Whig Party in 1840 and 1848, and served as a delegate to the 1856 Republican National Convention. In 1865, Lincoln's funeral train made three 15-second stops at Cambridge City; one was at Solomon's Oakland Farm to honor "a great personal friend."[7]

Solomon's visibility as the county sheriff and as a successful local businessman earned him sufficient credibility and recognition, which got him elected three times as a representative for Wayne County to the Indiana State General Assembly from 1846 to 1849.

By the mid–1840s, Solomon Meredith was well connected to influential people at all levels of government. Knowing the right people in the right places allowed him to garner important political appointments. In 1849, President Zachary Taylor appointed Solomon as the United States marshal for the District of Indiana, a position he held for four years. Solomon returned to state politics as a state representative in 1855, rising soon thereafter to the high rank of chairman of the Committee of Ways and Means.

The General Assembly approved articles of incorporation for Cambridge City on February 12, 1841, and Solomon became president of the city's first board of trustees.[8] Other publicly elected or appointed offices held by Solomon included Wayne County clerk (1859–61) and surveyor-general of the Montana Territory (1867–69). He seemed never to lose his connections with politicians at all levels. This was clearly illustrated through Virginia Meredith's recollections of one trip in particular:

> ... I recall the experience of a day in Washington [D.C.] several years after the [Civil] war. My husband, Mr. Henry C. Meredith, and myself were there with his father, General Meredith. It being my first visit to the capital, sight-seeing was naturally our occupation. General Grant was at that time President. Our call at the White House was by some inopportune occurrence delayed until after the hour when the President received, but for my gratification the call was undertaken so that I might at least see the interior of the White House. Just as we were approaching the entrance a man of rather commonplace appearance, wholly unattended, came out. After an instant of attentive regard on the part of each, he and General Meredith made a quick movement toward each other, cordially grasped each other by the hand and exclaimed both at the same moment, "General, I'm glad to see you!" and then in the most informal manner imaginable, outside the White House door, my husband and I were presented to General Grant, who at once, with the most kind and insistent manner, turned and entered with us, postponing his drive until he had talked with General Meredith and shown me the East room. I congratulate myself upon the informal introduction which so auspiciously gave me so distinguished a guide to White House scenes.
>
> That same day we took dinner with ex-President [Andrew] Johnson, who, like General Meredith, was a native of North Carolina. Their theme of conversation during dinner was their native state, its great sons, its colonial and revolutionary history—all those reminiscent lines into which men fall so naturally and unaffectedly when life has reached its zenith.[9]

While he was busy representing his constituents' interests, Solomon Meredith still found time to remain involved with livestock production.

> During the time he was discharging all these official duties, he found time to engage in agricultural pursuits, and has probably done more than any other man in southeastern Indiana to improve its live stock, having imported many rare breeds, particularly of sheep and cattle.[10]

Virginia Claypool Meredith wrote on May 12, 1897, that Solomon Meredith's "love for farming and his interest in advanced agriculture was deep and abiding. His public spirit in importing pure bred cattle and sheep, and also in promoting agricultural fairs, was of very substantial benefit to Eastern Indiana."[11]

Solomon Meredith's influence as a rancher grew in 1851 when he bought a 180-acre farm on the outskirts of Cambridge City. Purchased from the Ira Lackey estate at a sheriff's sale, it cost Solomon $6,500, which was two-thirds of its appraised value.[12] He named the property Oakland Farm. The farm included a beautiful Federal-style home built in 1836 about three blocks south of the National Road, the nation's first federally funded highway. The house was described as "a very handsome red brick structure of 20 rooms with the usual farm 'offices,' smoke house, milk house, wood house and out kitchen with large fireplace for boiling apple-butter, rendering lard, making soap and like accessories of farm life."[13]

General Meredith even had his own railroad stop at Oakland Farm. One report noted, "Many persons important in the political and civic life of Indiana disembarked from the railroad coaches at Meredith's private stop."[14] When the state legislature was in session, the general would often invite the legislators to attend parties at his home.[15] Virginia Meredith would remark, "Then, and many, many other times distinguished guests graced the handsome double parlors, with double doors connecting, with very beautiful mantels in each room."[16]

Raising livestock on Oakland Farm was Solomon's passion. The general purchased his first Shorthorns in 1851. In what would be a major purchase, he bought an English bull named Balco, which gave his herd great creditability among other breeders.[17] Soon, he was pasturing renowned herds of Shorthorn cattle and flocks of Southdown sheep, and even began importing these breeds from England to improve the genetics of his own animals. He raised other animals as well, advertising them all on his letterhead: "S. Meredith & Son. Breeders of Short Horn Cattle, Berkshire Swine, South Down and Cotswold Sheep."[18] Solomon held his first public stock sale in 1856 and soon became quite the expert on the breeds he raised, with people from around the country seeking his advice and purchasing his animals.[19]

Oakland Farm and the Meredith family became household names in the agricultural community, especially among those who raised purebred livestock. When Solomon sold his stock, it was recalled as a great event:

His stock sales on the farm, which attracted hundreds of people from his own and other States, will long be remembered. The sales resembled a great fair, in the beauty and variety of the animals exhibited. The feast which he prepared for the multitudes on such occasions, and the genial hospitality with which it was dispersed, always elicited the highest commendation.[20]

Solomon Meredith began showing his Shorthorns and Southdowns at county fairs in and around Indiana, and exhibited them at major livestock shows, state fairs, and expositions.[21] He not only competed but also won prize after prize for these breeds. In fact, he started winning within two years of establishing his Shorthorn herd.[22] Whether it was a local livestock competition or the highly contested Indiana State Fair, he always came back with blue ribbons, silver plates, money, other prizes, and accolades. Between 1853 and 1858, Solomon Meredith captured approximately 50 first- and second-place awards for his livestock, but most of all, he earned a reputation as a man who knew cattle and sheep.[23]

Solomon used his standing to further the advancement of agriculture in the east central part of the state. He was involved with the creation of a new association called the Cambridge City District Agricultural, Horticultural, and Mechanical Society, which represented ten counties in the area. The organization owned sixty acres near Cambridge City that were purchased from Solomon for $12,000.[24] The general would be elected as the association's first president.

In May 1872, Solomon Meredith helped organize the Indiana Short Horn Breeders' Association, which met for the first time to discuss the importing, breeding, feeding, and exhibiting of Shorthorn cattle.[25] He served on numerous association committees to select permanent officers during the first year and, in addition, helped write the rules for the association. He was also elected to the association's executive committee and, in 1873, to its vice presidency.[26] Much later, General Solomon would be inducted into the Indiana Livestock Breeders Association Hall of Fame.[27]

At the outset of the Civil War in 1861, Solomon Meredith formed a regiment of Wayne County volunteers. He had no military experience, but like many Civil War officers of the day, he had political connections to Indiana Governor Oliver P. Morton, high-ranking officials throughout the government, and other influential people.

There is little doubt that Solomon wanted to command men in battle. However, he indicated that if a command was not afforded him, he would still fight for the Union: "I am going to fight this war through; if a command is offered to me I will accept it; otherwise Captain Riley has reserved a place for me in his company, and I will go as a private soldier."[28]

Initially, Solomon made a direct request to Governor Morton to place him in command of his own regiment. Apparently, others did not think he was qualified and pressured Governor Morton to refuse the request. However, Solomon had even higher connections, so "with his usual energy, appealed to [the] President [Abraham Lincoln], who requested the Governor to appoint him a Colonel, which he did very promptly, giving him command of the famous Nineteenth regiment [of the Indiana Infantry], then just formed at Camp Morton."[29]

Solomon received his commission in July 1861. His regiment was assigned to the Union Army of the Potomac, where it was attached to what would become the famous Iron Brigade. The Nineteenth Regiment was involved in some of the hottest and deadliest skirmishes of the Civil War: Antietam, Fredericksburg, Chancellorsville, Gettysburg, the Wilderness, Cold Harbor, and Petersburg.

The Meredith family would pay dearly for their support of the Union. The older two of Meredith's three sons—Samuel and David—would die from wounds they received on the battlefield. Samuel died at Oakland Farm in January 1864, before his twenty-sixth birthday, from wounds received at Gettysburg.[30] Captain David Meredith died in 1867 at age twenty-seven in Mobile, Alabama, from his Chickamauga battlefield wounds.[31] Both sons were buried in the family cemetery at Oakland Farm. The surviving son, Henry Clay Solomon, would pass through the Civil War unscathed, serving on his father's staff as a second lieutenant and aide-de-camp.[32]

Solomon Meredith was himself wounded several times during the Civil War. While recuperating from a wound suffered in the battle of Gainesville in 1862, he was promoted to Brigadier General on October 6, 1862. He was the general-in-charge of the Iron Brigade at Gettysburg when the Confederates, under General Robert E. Lee, attacked at Seminary Ridge on the first day. The Confederates were repelled from the ridge but at great human cost. Nearly two-thirds of the Iron Brigade were wounded, killed, or missing. General Meredith was among the injured. According to the *Indianapolis Times,* "[T]he General was struck by a fragment of a shell which so shattered his nervous system that he never fully recovered from it."[33] These injuries took him out of service for four months.

The general took noncombatant military assignments in Cairo, Illinois, and at Paducah, Kentucky, in 1864 and 1865. At his request, he was relieved of command on May 28, 1865, to return to his farm in Cambridge City. Outside of a brief stint between 1867 and 1869 as a surveyor-general in the Montana Territory, he would spend the remainder of his life at his beloved Oakland Farm.

Solomon Meredith named his youngest son Henry Clay Meredith, because Solomon was an "active and zealous friend of Henry Clay, for whom he had an unbounded admiration."[34]

Born on July 17, 1843, Henry Clay Meredith received a well-rounded education, attending common schools for part of his training as well as attending Greenmount Boarding School in Wayne County and Fairview Academy in Fayette County. He would graduate from Indiana University in 1867.[35]

After graduation, Henry became a journalist, establishing the *Cambridge City Tribune* in 1869.[36] He managed the operations there until 1872, when he sold the newspaper to enter into business with his father "in breeding shorthorn cattle, Southdown sheep, and several improved varieties of hogs."[37]

Through visits to her grandparents' farm in Cambridge City, Virginia had known Henry as "a nearby farmer and childhood friend."[38] When Virginia Claypool married Henry Clay Meredith on April 28, 1870, it united two prominent, politically connected agricultural families. One newspaper reported it as ". . . an alliance between two of the old families of the state, the bride belonging to one of the oldest and wealthiest families of Eastern Indiana, and the groom being the only surviving son of Gen. Sol. Meredith, who has been prominent in state politics and a leading spirit in every thing that could help to develop the resources for our own and neighboring counties, all his life time."[39]

The wedding, held in Connersville at the home of Virginia's father, was quite the social affair. A local newspaper recounted the events of the day:

> Rev. Mr. Holliday, of Indianapolis, was the officiating minister. The bridesmaids were Miss Annie Steele, of Paris, Ill., and Miss Mary Claypool, of this city [Connersville]. The groomsmen were Capt. A. G. Wilcox, of the Richmond Telegram, and Mr. Schultz, of Cambridge City.
>
> The bride wore a trailing dress of white satin and looked beautiful under the bridal veil, and wreath of orange flowers. The bridegroom was attired in a plain black suit with white vest and gloves. . . .

In an adjoining room were displayed a large variety of bridal presents, consisting chiefly of silver ware, many of which were valuable as well as beautiful. The total value of the presents was some three thousand dollars.

A splendid supper was prepared for the occasion. The table besides containing almost every variety of cake, confectionery, tropical fruits, &c., was beautifully decorated with flowers.

The ten o'clock train on the Valley road stopped in front of the residence, and the newly married pair took their departure for Chicago [and Milwaukee]. May peace and love ever be with them.[40]

After their marriage, Virginia and Henry moved into Solomon Meredith's home. A two-story addition to the west side of the Meredith home may have been added at this time as the living quarters for the newlyweds.[41] As was customary for the women of prominent families of that era, Virginia was expected to help Henry's mother, Anna Meredith, manage the house, instruct the servants, and entertain the frequent guests—including politicians and important stock breeders—who visited Oakland Farm.

Just nineteen months after the wedding, tragedy struck the Meredith family. Anna died on November 11, 1871, leaving the management of the home entirely to twenty-three-year-old Virginia.[42] It was said in an unsigned note, "Her personality lacked the fine sensibilities and feminine touch possessed by his [Solomon Meredith's] wife, but right then the Oakland Farm needed a face-lifting and 'Miss Virginia' (as she was called) was just the one to do it."[43] Solomon Meredith would never get over the death of his wife, but his daughter-in-law helped fill the void. She became a close companion of Solomon's and learned much from him about raising purebred livestock, handling public sales, and establishing working relationships with the stock breeders who came to visit the farm.

In the post–Civil War years, Solomon Meredith had resumed showing his animals with great success. At the 1870 Indiana State Fair, he won first and second place for his Shorthorn bulls, heifers, and calves.[44] Virginia Meredith would comment that Solomon and Henry "began a new period of activity. The livestock industry was resumed and the farm entered on a term of fame and prosperity. Shorthorn cattle and Southdown sheep enlisted the time and energy of father and son."[45]

The year 1873 brought additional changes to the Meredith entries in livestock competitions. While Oakland Farm animals were, once again, winning everything in sight, the awards were now presented to "Solomon Meredith &

Son," indicating that Henry was taking more responsibility for the farming operations. The Merediths took first or second prizes in ten categories at the 1873 Indiana State Fair. A major win for the Meredith team was having the best bull of any age, with the animal being named the sweepstakes winner.[46]

Father and son would once again share the spotlight by winning a dozen or so awards at the 1874 Indiana State Fair, but it would be the last they worked together. In late 1875, Solomon Meredith became gravely ill and knew he would not live much longer. He made a final request that "the fine cattle in which he had taken so much pleasure and of which he was so proud, should be turned into an enclosure near his residence, that his neighbors and friends could see them."[47] Solomon Meredith took his last breath on October 21, 1875.

The funeral was at Oakland Farm on Sunday, October 24. Eight thousand mourners were said to have attended that day. His prominence in the community and the important role he played in local affairs were further evident on the day of his funeral, when local papers stated it "was not only the largest funeral ever known in Wayne county, but in the State."[48] Special trains carrying mourners came from around Indiana, "while wagons and carriages brought in hundreds from the country about Cambridge [City] and from the surrounding counties."[49] To honor his final request, his cattle were confined in the enclosure around his home for everyone to see.

Two horses led the funeral procession. Forty veterans from the Indiana Nineteenth Regiment were also part of the procession.[50] Solomon was laid to rest next to his wife and two sons in a private cemetery located on the Oakland Farm property about a quarter of a mile from his home.[51]

Following Solomon's death, his tradition of entering and winning livestock shows was continued by his son, much to the chagrin of others who had difficulty winning when the elder Meredith was alive. During the 1876 Indiana State Fair, Henry won a handful of awards, claiming first- and second-place finishes in ten categories.[52]

At the 1877 Indiana State Fair, Henry again won a half dozen or so awards for his animals. In later years, Henry Meredith continued to showcase his animals, but eventually he began to focus his energies more on judging the entries in those events that he had formerly won so many times as a competitor.

Like his father before him, Henry C. Meredith took an active role in politics. In 1879, he joined the Indiana State Board of Agriculture as the representative from the tenth district, having replaced his father-in-law, Austin Claypool, in that position. He worked hard within the organization, and soon his efforts were rewarded when he became president of the board in 1882. During his tenure, he was appointed to attend the Agricultural Convention at Washington, D.C., on January 10, 1882.[53]

Henry was also elected to the Indiana General Assembly in 1881. He became known for "taking special interest in all measures relating to agricultural questions."[54] He and Virginia traveled to Indianapolis in January 1881 to attend the inauguration of Governor Albert G. Porter.[55]

As Henry became more politically involved, Virginia was thrust into a more active role in managing Oakland Farm. Henry's long absences from the farm meant that she would take over much of its day-to-day operations. According to the 1880 U.S. Census of Agriculture, Oakland Farm now had 115 acres of pasture and 65 acres of tilled ground. Virginia and Henry had 21 acres that produced 60 tons of hay to feed their 50 Shorthorns. They also had a flock of 84 sheep on hand that June. During the previous year, they had sold 115 sheep at auction, and their sheep had produced 51 fleeces weighing 400 pounds.[56] By this time, the Merediths employed two Irish workers to help with the work: Anna Doughty, a twenty-two-year-old servant hired to take care of the home; and Thomas Fanning, a young man of twenty who was paid to take care of the stock and fields.[57] In addition, Virginia had hired additional field and livestock workers at a cost of $1,040.

Virginia soon became known as an expert in her own right as she started to advertise, show, and sell her livestock.[58]

> Mrs. Meredith welcomed them [stock breeders] graciously, talked intelligently, and in her husband's absence was able to display the stock and pedigrees and prepare the way for sales. It was not long until she was handling all the bookkeeping, the records, and the pedigrees, and was familiar with advertising and cataloguing.[59]

Virginia had been taught well by the Claypools and Merediths, and her training was about to be tested.[60] Her apprenticeships on the farms of her father, father-in-law, and husband would serve her well when thirty-eight-year-old Henry fell ill with pneumonia. He died unexpectedly on July 5, 1882, leaving her as the sole owner of Oakland Farm.[61]

At the age of thirty-three, Virginia Meredith suddenly had to "choose between returning to her father's home or carrying on the business of farming and stock breeding."[62] She would write (in third person):

The untimely death, in 1882, of Henry C. Meredith brought in another period in the history of the old home. The widow of Henry Meredith entered a new world for women. Being familiar with her husband's business she decided to "carry on" in the old home. . . .[63]

She quickly decided that she would manage the farm, a position that would have been "unheard of for a woman in those days."[64] It was here that she would establish herself as suited to the task of managing a sizable ranch and farm. She would move quickly from being locally notable to being a nationally recognized and respected speaker and writer of agriculture. She could not have known it then, but in 1882, she was about to embark on a journey that would place her in the spotlight for decades to come.

The Meredith Family Tree

Solomon Meredith (1810–1875) m. **Anna Hannah** (1812–1871)

    Children

    Samuel (1838–1864), **David** (1840–1867), **Mary** (1845–1846)

    and

Henry Clay Meredith (1843–1882) m. **Virginia Claypool** (1848–1936)

    Children

    Adopted **Mary Lockwood Matthews** (1882–1968) and

    Meredith Matthews (1887–1962)

The Woman Farmer from Cambridge City

CHAPTER 3

*I know of no other field which offers such opportunities to women.
Women, with a far greater genius for detail than men, have an ability
to concentrate their activities upon that which is essentially vital,
and the quality of close observations possessed by the average woman makes
for success in the raising of live stock and in all other departments of farm life,
and is an incentive to enter into this particular phase of the world's business.*

—Virginia Meredith, *Dignam's Magazine,* September 1905

VIRGINIA MEREDITH FACED tough times during the sweltering days of July 1882. Since their marriage twelve years before, Henry and Virginia had shared the ups and downs that came with running a large farming operation, especially after his father died in 1875. However, her husband's premature death at the age of thirty-eight that month had left her on her own. Virginia's days and nights were spent mourning Henry's death and wondering what she should do with the farm.

Oakland Farm was a landmark property, the legacy of General Solomon Meredith. As Virginia walked through the main entryway and around the home, she could see his Civil War paraphernalia prominently displayed. If she kept the property, she might never emerge from his shadow.

The days passed slowly as she thought about the Meredith men, but at the same time, she had to plan for a future without them. Work gave her comfort as she went about the business of feeding and caring for the herd of Shorthorns, flocks of Southdown sheep, and horses that grazed the farm's picturesque pastures. Farm work was routine, usually predictable, and always demanding.

Meredith's paramount concern was what to do with her farm and home. If she sold them off, how would she support herself? Still young at thirty-three, she could always remarry or teach in the local school system. But outside of teaching, the prospect for employment in the community seemed rather limited. Selling the farm would likely entail moving away from Cambridge City to find work to her liking, a prospect she did not relish. Another option was to return to her father's home. Ultimately, though, she decided in favor of keeping the farm, saying that it was "not with any hope of success, but because work was the only solace within my horizon at the time."[1]

Meredith and those she turned to for advice knew that in 1882 it was rare for a woman to own and manage a purebred livestock operation. One report noted, "[Her] decision to continue the type of farming which embraced livestock in pure bred lines was looked upon as something quite out of the ordinary career of a woman."[2] The 1880 United States Census supports this observation. Only 122 women nationwide referred to themselves as "stock-raisers" that year.[3] The picture would change fifty years later, when women in large numbers were calling themselves farmers, planters, ranchers, and farm managers. Women such as Meredith were in the forefront of agriculture in the 1880s, opening the doors to those who followed in succeeding generations.[4]

Virginia Meredith could not have foreseen how the decision to keep Oakland Farm would shape her life. Months became years as she settled into her role as farm manager and owner. She expressed to others that having the farm was an opportunity handed to her on the proverbial silver platter: "Indeed, with my exceptional advantages, I ought to have done very much more than I have done."[5] Her reputation grew, as did the status of Oakland Farm.

Meredith was practical in her thinking, well read on agricultural subjects, and had developed a good sense of what worked and what didn't—key traits in any successful businessperson. With her sights firmly set, she managed the farm with vigor and determination, but she must have questioned whether she had the skills, judgment, and tenacity to build on what her husband and father-in-law had accomplished at Oakland Farm. Surely the question "What would people think about her if she failed?" must have crossed her mind many times during the first few years.

In reality, Meredith was more than qualified to earn a living as a farmer and livestock breeder. She was a quick study, remembering much of what her father had taught her about farming. Her father's teachings were augmented by the many years that she had worked alongside the Meredith men. General Solomon Meredith had taken an interest in Virginia early on as someone with a keen interest in everything concerning the farm and its operations. She had

watched, asked questions, and learned livestock production and farming practices from two of the best animal breeders of their time.

The outside world knew Solomon Meredith and his son, Henry, as eminent
livestock breeders. Virginia herself could not deny that these two men had bred
some of the best Shorthorn cattle and Southdown sheep that money could
buy; the ribbons and silver cups scattered throughout the house were evidence
enough even to the novice livestock breeder. But it seems the men had been less
attentive to the financial oversight of the farm. Meredith examined the farm's
financial ledgers line by line, page by page. She was mortified to find that "[the]
business had not been managed so that the profits were such as they should
have been, and instead of being prosperous, it was, in reality, considerably
run down."[6]

It should not have come as a surprise to Virginia that Henry's financial
track record was less than stellar.[7] After Anna's death in 1871 and Solomon's
death in 1875, Henry and Virginia inherited Oakland Farm. The following year,
on February 10, 1876, Henry acquired 250 acres located two miles north of
Cambridge City for $15,000. Including Oakland Farm plus a few scattered acres,
the Merediths would now own a total of 450 acres. Unfortunately, the man who
sold Henry the 250 acres had never completely paid off the former owner for
that land. Just a year later, Henry was found to owe $7,497 to the former owner
of the acreage. This required Henry to take out a $10,000 mortgage from the
Richmond (Indiana) National Bank, using the entire 450 acres as collateral.
Henry and Virginia must have been in a financial bind when they acquired the
large tract of land, because Virginia had to borrow $2,900 from her father. That
same year Henry had paid to have a nearly forty-foot monument erected in the
family cemetery to mark his father's gravesite. Might the rather large loan have
been borrowed to help design and build the monument?

Things did not seem to improve for the Merediths. On January 1, 1878,
they mortgaged twenty acres to an individual in two promissory notes totaling
$1,000. But by January 4, 1878, the Merediths owed the Richmond National
Bank $11,843, which they found themselves unable to pay. Then on June 4,
1879, the unthinkable happened. United States Marshal W. W. Dudley deeded
to Richmond National Bank the 250 acres and Oakland Farm owned by the
Merediths. Henry and Virginia had lost the titles to their land.

On April 15, 1880, Oakland Farm sold to Phoenix Mutual Life Insurance Company of Hartford, Connecticut. Even though it sold, it seems that the Merediths continued to live on the farm. In September 1882, just months after the death of her husband, Meredith found herself in court again being sued for unpaid expenses. Somehow, Virginia must have worked out a deal to live on Oakland Farm while paying off the debt owed to the insurance company.

Virginia knew she had to realize a higher profit from the sale of the farm's livestock, her main source of income. She also had to trim expenses for the entire farming operation, including the home. Failure to do so would result in a shortfall of cash and lead to operational difficulties in the near future, which might prevent her from regaining control of the property. Her prospects for success appeared bleak.

She got a handle on the farm's finances by instituting an in-depth system "associated with the bookkeeping, records, pedigrees, and selling and advertising on the livestock farm. . . ."[8] She was a stickler for details and was "already intimately familiar with the details of pedigree in registry and record associations. . . ."[9] She based her analysis of how much of each dollar spent was returned to the farm on extensive records, including notes that described what worked, what worked better, and what didn't meet her expectations. The accumulation of detailed written notes allowed Meredith to calculate how much money she made from harvesting a crop or raising a calf in relation to the money spent to bring the product to market.

It took some years of hard work and difficult decisions to get the physical assets on the property repaired or replaced. But with the help of her meticulous farm records, she was able to pull the farm through some lean years.

> She put her ideas into effect and very soon began to elucidate them. The correctness of her views [was] demonstrated in her own experience. Within two years the business of Oakland farm became prosperous and the cattle and sheep raised there were eagerly purchased by breeders at high prices.[10]

It would take her nearly twenty years, but on August 27, 1900, Virginia Meredith's hard work paid off when she regained the title to Oakland Farm from the life insurance company.

Making a good showing in the highly competitive livestock ring was important to those who sold purebred animals. It was not, however, as important to
Virginia Meredith as it had been to her husband and father-in-law. Blue ribbons, premiums, and trophy cups did not pay the bills. Early on, she decided
that she would judge herself personally successful when livestock breeders and
farmers paid top price for the livestock bred and raised on the Oakland Farm.

For many years, she would advertise her livestock sales in such magazines
as the *Breeder's Gazette* under the name of Mrs. Henry C. Meredith. She understood the marketplace and so linked her sales to what was already familiar
to livestock breeders, which were the names of Oakland Farm and General
Solomon Meredith. One of her first advertisements stated:

> SHORT-HORN CATTLE.
>
> The OAKLAND FARM HERD was established more than 30 years ago by
> General Meredith, and afterwards continued by his son, the late Henry C.
> Meredith. The standard already established for the stock at Oakland Farm
> will be maintained. The herd consists of such families as Moss Rose, Hupa,
> Young Mary, Phyllis, Aylesby Lady, Raspberry, etc. A flock of Registered
> Southdowns also bred on the farm. Stock for sale. For information call on,
> or address MRS. HENRY C. MEREDITH, Cambridge City, Ind.[11]

By 1884, Meredith's herd had grown to about forty head of Shorthorns and
a flock of Southdowns numbering sixty, which were "one of the best flocks in
the country."[12] Virginia Meredith's first Southdown sheep sale on September 18,
1884, came two years after taking over the reins of Oakland Farm. She worked
off her nervousness the day before the sale, selecting and penning the
Southdown sheep that would be auctioned the following day. She waited anx-
iously that morning, wondering how many farmers would attend the sale at her
farm and what kind of prices her ewes and rams would bring. Slowly, the buyers
began arriving for the auction. She didn't have long to wait to get her questions
answered, because the veteran auctioneer, Colonel Judy, "cried the sale" as the
bidding took place and the sheep were sold to the highest bidders.[13]

> Mrs. Henry C. Meredith's public sale of the South Down flock at Oakland
> farm took place yesterday afternoon. The sale was quite largely attended
> by sheep raisers and stockmen from other States, and from the counties
> of Clinton, Madison, Randolph, Franklin, Rush, Fayette, Wells and Marion
> in this State. Some of the most prominent among them were J. H. Potts,
> of Jacksonville, Illinois; T. A. Stafford, of Ohio; Philip Miller, of Iowa. . . .
> The bidding was quite spirited, and the prices fully up to Mrs. Meredith's

expectations. The general average will be about $25 per head. There were forty-two head sold out of the lot of fifty-five advertised, Mrs. Meredith reserving the lambs of the flock. The fine imported ram was bought by J. H. Potts & Son, of Jacksonville, Illinois, for $100. This is the most extensive stock firm in the United States, and the liberal price paid for the animal showed that they appreciated the quality of the Oakland Flock.[14]

Meredith, during the morning, took time to answer questions about her Shorthorns, selling a few of them in the process. By 1 P.M., the auctioneer's voice and the bidders' calls gave way to the sounds of serving plates and the smell of freshly cooked food spread across numerous outdoor tables. Meredith was following a long-held tradition by providing lunch to the fifty or so buyers who had stayed until the last of her sheep were auctioned.

While Meredith was busy selling livestock, she was also active in purchasing new Shorthorns for her herd. Meredith published in the September 24, 1885, *Breeder's Gazette* a paragraph titled "A New Bull for the Meredith Herd."[15] Still calling herself Mrs. Henry C. Meredith, she informed the readers that she was improving her herds with the introduction of a rather famous Shorthorn bloodline. Her brief paragraph also showed how well she understood the jargon associated with purebred Shorthorn lineage:

> Mrs. Henry C. Meredith, of Cambridge City, Ind., recently purchased from T. Corwin Anderson, of Side View, Ky., the Bates Wild Eyes bull Wild Eyes Baron, a red of April 30, 1884, got by the famous Flat Creek sire Barrington Duke 37622, out of Wild Eyes Duchess 4th (Vol. XVIII) by exp. 2d Duke of Hillhurst (39748), etc., price $500. The dam of this young bull is the mother of three heifers that sold at public sale during 1884 for $1,600, $1,775, and $2,000 respectively, and one this year at $2,025.[16]

Nearly three years after her first sheep sale, the public had a chance to view Virginia Meredith's Shorthorns when her first cattle sale took place in the spring of 1887. She showed remarkable business savvy, advertising in farm magazines and newspapers the eleventh public sale of Shorthorns—her first cattle sale without the Meredith men—from the famed Oakland Farm herd. She correctly deduced that more prominent buyers would come if she linked her first sale to the past reputation of the farm. As was the case with the Southdown sheep sale, the quality of these Shorthorns derived from her decisions on which pairs to breed, their feeding regimen, and care.

Seven hundred people crowded around the auctioneer that day. It was said that it was "... such a crowd of Short-Horn breeders as has not been seen at any sale in this state for years."[17] Meredith appreciated the overflow crowd of would-be buyers on her farm. She especially was grateful for the professional compliments extended to her when ". . . so many distinguished breeders . . . praised her cattle, and especially the careful manner in which they had been bred and handled."[18]

Her cattle auction was nothing less than spectacular, a "grand success" by any measure, with "hers being one of the series of sales, and her average being from twenty-five to fifty per cent. better than that of any other sale in the series."[19] Meredith sold 35 head of cattle that day, bringing on average $120 for the heifers and $100 for the bulls.[20] If she wasn't confident about her skills or had any doubts before her first cattle sale, the day's bidding affirmed her position as a Shorthorn breeder on par with Henry and Solomon Meredith.

Comments were made about the reserve herd of Shorthorns grazing the lush pastures that day. It was noted that "her reserve herd of twenty odd head is much more valuable than that sold, and formulates, in pure pedigree, the foundation for one of the best, if not the very best herds in Indiana, headed as it is, by a pure Bates Wild Eyes Bull."[21] With this caliber of reserves in place, the future for Oakland Farm looked promising.

It was April 25, 1889, when Meredith hosted her second solo cattle auction of Oakland Farm Shorthorns. Seventeen Shorthorns were sold that day. The "animals offered were in excellent condition, well bred, suitable for any herd, and should have commanded much higher prices. Yet, when compared with the prices realized at other sales this season, the average is higher than any one yet made. The scarcity of money among the farmers and breeders of the country causes them to be less desirous to purchase than in other years."[22] Even during tough financial times, Meredith's Shorthorns brought better than average prices when compared to those sold by other breeders.

Each sale mirrored previous ones, with her animals yielding excellent returns. Virginia Meredith's sale in May 1891 grossed $2,000 from 27 cows and heifers. Seven bulls at the same sale put $540 in her pocket.[23] Even Purdue University's agricultural school purchased two Shorthorn cows and a bull for the university herd, which was "considered a great addition to the college herd."[24] The agricultural community quickly learned that their own Shorthorns would be judged and priced relative to Meredith's herd at Oakland Farm.

It was not until nearly a decade after her husband's death that she began selling cattle and sheep under her own name. For the May 1891 sale, she used her name in the advertisements, which read: "PUBLIC SALE OF SHORT-HORNS BY MRS.

VIRGINIA C. MEREDITH AT CAMBRIDGE CITY, IND."[25] By this time, her reputation as a livestock breeder had grown to the point that she was asked to speak at the twentieth annual meeting of the Indiana Short Horn Breeders' Association in Indianapolis. Her topic that day was "Facts relating to the combination of the beef and milking qualities of short-horns."[26]

Within rural communities, the midsummer county fair and early fall state fair are always circled on the calendar. Amusement rides, food, and 4-H exhibits make the fairs a traditional outing for farm families. However, behind the scenes there is fierce competition for the top livestock prizes.

Meredith was said to have won state and national awards for her livestock. Available records from the Indiana State Fair suggest her animals did well in competition, but she did not dominate the Shorthorn cattle and Southdown sheep classes as Solomon and Henry Meredith had done for decades. At the Indiana State Fairs held between 1882 and 1906, Meredith's Shorthorns placed near the top on those occasions when her livestock competed. In 1895, she won second place in the category of one- to two-year-old bulls. In 1905 and 1906, she placed in several categories: second place for bulls aged between one and two; third place for heifer calves under one year old; and second place for bulls two to three years old.[27]

Meredith did not always enter her livestock at the state and county fairs. She wrote that she was not an "extensive exhibitor," but instead attended "exhibitions with frequency...."[28] When she began showing her purebred Shorthorns and Southdowns at agricultural fairs in Indiana, Ohio, and Illinois, people were unaccustomed to seeing a woman livestock breeder. They were surprised that her animals competed well against the established, male-dominated livestock breeders of the state.[29]

> It was not [un]til she began to exhibit her stock at the county and State fairs that Mrs. Meredith came conspicuously before the public. In many places such a thing as a woman stock-breeder had never been heard of and, as might have been expected, she sometimes met with criticism and ridicule. But she was not dismayed. For business reasons, she needed a reputation for her stock, and that reputation she determined to earn at the sacrifice, if need be, of her personal feelings. Last year she sold and shipped stock to Wisconsin, Minnesota, Mississippi, Virginia, Kentucky, Ohio and Illinois, as well as her native State, Indiana.[30]

While her reputation was partially linked to livestock shows, Meredith contended throughout her life that she was successful not for the ribbons and trophies her animals won but because her purebred livestock outperformed comparable animals from other breeders at sale time. One source noted that Meredith's "public sales were important enough to command more than average prices and high class buyers."[31] By 1900, Virginia Meredith would be listed with four other women under the Chicago newspaper headline "Women Who Run Their Own Farm and Make Them Pay."[32] Virginia Meredith had arrived as a successful farm manager.

Meredith was left childless at the time of her husband's death in 1882. That would change in 1889. She was sitting at the bedside of a gravely ill friend, Hattie Beach Matthews, when the conversation turned to the woman's children.[33] Meredith eased Matthews's worries by promising that her daughter and son—seven-year-old Mary and two-year-old Meredith—would live at Oakland Farm if events warranted such action. The children's father had died previously.

When Hattie Matthews died later that year, forty-year-old Virginia became a mother overnight. She welcomed Mary and Meredith to their new home at Oakland Farm, and she later wrote that she found the children to be an "untold blessing."[34]

While official adoption papers were not uncovered, evidence indicates that Virginia Meredith likely adopted the children. The 1900 United States Census lists the children as "wards," which meant Virginia Meredith had official custody of them. One article about Meredith mentions "[t]hese two little children she adopted."[35] Her obituary also points toward adoption, stating, "Surviving, besides the adopted daughter, is an adopted son, Meredith Matthews, both of whom she took [in] as small children upon the death of their mother."[36] Lastly, Mary Matthews wrote a three-page biography of Virginia Meredith that stated: "No children of her own. Adopted two children of a friend—Mary L. Matthews and Meredith Matthews."[37]

Meredith's role as mother must have expanded her thinking about the importance of keeping the home: cooking, child rearing, hygiene, money management, and clothing. Years before, Meredith had published a short article that described the importance of the home. In 1879, Meredith was asked as an alumnus of Glendale Female College to represent her graduating class of 1866.

She and others wrote a collection of stories printed into a pamphlet called "The Quarter Century Reunion for Glendale College."[38] Meredith referred to herself as "Jennie," which was what family and friends called her: "Jennie Claypool, now Mrs. Henry C. Meredith, of Cambridge City, Indiana, as the wife of a progressive farmer, finds the world beautiful, and is grateful every day for the education and training received here that has given [her] the ability to see the beauty in Nature's mysteries."[39] She wrote:

> Fifteen years ago we wrote essays about "The Uses of Adversity," "Woman's Sphere," "The Pleasures of Hope," "Memory," and such other serious themes as readily present themselves to the youthful mind. Since then experience has modified our view, chastened our spirit, and enlarged our comprehension of the affairs of life; indeed, all there is of education is its power to enable us to meet the evil and good of life with equanimity; when it fails of that, it fails utterly.
>
> When an unimpassioned review of life thrusts itself upon the student or philosopher, he is not concerned that he has discovered a new element; but he does congratulate himself upon the persistent application which has brought him through a long series of studies and investigations to worthy success. And so it is that the acme of culture and refinement is not unworthily employed in housekeeping and home-making. The poet, often quoted, has said, "That she who sweeps a room as by divine command, makes that and the action fine."[40]

Under the influence of the two children, Meredith worked out a lifelong belief that managing a farm home was equal to the work done on a farm to make it productive and profitable. Her new thinking put into play a new phase in Meredith's life that would forever link her to promoting home economics as a career for college-bound rural women.

The life of Mary Matthews (1882–1968) is relatively well known. Mary's career path and chosen profession mirrored the part of Virginia Meredith's career that was related to the scientific and practical study of the home. She was born at Peewee Valley, Kentucky, on October 13, 1882.[41] While growing up at Oakland Farm, Mary attended Farmers' Institutes with Virginia Meredith. Mary followed her mother to the University of Minnesota when Virginia was made the preceptress in the School of Agriculture, where Mary attended high school and later the university. In 1904, Mary Matthews had the distinction of being the first undergraduate woman at the University of Minnesota to earn a bachelor's degree in home economics. She would go on to enjoy a distinguished career that, at times, would coincide with that of Virginia Meredith (see Chapter 7).

Meredith Matthews's life (1887–1962), unlike his older sister's, is filled with many unanswered questions. He was probably born in Indianapolis, Indiana, on September 29, 1887.[42] Hattie Matthews named her son after Virginia Meredith as a sign of their close friendship.[43] When Virginia Meredith left the University of Minnesota in 1903 to return to full-time farming in Cambridge City, Mary stayed behind to finish her degree. Meredith Matthews, however, moved back to Cambridge City with his mother to attend Central High School, where he graduated in 1906. He attended Purdue University for at least one semester in 1907.[44]

Meredith Matthews lived in various locations during his lifetime. He worked in Springfield, Massachusetts, in 1908, but later that same year, he relocated for a job in Atlanta, Georgia. It is unknown how long he remained there, but the year 1920 found Meredith Matthews working as an engineer in San Francisco, California, where he lived with his wife, Dorothy. By 1930, he resided in Alameda County, California, where he listed his occupation as a real estate agent.[45]

Meredith Matthews served in the United States military from December 14, 1917, to July 24, 1919. Whether or not he was an active combatant during World War I is unknown. On February 1, 1962, seventy-four-year-old Meredith Matthews, a widower, died at the Veterans Administration Hospital in Oakland, California.[46]

As if managing Oakland Farm and the children wasn't difficult enough, Meredith was becoming increasingly involved with community projects, political activities, public speaking engagements, and association and club work. These projects not only took time, but also required her to leave the farm for extended periods.

The farm prospered in spite of her extended absences because Meredith had a good eye for hiring well-qualified workers to care for the farm's Shorthorns, Southdowns, and horses. One exceptionally experienced and well-known herdsman who worked for Meredith was Joseph Edwards, who was mentioned in newspaper accounts describing Meredith's sales. One 1887 article noted "the pains-taking and watchful care of her excellent herdsman, Mr. Joseph Edwards," while, two years later, a report on her 1889 sale stated that the "fine condition of the animals reflected much credit upon Mr. Joseph Edwards. His knowledge and experience as a herdsman is not surpassed by anyone."[47]

Meredith was very aware of the public praise Edwards received. She made it quite clear that while Edwards and the rest of her hired staff took wonderful care of her herds, farm, garden, and home, she was the one making the critical decisions. In a 1902 interview, Meredith told a reporter that she "manages the farm personally. She has a herdsman and farm hands, but the management she has never delegated to any one."[48]

Many were curious about Meredith's employment of men; more specifically, they wanted to know how men responded to job instructions from a woman. Meredith was successful because she paid well, restricted the workday, and respected the men. She herself noted:

> The labor question has not proved a difficulty with me, as it has with many men. I am always able to secure good service at reasonable wages. I never board farm hands, and I never expect them to work more than ten hours a day, unless in very special cases. My observation is that the labor[er] respects a woman's dollar as much as a man's dollar, and will render an equivalent in one case as quickly as in the other—and as faithfully. I have employed many men, and among them a large number in whom I could place the greatest confidence.[49]

Meredith, as a general principle, preferred not to provide room and board to employees. She strongly believed that doing so would deprive the children of a proper upbringing: "[A]long with this experience came some clear convictions regarding farm help and responsibility for conditions that would encourage farm laborers to live in separate homes where children might be educated and grow into useful citizens."[50]

Meredith's comfortable lifestyle at Oakland Farm was turned upside down when she was asked to sell the farm in 1902. The farm sale was precipitated by events in 1897, when she accepted a full-time position with the University of Minnesota "to organize the women's work on the campus. . . ." (see Chapter 7).[51] The university administrators had arranged for Meredith to teach between the months of September and March, which left her a full six months from early spring to early fall in which to farm. Meredith accepted the position, knowing that it could help her pay off the mortgage on Oakland Farm.[52]

After following this routine for five years, Meredith returned to Oakland Farm to prepare for planting season in April 1902, only to be faced with a sudden turn of events:

Shortly after arriving home Mrs. Meredith dreamed that she was standing on the lawn and a strong wind blew down a favorite tree that stood near the house. She also dreamed that upon the same day that the tree was blown down she sold her farm. The dream did not impress Mrs. Meredith at the time, but a few days later, during a gale of wind, the very tree she had dreamed was destroyed, was actually blown down and later on the same day Mr. Wright came and offered her such a price for the farm that she could not refuse his offer. The coincidence of the dream and the actual occurrence furnish food for comment for those who delight in such themes. . . . [53]

With her mind on planting her crops, she was surprised when Cornelius T. Wright, the local mortician, asked to buy Oakland Farm. To his surprise, Meredith agreed to think over his offer. The local community was shocked that she would even consider selling the farm that had been in the Meredith family for fifty years.

Why would Meredith consider selling the iconic Oakland farm? The farm was more than just property to her. It had given her independence as a woman and a reputation as a lady of importance. Deciding to keep the farm in 1882 was, no doubt, a tough choice at the time, but twenty years later, selling it became a gut-wrenching decision. "[F]or Mrs. Meredith to part with its ownership is a hard trial," reported one newspaper.[54]

The dream notwithstanding, Meredith cited numerous reasons throughout the years as to why she finally agreed to sell the farm. Wright's offer was "so tempting that she could not refuse to sell" was the most mentioned.[55] For the land, house, and outbuildings, she received $17,250 from Wright, which amounted to $115 per acre.

Still, making a profit was not the only reason Meredith ever mentioned for selling the legendary farm. A local newspaper reported that it was ". . . because of the fact that the scene of her labors for the great majority of the year is distant from the farm. . . ."[56] So it seems that Wright may have caught Meredith at a time when she was overcommitted; by 1902, in addition to working at the University of Minnesota, she was traveling as a speaker and writing for magazines and newspapers, which must have made managing the farm exceedingly difficult.[57] And still on another occasion, Meredith gave yet another reason, stating that she "concluded I wanted to make a farm myself."[58] It might be that Virginia was just tired of the financial struggles that she had fought for twenty years in order to make Oakland Farm solvent. More than likely, it was probably the combination of all of these reasons that led her to sell Oakland Farm.

Word quickly spread through the agricultural community that Meredith
had come to terms with Wright. The sale became fodder for the papers as
"the news was flashed over the entire state that Oakland Farm, made famous
by the Meredith family . . . had been sold and every paper of any consequence
carried the story to its readers."[59] She told Wright that the property would
be vacated in September 1902, in preparation for her return to the University
of Minnesota.

Selling off the remaining herd became Meredith's immediate concern. One
newspaper announced that final sale, with a front-page headline: "Great Herd to
Be Sold, The Meredith Short Horns Will Go At Auction."[60] The story itself noted,
"The sale of this herd is a matter of considerable historic interest, especially to
this part of the country, and to the state and nation at large."[61]

The September 9 auction turned into a social event. Neighbors, friends,
and former sales attendees wanted to have one more look around the place
before it was sold to Wright.

> The dispersion sale of Shorthorn cattle by Mrs. Virginia C. Meredith,
> Tuesday afternoon, drew a large crowd of visitors and buyers to Oakland
> farm. Many home people went because the day was pleasant and not a
> few who had been going to sales at this famous old farm for a quarter of a
> century or more. Of buyers and noted breeders from a distance, were O. C.
> Biger, of Hardwick, Iowa, the largest breeder in the Northwest, and whose
> herd comprises some three hundred head. . . . The first offerings were nine
> head imported by Messrs. Robbins & Son, and recently purchased by Mrs.
> Meredith. The average price she received for this importation was $883.
> The total for 31 head was $12,705, an average of $410.[62]

She would sell all of the rest of her property at a private sale.[63] Meredith
closed the door to the old house for the last time on Monday, September 15,
1902. No one will ever know what she felt as she walked away from her home
of thirty-two years; she never once wrote or spoke about it.[64] But while the
ownership of Oakland Farm had changed, the Merediths' connection to it
never would.

Not long after selling Oakland Farm, Virginia Meredith worked out a deal to
purchase 159 acres about a mile southwest of Oakland Farm. On July 3, 1902,
Meredith received the title to her very own farm for $9,600. She would christen
her new place Norborough Farm. The name represented Norborough Manor,

the "ancient seat of the Claypools and the home of Sir James Claypool, the founder of this branch of the family."[65]

After spending the winter teaching in Minneapolis, Meredith's first task upon her return to Indiana in April 1903 was to improve her living quarters at Norborough Farm. The property included a two-story farmhouse with outbuildings on the ridge above Simon's Creek. The home was at the end of a long lane south of Hunnicutt Road. She had the farmhouse repainted and was settled in time for her women's club to close its season there on June 11.[66] Meredith, who was accustomed to a much more splendid home, was determined to build a new house on her land; however, this dream never materialized.[67]

Meredith had become a local celebrity by this time. What she did and said, where she traveled, who visited her, and what she bought seemed to find its way into the local newspaper. Even one of Meredith's most harrowing experiences—when she lost control of the horse that was pulling her buggy—made the local paper:

> Mrs. Meredith had rather a remarkable experience one day last week. She was driving her family horse [hitched] to a buggy coming to town. As she was coming down the hill in the road through the woods, the horse became frightened at something and started to run, and when he came to the gate under full speed, he jumped over the gate, taking the buggy, with Mrs. Meredith in it, with him, and continued running away, and she was not able to control and stop him until he had run a half mile. Upon examination it was found that the buggy, horse or harness had not sustained the slightest damage. It is a Manlove gate, made from gas pipe and is four feet high, and the only damage done was a slight bending of the top pipe. Israel Morrey, who was driving near by, was an eye witness to the scene. Mrs. Meredith had a narrow escape from what might have been a serious accident.[68]

Each story provided an important and meaningful glimpse into Meredith's life at the Norborough Farm.

> Mrs. Meredith is now comfortably and pleasantly located in her new home on Norborough farm. She has already made numerous improvements which greatly adds to the general appearance of the place. This, however, is just the beginning, and in the organization of her plans she is looking forward with great satisfaction and interest in their execution and perfection. In time she hopes to make this one of the most valuable and attractive Short-horn breeding farms in the State. It is well adapted for the purpose and with her experience and ability, makes it possible for the realization of every desired anticipation. It can and will be made a model farm.[69]

In 1905, Meredith offered a carriage tour of her property to a reporter from *Dignam's Magazine,* a publication for women published in Richmond, Indiana. The reporter's description of Norborough Farm seemed to chronicle Meredith's progress:

> . . . a winding roadway through a vanishing woodland of beeches and out over a level stretch of meadow; a low-ceiled old house with a veranda overlooking a picturesque bit of landscape—old-fashioned garden flowers near, a slope to a stream with hills on the farther side covered with trees which make a flame of color in the autumn, while groups of cattle disposed to one side seem purposely placed for an artist's composition.[70]

It was obvious that Meredith was proud of her farm. As they went along, she pointed to the cattle, horses, sheep, and fields of alfalfa rippling in the breeze.

Though Meredith had only resided on the farm for a short time, she was already continuing the success that she had first enjoyed at Oakland Farm. In the fall of 1903, shortly after taking up residence at Norborough, she had traveled to Anderson, Indiana, to attend a Shorthorn sale at the farm of J. M. Donnelly. There she purchased two 2-year-old Shorthorn heifers named Royal Cherry and Red Rose that were said to be some of the best animals auctioned that day.[71] She paid Donnelly $155 for each heifer. Soon she would establish a "large stock farm [Norborough] on which high-grade cattle and sheep are raised."[72]

Meredith was extremely pleased with the progress of her farm, saying, "I have never been happier than in the past two years."[73] She had converted eight to ten fields that previously had been planted to corn into "a great pasture" for her prized cattle and sheep. She lived the maxim "Good live stock in rich pastures is the symbol of a high type of farming and comfortable living."[74] And she indulged her lifelong passion for books with her library of five shelves "devoted to herd records, with many volumes aside from these, the literature on these subjects being extensive."[75]

But while things seemed to be going well for Meredith at Norborough Farm, it is possible that she was still having a difficult time with her finances. In January of 1904, she had tried to secure additional speaking engagements without success.[76] Having no luck on that front, she then attempted to secure her father-in-law's war pension through political contacts. She wrote to Indiana Senator Charles Warren Fairbanks, asking about General Solomon's pension:

February 20, 1904
Norborough Farm
    Cambridge City, Ind.
Senator Fairbanks
    Washington

Dear Mr. Fairbanks

I am writing you, after consultation with Col. W. W. Dudley, in reference
to the propriety of seeking a pension for myself though a private pension
bill. You probably are familiar with the conspicuous military services of
General Solomon Meredith and his sons Lieut[enant] Samuel H. Meredith
and Major David M. Meredith—my husband Henry C. Meredith was the
youngest son, he was commissioned a lieutenant in the 160 Regh Indiana
Militia—all are now deceased.

Col Dudley was in Gen Meredith's "Iron Brigade" and is familiar with the
services of the Meredith family and my circumstances. If you would not
consider it an intrusion I would like to have him call upon you to present
the merits of the case.

I hope that you will be inclined to take up the matter for me—I will appreciate your consideration of the subject and also any advice on any questions which you may be kind enough to give me.[77]

Was it possible that she had spent the proceeds from the sale of Oakland
Farm on buying Norborough Farm, renovating the home there, and purchasing
livestock for her new herd?

By the latter part of 1905, Meredith had already resumed her public sales
of Shorthorns.[78] Other sales would follow. On April 10, 1912, she was again
making an offering to sell Shorthorns, this time sired by Golden Dale, one of
the "best breeding sons of the champion Avondale and grandson of the famous
Whitehall Sultan."[79] Interestingly enough, Meredith included the three-year-old
Golden Dale, her prized bull, in the same sale, but it is unknown whether this
decision was related to possible financial difficulties, a management strategy
for her herd, or for another reason entirely.

While at Norborough, Meredith continued to exhibit her animals at fairs. She
did well at the 1905 Indiana State Fair, when she took one first-place and
two second-place premiums for her Shorthorns.[80] She spent her time at the

fairs simply enjoying the occasion and looking over all of the fine animals
entered into competition. In December 1906, she attended the ten-day National
Livestock Show in Chicago.

Meredith made the 1908 Indiana State Fair a special moment in her life.
Fair officials announced that $58,663 worth of premiums would be offered
to those winning certain livestock categories. Meredith herself would offer a
once in-a-lifetime chance for a Shorthorn exhibitor to win a silver cup that
General Solomon Meredith himself had won more than fifty years earlier for
the top yearling Shorthorn heifer.[81] One account stated, "Only a woman of Mrs.
Meredith's loyalty to Short-horn interests would have parted with such [a] historic plate."[82] Another account provided more detail about the award:

> The Meredith cup was won by Gen. Solomon Meredith at the fourth
> Indiana Fair, held in 1855, and the award was made to him on Shorthorn
> cattle. For several years General Meredith drove his blooded Shorthorns to
> Indianapolis from his farm, the route being over the old National road, and
> the distance was fifty-three miles.... Mrs. Meredith has twenty heavy silver
> goblets and four pitchers, as well as an entire solid silver service of coffee,
> sugar, cream and water bowl, all of which were won by General Mere-
> dith at Indiana fairs. The cup she offers is one of the choicest of the
> Meredith collection.[83]

Meredith offered the cup for the top Shorthorn yearling bred in the state. The
lucky winner of the Meredith cup was a Mr. Bowen, who won with a roan heifer
named Countess Selma 2d, "which was also declared the best female under
three years old in the show, all breeds competing, by a committee of stockyards
men in awarding a stockyards special."[84]

Meredith's stature grew with each passing year at Norborough. Many
younger men and women came to her home seeking advice about livestock and
farming. Earl Robbins, a family friend, wrote that she "advised many young
men who were contemplating farming to utilize their farm products with purebred live stock instead of scrub."[85] Meredith would live on her farm for fourteen
years, immersed in agriculture, offering advice to a younger generation, raising
animals, attending fairs, and becoming a much-sought-after national lecturer.

Meredith had left unfinished business behind when she sold Oakland Farm and
moved to Norborough. While the home and property that the Merediths had
owned for fifty years was no longer hers, there remained on a hill overlooking

Oakland Farm a private family cemetery where Solomon Meredith; his wife, Anna; and sons Henry, David, and Samuel were buried. It was surrounded by a white picket fence that could be seen from the front windows of the house. Located next to the town's original Capitol Hill Cemetery, it was a fitting memorial to the Merediths.[86]

Towering above the cemetery was a monument to Solomon Meredith. Henry had contracted with Lewis Cass Lutz, a local artist, to design this tribute to his father. John H. Mahoney was commissioned for the work.[87] The monument was described as a "lofty column, surmounted with the statue of Gen. Sol. Meredith, in heroic size. It is a prominent object [forty feet tall], and can be seen from the surrounding country at many points miles away."[88] The statue depicted General Meredith in his Civil War–era Iron Brigade uniform.

Just to the west of the monument were the graves of three Civil War horses—Barney, Tom, and Turk—who Meredith affectionately described as "pensioners on Oakland Farm."[89] She offered this description of the horses:

> Horses were far more important then than now. We had on our home farm [Oakland Farm] three pensioners, horses that had seen service in the Army of the Potomac. Barney, a gaited saddle horse, shared Indiana honors in the battle of Gettysburg. Barney was one of the noted horses of the Army of the Potomac with speed and endurance; at the battle of Gettysburg Barney was the only horse of the Iron Brigade that escaped with his life. He was then sent to the home farm to end his days in Indiana.
>
> On those historic days of [18]63—July 1, 2, and 3—the Rebel General Lee rather surprised the northern army by his rapid advance and it became imperative to "hold" the Rebel army by engaging it in battle until the Union troops could be placed in position. For this duty the "Iron Brigade" was chosen because it had seen service and proved itself; in that brigade, First Division, First Army Corps, was the 19th Regiment Indiana Volunteers. Barney belonged to Lieutenant Samuel Meredith and shared the glory of the day....
>
> A second pensioner was a big roan, Tom, sent home from Gettysburg. In the early days after Appomattox there was a constant stream of soldiers coming to our home in a very active effort to qualify for Government help, and every old soldier wanted to see "old Tom" and stroke his glossy shoulder.
>
> And there was still another pensioner—a handsome bay horse given to General Meredith—Turk. . . . These three pensioners had the freedom of the pasture.[90]

[Turk] was a large, fine bay, a rapid mover, a trusty, serviceable horse. He saw active service during the latter part of the war in the army of the Potomac, and in the Southwest. During Gen. Meredith's life at home on the farm, this was his driving horse. . . . Turk was led in the procession, with empty saddle, at the burial of Gen. M. He was over 25 years old."[91]

In 1905, the Meredith cemetery was visited by the Indiana Nineteenth Regiment, part of the famed Iron Brigade. Surviving members had come to Richmond, Indiana, to meet with old friends. At their reunion, Virginia Meredith was not only made an honorary member of the regiment, but she was presented with a badge made of iron collected from the Gettysburg battle. A large contingent of soldiers from the regiment went to Cambridge City to pay their respects at the grave of their former leader, General Solomon Meredith.[92]

With few living relatives to assume the burden of maintaining the graves, Virginia became concerned that the Meredith cemetery would fall to neglect after her own death. Something had to be done to remedy the problem that she had created by selling Oakland Farm.

She became preoccupied with having the Meredith cemetery moved from its hilltop site to a public cemetery. Word quickly spread that Meredith wanted to move the graves of General Meredith and his family to a new location. Public cemeteries outside of Cambridge City approached her about the matter. The Crown Hill Cemetery in Indianapolis along with Glen Miller, a city park in Richmond, showed strong interest in interring the Meredith family.[93] They wanted one of Indiana's best-known Civil War generals added to the list of distinguished persons buried within their respective cemeteries.

Her final decision was to re-inter the Meredith family in the Riverside Cemetery in Cambridge City. She "always felt that this was the home of the family through life, and it ought to continue. . . ."[94] This was also fitting since Solomon's wife, Anna, was president of a group of ten local women who helped raise the funds to purchase the land that would become Riverside Cemetery.

Meredith announced her intentions on July 23, 1907, and said that the monument and family graves were to be relocated to Cambridge City's Riverside Cemetery.[95] Her announcement was timed to coincide with the dedication in Indianapolis of a monument to Oliver P. Morton, the Civil War–era governor of Indiana. Morton, a personal and longtime friend of Solomon Meredith, had been at Solomon's bedside at the time of the general's death.

Meredith's announcement required her to work out the details with the Cambridge City trustees, as they were responsible for the care and maintenance of the Riverside Cemetery. Meredith and the trustees came to an amicable agreement in August 1908, when she accepted a large piece of ground known as park lot seven from the trustees. Not only was the plot large, but it was also a focal point of the cemetery. In addition, the trustees gave her the assurance that no others—outside of General Solomon, his family, and Virginia—would ever be buried in this plot.[96]

Meredith agreed to pay the expenses for relocating the graves and monument. In the fall of 1908, some thirty years after the general's death in 1875, the final move began. George Boden was hired by Meredith to move the huge stone monument to its new site, a distance of approximately one mile. Boden and his son began the process early that November, when they loaded the monument's shaft on "two (2) sets of four-wheel wagon running gears and it was pulled by four horses."[97] After the monument was placed at Riverside Cemetery, Boden then moved the five caskets and placed them west of the statue, completing the work by November 19.

Twenty years later, Meredith would renew the Meredith family's ties to the Cambridge City community through a special donation. Virginia was always proud of her association with her father-in-law, General Solomon Meredith. She also understood the importance of the man and legend to the people of Cambridge City. At the 1928 Memorial Day ceremonies, she gave to the Cambridge City library the general's sword so that it could be displayed in the community.[98] With the gift, Meredith wrote the attached note:

> To the Public Library Board, Cambridge City, Indiana
> I have pleasure in giving to the Public Library as a memorial to the Civil war history of General Meredith the jeweled sword and its case which was presented to him when in command of the western district of Kentucky 1864–5, together with military sash, belt and spurs; also his commission as Brigadier General, signed by Abraham Lincoln, president.
>
> The loyal interest of General Meredith and his family in their home town makes Cambridge City a fitting place for this memorial, therefore, believing that it will be appreciated and its care suitably guarded, I am gratified by your acceptance of the gift.[99]

Meredith's choice of farming as a profession may have been unconventional for a woman in the late 1800s, but she embraced it and even excelled at it. This gave her a sense of great accomplishment, which she addressed in one of her speeches: "There is one time when I feel proud, very proud, and it comes once in ten years, and that is when the census taker comes around and says, 'What is your occupation?' And I say, 'Farmer.' And he usually says, 'You don't want me to put your name in as a farmer, do you?' I certainly do, for I am a farmer, and I have an opportunity to gratify my pride once in ten years."[100]

In fact, Meredith wanted more women to consider farming as a legitimate career choice. One newspaper interview reported that Meredith's views were that farming "furnishes those conditions of life which the average woman craves, a home, a safe and sure income, independence. She admits that there is no prospect of amassing a fortune, but believed that women care less for wealth in itself than do men; and that therefore the vocation has become one of the few open to women which are not already over-crowded."[101]

Meredith felt that women had many of the attributes that made farming a perfect profession for them. She thought women and farming went hand in hand because, as she noted, "[women's] work is not discounted on account of sex. A bushel of wheat brings market price; a cow makes as many—or more pounds—of butter when owned by a woman, as when owned by a man."[102]

And Meredith actually thought that farming was easier than managing a farm home. She said if "a woman can make bread and direct some one else how to make bread, she can do the infinitely simpler thing—make hay. If she can make butter or teach another the delicate process that involves painstaking care and sound judgment, she can certainly accomplish the comparatively simple process of growing corn. If she can take care of boys and girls, how easy is it in comparison to maintain the health and promote the growth of cattle, horses and sheep."[103]

The farms at Cambridge City remained central to Meredith's life for forty-six years, but her time there would eventually draw to a close. She once said, "I have always felt that if you cannot live on a farm you should sell it to somebody who can live on it."[104] So Meredith sold Norborough Farm and left Cambridge City to move in with her daughter, Mary Matthews, in West Lafayette in 1916, at the age of sixty-seven.

In Cambridge City, Meredith had availed herself of opportunities and become an independent woman at a time when few women had. She used the experiences gained at Oakland and Norborough Farms—in livestock breeding, farming, and political and community influence—to expand her own career horizons, achieving great success in the process. Her success would continue in the years ahead as she continued to draw upon and apply the lessons she had learned at Cambridge City.

A Voice for Rural People

CHAPTER 4

*We seek to emphasize what we truly believe,
that the farm and its home offer an opportunity for
"the investment of all that manhood is or may be"—
for the "investment of all that womanhood is or may be."*

—Virginia Meredith, from a speech given at the
Annual Conference of Farmers' Institute Workers,
West Lafayette, Ind., October 1910

M EREDITH WAS IN HER THIRTIES when her name became synonymous with women who broke down barriers placed in front of them. She was a woman to be reckoned with in her early life, thanks mainly to her love of agriculture and livestock. When others spoke of women farmers in agriculture, Meredith was singled out by name. She represented only a handful of women at that time who were successfully running their own crop production and livestock operations. Meredith and Oakland Farm were nationally known. As an agricultural businessperson, she had no equal among women and, some argued, could stand toe-to-toe with most men of her day.

Her well-managed and financially successful Oakland Farm opened an additional and very influential door that soon made Virginia C. Meredith's name well known across Indiana and the Midwest. She achieved yet another first when she began speaking on livestock issues in front of audiences consisting primarily of male farmers. One of Meredith's earliest documented talks was at an 1884 program hosted by the Gibson County Agricultural Society in Princeton, Indiana.[1] Her assigned topic was "Improved Breeds of Cattle," with special reference to Shorthorns. Just a year later, she was asked to speak at the Farm and Home Week at Purdue University.[2]

Meredith's successful work as a livestock breeder, farmer, and business-woman soon led to a constant stream of requests to address agricultural audiences on livestock production. Coincidentally, her rise in popularity as a public speaker on agricultural subjects occurred as the need for educating the farm populace became a priority for the Indiana State Board of Agriculture, an organization that represented the interests of the strong and influential agricul-tural sector of Indiana. It was this same quasi-governmental organization that Virginia Meredith's husband, Henry, had served from 1879 to 1882—including as its one-time president—and that her father, Austin Claypool, had served from 1869 to 1879.

With funding provided by the Indiana General Assembly, the representa-tives on the agriculture board were appointed to better define the needs of agriculture and farmers, and to bring about long-term improvements in the farm economy, farmer education, and the farm family. The board members decided to offer programs known as Farmers' Institutes. These locally based meetings, a forerunner of similar services that would eventually be provided by the Cooperative Extension Service, offered opportunities for farmers to learn more about the latest developments in agriculture and to use this information for improving their businesses. Henry Meredith was a strong proponent of making these programs available in Indiana and guided the passage of a series of resolutions creating the state's first Farmers' Institutes.

While the Indiana State Board of Agriculture sponsored a handful of institutes as early as 1882, for many reasons—including political infighting and limited state funds—it was ineffective at managing the program, so the Indiana General Assembly passed the Farmers' Institute Act of 1889, which turned over the management reins for the institutes to Purdue University. William C. Latta, the professor of agriculture at Purdue, was assigned the job of creating institutes where farmers would receive the latest science-based views on agricultural production.[3] The institutes managed by Latta would launch Meredith's career as a speaker and writer.

During the first two years in which Latta managed the program—from 1889 to 1891—approximately half of Indiana's counties participated by holding at least one program, but by 1893, institutes were being offered in all ninety-two counties.[4] Many Purdue faculty members participated in those early institutes, but with so much ground to cover, Professor Latta recognized early on "the impossibility of supplying all the meetings with trained speakers and scientific experts," noting instead that his aim was "to develop practical workers from the ranks of the everyday farmers."[5] To ease the burden, he recruited experienced and successful agriculturists to participate as Farmers' Institutes speakers.

By November 1889, Latta had selected "nearly one hundred active institute workers, including farmers, horticulturists, stockmen, and the specialists of the Agricultural Experiment Station" to present the first year's programs.[6] It has often been said that Virginia Meredith, as one of the first speakers to be invited, was the "first woman employed by Agr. [Agricultural] Extension Dept. of Purdue University."[7] Latta always considered her to be one of his best institute speakers. She remained a dedicated and willing speaker for twenty years, which Latta noted in his 1904 annual report: "She still continues in active and effective service, as an Institute speaker, and is the only member of the corps of early Institute workers to whom this distinction belongs."[8]

Throughout the years, she became a trusted colleague from whom Latta sought advice on how to improve the Farmers' Institutes:

> I quite fully agree with you that the farmers have not as yet reached the higher levels. There will be a good deal of patient plodding and grubbing necessary before we shall realize our hopes. . . . I will appreciate it at any time if you can offer suggestions that will be to the betterment of the work. I am especially desirous to find but where the weak places are. We have a few veritable sticks of chairmen, but I think you did not strike them in this series. . . . [If] anything occurs to you as to how the interest may be increased, I shall be very glad indeed to receive your suggestions.[9]

Meredith and Latta had become a team that would last a lifetime.

During the formative years of the Farmers' Institutes, speakers were not compensated outside of their expenses. Latta said that in the "first year these workers, without exception, donated their services. The second year a few, and the third year quite a number made a moderate charge when engaged in Institute work outside of their own counties."[10]

Meredith and James Mount, who would later become the governor of Indiana, were specifically recognized by Latta for volunteering their time. Latta wrote, "Mrs. Virginia C. Meredith and the late lamented Governor Mount attended many of the Farmers' Institutes during the first two years [1889–91] that the work was conducted under State [Purdue] control. They not only freely donated their services, but they proved especially helpful in performing the duties assigned them on the programmes and in informal discussion as well."[11]

Undoubtedly, Latta must have wanted to pay Meredith at some point in the second year but was not permitted to do so. Meredith herself was quoted as saying, "One of the board members protested against paying any woman for any kind of work."[12] The board to which Meredith referred was the Purdue University Board of Trustees, which was the only board that Professor Latta answered to in an official capacity. It was this board that ultimately controlled the funds provided by the Indiana General Assembly to Purdue for implementing the Farmers' Institutes. This disappointment notwithstanding, Meredith continued to speak for free until such time that all institute speakers were paid for their efforts.[13]

Speakers in the early days were paid two to ten dollars for each two days' worth of work. Meredith and the other speakers often worked a grueling six-day week. Apparently, partway through the 1895–96 institute season, Meredith must have had doubts about doing all of the speaking engagements that she had agreed to do. Latta let her know in no uncertain terms that "[y]es, I expect you to take all the work assigned you in the schedule, and the local authorities are also expecting as much. Please do not disappoint us."[14]

Outside of their salary, Professor Latta's state funding paid for speakers' expenses, such as train fare, carriage rentals, meals, and lodging. Speakers would travel by train from town to town, then be shuttled to meeting locations, often by carriage. Latta secured the rates for the trains and worked with speakers to make the necessary travel arrangements. Latta wrote one particular letter to Meredith that provides insight into these arrangements:

> I have asked the G.P.A. [general passenger agent] of the Big 4 Ry. [Railway] Co. to grant you half rates for the following trips: Dec. 14, Indianapolis to Lafayette; Dec. 21, Crawfordsville to Indianapolis. Each ticket is to be good for five days from date of sale. You will therefore please ask the agents at the respective starting points for half rates in accordance with this schedule.[15]

Early on, Meredith and the other speakers read papers they had prepared and took questions.

> The papers, or essays, were somewhat formal in character, and the audience seldom took an active part in discussing the subjects presented.... As a rule, the speaker takes about half or three-fourths time allotted to a given subject, and then gives way for questions and informal discussion by the audience.... Inexperienced speakers are requested to write brief papers, not exceeding twenty minutes in length.... The decided preference of the audience is, however, for the speaker who can discard paper and notes

and speak extemporaneously. The more experienced and more effective workers use only outlines....[16]

Meredith remained active as an institute speaker between 1889 and 1920, except for a period of six years when she was at the University of Minnesota (see Chapter 7).[17] Starting with the first institute in 1889 and continuing through 1892, Meredith traveled to nearly every county in Indiana.[18] It didn't take long for the county organizers to personally request the lady livestock manager from Cambridge City for their programs. According to one historian, "the invitations came more frequently and she acquired more than a local reputation as a public speaker."[19]

Meredith left little record on how she was treated as the first woman speaker addressing predominantly male agricultural audiences. No doubt, a few eyebrows were raised and more than a few whispers could be heard in the audience when she took to the podium to speak about her experiences raising livestock. Obviously, the men first had to get beyond their prejudices about a woman being able to raise purebred livestock. But once they looked past Meredith's gender, they began to earnestly listen to her advice on producing better animals that sold for higher prices in the marketplace. Her audiences came to understand that the woman speaker in front of them was more than ready for the challenge.

There is little doubt that her influence on audiences and her reputation as a speaker grew by leaps and bounds each time she made a public presentation. Following a series of lectures about cattle production to animal sciences students at Purdue University in January 1890 and again in 1897, it was reported that audiences at the university found her to be one of "the most compelling and popular speakers who comes to the campus."[20]

Meredith's knowledge, speaking style, and demeanor contributed to her success as an institute speaker. One article noted, "To those who had not made her acquaintance, her knowledge of her subjects and her gift as a speaker were a revelation."[21] Even Meredith's appearance seemed to be of note: "[Meredith] is a woman who would attract attention anywhere....At middle age, she is a handsome woman, tall, erect, and splendidly proportioned."[22] Off stage, she was a quiet and modest person, but when she took to the podium, her presence was undeniable.[23]

The *Indianapolis News* described her as having an "individuality about her, an atmosphere of inexhaustible strength, of calm confidence in herself—arising, no doubt, from her long habit of self-reliance, but never merging into arrogance or egotism—that stamps her at once as 'somebody.'"[24] Others talked about her passion for agriculture and persuasiveness coupled with a "rich voice and power to carry an audience. . . ."[25] Her talks were said to be of ". . . inspirational quality. There is fire at the heart of her which fires other people. Born with a rare gift for thinking, she has been willing to use it,—to wrestle with an idea, as Jacob wrestled with the angel, until it yields its blessing. Accordingly her talks are shot through with that most magical of all the elements—thought. And behind that is her hundred horse-power earnestness."[26]

Thus, it was not by accident or luck that Virginia C. Meredith became one of the country's most popular agricultural speakers of the late nineteenth century. But while Meredith gave the impression that she was a very confident woman, in her early days as a speaker she questioned what impact she was having. In 1894, just prior to her institute work, she confided to Latta that she was concerned about her effectiveness as a speaker. Latta's reply indicated that he often felt the same way. It was a rare confession between two popular speakers.

> Your brief note upon leaving Chicago came duly to hand. I can appreciate the feeling which you entertained upon starting out in the Institute work. I feel sure, however, that the kindly, if not always punctiliously courteous, treatment which you have received will, on this, have restored your complacency and equipoise. I know that your services will be appreciated this year as they have always been in the past, and, what is better still, I know that you will do genuinely good work which has the ring of the pure metal in it. Rest assured of my implicit confidence in the outcome and in your ability to do the best thing possible. Please do not lay too much stress upon either the absence or the methods of expression of approval. Farmers are frequently lacking in this respect, but their hearts are kind and I am sure your long familiarity with them will enable you to discern both their desire for improvement and their appreciation of those who strive for it. Sometimes I, myself, feel a little cast down, but I am encouraged almost all the while in the thought that a great good work is being done and that in the end it will be all right.[27]

In fact, Meredith had become so popular that Professor Latta soon needed to secure her services much earlier than other institute speakers.[28] By the early 1890s, Latta was competing with the World's Columbian Exposition for Meredith's time (see Chapter 6). He asked her in March 1893 about her availability during the upcoming winter. Latta also offered Meredith more money than he paid any other institute speaker from Indiana. She was now being paid what then Senator James Mount and T. B. Terry, his two top male speakers, commanded.[29] In his letter, Latta asked Meredith the following:

I recently sent out copies of the enclosed circular to the chairmen and secretaries of Institutes throughout the State. I find upon the return cards that your name is quite frequently mentioned and this is evidence of quite a general and earnest desire to have you actively engage in the Institute work next year. I therefore write you thus early in the hope of securing your services for say about a fortnight at a time at intervals through the season. I am sorry to say that we are not able to hold out strong financial inducements to you to enter this work. [*Authors' Note: Latta always believed he could never pay the speakers what they were worth.*] I am compelled, therefore, to appeal largely to your patriotism, pride in Hoosierdom and interest in the farming community generally to induce you to again engage actively in this work. The regularly assigned speakers will receive from $15.00 to $25.00 per week in addition to expenses, with the exception of Mr. T. B. Terry, of Ohio, who asks more. So far I have offered $25.00 to but one speaker within the State for next year. I realize that any person who is qualified to do his work as it should be done is worth more than our limited funds will warrant the General Manager [Latta] in paying.

The replies to my queries show that almost unanimously the institute officers will favor but three meetings per week, which will make the work more expensive than it was for this season just closed. This means that it is necessary to practice the utmost economy if we are to send out two speakers to each Institute and continue the direct apportionment of $20.00 to each county. We desire to secure the very best workers possible with the funds at our disposal, but will find it absolutely impossible to pay many of these workers $25.00 per week in addition to their expenses. I earnestly desire to have you lend a helping hand next winter and trust you will consent to an active participation in the work. If $25.00 per week and your expenses would not be a satisfactory remuneration I will pay you $30.00 in addition to your expenses. I would say, however, that $25.00 per week is, in my judgment, a full equivalent of $10.00 per Institute where you go out to a single meeting because each individual Institute attended will, on an average, take three days time. Please consider this matter carefully and give me an affirmative answer, if possible, on as reasonable terms as you can afford to engage in the work.[30]

Meredith signed on to do the upcoming work for the institutes.[31] Latta set the schedule for her, warning her about the difficulties she would face when speaking at three programs a week:

I have tentatively made the following assignments for you at Farmers'
Institutes next season, namely; the 1st, 2nd, 3rd weeks in December
[1894] and in 1895, the weeks beginning respectively Jan. 14th, 21st and
Feb. 4th, 11th and 18th. In assigning speakers I have, as far as possible,
assigned those requested, but this is not true in every case. Your name has
been mentioned by a majority of the chairmen and I am sure you will be
a very welcome visitor at any of the Institutes to which I have thus tentatively assigned you. It will hardly be possible for you to get home at the
end of each week as the meetings begin on Monday and close on Saturday.
You may, therefore, prefer not to have three weeks of continuous work
in December. Please let me hear from you as soon as convenient stating
whether I may make these assignments final or not....[32]

Meredith agreed with Latta that doing too many programs would take
her away from home for too long, so Latta honored her request to work no
more than two weeks in succession.[33] By August, Meredith knew her Farmers'
Institute schedule for the upcoming season:

I have made the assignments as nearly in conformity with your wishes
as I can. The assignments as they now stand are as follows: the first week in
December, Harrison, Floyd and Washington counties; the second week
in December, Jefferson, Switzerland and Ohio counties; the week beginning January 21st, Steuben, Dekalb and Allen counties; the week beginning
January 28th, Kosciusko, Noble and LaGrange counties; the week beginning February 18th, Whitley, St. Joseph and Elkhart counties. . . . As the
assignments now stand I have five weeks of Institute work for you....[34]

Latta was disappointed that Meredith's administrative duties at the World's
Columbian Exposition seemed never ending. The institute chairmen continued
to ask for Meredith. He knew Meredith's presence on even a few of the institute
programs would be a big draw. Early in June 1895, Latta asked Meredith to commit to doing a few days of institute work:

Can we count upon you to do some Institute work next winter? Although
many of the counties have not yet been heard from I find there is quite a
call for your services, and I am very desirous to have you in the work. Please
let me know from you at your early convenience and state whether the
terms of last year will be satisfactory in case you can engage in the work.
Hoping to receive a favorable reply, . . .[35]

By 1900, Meredith was accepting speaking engagements that went well
beyond the state's boundary. "Mrs. Meredith has this winter been invited to

address farmers' and breeders' conventions in New York, Illinois, Indiana, Wisconsin, Minnesota and Mississippi," reported the *Indianapolis News*.[36] Sometimes she even had to turn down her longtime friend, Professor Latta. He wrote to Meredith on September 9, 1899, at St. Anthony's Park, Minnesota, asking whether she could give a presentation at an upcoming Conference of Institute Workers that was held each year at Purdue University. This annual program was a way for Latta to update his speakers on the latest subjects relating to the Farmers' Institutes.

> We are planning to hold a conference of institute workers here Oct. 18 and 19. I write to ask if you could be with us on the 19th, at least, to present at a woman's session the subject of "women or woman in agriculture." My thought is to have three subjects presented, viz., "Women in agriculture." "Industrial education of women." "Needs of the farmer's wife and daughter." I hope to secure Mrs. [Nellie] Kedzie [Jones] of Illinois to present the second topic and Mrs. [Mary] Mayo of Michigan for the third.

> With the small amount at my command for meeting the expenses of such a meeting, I confess it seems presumptuous for me to ask your help. I trust however that your interest in the subject and your loyalty to the farmers of Indiana will induce you to make a strenuous effort to be with us.[37]

Meredith replied that she could not speak at the conference due to her commitment to teach classes at the University of Minnesota at that time. Latta tried again with a follow-up request: "Your kind letter of the 15th duly received. I greatly regret that you will be unable to attend our conference but I recognize the fact that so soon after the opening of your term, that it would hardly be practicable for you to get away. I would be greatly pleased to have you with us at least one session. I expect to be at the State Fair on Friday and hope to meet you then. I hope the year may be a pleasant and prosperous one in Minnesota."[38] Despite Latta's persistent efforts, Meredith did not attend his conference that year.

By 1903, Virginia Meredith had left Minnesota and returned to farming full-time at Norborough Farm. Consequently, she was able to resume her duties as a lecturer at the Farmers' Institutes in Indiana, making 1903 her most prolific year for institute work. With Meredith back in the state, Professor William Latta began promoting her to county chairmen at every opportunity, noting her versatility: "I think it would add to the interest at that session if you could have Mrs. Meredith's address on 'Special Education for the Home Keeper' or 'Fences,

Fields and Farmstead' or 'The Relation of the Home to Civic Life.'"[39] In one case, Latta wrote to tell Meredith of a special request made by one chairman:

> Mr. A. W. Shoemaker, of Daleville, desires to have you instead of Mr. Burkhart at his meeting to be held at Daleville, Delaware County, Feb. 1–2. I understand from his letter that he has spoken to you about this, and that you have no engagement to prevent. If you can go, I will pay your per diem and one-third of the week's salary agreed upon, and you will look to him to be reimbursed for traveling expenses. I make this arrangement because your charge is considerably higher than that of Mr. Burkhart.[40]

Shortly after the winter meetings had ended in March 1904, Latta began asking Meredith to commit to doing more institute work for him for the next year's institutes. He knew he was competing with organizations from around the country that also wanted Meredith on their programs. In 1907 Meredith did not make a single presentation at any of the Farmers' Institutes, but she did contract with Professor Latta to do more presentations in 1910, the last year that official records on the assignment of institute speakers were found.

As evidenced by her growing popularity as a speaker, Meredith was an excellent presenter who knew her material well. Indeed, Latta often tapped her for assignments because she would incorporate topics in her speeches that he thought were important. In 1904, Latta agreed to hold a District Stockman's Institute in Rushville, Indiana, and wanted Meredith to give two presentations, which she subsequently agreed to do.[41] In his letter to Meredith, Latta suggested what she might include in her speech on livestock:

> . . . We shall devote the evening session of the 12th to educational topics, under the following headings:
> (1) The Need of Trained Men and Women in Agricultural Pursuits;
> (2) What the Agricultural Colleges are Doing to Supply this Need;
> (3) Opportunities for Trained Men and Women in Agricultural Pursuits.

> I desire to have you take No. 3 above, and would like to have you discuss, also, the following day, "The most profitable cow for beef production." There is, I believe, a growing belief that the general farmer can not afford to maintain a cow simply for the calf that she will raise each year for the shambles [slaughterhouse], hence, there is something of a tendency to go into dairy stock and buy western calves for feeding. This idea will tend to discount the use of cows of a beef type in the production of butcher's stock.

Do you feel disposed to make a strong plea for the dual-purpose cow, like the milking type of Shorthorn, that shall produce calves for the general market, and also serve as a dairy cow? If you can support this proposition, I would be glad to have you take it up, or something like it.[42]

Meredith showed great versatility regarding the subjects she covered as a speaker, with her topics spanning both the field and home. She would cover such subjects as "General-Purpose Farming" and "The Farm Home" at the Tippecanoe County Farmers' Institute in 1897.[43] She carried through with the multiple themes of production and home at the 1902 special program on butchers' stock in Anderson, discussing "Lines of Progress in Animal Husbandry" and "The European Farmer and His Home."[44] At the New Paris [Preble County], Ohio, Institute in February of 1906, she made three presentations on what might have been the most important issues addressed throughout her speaking career: "The Farmstead Field and Fences," "The Business of Home-making," and "Standards of Living and the Use of Money."[45]

Throughout time, Meredith adapted to meet the changing needs of her institute audiences. Professor Latta asked Meredith in April 1904 to consider adding new topics to her repertoire. He included these new subjects on an updated list that was sent out to the chairpersons responsible for each county's meetings.

Would it be convenient and agreeable to you to do some institute work next Winter on the same terms as the past Winter? If so, I would be pleased to have you suggest at your early convenience any additions to your subjects or any changes which you care to make. I think the number of special subjects desired by chairmen will be larger than heretofore. If I mistake not, the tendency is in this direction. These special subjects will include, among other things, beef making, feeds and feeding, improvement of live stock, highway improvement, betterment of the schools, domestic economy, household management, etc. etc. If your subjects of last year do not cover the full range of your experience, observation and study, I will be glad to have you add others.[46]

One of Meredith's last agricultural talks occurred on August 3, 1920, when she was invited to speak by the Indiana dairymen at Martinsville, Indiana. At seventy-one years of age, Meredith had become a living legend in the agricultural community. Her part of the program was advertised in the *Indiana Farmer's Guide* with the following quote: "Mrs. Virginia Meredith, prominent club woman and influential speaker will be present to give a talk of interest to both men and women."[47] She was allowed to speak at that summer field day on a subject of her choosing.

In 1895, Virginia Meredith was invited to give a presentation about sheep at Vicksburg, Mississippi. It would be a talk that forever identified her as "The Queen of American Agriculture." A local newspaper announced the event:

> . . . [Meredith] goes from Chicago in a special car, with the governors of Iowa and Wisconsin, to the Inter-State Agricultural Institute at Vicksburg, Miss., this week, where she will respond to the address of welcome, and also deliver an address on sheep husbandry. We feel proud that Mrs. Meredith is a citizen of our town. The numerous deserved honors she has gained reflect credit upon our town and State. Her sister, Mrs. Earl, of Connersville, will accompany her on her trip South.[48]

Around 7 P.M. on February 20, the train arrived at the Vicksburg depot, where a crowd of approximately 250 people waited on the platform. As the passengers disembarked, the Warren Light Artillery gave them a military salute. The guests were then escorted to the Hotel Carroll by a volunteer band and a battery detachment.[49] This special touch of southern hospitality was one that the travelers from the Midwest never forgot.

After a quick supper at the hotel, the invited speakers and special guests went to the Opera House, where, "in the words of the proprietors, there were more persons in the building than ever known before."[50] Meredith took her seat on the stage alongside other dignitaries.[51]

The late-night meeting at the Opera House was the ceremonial opening of the Interstate Farmers Institute. The first speaker to the podium was Mr. P. Harding, the chairman of the executive committee of the institute. Welcoming addresses by Mississippi Governor John M. Stone, Vicksburg Mayor W. L. Trowbridge, and Murray F. Smith, who represented the Mississippi Board of Trade, were offered to the audience and to the guests on stage.

Some of the out-of-state guests were invited to offer a few words of appreciation to the crowd, thanking them for their kind invitation to Vicksburg. The *Vicksburg Evening Post* noted that the speakers included "Ex-Gov. W[illiam] D. Hoard, Wisconsin; Hon. J. M. Samuels, Kentucky; Gov. Frank D. Jackson, Iowa; Mrs. Virginia C. Meredith, Indiana; Gov. Murphy J. Foster, Louisiana."[52] Meredith gave the last presentation of the evening. The newspaper reported that a "fitting close to this most happy occasion was a few minutes talk from Mrs. Meredith a most brilliant and gifted lady, who charmed the audience with her words and most pleasing address."[53]

The educational program began sharply at 9:30 A.M. the next day. The agenda listed a wide array of topics, but the theme of the program was clearly evident: How could a profit be turned from farming? Meredith had been invited to the 1895 conference as a businesswoman who understood how to make money from her farming operation. Her speech, "Profitable Sheep Husbandry," was one of six offered that day by speakers from around the country. She followed a native Mississippian as the only woman speaker on the two-day educational program. Years later, Meredith remembered: "The remarkable thing about it was that in the South, up to this time, it had been thought 'not quite nice' for a woman to speak in public."[54] In fact, the only other woman speaker who had appeared on a Vicksburg platform was reformer and temperance leader, Frances Willard.[55]

The effort that Meredith had invested in the conference—from the long train ride to Vicksburg, to preparations for her talk, to the social events surrounding the institute—paid off. Her speech encouraged, engaged, and energized the audience.

> Her paper captivated the audience completely. From a purely literary point of view the paper was a gem, and charmed from the exquisite manner in which the subject was handled, while from a practical point of view it could not be excelled. It evinced a thorough, intimate and detailed knowledge of the subject. Its delivery was perfect, every word being distinctly heard by the entire audience.[56]

The last day of the program was a long session that opened at 9:30 A.M. and ended around 10 P.M. The crowds were some of the largest ever recorded for such meetings. As one person recounted, "Every seat was occupied; some persons brought folding chairs with them and filled the available space in the aisles, and many were glad of the opportunity to secure standing room."[57]

The highlight of Meredith's visit to Mississippi occurred as the conference neared its end late that evening. The secretary of the Mississippi Board of Trade's executive committee, J. A. Conway, stood up to give the closing remarks. He began reading his prepared address to the audience, occasionally glancing over at Meredith, who was seated at his side. It didn't take long for Meredith to realize that his speech, while read to the audience, was actually directed at her.

There are three simple words in our good English tongue at the sound of which the chords of every manly heart should beat with a stronger, fuller tone—Mother, Home and Woman. In all ages, in all civilized lands, men have paid tribute to women and woman has looked to man as her natural protector. In this Sunny Southern land of ours we have a peculiar pride and glory in the grace, the charm, the intellect, the sweetness and the beauty of our women; we delight to honor ourselves by honoring them, and they rule us more than we will allow ourselves to believe. With senses quickened by the fondness and the love we have for our own fair women, it is but natural that we should be keenly alive to the intelligence and beauty of our charming visitors from the Northwest, and to-night it is my pleasant privilege to present to one of their number a souvenir of our admiration and respect.

Mrs. Virginia C. Meredith: You have contributed so largely to our entertainment and instruction during these two days of our Vicksburg Institute that our people do not care to let you go without taking with you a testimonial of our appreciation. I take the greatest pleasure in handing you in behalf of the citizens of Vicksburg this token, and venture the hope that when you return to your thoroughbred "Southdowns," and the friends in your own fair home in Indiana, it may serve to remind you of the admiration we all feel for your high attainments and genial womanliness.[58]

Meredith was "flabbergasted" by his remarks.[59] The token presented to her was a gold medal made by Robert Ernst inscribed across its face with "The Citizens of Vicksburg, Miss., to the Queen of American Agriculture, Mrs. Virginia C. Meredith, Interstate Farmers Institute, Vicksburg, Feb. 20–23, [18]95."[60] She was genuinely moved by this gesture. At that point, "Mrs. Meredith's graceful response, spontaneous as it was and emanating from one utterly surprised, cannot adequately be presented. She was evidently deeply touched by the tribute of her Vicksburg friends."[61]

The Hotel Carroll hosted a grand ball later that evening. Important women and men from the Vicksburg community attended this special event to honor the speakers, including Meredith. She and the other guests then departed Vicksburg by train early on the morning of February 25.[62]

Meredith's impact as a public speaker was on those who attended her programs and listened intently to her ideas. Those ideas deemed worthwhile may have been spread further as audience members interacted with their families, friends, and neighbors. However, it was not until Meredith began writing her essays for agricultural magazines that her notions about farming, the home, and community reached a wider audience.

Meredith's most popular article, "Farm Life: Its Privileges and Possibilities," was published in "every English speaking country throughout the world."[63] It describes a love of farming, rural people, and a way of life that Meredith often addressed (see appendix 1 for full text of essay).

> What is farming? Its realities assume phases in harmony with one's own nature. One will tell of all its hardships, another of its charm in the lovely June time, "knee deep in clover." City folk will talk of its independence—country folk of its drudgery. What is farming? It is an art, a science and a profession. With such scope, should not privileges and possibilities cluster about the farmer? As a vocation farming allows the widest range for individuality. Here, more than in any other calling, can one have liberty to exercise the power of choice, that greatest privilege of existence, and also the greatest responsibility of life, because the *power of choice* involves the possibility of making a mistake. [italics in original] All conduct, intelligent or otherwise, rests upon the power of choice. We choose high or low thoughts, aims, friends, methods of farming. Choice never denied us. We are sovereigns with our own acre and with our own brains. If we exercise our high privilege and choose knowledge rather than ignorance of breeds and their adaptations; knowledge rather than ignorance of crops, soil and cultivation, we shall get the last ounce of value from our acre.

Meredith always seemed to note that members of the agricultural community had in their reach choices that they could make to improve their lives and increase the profitability of farming. She wrote in "Farm Life" that putting knowledge to work was the issue at hand if the people who called themselves farmers were to prosper:

> As farmers, we need to be practical; to be concerned about *facts*. [italics in original] Our corn is a fact that must be got into a bushel measure and for which we must get dollars. But is that all? We raised lots of good fodder when we raised the bushel of grain—how about ideas? . . . May not our mind have some activity in changing facts into ideas? . . .

> We are to seek truth—knowledge—in all the lines that center upon the farm. Acquire information, in order to discover what is best for our own acre—and our own brain. Our tastes and preferences are to be candidly considered. Patient study is being bestowed upon the problems of soil and heredity, and farmers coming after us are to be congratulated upon the

opportunities that will be theirs. Each of a dozen lines of farming appeals to the active and intelligent mind. The farmer may become a manufacturer. Webster's definition of a manufacturer is "one who works raw materials into wares suitable for use." In political economy, that nation is most prosperous and illustrates the best civilization whose exports leave her shores in the form fitted for ultimate consumption. Is not something of the same nature true of the farm? And is it not notably the privilege of the farmer to work the raw material of the soil into food suitable for use? Prof. Roberts says that history does not furnish a single example of a nation rising to any degree of civilization whose food was a few unconcentrated products. Better food makes better men. To produce and improve the food of the world is notably the privilege of farmers in this latitude.

It lies within the providence of the farmer to be an artist; his business has to do with life; he makes or brings about the conditions of its creation or development. We note a great contrast in the laws that govern the reproduction of wheat and those that rule in the animal kingdom. In the wheat we observe an exquisite wonder of nature controlled by an unvarying law. But when we turn to the domestic animals we discover the law of variation which opens a grand domain for the exercise of intelligence. Here the artist may use his creative faculty and we find him molding into beauty, and into value, the "red, white and roan," the Jersey, the thoroughbred horse.

We plant, and sow, and reap. We may also think. Let no one say he must leave the farm in order to be near the great currents of thought. Mental vigor is not denied an outlet on the farm....

James Parton said, "If any young man were to ask me: Shall I become a farmer? I would have to reply by asking him another question: Are you man enough?" Think of that. Recall how from a crude form of farming has been evolved agriculture as a profession, directed by intelligence and sustained by capital. There is too much talk of farming as an exhausted industry, when really we have the most inadequate conception of its possibilities as a profession and an industry. We should distinguish between the farmer and farming—farming goes on forever. Let us dignify our calling, but more than all let us exalt our home on the farm. Let us make much of our farm and our farm life, cherish its privileges and realize its possibilities.[64]

By 1893, the editors of the *Breeder's Gazette,* a popular weekly livestock trade magazine, had invited Meredith to write for their publication. The December 13 issue carried the following introduction:

> We have pleasure in announcing that we have arranged with Mrs. Virginia C. Meredith of Indiana for a series of articles upon the subject of the relations of women-folk to the farm and farm life. . . . Mrs. Meredith occupies an unique position in relation to American agriculture. . . . The *Gazette* has provided an unusually large store of original matter from the best sources for the coming year, a large proportion of which is as usual of the strictly practical sort; but while we are studying out the multitudinous problems presented by various branches of the breeder's and feeder's art we can certainly devote a little time very profitably to following what Mrs. Meredith has to say about farming and farm life from the standpoint of a woman who knows something practically whereof she speaks.[65]

Meredith described her eight articles as being "on the relation of women to farming, and inferentially to the future of society."[66] Meredith's career would bring her into contact with many influential women and men. However, her "Women and the Farm" series brought her work to the attention of working farm women and men across the nation.

The series addressed four lines of thought: farming is a vocation well-suited for women; women should immerse themselves within their communities; taking care of the home is honorable; and farm women need to invest in furthering their education.[67]

According to Meredith, farming brought women "into business relations with a class of men who have a genuine respect for women, and who have also the habit of mind that considers directly the result and not the incident of who accomplished that result."[68] She argued that buyers of farm commodities look more at the quality of the product rather than at who produced it. She noted, "Away from the farm women in endeavoring to carry on an independent business encounter a serious barrier in the fact that men generally are so in the thrall of sex-bias as to be unfit to do business with."[69]

She linked the success of a farm directly to an educated farm woman:

> Every well educated woman masters the fundamental laws of physics, and is perfectly able to understand why the plow point runs too deep; she can readily see when the traces and double-tree [for horses] need to be

readjusted. . . . A woman is certainly competent to know the how and why of these elementary farm exercises, and knowing why, she is no less becomingly employed when she directs the laboring man out in the sunlight of the field how to use the principle of gravity than when directing the laboring woman in the bright kitchen about the application of the principles of chemistry.[70]

Meredith noted that a woman who learns the basic principles of farming could more easily direct the work assigned to men:

Farming is the business of cultivating land. The popular definition and conception of farming as the mere *process* of cultivating land is not correct. The agricultural colleges have encountered some opposition, because with a certain class of the farm *doing* is exalted above *directing*. The best farming does not consist in doing but in directing. It is not necessary to hold the plow-handle, but it is essential to know how deep the plow point should run, and why. It is not necessary to ride or drive the cultivator but it is essential to know when and how and why the corn should be cultivated. ... Driving the mowing machine, raking, loading, and stacking are incidents of the business and laborers may be had for a dollar a day to do those things, but the directing of a hay harvest combines an exercise of intelligence and an enjoyment of pleasure, indeed too great to be monopolized by men! [italics in original][71]

Meredith also expected that a successful woman farmer would want to improve her community:

When the daughter believes that farming is a learned profession, a fine art and an exact science suitable for her endeavors, will she not cease to turn longing eyes toward the town? When she discovers that a woman may have a positive vocation, a definite purpose and a remunerative business in farming, she will find charms in country life, she will become so interested in good roads, good schools and good society that she will seek sure methods of bringing them, each and all, into existence in her neighborhood.[72]

Meredith maintained that women could make significant differences in the community when they expressed their well-reasoned opinions. For example, good roads became a central theme in her series. Good roads, in her view, directly led to improvements for schools, social life, churches, and businesses. Meredith pointed out that demanding good roads is "the high privilege of his [a farmer's] daughter and his son's wife to study these questions and to bring all men to a correct way of thinking."[73]

Meredith also challenged her readers to take immediate action by getting involved in their schools:

> Women of the farm must make it a business—a vocation, to see that the schools are *steadily improved;* beginning with the present conditions, proceed to make them better. . . . [O]ne who will read, study, and think on this subject may become a mighty influence in her own locality. [italics in original] If every one were to take a vow of devotion to the interests of her own locality what think you would be the effect?[74]

She was concerned that rural schools were not only hiring unqualified teachers but that the system put in place to educate children was anything but educational: "Instead of education adapted to the child, we find the child manipulated until he fits the system."[75]

While the need for women to seek education and to answer the call to public action filled her first articles, Meredith never wavered in her belief that the greatest occupation was the "making of a home."[76]

> It is to be regretted that nature and society do not allow every woman the privilege of making a home, and it must be in lieu of this privilege denied that she seeks other privileges—the privilege of self-support, of earning a competence, acquiring a profession, conducting a business, and other like privileges—which, desirable as they may be, must always in the estimation of every woman be considered as of secondary importance when compared with the privilege of making a home.[77]

Meredith was worried that women who manage the affairs of the home greatly underestimated their value and worth.

> Each woman who is the head of a well-kept home is aware that she has inaugurated and is maintaining an institution of the most complex nature—an institution demanding the most varied qualities of mind and the most diverse accomplishments of hand. She is aware that she marshals all her forces in so successful a manner that those nearest think it all a matter of course, never giving a serious thought to the contingency of having it otherwise than orderly and agreeable.[78]

She wrote about men who have become important but "have achieved distinction with less ability and with less application than she [a woman] exercises in her vocation of home-keeping."[79]

Given her own upbringing, Meredith thought the farm was a wonderful place to raise children. She probably reflected back on her own experiences on her parents' farm as she wrote on this subject.

Family life is accented in the country as nowhere else. The isolation renders dependence on others impossible. Three times a day at the table and in the evening the entire household is together. The father's business is transacted at home and naturally the association between parents and children is very close. The events of the day and of the season are the mutual topics of conversation for old and young, the subject of childish inquiring and philosophic comment. In the country older people have time to talk to children sensibly and to take them seriously. The long drives and walks alone with father on the farm would in the confessions of many a man and woman be acknowledged as the determining point of an after career. . . . In the country the child may be alone with its father or mother often and the cardinal points of life are decided in these tender years.[80]

Meredith advocated women banding together socially through clubs because she believed it led to a "broadening of vision and of companionship [that] is of inestimable value to the individual and is inevitably felt in the whole community."[81] She went on to explain how women of that time were different than their mothers: "We are constantly being exhorted to *do* something, while in the preceding century men and women were persecuted for merely *believing* and *thinking* certain things. That has all passed away, happily." [italics in original][82]

She wrote that "literary culture, the acquisition of knowledge and social advancement" are personal benefits that each woman gains by belonging to a club.[83] She observed that reading and discussing novels at club meetings helped elevate a woman's status in her own home.

Nowhere else does conversation need to be so studiously guided and guarded, directed and encouraged as in the country home—and here the supreme tact of the woman is exerted or her supreme unworthiness demonstrated. In the country topics for conversation must be supplied by intelligent effort or else conversation will flow with the dull and dismal motion, eddying about the commonplace and stupid duties of the day. The club will furnish topics for conversation.[84]

Meredith often wrote about the accumulation of money by men and the spending of money by women. Supporting the theme espoused by club work and community involvement, it is not surprising then that she believed money should be dedicated to projects that benefit the community.

The accumulation of wealth is the problem and pursuit of men, but a greater problem is the proper consumption of wealth. When one has learned how to earn a dollar he has acquired a valuable lesson, but far transcending that knowledge in importance is intelligence in using the dollar after it has been earned; and this latter is fittingly a responsibility that women should assume—assume conscientiously and intelligently. Use the dollars for education rather than for reformation, for library rather than asylum, for gymnasium rather than prison, for recreation rather than for healing, for beauty rather than for pride, for sweetness and strength rather than for ambition. Use the dollar for good schools, good roads and good society.[85]

Meredith's final column, written in 1894, returned to the pleasures she found in reading and learning. Meredith believed that the knowledge gained from reading acted as a powerful and motivating tool that could impact local discussions and community action.

It will probably always be true that books influence us more than the people who write them. Books are inestimably useful, and a taste for reading is the greatest boon that can be conferred upon a child. . . . The women of the farm have a superior opportunity for knowing the best books and being influenced by them. The seclusion of the study with its opportunity for consecutive thought is their birthright. In these times when public sentiment rules State and society, and when public sentiment is so quickly formed it becomes women to have a reserve of intelligence. Now no question so new or so unexpected can be projected into the public arena but at once advocates and antagonists fully-armed spring forward. One cannot shirk responsibility by pretending to say that public sentiment is formed in some far-away spot; it is formed here, and now. We who read and write these lines do not rise to our responsibility and duty if we have not defined and correct ideas upon all questions that concern our schools, our society, our homes and our State.[86]

Throughout the years, Meredith wrote for or was interviewed by many of the leading agricultural newspapers and magazines in the United States. Meredith's business sense, practical experiences, and travels around the country told her that farmers were not giving enough attention to the business side of production. She and her husband had faced their own financial difficulties, and after his death, she had to evaluate her farm-related expenditures very carefully to see where she could earn a better return on her investment. She shared her hard-won wisdom with her readers, explaining how accurate and up-to-date records made the business side of farming more efficient and profitable. One account of her management skills noted, "A talent for detail soon led to the keeping of accounts with field crops and in a few years she had accumulated data regarding the labor cost of growing crops as well as methods of utilizing them on a livestock farm. . . ."[87] Another pointed out that "Mrs. Meredith's methods were copied by many old-time breeders and thus the practical side of her views was demonstrated."[88] Her livestock work made her money, but her insights on business matters got her quickly noticed.

It bothered her that farmers left their cornstalks in the field after throwing the ears into the grain wagon. She wrote, "The corn stalk contains 45 per cent. of the whole value of the plant. Farming is the only business in the world that will allow a man to lose 45 per cent. of his capital stock, and at the same time live, and yet, strange as it may seem, there are hundreds, yes, thousands of just such farmers in the State of Virginia. A woman knows better than to farm in that way."[89] It also bothered her when a grower would not run his cattle or other livestock through the fields to pick up the wasted grain or to eat the corn plants left standing. Instead, she encouraged farmers to be innovative in their thinking: "We need interpreters of life. A new thought about an old fact sometimes has a thrilling power. It may indeed build a bridge over which we go safely to new roads."[90] Early on, Meredith began expressing the need for the agricultural community to become educated about the science behind the farming practices used.

> Another way of putting the question is: Are we satisfied with what the acre is doing for us? Are we satisfied the acre is bringing us its very best returns? Do we think we are getting enough wheat, enough corn; . . . Does everyone have as many apples as they want, as many strawberries? Are there any needs along this line? Is the acre doing for us all that it should? . . .
>
> Down in our county we had a yield of wheat of from five to seven bushels [per acre] average. The people are taking five or six acres to raise what ought to be raised on one acre of ground. Who gets the thirty bushels of wheat to the acre? I have a neighbor—a woman farmer—who got thirty-two and one-half bushels to the acre, instead of five or six. How did she get thirty-two and one-half bushels to the acre? Was it luck, or did she make herself a student of seed vitality and the right kind of seed for her soil? I say she got thirty-two and one-half bushels to the acre because she studied the subject of seed vitality and the amount of seed to be sown on her soil. It was not luck. So, then, there is a way of getting over thirty bushels of wheat to the acre. Then there must be special training.[91]

Meredith offered specific advice on what it took if one expected to raise livestock profitably. She described the real costs associated with bringing livestock to the market (see appendix 2 for full text of essay):

The business to be profitable requires an investment in courage and patience as well as investment of money in cattle. . . . Beef breeds of cattle can not be profitable except they have good pasture—and good pasture is itself a matter of years—of a long period of time.

If one asks what is the trend of the beef markets today—asks what is the outstanding point in the situation—the answer comes clearly, unmistakably—the demand for the ripe yearling—and he ought to be profitable, for a penny saved is two pence earned and the steer that does not go to the market until two or three years old often has pounds laid on and then lost. When these pounds are laid on for the second time each pound represents the cost of making two pounds. There is then a practical argument in favor of the ripe yearling pushed from birth to block. . . .

What does the farmer invest in his cow? Feed, shelter, care and a purchase price. The purchase price usually indicates the quality of the cow, that is, the amount and kind of pure blood she carries. It would be easily demonstrated that the ratio between the purchase price and the amount invested in feed, care and shelter is a shifting one. At the end of five years, ten years, the greater part of the investment is in feed, care and shelter—but unchanging and immutable is the potency of her breeding, her quality as represented in the purchase price, as a factor in profit and loss. Our farmer will find then, if he invests $1,000 in feed, shelter and care, that the supremely important thing in the transaction is the purchase price of his cows; and it is for him imperative that he know positively which breed is best for him on his farm. . . . The profit which the farmer expects on his investment in feed, shelter and care depends upon his judgment in paying the initial purchase price for his cows and the sire of their calves.[92]

In addition to promoting good business practices on the farm, Meredith also promoted the farm itself as a good opportunity for women. Meredith strongly believed that women could do as well as—if not better than—men at farming. She encouraged women who wanted to start their own farm to get the same agricultural education as men:

I wonder if you would be shocked if I were to say that I think there is a special need for the training of women to be farmers. I live twelve miles from my father's, and I drive that many, many times in a year, and for six miles on every side of the road every farm is owned by a woman, and only one woman lives on her farm. She is a German woman who was left a widow with several children, and she was enabled by this farm to raise and educate these children. Some of these women who owned these farms

longed to live on them, but they didn't know how to manage them. One of
the greatest changes which has come to us in the last fifty years has come
through the inheritance laws of the United States, which allows a daughter
to inherit equally with the sons, and so it has come to pass that girls inherit
farms. Sometimes they do not know what to do with them. There are a
great many women who never get married for the very best of reasons.
May be you don't know what they are. There are not enough good men to
go around. This woman would like to live on the farm if [she] could make
things go, and there is no business to my mind so suitable to women as
farming. She is removed from competitors. If she undertakes to be a doctor, medical students will not have a woman in the class if they can help
themselves. Ministers will not permit women to preach. Men do not want
women in the professions, and I for my part, do not want my girl to be a
clerk, or do any of the things girls do down town. I would so much rather
she would farm, because I know that every good man on a farm will help
her if she needs help, and will do it in the very best spirit in the world. We
have all seen this many times. If a woman is left a widow every man wants
to help her. They do not say: "You shan't farm here in my neighborhood." I
know a woman who lives on an eighty-acre farm that has put four children
though the University at Bloomington [Indiana University]. Wouldn't you
rather see your daughter managing a farm, a little one or a big one, than see
her working down town? I think it is a fine thing. Since girls can get that
sort of an education, why not give it to the girl that wants it? [93]

Meredith continued to write on the subject of homemaking, including contrib-
uting a chapter called "System in Farm Housekeeping" in a 1918 textbook titled
Farm Knowledge: A Complete Manual of Successful Farming. The editor of the
book, E. L. D. Seymour, wrote quite an introduction for Meredith:

> ... By Mrs. Virginia C. Meredith of Indiana who can lay claim to the titles of
> teacher, writer, editor, lecturer, farmer and farm woman in all that the name
> implies. After the death of her husband in 1882, she assumed the active
> management of their farm—one of the oldest in the region—and its herd
> of purebred Shorthorns and flock of Southdowns. Here for 30 years, and
> later on a new farm which she herself developed, she has achieved notable
> success as a breeder and exhibitor. Meanwhile she also became deeply
> interested in the modern development of home economics, and, when the
> University of Minnesota opened its school of agriculture to women, she was

called there to start the work, with which she remained for 6 years. During that time the expansion of the field of extension work offered an attractive opportunity for further service, and she has ever since been active as a speaker in Institute and Short Course work in many states. Meanwhile she has become a contributor to the agricultural press, her writings covering a wide range of subjects relating to livestock, the farm in general, the farm home, and the farm family. Her acquaintanceship among successful breeders, and her activity in progressive organizations have had a further broadening influence that increases her ability to tell other farm women the things they want to know, in the way they want to be told them.[94]

In 1921, the editors of the *Breeder's Gazette* asked Meredith if she was interested in writing a weekly column aimed at rural women, similar to what she had written for the publication in 1883. She agreed, and on May 12, 1921, the seventy-two-year-old Meredith became the editor of the "Virginia C. Meredith Page." A headline announced the arrangement: "One of 'The Gazette's' Most-Esteemed Contributors This Week Assumes Editorial Charge of a Page to Be Devoted to the Women and the Boys and Girls of the Stock-Farm Home."[95]

Meredith contributed 124 weekly columns between 1921 and 1924. Throughout the years, the name of her column changed four times: The Virginia C. Meredith Page; In and About the Farm Home; The Farm Home; and The Home.[96]

Meredith provided space in her weekly column for readers to share stories and offer opinions. One young girl, for instance, wanted to point out that she could do what the boys did: "Last fall when the district superintendent was laughing at the boys for letting a girl beat them I decided to join the pig club. I wanted to show my brothers that I could do as well at raising pigs as they could at growing corn."[97] It surely pleased Meredith to see young girls challenge the status quo.

Meredith's articles covered an array of subjects, including topics such as home design, rural schools and teachers, boys and girls' clubs, and canning and raising vegetables. Her readers included men and women. One male reader wrote, "When the *Gazette* announced that it would inaugurate a department for women, with Mrs. Virginia C. Meredith as its editor, I was much pleased, as I had often thought that such a department would perfect our best paper, but I did not feel competent to suggest it. We older stockmen know personally or know of Mrs. Meredith, so that we began at once to read her department. We have not been disappointed."[98]

Her writing was normally rather straightlaced and serious, but occasionally she would give her readers something to laugh about. Examples of amusing stories Meredith passed on to her readers included:

> • An underweight child drinking milk at school in the usual way through a straw from a bottle when questioned said that he did not drink milk at home. Pressed for a reason, after many evasions, he said, "Well, we have no straws at home!"[99]

> • A woman in our community, when celebrating her 100th birthday . . . led her to ascribe her long life to the daily use of Duffy's whiskey. The local temperance society was shocked and appointed a committee to investigate. It asked the direct question, "Do you really believe your long life is due to the daily use of Duffy's whiskey?" She replied promptly and with fervor, "O, no; any other whiskey would have been as good!"[100]

> • . . . a little boy in his first term who, after a week's illness, refused stubbornly to return to school. He said that if he went back the teacher would "throw him into the furnace." The mother interviewed the teacher, who indignantly denied any foundation for the story, but after a time she was able to recall what she had actually said, namely, "Any child absent from school one week will be dropped from the register!" Not only children, but older ones, often are limited in their power to understand. Sometimes it seems that no two persons ever speak the same language with the same understanding, and much time must be spent in explanations.[101]

Meredith wrote repeatedly about the advantages of country living:

> The supreme value of life on the farm for women and for men and most especially for children is nearness to the manifestation of life in the varied forms of plant and animal; life beautiful and perhaps life destructive. . . .

> The splendor of that beauty which lies about us in nature's day, the flush of sunrise, the glow of sunset, the shadow of trees, the miracle of grass; the glory of action, reflected in the quality of herds and flocks, in children nurtured and homes kept; the bliss of growth toward understanding of it all, toward enjoyment of its beautifully distinct aspects. Here truly lie all the varieties and realities of living, the rose garden in June, the garnered harvest in autumn, herds and flocks safely in stall and fold when winter blasts bite, and, forever, the solitary set in families.[102]

Meredith understood that living and working on a farm was not a life that every child would want. In response to a question posed by a reader, she noted:

The farm does not need all the boys and girls born there, but it does need the competent ones; it needs those who have had an opportunity of getting the great vision of the meaning of life when it is joined to productive activities and spiritual forces. To abandon the prestige that belongs to a high-class business like the breeding of purebred stock with all its associations, with its history, stability and opportunities, is not a course to be urged by a thoughtful mother. Have mothers on stock-farms been underestimating the business?[103]

Repeating a familiar refrain, she cajoled her readers to acquaint themselves with how their local schools were run. Meredith had long argued that rural children often were shortchanged when it came to education.

A principle of growth that appears to be universal is that it [change] must proceed from within outward. Community growth is no exception to this law. It is observed that the best comes to pass, especially in schools, wherever the community is alert in laying hold for itself of good methods and firm in backing those who propose progressive plans. . . . Teachers are the vital inner life of the school.[104]

The subject of many of Meredith's articles was her support of the boys' and girls' clubs.

Among all the distinct features of agricultural teaching that have been developed during recent years—and they have been many and important—none have been more pronounced as a change in attitude and method, fundamentally new and fuller of promise for farm life, than the teaching given to young people which has taken form in boys and girls' clubs of many descriptions, with a range of projects so wide that no talent nor aptitude, no taste nor capacity, need lack an outlet.[105]

Meredith wanted youth to involve themselves in club projects, which, in her opinion, would "engage the mind and the hand and through which to measure capacities and aptitudes."[106]

Meredith had not forgotten the importance of maintaining a home. She never lost her enthusiasm for the subject or her appreciation for its challenges.

To be able to manage the affairs of a country house so that its machinery runs smoothly demands qualities of a high order, because the complex problem of a country home embraces a bewildering multiplicity of important things. . . . Probably the outstanding and recurring ceremony of meals, which someone calls "three blessed epochs every day in the year," demands a more versatile capacity on the part of the country-house mistress than any other section of her household management. Long before the meal is in course of preparation there has been a vegetable garden organized and tended, a poultry flock selected and cared for, and a dairy established and operated. These may be on a scale far from elaborate, yet the germ of each business is there, and requires a knowledge of its fundamentals, with enough executive force to bring them all into harmony with the housekeeping plans. . . . Fortunately, most come by easy stages to the arduous task of planning and preparing meals. . . . If any one is in danger of thinking this performance of three meals a day an easy one, it is but necessary for the correction of that opinion to look on at the attempts of one without experience who seeks to bring a properly-selected and cooked meal promptly to table.[107]

Meredith kept up with current developments in home economics as nutrition and child development education began to emerge as serious disciplines within the field. She wrote, "The enlarging scope of home economics as a subject of instruction justifies the definition that it is sometimes given, namely, the right care of human life in the home. It is, therefore, to be expected that home economics in the college curriculum should include courses dealing with the care and management of the child, quite aside from the valuable and extensive study of nutrition."[108]

Part of Meredith's concern was that many adults lacked reliable information on raising children. She noted, ". . . it remains a fact that helpless little babies continue to be the victims of ignorance and superstition, that a cord of red yarn is still tied about the baby's neck to ward off contagion, and that undernourished babies are still 'measured' by old women with a reputed 'gift.'"[109] She summed up her position by saying, "[T]he after-value of the child is determined largely by the nourishment of his body in early years, a realization that physical health and mental strength in mature years are largely the result of eating, during childhood, the right foods properly prepared."[110]

Meredith tried to personalize her stories in an effort to make them more meaningful to her readers. She titled one such story "The Motherless Child." The setting of the narrative is a brief lunch shared by a town's orphans and a group of women volunteers. The moral of the story was a call for personal involvement.

An afternoon was planned by a town club to give pleasure to the children in the local orphanage, and with the most satisfactory results in the way of mutual pleasure. The plan was that a number of women corresponding to the number of children in the orphanage should each agree to play "mother" to a certain named child. There was to be a luncheon, together with some other features of interest. . . .

One woman in describing the occasion said that it was one of the most pathetic experiences of her life: the eagerness of the child to be claimed even by a play mother, the hunger for a personal love and attention, the clinging of the child to her hand; even at the luncheon, she said, the child reached out under the table and stroked the lap of this very brief "mother." . . . Some such plan as this could be easily carried out in a country community.[111]

In one article, Meredith described Nobel Prize Laureate Madame Marie Curie, who was traveling to the United States to pick up a gram of radium for her experiments. It was a special gift purchased with $110,000 that had been raised by American women. Meredith's reason for writing the article was to mention that this woman was both a famous scientist and a mother of two girls. She noted, "There came with Madame Curie her two daughters, for it seems that she has had time to be a mother and to enjoy her children while pursuing scientific research. She has felt, too, the compelling obligation to do her best in science without deserting the usual avenues of a woman's activity."[112]

Meredith railed in a column about the lack of respect for women with children. Her target was the U.S. Census.

The taking of a census has been a Federal function for more than a century without any recognition of homekeepers in the classifications, except to count them as persons of "no occupation." Since the ballot has been given to women, however, things are changed or, at least, mentioned with respect. For example, just now, when Congress is in the periodic throes of creating a tariff measure, politicians find themselves particularly clear about the effect of each item upon the home budget and their serious concern takes the form of appealing to women "to vote" right! The appeal is made to women "as executives of the greatest industry in the world, who spend 90 percent of the money through the administration of the family income." These women who conduct "the greatest industry in the world" appear to need guidance, and are getting it in advice to protest in the right place against "fines levied by American men upon American women and upon American children." The question arises, "What shall be done for the salvation of the said 'American men?'" The gravity of the situation is almost lost in the comedy of the somersault turned by the politician![113]

Meredith challenged her readers to make their voices heard within their communities and by their elected representatives in Washington:

> It is within the power of farm women to bring to every needy mother in every township in the United States the counsel and the active help of a person informed in every phase of maternity—to those who are needy, not only on account of poverty, but for the lack of a reliable friend. It is idle to deny that there are many who believe that the child of the poor and the degraded is not worth saving; and in consequences those who believe otherwise have a heavier burden in finding help for the lowly and the ignorant. Farm women have it within their power to secure the passage of the Shepard-Towner bill, now before Congress [1921], which provides in a national way maternity counsel and aid. Farm women can do this because they are capable of sustained effort in such a cause, and because senators and representatives in Congress are more impressed by a personal letter of request from this farm woman back home, who votes, they are more impressed with her potential memory than they are likely to be impressed by resolutions or organized groups elsewhere. Those who are in touch with political matters are conscious of a great reaction in both political parties against the wishes of women voters; last year both parties were vehement in their advocacy of the Shepard-Towner bill, now both are virtuously declaiming against its "bureaucratic tendency," as though that were more criminal than ignorance and superstition that can destroy children before they are a year old. The cost involved in the Shepard-Towner legislation is very great, but as it is the first proposed expenditure of this nature it is worth trying, and may, indeed, lead to the cutting off of some other colossal governmental expenditures that are hoary with age.[114]

Meredith showed her impatience in 1923 with the administrators of the Cooperative Extension Service, who she believed were paying too much attention and money to the production side of agriculture at the expense of better understanding the farm home and family:

> It is rumored that some observations in the field of agricultural extension work indicate that whenever the work of agriculture is stressed and the welfare of the home ignored there is sure to be reached a place, or point, where advancement halts. On the other hand, the states and the communities in which the improvement of the home has consideration, along with the improvement of crops and live stock, are precisely the places where the greatest advance has been, or is being made in agricultural extension work.

Few of the directors of agricultural extension work are able to make a fair division of the funds available for the work, because they sincerely think that production on the farm is more important and must precede improvement in the farm home. They have not grasped the proposition that one must learn to eat and sleep and talk in a right way before he arrives at a place where he can think and do in a right way. . . . So it is that men high up in the Federal Department of Agriculture, in state agricultural extension work, and county agents have their eyes holden so that they do not see that nutrition is the big subject to be learned and taught. Too often they do not even understand what is meant by the word [nutrition]. Educated women and informed women everywhere are impatient with the apparent lack of sincerity in the promises made about a fairer division of Federal funds, while at the same time there continues a persistent and consistent opposition to any legislative measure which contemplates a place of responsibility and authority for trained women in the Government service.[115]

Through her articles, Meredith campaigned for establishing a home economics department in the United States Department of Agriculture. She had gotten word in 1922 that the USDA would make such a move in the future. Meredith pushed for a competent woman to be given the authority to manage the affairs of such a department:

Trained women have had much to complain of in the subordinate position given to home economics, both in the division of Government funds and in the methods of administration. Naturally men are absorbed with their own problems, and rarely are those in authority able to comprehend the advance which has been made in scientific knowledge pertaining to the affairs of the home; nor do they understand fully the importance and the far-reaching influences of the fundamentals of food, clothing and shelter. It is a promise of better things when competent women are put in official charge of whatever contacts she and local governments have with the welfare of women and children.[116]

The USDA finally relented and hired Dr. Louise Stanley as the head of the new Bureau of Home Economics. Stanley was formerly dean of the Missouri College of Agriculture Home Economics Department.[117] Meredith seemed pleased with the appointment, saying, "Dean Stanley has the farm point of view, and has been technically trained in home economics. Women everywhere welcome the new bureau, and look forward to its development under capable leadership."[118]

On February 7, 1924, the *Breeder's Gazette* announced that Meredith was stepping down as editor of the women's section. At the age of seventy-five and with competing responsibilities as a trustee for Purdue University (see Chapters 8 and 9), Meredith decided to cut back. The editors of the *Breeder's Gazette* informed their readers of Meredith's decision:

> It is with deep regret that we have to announce this week that we are no longer to have the valued help of Mrs. Meredith in the conduct of this department. Under her capable direction it has been made one of THE GAZETTE'S most popular features, and the editors invite the active cooperation of all who are interested in it, to the end that it may continue to sustain the high character already attained. Mrs. Meredith, it will be understood, is merely relinquishing the personal direction of the Department, and continues as a special contributor.[119]

Meredith only wrote a couple more articles for the *Breeder's Gazette*. One reminded the readers of the many scientific advances made over the course of her lifetime:

> My childhood was lived on a farm beside the "Old National Road," and I heard thrilling stories of the remarkable benefits that followed the construction by the Federal Government of this roadway; but probably contributing more to comfortable living today is the power service given to farm homes by the electric railway that now runs along the grand old highway. Many a farm home now sees the marvel of "pressing the button" and beholding the home-made candle—the kerosene lamp—drop out of existence. Very splendid is the electric light and the oil-burning furnace with telephone, and radio to add the social note whenever it is wanted, and there is the garage with a dependable automobile that gives me more luxury and pleasure.... Then, too, I have the joy of a bath-room with running water, hot and cold.... And what a bed I have to sleep on! ... And let me not forget the wholesome white bread that I had at dinner, baked perfectly in a controlled oven—a culinary conquest.... What surpassingly rich gifts of comfort and luxury are mine this year when science, invention and organized industry unite to serve me; it would be quite beyond the limits of human nature to walk humbly and refrain from boasting![120]

Meredith's old page lingered for a number of years as a progression of other writers attempted to make a go of it. In 1931, Lucy Ruth Guard took over as the women's editor under the banner of "One Woman to Another." She wrote her first column after visiting Meredith's home in West Lafayette, Indiana, where she had moved in 1916. Much of Guard's first article was based on an interview with the eighty-two-year-old Meredith:

The cool quietness of her living room was in direct contrast to the shimmering heat outside. Old furniture, selected by one who knows beauty of line and cared for by those who love it, bespoke permanence. There was a world of dignity about that room, making it a fitting background for the personality that filled it. There was no clash of blatant reds and brazen yellows, no modernistic wall coverings; instead, soft browns blended into tans and these into creams. Within easy reach of her favorite chair were many books and later copies of the better magazines, all satisfying food for an alert mind. . . .

I asked her, "What are the major interests of our *Gazette* women?" "Everything! Home! Community! Anything the men are interested in. After all, men will not go farther than women's sympathy will carry them."[121]

Guard offered this summary of her visit with Meredith: "This, then, is her philosophy of rural living. It implies that the farm home is the center of family interests, and from this home should radiate all the activities connected with farm life."[122]

Meredith's last article for the *Breeder's Gazette* appeared in the April 1932 issue. She was asked to write an endorsement for the publication. The *Gazette* had merged with the *Dairy Tribune* and, in doing so, had become a monthly instead of weekly publication. Meredith took the opportunity to tell her readers her hopes for a better rural life:

Endowed with ample acres, intelligent use of soil and livestock, an understanding of the obligations to contribute to the needs of the race and very specially to develop the child, there may be realized with these a better mode of life—a mode of life inspired by the ideals of the new farm woman and the new farm man. Whence cometh this new farm man, this new farm woman? you ask. Well, here at least, we are on safe and firm ground, for the answer is to be found in the surpassingly fine impulse and urge of the 4-H Clubs, the classes in vocational agriculture. Capable and coming, these may be able to maintain a mode of life suited to the family living in farm homes.

And so we are wishing for this new *Gazette,* a three-fold blessing—plenty of paying advertisers, a staff of sympathetic and informal writers, and a host of appreciative readers! With all of these, all the time, talking about whatever is good in *Breeder's Gazette,* the good promise will come true![123]

Being first might establish a legacy, but often pioneers have to endure great difficulties until they are accepted by those who initially fought them. While it is true that Meredith became an expert livestock producer, a very popular speaker at the Farmers' Institutes, and a respected writer for agricultural publications, first she had to overcome the stereotypes and biases that faced women like her who were breaking down gender stereotypes. Her gender meant that she was not well accepted as an agricultural spokesperson at first, for many men would have wondered out loud or, at least, to themselves why a woman was lecturing to them about livestock. What in the world could a woman tell them about livestock that they didn't already know?

While Meredith had made a fairly good living raising livestock, the practical skills developed on the farm were tested as she lectured in front of men. With practice and perseverance, she not only succeeded as a public speaker and writer, but she excelled. One newspaper account stated, "Her work carried her outside of Indiana and while women speakers were not popular 50 years ago she braved hostile sentiment and made a name for herself and worked her way into the hearts of the public."[124] She would hold that public podium, the "bully pulpit," for decades to come, as she used it to advance agriculture as a profession, the home environment as a worthy field of collegiate study, and women as equal partners in American society.

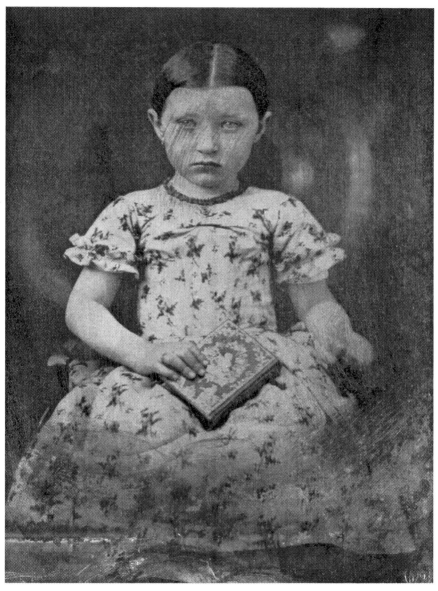

Eight-year-old Virginia Claypool poses for a photograph in 1856.
Courtesy of Purdue University Agricultural Communication, J. C. Allen Collection.

Virginia Claypool credited much of her success to her father, Austin Claypool (1823–1906). Reproduced from *The History of Fayette County, Indiana.*

Virginia Claypool's childhood home, Maplewood Farm, near Connersville, Ind. Reproduced from *The History of Fayette County, Indiana.*

Sixteen-year-old Virginia Claypool was known as "Jennie" to her friends and family.
Courtesy of the Robert Miller Family.

Virginia Claypool graduated from Glendale Female College near Cincinnati, Ohio.
Courtesy of Glendale Historic Preservation Society, Glendale, Ohio.

Virginia Claypool, age twenty-one, in 1870.
Courtesy of the Robert Miller Family.

Virginia Claypool at the time of her marriage in 1870 to Henry Clay Meredith. Courtesy of the Robert Miller Family.

Henry Clay Meredith (1843–82) was a lieutenant in the 108th Regiment Indiana Militia, circa 1863. Courtesy of Cambridge City Public Library, Cambridge City, Ind.

The Merediths were quite proud of their Oakland Farm home in Cambridge City, Ind., shown here circa 1905. Photograph used by permission of *Indiana Prairie Farmer.*

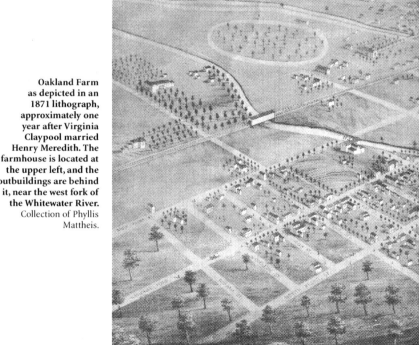

Oakland Farm as depicted in an 1871 lithograph, approximately one year after Virginia Claypool married Henry Meredith. The farmhouse is located at the upper left, and the outbuildings are behind it, near the west fork of the Whitewater River. Collection of Phyllis Mattheis.

An undated Civil War
photograph of General
Solomon Meredith,
circa 1863. Courtesy
of the Robert Miller
Family.

A family photo shows Solomon Meredith (center) and wife, Anna (right),
with sons Henry (front left), David (back left), and Samuel, circa 1847.
Courtesy of the Robert Miller Family.

Trophies won by Solomon Meredith at the 1853 Wayne County Fair, Cambridge City, Ind. Courtesy of the Robert Miller Family.

S. MEREDITH & SON.,

BREEDERS OF

SHORT HORN CATTLE,

BERKSHIRE SWINE AND SOUTH DOWN SHEEP.

Cambridge City, Ind., Aug 7 _____ 187 _____

A letterhead shows Solomon and Henry Meredith were partners in the Oakland Farm operations in 1877. Courtesy of Indiana Historical Society, Indianapolis.

Henry Clay Meredith served as president of the politically influential Indiana State Board of Agriculture in 1882. Reproduced from the Indiana State Board of Agriculture.

Henry C. Meredith advertised a livestock sale in the *Ohio Farmer* shortly before his premature death in the fall of 1882. Reproduced from the *Ohio Farmer*.

93

This photograph of Virginia Meredith accompanied her "Women and the Farm" series, published in the *Breeder's Gazette* starting in January 1894. Reproduced from the *Breeder's Gazette*.

A THREE DAY'S SESSION

OF THE

◁ LAGRANGE COUNTY ▷

FARMERS' INSTITUTE,

WILL BE HELD IN THE

Court House, LaGrange, Ind.,

JAN. 22, 23, 24, 1891.

PROGRAM.

THURSDAY.

10.30 A. M.	Address of Welcome by O. L. BALLOU. Response by J. N. BABCOCK.
11.20.	Miscellaneous Work—Reports of Treas. and Sec'y.
1.30 P. M.	Paper, "Tile Draining." T. E. ELLISON. Discussion, General.
3.00.	Paper, "Sheep Raising." HENRY PRICE. Leader in Discussion. J. Q. A. BOOTH.
7.30.	Address by J. N. BABCOCK. Subject—"The Farmer as a Citizen."

FRIDAY.

10.00 A. M.	Paper, "Dehorning Cattle." MARVIN FORD. Discussion, General.
10.30.	Paper, "Bee Culture." G. W. NEIHARDT. Discussion, General.
11.00.	Paper, "Ensilage and Silos." C. M. CASE.
1.30 P. M.	Paper, "Why should Farmers Organize?" D. N. STOUGH. Discussion, General.
2.15.	Paper, "Farm Fences." ROBERT KENT. Discussion, General.
3.00.	Paper, "Farmer's Reading Circle." H. S. BARTHOLOMEW. Discussion, General.
7.30.	Address by HON. MILTON TRUSLER, Master State Grange. Subject—"What can Co-operative Effort do for the Farmer?"

SATURDAY.

10.00 A. M.	Paper, "Value of our Native Birds, and a Plea for their Preservation." MRS. LAURA MANNING.
11.00.	Topics of General Interest and Election of Officers.
1.30 P. M.	Paper, "Privileges and Possibilities of Farm Life." MRS. VIRGINIA C. MEREDITH. Discussion, General.
2.30.	Paper, "Mixed Husbandry vs. Grain Farming." J. R. MERONEY.

NOTE.—Mrs. Meredith will probably favor the Institute with another paper. Also other work may be expected from Mr. Trusler.

    SECRETARY.

Meredith delivered one of her most popular talks, "Privileges and Possibilities of Farm Life," to an audience attending the LaGrange County Farmers' Institutes in 1891.
Courtesy of Archives and Special Collections, Purdue University Libraries.

NOBLE COUNTY

FARMERS' INSTITUTE,

ALBION, INDIANA,

Wednesday and Thursday,

JANUARY 30 AND 31, 1895.

PROGRAM.

WEDNESDAY.

10:30—Come to Order.
    Music.
    Prayer.
    Address.................Hon. James Roscoe, President of the Institute.
        Adjourn for Dinner.

1:00—Music.
    Address.....................J. A. Mount, of Montgomery County.
  "To What Extent Is a Farmer Responsible for His Lack of Prosperity."
        Questions may be asked and answered.
    Address..................Mrs. Virginia Meredith, of Wayne County.
  "Live Stock the Basis of all Great Agricultural—Sheep and Shepherd."
    Followed by Discussions.
        Adjourned.

THURSDAY.

9:30—Address...............................J. A. Mount,
  "The Successful Farmer of the Future—Element He Must Possess—Mutual
    Interdependence of Agricultural and Other Calling."
    Followed by discussions.
    Music.
    Address........................Mrs. V. Meredith,
  "The Influence of the Farm. Home on National Advancement. The Re-
    lation of Women to the Farm."
    Followed by discussions.
        Adjourn for Dinner.

1:00—Election of Officers for next year.
    Music.
    Address........................J. A. Mount,
  "Knowledge the Spring of the World's Activity and the Key to Success."
    Followed by discussions.
    Address........................Mrs. Meredith,
  "Time and Money the Terrors of Farm and with a Difference."
    Followed by discussions.
        Adjourn.

Virginia Meredith and James Mount, a future Indiana governor, were often paired as speakers at Farmers' Institutes. This Noble County program shows Meredith's versatility as a speaker. Courtesy of Archives and Special Collections, Purdue University Libraries.

FARMERS' INSTITUTE

Friday and Saturday,

FEB. 1 & 2, 1895

AT RUICK'S OPERA HOUSE,

LAGRANGE, IND.

PROGRAMME:

FRIDAY FORENOON.

Address of Welcome......................ANDREW ELLISON
Response.................................J. N. BABCOCK
Reading of Minutes of Last Meeting.

AFTERNOON.—1:00 O'CLOCK.

Music.
Address: "Management of Hired Help on the Farm,"....HON. J. A. MOUNT
Discussion.
"Drainage"................................JAMES CLUGSTON
Music.
"Appearance of Our Farms From the Road, Including the Road,"
J. J. GILLETTE

EVENING—7:30 O'CLOCK.

Music.
"Time and Money—The Twin Horrors of the Farm and Town, with a
Difference".........................MRS. VIRGINIA C. MEREDITH
Music.
"Mutual Interdependence of Agriculture and Other Callings,"
HON. J. A. MOUNT

SATURDAY FORENOON.

"Shall we Warm Water and Cook Food for Stock?"............L. E. DEAL
Discussion.
"Does It Pay to Feed Wheat? If so, How Shall we Feed It?"
PLINY HUDSON

AFTERNOON—1:00 O'CLOCK.

Music.
Election of Officers.
"Relation of Women to the Farm"..................MRS. MEREDITH
Music.
Query Box.
"Is the Silo a Success?".........................H. L. TAYLOR
Discussion.
Adjournment.

Virginia Meredith covered topics ranging from production agriculture to women's issues at Farmers' Institutes, which were the forerunners of the Purdue University Cooperative Extension Service. Courtesy of Archives and Special Collections, Purdue University Libraries.

SHORT-HORN CATTLE.

THE **OAKLAND FARM HERD** was established more than 30 years ago by General Meredith, and afterwards continued by his son, the late Henry C. Meredith. The standard already established for the stock at Oakland Farm will be maintained. The herd consists of such families as **Moss Rose, Hilpa, Young Mary, Phyllis, Aylesby Lady, Raspberry,** etc. A flock of **Registered Southdowns** also bred on the farm. Stock for sale. For information call on, or address MRS. HENRY C. MEREDITH, Cambridge City, Ind.

Virginia Meredith advertised this sale—possibly her first following Henry's death—under the name of Mrs. Henry C. Meredith in the 27 December 1883 issue of the *Breeder's Gazette*. Reproduced from the *Breeder's Gazette*.

The entrance lane to Virginia Meredith's Norborough Farm in Cambridge City, Ind. The device in the lane would automatically unlock the gate when her carriage crossed over it. Reproduced from *Dignam's Magazine*.

A black-and-white sketch of the home at Norborough Farm.
Courtesy of Cynthia Marshall-Heller.

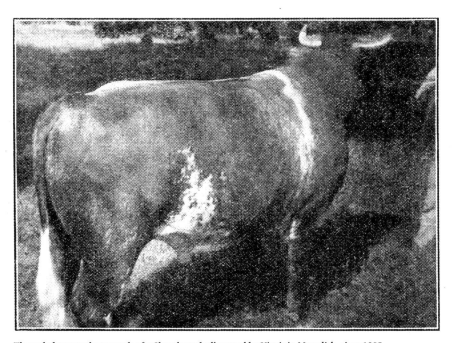

The only known photograph of a Shorthorn bull owned by Virginia Meredith, circa 1905.
Reproduced from *Dignam's Magazine*.

After Virginia Meredith sold Oakland Farm, she arranged to have this monument to General Solomon Meredith and the family gravesites relocated to Riverside Cemetery in Cambridge City, Ind. Photo by Frederick Whitford.

RICHMOND PALLADIUM
AND SUN-TELEGRAM.
RICHMOND, IND., THURSDAY EVENING, NOVEMBER 5, 1908.   SING?

Meredith Monument Moved to Cambridge City

SOLOMON MEREDITH

MRS VIRGINIA C MEREDITH, DAUGHTER-IN-LAW.

Moving General Solomon Meredith's rather large statue from the family cemetery at Oakland Farm to the Cambridge City Riverside Cemetery made front-page news in the *Richmond Palladium and Sun-Telegram* on 5 November 1908. Reprinted with permission from the *Richmond (Ind.) Palladium-Item*.

Virginia Meredith received this medallion in 1895 at the conclusion of
a Farmers' Institute program at Vicksburg, Miss. The medal is inscribed
"The Citizens of Vicksburg, Miss., to the Queen of American Agriculture,
Mrs. Virginia C. Meredith, Interstate Farmers Institute, Vicksburg,
Feb. 20–23–[18]95." Courtesy of the Robert Miller Family.

William C. Latta, Purdue University professor of agriculture, and Virginia Meredith, Purdue University trustee, appear together on the cover of the Farmers' Institutes schedule for 1924–25. Courtesy of Archives and Special Collections, Purdue University Libraries.

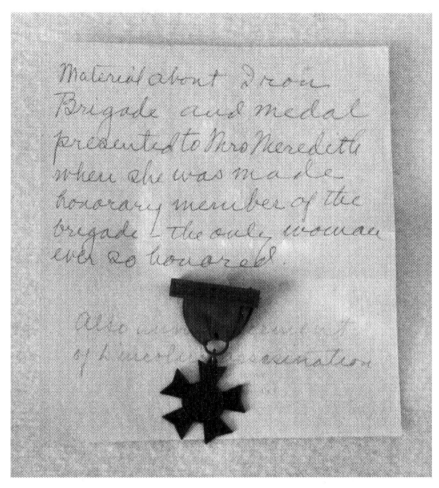

This medal made from Civil War iron collected at the Battle of Gettysburg was presented to Virginia Meredith at a Civil War reunion of the Iron Brigade at Oakland Farm. The five extensions on the medal represent infantry units from the Iron Brigade, including (clockwise from top): 6th Wisconsin Volunteer Infantry; 7th Wisconsin Volunteer Infantry; 24th Michigan Volunteer Infantry; 19th Indiana Volunteer Infantry; and 2nd Wisconsin Volunteer Infantry. Courtesy of the Robert Miller Family.

Community and Service

Empowering Women
Through Club Work

CHAPTER 5

As has been well said no man can do much for the future unless
he is indebted to the past—is it too much to say that
the past has no existence except as it is found in the book?
The book is the satchel that holds the advance of the race.

—Virginia Meredith, from a speech given at the
dedication of the Connersville (Ind.) Public Library,
Connersville Evening News, 13 April 1909

DURING THE LATE 1800s, Meredith garnered a name as "a pioneer in women's club work."[1] It was an exciting time, when women by the thousands were joining hundreds of local clubs. The club movement was a phenomenon that was sweeping across the country, and early on, Meredith was an integral part of that movement in Indiana.

Her own growth and personal development from an agricultural advocate into a campaigner for women's issues can be readily traced through the groups she helped charter and associations she took a personal interest in: the Helen Hunt Club of Cambridge City, the Indiana Union of Literary Clubs, and the Indiana Federation of Clubs. She also became an important volunteer in the Society of Indiana Pioneers, League of Women Voters, Altrusa Club, Indiana Tuberculosis Association, and Indiana Historical Association.[2] Meredith's club work was so important that by 1900, at the age of fifty-one, it would help earn her recognition as one of the hundred most influential Indiana citizens.[3]

Women in the latter half of the 1800s experienced more than their share of difficult times and trying moments in American society and culture. It seemed that the political establishment, legal system, and, some argued, social attitudes worked against them at every possible intersection in the road. Voting in public elections was out of the question, marriage and divorce laws favored their spouses, some universities prevented women from enrolling, families were often not convinced that their daughters needed a college education like their sons, and owning property outright was, to say the least, challenging.

Women saw themselves as second-class citizens under the statutes and the customs of the day. Compounding this situation was their belief that issues important to them—issues affecting their children, homes, and communities—were not taken seriously by government.

As the status quo remained unmoved, unfazed, and unsympathetic, the women's sense of fair play—or perhaps, foul play—brought them into the open, speaking out for reform. Many thought that if more women got involved at all levels of society, the condescending view of women would diminish. A better opinion of the role of women in American society would create a culture whereby women would be treated more as equals in the arenas of family, business, politics, and law.

If the doors were closed in a certain venue, women wanted them opened— now, rather than later. Each passing year brought them only limited opportunities in all aspects of American life; change seemed ever so slow to women of the nineteenth century. As their anger and frustration increased year by year, their voices became amplified as women joined organized clubs in large numbers. Groups of women soon began speaking out against the status quo. An organized movement with a stronger, more unified voice began telling their side of the story and explained to all who would listen—including to other women—their agendas for a better America. Women who would never have thought of participating in civil disobedience and community activism became actively involved in these newly formed community clubs. In fact, the clubs became a sisterhood of all age groups, and professional women as well as homemakers banded together as they called for reform throughout American life.

These grassroots organizations addressed hundreds of issues, such as improving living conditions in orphanages, providing books for schoolchildren, building libraries, and improving schools. In fact, there would be few issues that these groups would not address at the local level.

Some problems, however, were much larger than what local women could ever expect to tackle on their own. They had the will and energy, but for these larger problems, they lacked the necessary political influence. As women became empowered in their communities, they saw a need for their clubs to work with other clubs to confront larger state and regional problems. As a result, local women and clubs from around the state merged into larger organizations whose leaders understood that their influence within political circles rested with strength in membership. The larger clubs could negotiate with a single voice, knowing that their members would support them when they spoke to elected officials at all levels of government. Not long after that, the women who were initially dissatisfied with the slow pace of change began seeing gradual gains, which only encouraged them to continue their pursuit for reform. Each success—whether accomplished by small steps or large leaps—emboldened them to work harder for more changes.

While Virginia Meredith's views were consistent with those of the leaders of the national women's movement, her actions could be described as more moderate and centrist than the actions of those leading the suffrage movement. While her more activist-minded friends frequently publicized their message by challenging politicians through newspapers or through public demonstrations, Meredith used repeated and constant education to alter public opinion and effect change. In 1895, Meredith took to the speaker's podium at the Indiana Union of Literary Clubs convention in Huntington, Indiana, where she told her mainly female audience that sustainable changes would occur only when public opinion agreed with women's viewpoints:

> . . . Public sentiment is the great force that accentuates and accelerates human advancement. It has been said that statutory laws not only indicate public sentiment and thus become a record of advancing civilization, but they are the power that holds the advance—the power that conserves the advance—the power that keeps civilization from slipping back. . . . Let the club make public sentiment and just laws will easily follow.[4]

Changing public sentiment through dialogue and education was Meredith's guiding principle throughout her long and distinguished public career. Meredith told others that when they became frustrated that their advocated changes were not being thoughtfully considered or duly implemented, it only meant that they had to redouble their efforts to convince the public to support them.

In 1920, the ratification of the Nineteenth Amendment to the United States Constitution guaranteed women a place in the voting booth, which, in turn, strengthened their political influence. Much of the credit for the ratification is often attributed to outspoken women's rights advocates, chiefly New York's Susan B. Anthony (1820–1906) and Elizabeth Cady Stanton (1815–1902). Anthony, Stanton, and scores of lesser-known women across Indiana and the nation waged a long and difficult battle to win the right to vote. The issue galvanized women from different socioeconomic levels of American life; it was a thread that ran through and linked most organizations to one other.

While Anthony, Stanton, and other women of their generation would not live to see their dreams of an equal vote for women fulfilled, they did build a permanent framework for the next generation to use in advancing the causes important to women. Their legacy still continues in many organizations concerned about the important issues for women today, including the Indiana Federation of Clubs and the General Federation of Women's Clubs, organizations that, at one time, claimed Meredith as a member.

But while getting the vote was an important historical milestone in the women's movement, it was only one issue that the women were tackling on multiple fronts. Women's clubs were trying to broaden the thinking of government officials, elected public servants, and truthfully, American citizens, getting them to listen more intently to the voice of women in the decision-making process. To be sure, women would use the vote as a tool for promoting change, but another important tool would be the united voice that the women found through organized clubs. From these organized clubs would come sustainable change.

Virginia's first serious endeavor into club work was as a member of a small local group called the Helen Hunt Club of Cambridge City, Indiana.[5] It was 1889, a short seven years since she had taken over full control of Oakland Farm. While she enjoyed farming, she wanted the opportunity to discuss literature, art, geography, and cultural issues with other women.

At the age of thirty-nine, Meredith co-founded the Helen Hunt Club, which still meets today. She wrote the following about the club's inception:

> When recalling the beginnings of the Helen Hunt Club I remember the first suggestion of a study club that came to me was in a note, in the fall of 1888, from Mrs. John W. Marson [Sue Logan]—this brought out an agreement of views on the subject and led the two of us to call on Mrs. [Ophelia] Shults in order "to talk it over," and then later to a meeting at Mrs. Marson's home to organize.[6]

A number of local women were invited to attend an organizational meeting held in June 1889. At this meeting, Meredith, Marson, and Shults, along with Libbie Ballenger, Sue Wilson, and Dora Garvin became charter members of the club. At first, the club was called the Two O'clock Club, but it was soon renamed in honor of author and advocate Helen Hunt Jackson.[7]

[A]fter a very few meetings we were requested by our president, Virginia C. Meredith to each bring a name that a more fitting one might be chosen. The honor fell to Mrs. Meredith and so the new beginning was named Helen Hunt, after a woman whom all American women should be proud of.[8]

The membership numbered, at any given time, twelve to forty women.[9] For the first eight years, meetings were held each Monday afternoon in members' homes, starting at two o'clock and lasting two hours.[10] The group selected Monday as a protest that women had to do laundry on Mondays.

Initially, the club members studied local history and discussed the works of William Shakespeare. As one member explained, "Our first work was reading a book, then we took up the formation of our government and the presidential administrations."[11] The group also hosted special speakers at community lectures.

Within a decade, the members had taken an active interest in improving the Cambridge City community.[12] One of their first civic projects was to encourage the town board to pass a curfew ordinance, ". . . and for many years afterward, the fire bell was rung every night at 8 o'clock," according to a local newspaper.[13] The Helen Hunt Club also put on children's plays, built a children's playground and park, and taught children how to grow flowers. However, it was their work on getting a public library started in 1912 for Cambridge City that bore testimony to the civic-mindedness of the club members.[14] Meredith said that "[very] soon after its organization there was begun an agitation by the club for a public library in Cambridge City which did not cease until accomplished."[15]

The club made its first attempt at securing a library in February 1892, when Meredith appointed a committee from the club membership to look into regulations regarding building one. But the law actually prevented further movement when the "committee, acting in conjunction with the school board, discovered that it was impossible, under the then existing law, to perfect a library organization."[16] By October 1911, the law was changed as it related to the building of public libraries, so once again, the Helen Hunt Club took action. The members organized a town meeting with officials of the State Library Commission to discuss what Cambridge City officials and citizens could do to build a library.

Immediately after the meeting, a committee consisting of William Creitz as the chairman along with Mrs. J. W. Judkins and Mrs. William H. Doney were appointed to select a larger committee to study the issue in greater detail.

Meredith was included in this larger committee. The group soon realized that building a public library was beyond their financial means.[17]

But the idea had merit, and the community wanted a library. Cambridge City citizens raised $1,000 by 1913, which was more than what was required by state law. On June 19, 1913, the library "was installed in quarters located in the Boyd room [part of a local bank]," and the community donated 500 books to get the library started.[18]

It was not until 1936 that the library would have its own building. In May 1934, there was a generous donation of $10,000 toward a library building from the estate of Joseph Hollowell. The community had to raise $5,000, a goal that was eventually exceeded by $1,000. The land was donated, and a government grant of $13,000 completed the funding for the building, which opened in the fall of 1936.

Meredith took great pride in her association with the club, writing:

> I cannot forbear saying that personally I count it among the greatest privileges of my life to have been elected president of the club for nine consecutive terms. The opportunity for service and the association with women at their best, was for me, during those years, a rich source of inspiration. The affectionate regard that its membership generously expressed for me on many other occasions took a tangible form when the club presented to me the handsome and choice tea set which it had commissioned the Overbecks [four sisters in Cambridge City who became famous for their pottery and glazes] to design and make; aside from the distinction of having, for my very own, pottery unmatched and unmatchable, I prize it beyond estimate as a testimonial from the Helen Hunt Club.[19]

Soon after the Helen Hunt Club started meeting in Cambridge City, representatives from literary clubs around the state were invited to attend a meeting in downtown Indianapolis to discuss the benefits of forming a statewide literary association. The invited clubs were asked to send two delegates to the organizational meeting. The Helen Hunt Club selected Meredith and Mrs. J. S. Garvin to attend.

On the evening of October 4, 1889, delegates from clubs around the state were hosted by Laura F. Hodges at 152 North Meridian Street. Clubs represented there included:

Ladies' Literary Society, Brazil
Woman's Reading Club, Brazil
Helen Hunt Club, Cambridge City
Frankfort Woman's Club
Tourists' Club, Frankfort
Catharine Merrill Club, Indianapolis
Clio Club, Indianapolis
College Corner Club, Indianapolis
Fortnightly Literary Club, Indianapolis
Indianapolis Woman's Club
Ladies' Matinee Musicale, Indianapolis
Tuesday Club, Indianapolis
Afternoon Club, Lafayette
Monday Club, Lafayette
Parlor Club, Lafayette
Woman's Club, Muncie
Aftermath, Richmond
The Cycle, Richmond
Decorative Art Society, Terre Haute
Terre Haute Reading Club
Round Table, Wabash [20]

The attendees agreed that a state association was warranted, naming it the Indiana Club Union. Later called the Indiana Union of Literary Clubs, it was the first state organization for general clubs in Indiana and would include the Helen Hunt Club as a charter member.[21]

The group's first constitution was broad in purpose, indicating that the group was open to ". . . all questions pertaining to social, educational, or literary matters. . . ."[22] By all accounts, however, the group initially focused on self-improvement of members rather than community involvement.

The Indiana Union of Literary Clubs held its first convention June 3 and 4, 1890, at the First Presbyterian Church in Richmond, Indiana, with Meredith in attendance as one of two Helen Hunt delegates. The program was simple, as compared to later conferences, and included a presentation by Meredith on "A Programme for Club Work."[23] By the next conference in 1891, Meredith's name would be placed on the ballot for president, though the honor ended up going to Elizabeth Nicholson from the Indianapolis Woman's Club.[24]

Meredith continued to be very active in the new organization, giving the occasional presentation when asked and helping the club's organization through her appointment to boards and assignments to committees. At the third annual conference hosted in Lafayette in 1892, Meredith was part of a symposium titled "Woman as a Factor in the World's Progress."[25] She was asked to speak about her then involvement with the upcoming World's Columbian Exposition in Chicago (see Chapter 6), including an impromptu presentation on "What Indiana Women Will Do at the World's Fair," as the exposition was also known.[26] At the conclusion of the meeting, she and five others were nominated to develop the agenda for the group's 1893 annual conference at Fort Wayne.[27]

In 1894, at the age of forty-five, Meredith received a pleasant surprise when her colleagues elected her as the sixth president of the Indiana Union of Literary Clubs.[28] She captured enough of the 130 votes to win the election over Mrs. W. W. Woolen.

> . . . and it was something in the nature of a surprise that a farm woman, Mrs. Virginia C. Meredith, should have been chosen president and especially that she should have come from a small club, the Helen Hunt Club of Cambridge City, a small town.[29]

As president, Meredith presided over the group's sixth annual convention May 14-16, 1895, in Huntington.[30] During her term as president, she increased membership by twenty-three new clubs.[31] Meredith noted the progress with pride:

> I congratulate the members of the Convention upon the increasing strength of the Union—organized five years ago in Richmond with a membership of twenty-six clubs and holding annual conventions consecutively in Terre Haute, Lafayette, Ft. Wayne, and Indianapolis, the membership has steadily increased until now the Union consists of one hundred and sixteen clubs, representing forty-seven towns and forty-five counties.[32]

The Huntington convention featured a display of paintings by Indiana artists Wayman Adams, Theodore Forsyth, Richard Gruelle, Otto Stark, and T.C. Steele.[33] The simple program that marked the occasion of the first conference in Richmond had, by 1895, become broader in scope and depth. Literature, history, and travel topics were the main themes in Huntington:

- Practical Hints for Efficient Club Work
- The Place of the Study of the Classics in Modern Education
- Helen and Penelope

- The Other Side of the Line
- Discussion on Dialect Literature
- Modern Italy
- Tendencies of Modern Art
- Read the Best Books
- Napoleon[34]

Meredith delivered the opening remarks, which she focused on the need to improve school classrooms:

> I have known a mother to take her child on a long journey of fifty or a hundred miles to consult with an oculist, and to have the child "fitted" with spectacles. An expensive and tiresome journey—the expensive and tiresome habit of wearing glasses—a maimed child! The mother would not presume, and certainly the father would not presume—and perhaps it would be presumption—to suggest to the school trustee (who lives next door) that an architect who understands the relation of light to the eyes—of air to the lungs and of temperature to the circulation—should build the school room. Men would better be architects than oculists. Learned men have written learned theses on "The effects of posture on school children." Near-sighted, round-shouldered, weak-chested men and women seem to be among the effects. It is within the bounds of possibility and propriety for the Clubs to accumulate knowledge and to disseminate sentiment to these near-at-hand, homely and essential subjects. The embellishment of school rooms is a fascinating theme.[35]

Meredith's inaugural address alluded to the fact that the union was becoming more focused on community service.

In October 1905, the sixteenth annual convention in Indianapolis found Meredith once again nominated for president, this time facing two opponents, Mr. W. A. Bell of Indianapolis and Mrs. Charles B. Woodworth of Fort Wayne, though the latter withdrew her name from consideration.[36] Meredith was elected and became the only two-term president of the Indiana Union of Literary Clubs.[37] She would also be the last president, because the following year the group merged with the Indiana Federation of Women's Clubs.[38] In early 1906, Meredith wrote to the member clubs, inviting them to the October conference and explaining the situation regarding the possible merger:

GREETINGS:—

The Seventeenth Annual Convention of the Indiana Union of Literary Clubs will be held October 9th, 10th, and 11th, at Winona Lake. This postponement of one week was determined upon by the Business Committee, mainly to meet an expressed sentiment that in view of the proposed consolidation of the Union and the State Federation of Women's Clubs it would be desirable to have both organizations in session at the same time. . . .

The vote upon consolidation will be taken Wednesday morning. In the event that consolidation carries in both conventions the Club League of Fort Wayne invites the Joint Committee of fifty (25 from the Union and 25 from the Federation) to meet in Fort Wayne to perfect the new organization. . . .

The Constituent Clubs are earnestly urged to send a full representation—two delegates from each club—to the convention, as this will be an important occasion in deciding the destiny of the Union. Delegates with wise views and the judicial temperament should be selected. . . . [39]

Meredith presided over the seventeenth convention of the Indiana Union of Literary Clubs at Winona Lake that fall.[40] Her presidential address—"Is the Club Worth While?"—discussed the need for clubs to work together to identify and complete worthwhile projects, noting: "In organization we find strength. . . . Together we may discuss important questions, together we may reach sane and safe conclusions and together we may do efficient work for humanity."[41] Key papers presented at the Winona Lake conference indicated that the group had, indeed, begun to broaden its mission by looking at the world around them. Topics included:

- The Modern Spirit in Civics—Mr. Edward H. Davis, Instructor in History and Economics, Purdue University
- Social Unrest in Current Verse—Prof. Thos. H. Briggs, Eastern Illinois State Normal, Charleston, Illinois
- Complete Education for the Masses—Hon. Fassett A. Cotton, State Superintendent of Public Instruction, Indianapolis
- To Preserve Health Is Better Than to Cure Disease—Dr. J. N. Hurty, Secretary, State Board of Health, Indianapolis
- Pure Foods and Drugs—Prof. H. C. Barnard, State Chemist, Indianapolis

Also on the agenda was the need to address the proposed merger with the Indiana State Federation of Women's Clubs.[42]

The goals of the Indiana State Federation of Women's Clubs were similar to those of the Indiana Union of Literary Clubs. Founded on March 7, 1900, it was formed with the intent of representing Indiana in a larger national organization called the General Federation of Women's Clubs. There had been previous discussions about merging the two state groups, and the Indiana Union of Literary Clubs had actually contemplated joining the national organization as well, but the General Federation of Women's Clubs excluded men from membership. This presented a problem, since the Indiana Union of Literary Clubs allowed men to participate as speakers at their conferences, be nominated for elected office, and be assigned to committees. While there were relatively few men in the organization, they were treated as full members with the same voting rights as women members. Consequently, organizations such as the Indiana Union of Literary Clubs were known as mixed clubs. A club publication noted:

> The Indiana Union of Literary Clubs, formed in 1890, included in its membership "mixed" clubs, numbering on the rosters of these clubs the most brilliant men as well as the women of our state, who participated in the annual meetings. The same year that the "Union" was formed, the General Federation of Women's Clubs was organized; so greatly enjoyed were the discussions of our "mixed" groups that the "Union" was disinclined to lose its identity by affiliating with the great woman's organization.... [43]

As a mixed club, the Indiana Union of Literary Clubs could not join the General Federation of Women's Clubs without dropping the men as members, an option its members would not take. According to a one-time club president, "The Indiana Union considered the influence of the mixed clubs of greater value than membership with the national body, and at that time believed that mixed clubs could not be retained if the Union became affiliated, and consequently, these appeals [to merge with the Indiana Federation of Women's Clubs] for years fell on deaf ears."[44]

In 1899, the leaders of the Indiana Union of Literary Clubs directly asked the General Federation of Women's Clubs if their group was eligible for membership in the national organization. The request provoked quite a discussion, but eventually, the reply indicated that the group was eligible.[45]

This was the backdrop in Winona Lake on the morning of October 10, 1906, as President Meredith approached the podium. Her words were carefully chosen, brief, and pointed. She asked the membership to think about the "all important question" regarding consolidation that would be presented for a vote during the morning session.[46]

While Meredith's group ultimately accepted the consolidation and accompanying recommendations made by a joint committee representing both groups, it was not done without debate. The final vote was 84 in support and 14 against, with four members strongly opposed to the merger.[47]

After the vote, President Meredith wrote to Mrs. Mummert, president of the Indiana State Federation of Women's Clubs, to share the news.[48] Grace Julian Clarke, who was attending the federation's meeting, had this to say: "I distinctly remember the sense of relief and joy occasioned by the reading of that message. It seemed as if we had come out of the woods of doubt and uncertainty into the sunshine of assurance."[49]

Fifteen members from each group met at the Fort Wayne courthouse on October 12, 1906, to work out the details of the merger.[50] As president of one of the two groups, Meredith participated in the process. After officially accepting the consolidation, the participants agreed to accept the constitution of the Indiana State Federation of Women's Clubs with some modifications for the new organization.[51]

The modification entailed what to call the new group. The delegates representing the Indiana State Federation of Women's Clubs felt that the name of their group was more than adequate for the merged group. In fact, the federation delegates had been told by their executive committee that they were to do everything within reason to keep that name.[52] Meredith, who had friends in both camps, must have known that the other side had been given strict orders to keep its name at all costs. In spite of this, she offered the motion that the name be only slightly altered to the Indiana State Federation of Clubs. The removal of "Women's" from the title set the stage for a firestorm of debate, but a gender-neutral name was fair to the male and female members Meredith represented. This said, it was curious that no men from the Indiana Union of Literary Clubs were picked as delegates to the consolidation meeting.

Meredith's motion caused a significant rift between the two camps, bringing the meeting to an absolute standstill. Multiple votes were cast even within committees, with the results repeatedly ending up deadlocked in a tie. It appeared that a compromise was impossible. Various members offered motions to dismiss the meeting for one month, giving both sides time to regroup. But time after time, the motion to go home was voted down by a majority of the delegates. They wanted the group to arrive at an immediate agreement.

Meredith then asked for a ballot vote instead of another voice vote. Had someone from the federation told her that if she could get a ballot vote, they would side with her on the matter? The answer to that question remains unknown, but one person changed her vote, and the name of the organization became the Indiana State Federation of Clubs.[53] In 1910, the word "State" was omitted from the title, establishing the name that is still used today.[54] A 1927 magazine article noted, "Our state federation is, therefore, today, so far as the writer knows, the only state organization that does not have the word 'Women's' in its name, and there are yet remaining in the Indiana Federation several 'mixed' clubs."[55]

The General Federation of Women's Clubs immediately approved the consolidation, admitting the newly consolidated Indiana group as a member of the national organization. The name change notwithstanding, merger and acceptance into the national organization meant marginalizing male club members. Men retained their status as club members in the state but were denied the ability to participate in national representation.

Meredith was acclaimed for her work in getting the two groups to successfully meld their organizations into the Indiana State Federation of Clubs. A historical account of the group noted, "To Virginia Claypool Meredith goes much credit for effecting the merger. The Indiana Union [of Literary Clubs] was the first state organization of clubs, and Mrs. Meredith saw advantages in unified efforts...."[56]

The Indiana State Federation of Clubs brought 185 clubs under a single umbrella.[57] The group adopted the slogan "The union of all for the good of all."[58] With a combined membership of 7,000, the new club now had the strength to impact state politics.

The first order of business was to establish the administration of the organization. The first executive committee met October 30–31, 1906. As the former president of the Indiana Union of Literary Clubs, Meredith was extended an invitation as a matter of courtesy. Mrs. E. E. Mummert of Goshen, former president of the Indiana State Federation of Women's Clubs, was also invited but could not attend.[59]

The executive committee voted on the board of directors and elected O. P. Kinsey of Valparaiso as the first president.[60] In order to give a voice to all members, the committee divided the state into thirteen districts, each represented by a district vice president.[61] Meredith was selected to represent the Sixth District.[62]

Before long, the federation had formed standing committees to coordinate program activities and to further the work of the organization. Based on committee titles, the new group had a much more ambitious agenda than the Indiana Union of Literary Clubs. Committees included Art, Civic, Civil Service,

Education, Forestry, Home Economics, Industrial and Child Labor, Legislative, Library, Music, Pure Food Investigating, and Reciprocity.[63]

Two examples of the federation's agenda can be found in the following measures, which were passed while Meredith chaired the Resolutions Committee:

RESOLUTION 1
Whereas, The 1911 legislature passed a law on anti-child labor, believing that it falls far short of the status we would like to see prevail in our fair State of Indiana, therefore be it

Resolved, That we continue to agitate and educate more for the conservation of the child, and ask that a better child labor law be enacted at our next General Assembly that Indiana may rank among the foremost in good anti-child labor laws.

RESOLUTION 2
Whereas, the 1911 session of the Legislature created a new State Bureau of Inspection of Factory, Mining and Boiler Bureau, and

Whereas, On account of the great number of women and girls, who are now employed in factories and workshops throughout the state, therefore be it

Resolved, That we petition the Governor and the Chief Factory Inspector that some women be appointed on this board.[64]

Clearly, this larger, more organized association was using its increased membership to exert pressure on the state's General Assembly. The group also used its influence to get the girls industrial school removed from the men's prison and to encourage schools to offer instruction in home economics and vocational training.

In time, Meredith held many positions of importance and leadership within the organization. Though she never served as its president, she served as first vice president. Some of the appointments she held included board member, chairperson of the Revision of the Constitution Committee and of the Resolutions Committee, and an occasional delegate to the General Federation of Women's Clubs.

One of the more important positions that Meredith held was that of a two-term trustee of the federation. Meredith was placed on the board in 1912 and was subsequently reelected in 1914 for a full three-year appointment. Her fellow trustees chose her as the board secretary every year of her service.[65] During her tenure, she helped the fledging organization establish necessary procedures and policies that were lacking and to revise those that were cumbersome to implement.[66]

The trustees generally gathered sporadically at the then famous Claypool Hotel in Indianapolis. In the beginning, the trustees had to deal with an organization that was outspending its revenue. From the outset, the federation seemed to have trouble keeping its financial ledger in the black. In order to help move it to solvency, the members placed the trustees in charge of financial decisions at the federation's sixth annual conference, held October 2–5, 1912. Meredith and her fellow trustees had to approve payment for bills that had not been preapproved, such as for the payment of "$68.25 for printing the unauthorized and extravagant programs of the Convention."[67] They had to approve all expenditures, including the printing of the annual yearbook, postage, and stationery for the various committees. The trustees even requested that the annual convention be shortened as a cost-cutting measure.[68] It would take many years of restraint spending to get the organization's finances in the black. In 1915, the trustees notified the executive committee that the Indiana Federation of Clubs was finally on the right track after nine years.[69]

Along with managing the general affairs of the federation, the bylaws mandated that the trustees administer the Education Loan Fund, established as a way for the organization to help young women borrow money to pay partial costs for a college education. When the trustees were given this responsibility in 1912, they had $575 to loan to students.[70] In addition to the loan, the federation had gotten many state universities to provide one or two scholarships that the federation could fill through the trustees.

Making loans was difficult at best, and only one loan was made from among the first five formal applications. The first loan was to Carrie L. Quinn for $100 in 1912, enabling her to finish her undergraduate teaching studies.[71] At times a lack of coordination among the trustees and committee chairpersons meant that too many scholarships were approved. Other times, the trustees seemed unable to act. It was finally decided in 1914 that it would be easier for the trustees—and more efficient—if a contractual agreement between the federation and the state's universities could be written, thus allowing the university to loan the federation's money based on criteria established by the federation.

By 1915, the trustees had released $300 to Purdue University and to Indiana University to loan to women students.[72] The trustees received a letter from Purdue President Winthrop Stone indicating loans of $100 each were made to two senior students to help them finish their college education. A few months later, President William Bryan from Indiana University indicated that "six loans of $50 each had been made to six worthy young women" at his school.[73] In later years, the federation would provide the same funds to Anderson College, Ball State University, Butler University, DePauw University, and Earlham College as a means of helping women students across the state stay in college.

The Indiana State Federation of Clubs held its first convention in late October 1907 at the Denison Hotel and Propylaeum in Indianapolis. While this marked the first convention since the merger, the federation had already generated interest among politicians. Governors and other high-ranking officials took part in the meeting. Soon their attendance would become the norm rather than the exception.

Indiana Governor J. Frank Hanly readily accepted the federation's invitation, welcoming the conference attendees to Indianapolis in 1907:

> You represent the culture and aspiration of the entire State. . . . Woman's influence in social life of people can not be overestimated. Men may build strong structures, but it requires delicacy and culture to give beauty and character that soften, refine and uplift. . . .[74]

Representatives from the thirteen districts were asked to brief the attendees on the work being performed within each district. Meredith gave the report for the Sixth District in eastern Indiana:

> The club spirit is strongly expressed in this district, the total number of clubs probably being as large as in any district of the state. Several of the counties are well organized. Henry county has an active Federation which holds regular conventions. Shelby county is organized and is doing excellent work in municipal lines. Hancock county has a prosperous League and now has in hand a plan for the reform and reorganization of the county asylum for the poor that not only deserves to succeed, but to be copied by other counties. Fayette county is not organized, but the numerous clubs are doing practical and efficient work in behalf of a public library. In this connection I may state that the clubs in no other section responded so generously to the appeal made in behalf of the Robert Dale Owen Memorial fund as did the Connersville [Fayette County] clubs. . . . The Domestic Science club of Richmond is doing aggressive work in its line, providing classes

and arranging strong programs to which the public is invited. The Helen Hunt club of Cambridge City last winter took the initiative in organizing a civic center with reading rooms, rooms for games and music, with classes in physical culture and free public lectures.[75]

At an annual convention in Richmond, Indiana, a few years later, Meredith, as the first vice president, was asked to give the customary follow-up speech to those who had earlier welcomed the attendees to the conference. In this speech, it is important to note her implication that social change results from efforts that first change public sentiment:

It is gratifying to recognize that your hospitality goes beyond this beautiful room for the convention; beyond the good cheer of the homes that welcome us; goes beyond these and reaches the point of being hospitable to the ideas and aims that the Federation seeks to promote. Our clubs are very much in earnest about the welfare of the child, but we are not revolutionary. Indeed, I think we stand where Stanley Hall does when he declares: "Everywhere there is need for a regeneration so radical that it must be accomplished by slow methods of practical ethical education. Regeneration is not to be effected by endowments, legislation or new methods, but, as Pestalozzi thought, by the love and devotion of noble women overflowing from the domestic circle to the community."

I take it that this High School building, which is without a peer in the state, did not come to pass until the love and devotion of noble women began to overflow from the domestic circle to the community. . . .

Twenty-one years ago in this city was accomplished the first organization of the clubs of the state; of any state, indeed. We are not boasting of the heights we have reached; on the contrary, we are properly humble; but we are rejoicing over the long way we have come in twenty years. We recognize more clearly than we did, even ten years ago, that the changes we seek to have made are so radical that they must be made slowly. We recognize that the mighty force adequate for the betterment of childhood is the love and devotion overflowing from the domestic circle to the community. Therefore, we meet in annual convention to counsel together and to encourage each other.[76]

By the time the federation held its eighth annual convention October 20–23, 1914, in Evansville, the topics on the agenda showed just how far the federation had come on issues of importance:[77]

- A Plea for the Birds
- A Few Specific Reasons for a Barge Canal
- Pure Food
- Indiana's Dependents, Defectives, and Delinquents
- Fire Prevention
- The Practical Value of Art in the University Education
- The Value of Art Commissions to City and State
- The Great Need for Counting Babies
- The Indiana Girl's School
- War Against Disease
- A Private in This War
- Public Health
- Nurses and Citizenship
- The Need of a Constitutional Convention
- Playgrounds and Good Citizenship
- A Community's Disinherited
- Things that Puzzle the Humanitarian
- The Purpose of a Commission on Working Women in Indiana

It is interesting to note that one of the more active and outspoken members of the association was Meredith's sister, Elizabeth Claypool Earl. In a 1913 speech to the Indiana Federation of Clubs at Fort Wayne, she addressed some of the issues the group faced:

> Until the homes of Indiana can give the child a fair chance in life to breathe pure air, to eat wholesome food, and to be governed by a sober, industrious and intelligent parenthood, we must have legislation along the lines toward the accomplishment of this ideal; and of a necessity, women have need to become a strong factor in the struggle for humanity; and strange to say, the most hopeless outlook in all these vital questions of the day, are the women themselves. It is not easy to realize what a large per cent of the women of Indiana (among the club and leisure classes) are not thinking very much about the conditions of the other women. They seem never to feel the sting of the humiliation of a drunkard's home, the anguish of a White Slave victim, the groan of an oppressed bread winner; and until they do awaken to consciousness, it will be an uphill fight, a struggle by the few for the many.[78]

Meredith attended as many annual conferences as possible, missing only when her health prevented her from traveling. And throughout the years, she remained actively involved with the federation. For the 1916 conference, at the age of sixty-seven, Meredith prepared a presentation called "Indiana Women of a Hundred Years," a look at famous women from the state and their accomplishments. Mrs. Frederick Blaine Clark and Mary Flanner presented her work at the conference:

> The women talked of were represented by living pictures. Among them were the following: Mary Kern, a pioneer woman of Fayette County, represented by her granddaughter; Julia Dumont, the first woman teacher; Catherine Merrill, of whom it was said "to know her was a liberal education"; Lucy Stone, Susan B. Anthony, Mrs. Henry S. Lane, who attended all Republican conventions; Zerelda Wallace, early advocate of suffrage and temperance; and Sarah K. Bolton, poet laureate of Indiana.[79]

In many ways, Virginia Meredith had become a living legend in the organization, and a magazine article described "the members rising in reverence" when she arrived at the annual meeting.[80] One of these occasions occurred in 1918, when Meredith, two-time president of the Indiana Union of Literary Clubs, and Sarah Kinsey, first president of the Indiana State Federation of Clubs, were given a standing ovation as the two women, side by side, received the first honorary president titles that the federation ever bestowed.[81]

Eighteen years later, Meredith used "Honorary President" as her title—indicating the importance that she placed on that recognition—when she wrote a short letter to be included in the federation's annual yearbook for the 1936 annual conference. Ill health had kept her from attending in person, but it wouldn't keep her from addressing the convention.

GREETINGS TO THE FORTY-SEVENTH ANNUAL CONVENTION
Mrs. Virginia C. Meredith, Honorary President
Dear Mrs. Balz:—

I am sending greetings to the Forty-Seventh Annual Convention of the Indiana Federation of Clubs. I am congratulating the Federation upon the long series of conventions since that first fine meeting held in Richmond. It was a splendid group that met and organized at that time,—it is doubtful, however, if any of those present would have predicted the long life and the usefulness that some of us have had the privilege of knowing in detail.

With all good wishes for continued growth and service, I am,
Very truly yours,
VIRGINIA C. MEREDITH
Lafayette, Indiana[82]

Within the year, Meredith passed away at the age of eighty-eight. The following year, Meredith would be remembered at a memorial service as someone who made contributions to the women's movement of the late nineteen and early twentieth centuries through encouraging women to actively participate in the decisions being made within their communities:

> It is in her achievements as an active clubwoman that we are particularly interested. Mrs. Meredith belonged to that group of women who asked for so little and achieved so much. They asked for the privilege of expressing their ideals and beliefs, for the privilege of helping to shape the laws under which they must live—and they have made life a better thing for us to live. She showed to women something which they did not then realize—that whatever affects the community affects the life within the home as well and that the community's problems must become each woman's if she would have hers a well-ordered home life.[83]

The Indiana Federation of Clubs also paid tribute to her in its annual yearbook. The president that year, Arcada Stark Balz, a longtime friend and admirer of Meredith's, wrote the following to the membership as a lasting tribute to Meredith:

> With the passing of Mrs. Virginia Claypool Meredith, our esteemed, beloved Honorary President, we lose our last link between those women of the beginning club movement in Indiana, so long ago, and before our own time. Mrs. Meredith, whose sagacity we all recognized and so highly appreciated, had great part in the very foundations, as well as in the later structure of this organization of ours, and much of that which is fine in Indiana club life today, we owe directly to her fine thinking. She pioneered in so many of Woman's fields—in education, in business, in club organization, and in professional education for home making.
>
> Where shall we turn to find a woman who will carry on as she has done? Ever must we cherish and hold fast that which she has given us, keeping it a living thing, upon which we shall build,—if we would keep faith with her.[84]

Balz, who would distinguish herself as Indiana's first woman state senator in 1943, wanted more done for Meredith than just a few passing words printed in a yearbook that few would ever return to read. With her term as president nearly over, she asked the federation to fund a memorial library that would be "established at Purdue University, honoring Mrs. Meredith, and that $200 be set aside for the purchase of such books. . . ."[85] Balz then "recommended that these books be upon subjects of special interest to women in whose field Mrs. Meredith had pioneered, and that they be held subject to the use of women students in the University."[86]

Balz paid further tribute to her friend when she proposed that the federation plant a forest in honor of Meredith. Balz hoped that the dedicated forest would be "somewhere upon the highway south of Indianapolis, and leading to the Old Fauntleroy Home, over which women will be passing from time to time, through the coming years."[87] The actual site would be chosen by the president of the Indiana federation along with a committee of her choosing and the supervisor of federal forests in Indiana.

By February 1938, the federation had worked out a deal with the United States Forest Service. The terms of the agreement were straightforward. The federation agreed to purchase and donate 175 acres to the forest service to add to the Hoosier National Forest. They also agreed to purchase red, shortleaf, and Virginia pines from the forest service to use in replanting the tract of land. The forest service advised the federation about which species of trees would help restore fertility to the land.[88] In return, the forest service "agreed to mark the area with a suitable sign, to protect it from fire and other damage, and to administer this Memorial Forest in the same manner as it administers the other forest lands within the Hoosier National Forest Purchase Units in Southern Indiana."[89]

On April 19, 1938, the Indiana Federation of Clubs purchased the 175 acres at four dollars per acre. However, clubs and individuals continued to send in additional contributions so that, in the end, the federation was able to add a total of 460 acres of land to the Hoosier National Forest.[90]

A special preconference tour of the site in June 1938 was organized "in order that the club women might see the need of the replanting of these rain-washed hills, such as would be done in the Meredith Memorial Forest."[91] Mrs. Edwin I. Poston, then president of the federation, led a group of approximately 100 club women about three miles southeast of Shoals on U.S. Highway 150 for the dedication of the Virginia Claypool Meredith Memorial Forest on

May 27, 1938.[92] Mrs. Russell O. Cramer of Sullivan, who was the president of the federation's Second District, welcomed those who attended the program. Guest speakers were Mary Matthews, Meredith's adopted daughter, and Margaret March-Mount of the U.S. Forest Service.[93] Mary Matthews said "that the dedication is being held under a tulip-popular tree, which was the favorite tree of Mrs. Claypool Meredith."[94]

Poston presented the land to Paul Newcomb, who was the forest supervisor. The ceremony included a formal dedication and the placing of a marker at the entrance of the Virginia Claypool Meredith Federated Forest.[95] Each club woman was then invited to plant a Virginia pine as part of the concluding ceremony. Balz's dream of "a memorial to her [Meredith] who pioneered in so many of woman's fields, chief among which was the woman's club movement in Indiana" was realized.[96] While the trees that were planted then have since been harvested, the land is still known today by the local people as Virginia's Hill.

The following year, Meredith's role in the Indiana Federation of Clubs was also remembered during the organization's fiftieth anniversary in 1939. The federation honored its past by placing bright gold covers on the yearbook, *Clubwoman* magazine, and club programs.[97] At its conference, the federation honored and paid tribute to its pioneers. Gold medals were presented to Mrs. Daniel Sprang of Decatur, Indiana, who had been a club member of the federation for fifty years, and to Mrs. Felix T. McWhirter for her service and leadership. The third recipient was Virginia Claypool Meredith, who was given a posthumous award for outstanding service.[98] Meredith, in memoriam, was also one of five women named as a Pioneer Club Woman, which credited her for her leadership and contributions in promoting the club movement in Indiana.

Meredith found strength and purpose in her own life through her work in the Helen Hunt Club, the Indiana Union of Literary Clubs, and the Indiana Federation of Clubs. She gave time to elected offices, committee assignments, and whatever was needed to help these groups succeed. While she herself seldom mentioned it, Meredith relished the idea that she was a leader and part of the movement that advanced issues important to women. She took pleasure from participating in organized club work and in helping the organizations move their agendas forward. This is supported by the fifty years that she gave to club work.

In return, she greatly appreciated the respect and admiration that she had earned from fellow women for whom she had worked so hard throughout her own life. She enjoyed the attention when she was greeted by a standing ovation from the other club members. She took every opportunity to sign many of her club letters with her title of honorary president. For Meredith, providing hope and inspirational messages to others were important, but she was also grateful for the many accolades she received for her work.

Meredith made a good living and acquired a national reputation raising livestock and making day-to-day farm decisions, but it was her work with other women that gave her life meaning. She had become a woman of importance that Indiana and national women would speak to about the issues of children, women, and community. Her home became a place to visit when issues were being discussed and strategies planned. Sometimes her name and experiences were given as an example, to show what a woman could achieve if she only pushed forward.

She was successful in club work in part due to her successes in life. Meredith availed herself of the opportunities she had. She believed that she could do whatever she wanted to do in life. It was her choice, her right to succeed or fail, based on her mastering the subject at hand. She never saw gender—female or male—as a sole reason for failure or success. She clearly saw no distinction between what a man could accomplish and what a woman could do and achieve, believing to her last days that one's success and failures should be solely dependent on individual skill, decision-making abilities, and the amount of effort put forward.

*The Lady Manager from Indiana
at the Chicago World's Fair*

It is not likely that there will ever again be any distinction so artificial as that of sex between the skill of men and women—unlikely that there will ever again be a woman's department in any World's Fair.

—Virginia Meredith, from a speech given at the
Indiana Union of Literary Clubs meeting,
Lafayette, Ind., May 1892

THE WORLD'S COLUMBIAN EXPOSITION, hosted by the United States at Chicago in 1893, commemorated the 400th anniversary of Christopher Columbus's first voyage to the New World. The nation's best inventors, artists, writers, and manufacturers showcased their talents alongside their counterparts from other countries from May 1 to October 30 that year. Twenty-eight million people visited the exposition, which is commonly known as the Chicago World's Fair. It was a defining moment for the city of Chicago and the United States.[1]

It would also be a defining moment for Virginia Meredith, who would represent Indiana at the World's Columbian Exposition. It was here that Meredith made contact with women of influence from around the world. She would befriend many important women and men of the exposition. Meredith's work at the World's Columbian Exposition was frustrating at times and rewarding at other times. However, her work on important committees, visibility among the influential, and advocacy for the accomplishments of women throughout the world during the 1890s brought her national prominence.

Nearly a year before Meredith began her work, though, the Fifty-first U.S. Congress had to decide which city would receive the exclusive rights to host the exposition at the end of the nineteenth century. New York and Washington,

D.C., were serious contenders, as were Chicago and St. Louis. Competing cities became fierce rivals as representatives for each leveraged what they thought would land them the event. City officials organized committees, made political connections in Washington and within their statehouses, and raised money to support their respective bids before Congress.[2]

Following months of intense political maneuvering, the vote on the exposition's location came before the House on February 24, 1890, in front of a standing-room-only crowd in the public galleries.[3] After an arduous process with multiple ballots in the House and legislative revisions made by the Senate, Congress named Chicago, with its multimillion-dollar commitment to the project, as the site of the World's Columbian Exposition.[4] On April 28, 1890, President Benjamin Harrison signed the final bill, which would be commonly known as the World's Fair Bill.[5]

Congress never entirely relinquished control of the World's Columbian Exposition to the community leaders of Chicago. Instead, through legislation authorizing the exposition, Congress created an oversight committee known as the World's Columbian Commission, which consisted of 108 male commissioners. In addition to eight at-large commissioners appointed by President Harrison, two commissioners each were appointed by state and territorial governors, and by the chief executive of the District of Columbia.[6] Indiana Governor Alvin Hovey selected Elijah B. Martindale, a Republican from Indianapolis, and Thomas E. Garvin, a Democrat from Evansville, along with two alternates as Indiana's commissioners.[7] President Harrison made all of the appointments official on May 26, 1890.[8]

While these commissioners were responsible for issues of national significance and international implications, they would have to work with organizers from Chicago to bring the exposition to life. Ultimately, several organizations would have to work cooperatively to create an international event that would turn 586 acres of unimproved swampland into Chicago's "White City," complete with impressive buildings and equally impressive public displays that would draw the attention of the world.

Illinois Representative William Springer was responsible for an important amendment to the World's Fair Bill of 1890:

> And said [World's Columbian] Commission is authorized and required to appoint a Board of Lady Managers, of such number and to perform such

duties as may be prescribed by said Commission. Said Board may appoint one or more members of all committees authorized to award prizes for exhibits which may be produced in whole or in part by female labor.[9]

While his colleagues initially thought this was of little importance, in due time it brought national attention to women in ways that Springer could not have imagined. Springer's amendment authorized the commission to create a women's board to determine how contributions by women would be managed at the exposition. Congress's only direction was to suggest that the commission appoint female judges to any committee assigning awards to exhibits where women were instrumental in their development, design, or construction.

The commissioners created a Board of Lady Managers that, unfortunately, was modeled after their own unwieldy group. They decided that the forty-four states, the District of Columbia, and the four western territories—Arizona, New Mexico, Oklahoma, and Utah—would be represented on the board by four women each, which included two primary members and two alternates. The commissioners also selected nine delegates from Chicago, supplemented by eight at-large lady managers appointed by the president of the United States.[10]

And so it was in 1890 that the commissioners began the difficult process of identifying four women to represent each state on the Board of Lady Managers. The women being considered by the commissioners as potential lady managers were often, but not always, influential or important within their own states. Some were politically savvy in their own right or were well connected to prominent organizations, businesses, and leaders. The women came from all walks of life. According to a writer who was present at the exposition, "[S]ome were business women, school teachers, farmers, lawyers and physicians while one woman was successful as a real estate dealer, and another had charge of a valuable plantation in Louisiana. Several owned or edited newspapers, but by far the greater number were the wives and mothers who had come, for the first time, to take part in public affairs."[11] It should be pointed out that many of those "wives and mothers" were married to governors, prominent politicians, successful entrepreneurs, and influential farmers.

With their final votes cast and recorded, the commissioners selected an impressive list of women along with an equal number of alternates to constitute the full quorum for the Board of Lady Managers.[12] Judge Elijah B. Martindale, an Indiana Republican on the commission, recommended Virginia Claypool Meredith to become one of the two primary lady managers from his state. Martindale and Meredith were longtime friends, and both were active in the

Indiana Short Horn Breeders' Association. Indiana's second representative on the Board of Lady Managers was Wilhelmina Reitz from Evansville, with Mary H. Krout of Crawfordsville as Meredith's alternate and Susan W. Ball of Terre Haute as Reitz's alternate.[13]

Meredith's activities at the World's Columbian Exposition typically receive scant summary:

> . . . Mrs. Meredith demonstrated her grasp of the possibilities and formu-
> lated what afterward proved to be the policy of the board. She was elected
> vice-chairman of the executive committee,—with Mrs. Potter [Bertha
> Honore] Palmer, president of the board, chairman *ex officio*,—and in that
> position had a large share in formulating the plans and methods which at
> last embraced the extensive interests of women all over the world.[14]

Such descriptions about Meredith's role are superficial and fail to convey her efforts and accomplishments as a member of the Board of Lady Managers. To fully appreciate Meredith's role requires an understanding of her relationship with the president of the Board of Lady Managers, Bertha Palmer.

Letters between the two women reveal that they were confidantes who shared a close working relationship. Their correspondence often contained references to them meeting to discuss the business of the board. When Meredith stayed in Chicago, she was expected to meet with Palmer to dissect emerging issues and discuss their ramifications. In quick order, Meredith became one of Palmer's circle of advisors, dubbed the "favored few."[15] Through Palmer's confidence and trust in her, Meredith learned the details of how the Board of Lady Managers operated and the personalities of the other lady managers.

A letter from Palmer on February 28, 1892, to Meredith fully supports the supposition that the lady manager from Indiana was an integral player in policy decisions that Palmer made for the board:

> When I went to the office on Wednesday I looked for you and was much dis-
> appointed that I did not see you. As soon as I returned home I telephoned
> to the hotel to ask you to spend the afternoon with me to talk about busi-
> ness matters, but I was sorry to learn you had left there the night before
> and I supposed you had gone to your friends in Hyde Park. When I went to
> the office on Thursday morning, I was disconcerted to learn you had left the
> city, as I felt that we had not accomplished as much as usual owing to
> the many interruptions.

Of course I feel that your talks to the Congressmen were really more valuable than any business details that we would have discussed, and I am delighted that we had you here to help us, but I regret very much that we did not have more opportunity to talk over the work.

I fear that you felt your visit to the city was not utilized, and I have that consciousness myself. I always consider it such a pleasure and privilege to have your advice and assistance that I am apt to be disappointed when we have not had our usual opportunities for conference.[16]

A letter dated six months later indicates just how much Palmer relied on Meredith's input: "Do come to the city . . . if you possibly can as there are many matters of importance that I should like to discuss with you. . . . We are much agitated over the situation in Washington which looks very threatening at this moment. We watch every change in the situation with the keenest anxiety but I still hope for the best. Trusting that we may have the pleasure of seeing you soon and begging that you will send me a line in advance that I may reserve my time during your visit."[17]

Discussions between Palmer and Meredith were generally in person and private. They were discreet, so as not to contribute to the rumor mill that always seemed to swirl around the board. Letter writing served as a way to continue and clarify their discussions. Sometimes when Palmer and Meredith corresponded, their messages were so cryptic that only the two of them really knew what was being discussed. It allowed them to write to each other with little concern over prying eyes. Still other letters contained lengthy descriptions about the behind-the-scenes efforts of the two women, including this April 1891 letter from Palmer to Meredith:

Your suggestions were read last evening, warmly commended, and opened a most interesting discussion. I presume your report in some measure supplements Miss Beck's, who suggested the organization of women and girls all over the country. The reading clubs you proposed were warmly commended with the addition, possibly, of an examination like the Chautauqua clubs,—the prize being the payment of the winner to Chicago. If an admission fee and yearly dues are paid, for membership in organizations, a sum will be provided that will be very useful in our work.

The promotion of the "Twenty Clubs" was also suggested; these clubs being organized to provide for the payment of the expenses of the members to Chicago during the Exposition.

I think also that we should approach at once all of the organizations of women in the country, especially the industrial associations, asking their interest in and cooperation with the work we are doing and their suggestions as to how the B. of L. M. [Board of Lady Managers] can promote their interest at the time of the Exposition.

Our Board should also communicate with the R.R.s [railroads], to know at what rate they will transport industrial women to Chicago. Perhaps they would bring fifty or one hundred from each state free, and so many more as we can make arrangements for, at a nominal price.

I think that as a Board we should ask these favors, instead of going indirectly, through some man, or men. Of course we should bring all the [   ] to bear that is possible, in order that the decision may be favorable. I think our usefulness will be largely judged by the plans which we send out for state work and other practical matters, and we must make a good impression on the country, in order to wipe out "the blot on the 'Scutcheon.'"

I hope therefore that you will make your report tomorrow as full and suggestive as possible. I like it extremely as it is, but beg that you will have it under consideration till the last moment and add every thought that may be valuable.[18]

Palmer was a woman to be reckoned with. During her tenure as president, she constantly dealt with internal disagreements, personality conflicts, individual aspirations, political spats, and personal feuds. She may have been a political novice in the beginning, but she quickly became politically astute, seeing to it that women were well represented at the exposition in spite of the sometimes-argumentative lady managers and uncooperative male commissioners.

Meredith stood ready to assist her in moving board projects forward. Palmer assigned Meredith the task of working with foreign dignitaries, lobbying Congress, soothing ruffled egos, getting projects off the ground, and writing reports. Meredith would later state that Bertha Palmer "was one of the brainiest women I ever knew."[19]

Palmer would reward Meredith's loyalty and dedication by appointing her to various positions, the most important one being the chair of the Board of Lady Managers Committee on Awards in the fall of 1892. Through her work, Meredith attracted national and international attention. Her efforts on the World's Columbian Exposition brought her and many other lady managers a celebrity status that followed them throughout their lives.

On November 19, 1890, the Board of Lady Managers convened its first meeting in Chicago with 115 women in attendance.[20] The World's Columbian Commission had arranged for the lady managers to hold their business meetings at Kinsley's Restaurant located on Adams Street.[21] Meredith and the other lady managers were "paid six dollars per day for each day necessarily absent from home engaged in the work of the Commission," plus their transportation expenses.[22]

The president of the World's Columbian Commission, Thomas W. Palmer, called the first day's meeting to order, then commission secretary John T. Dickinson presented the lady managers and their alternates with a large parchment certificate marking the occasion. Palmer, who was not related to Bertha Honore Palmer of the Board of Lady Managers, noted the importance of the work that the women were about to embark on:

> All that American women ever lacked—opportunity—is here, and from every State and Territory the women of the hour are here to take advantage thereof. It needs no gift of prophecy to enable one to predict that the future will justify the wisdom of the creation of your Board, and the selection of its individual members.[23]

With the first day's pomp and ceremonial speeches behind them, the lady managers spent their weeklong conference posturing for control of leadership positions and influence on the board. Meredith voiced her very strong opinions, becoming a lightning rod. Her outspoken manner made her a friend to many and an opponent to others.

The first order of business on the next day was to elect a leader for the Board of Lady Managers. Bertha Honore Palmer, who was one of the nine at-large members appointed from Chicago, won without much opposition. She was a prominent woman who "had social and political connections and great wealth; she had also, . . . a magnetic personality and good deal of charm and tact."[24] Palmer's title would be president of the Board of Lady Managers of the World's Columbian Commission.[25] After the election, President Palmer officially called the meeting to order. She welcomed the lady managers to Chicago, telling them of the countless opportunities that awaited them.[26]

The messy struggle for power surfaced as the process of drafting a constitution, writing the bylaws, and assigning duties and responsibilities began in earnest. Women such as Palmer and Meredith believed women's suffrage was important, but reforms in women's education, commitment to public service within the community, and charitable work were also key issues to address.

This put them at odds with those lady managers who were suffragists first. The women's suffrage faction diligently campaigned to weaken Palmer's power. In fact, the November conference was more about competing resolutions that would establish how much power President Palmer would have.

The key to the power struggle rested in the establishment of the board's executive committee, a group that would concentrate the decision-making abilities of the full organization into the hands of a precious few of its members. While Palmer and Meredith's opponents wanted representatives to this committee to be elected by the full board, the two women fought to maintain President Palmer's control, proposing instead that she retain the right to approve all committee appointments or, in the case of one proposal, to simply choose them outright. This would be the first of many power ploys within the group, but with help from Meredith as her parliamentarian, Palmer ultimately gained the upper hand in her quest for full management over board affairs.

After much wrangling, the lady managers gave Bertha Honore Palmer what she wanted. Not only would she be a member of the executive committee, but she would also appoint the other members.[27] The structure of the executive committee outlined in the bylaws consisted of Palmer as the president, nine regional vice-presidents, and a vice-chairman, plus additional members from the various working committees.

The newly created vice chairman's position would "perform, in the absence of the President, the duties normal to such officer."[28] Essentially, the vice chairman was second in command to the president, making it a powerful position indeed. It would take six ballots at a later meeting, but Meredith would eventually claim this position as her own. This would afford her power, position, and visibility among the Board of Lady Managers, elected officials, dignitaries, and the press, and build her reputation exponentially across the country.[29]

Palmer achieved another victory when the Board of Lady Managers voted her as chairman of the executive committee by virtue of her presidency.[30] With the executive committee now firmly in her control, Palmer further extended her authority, establishing that:

> . . . when the Board is not in session, [the executive committee] shall have all the powers of the Board of Lady Managers. Ten members shall constitute a quorum, and the Committee may make such regulations for its own government and the exercise of its functions through the medium of such sub-committees as it may consider expedient.[31]

Exercising her power, Palmer would work throughout the winter of 1890 and spring of 1891 to select executive committee members who would cooperate with her.[32]

The World's Fair Bill provided no guidance on what Congress expected the Board of Lady Managers to accomplish. The vagueness in the law created confusion and dissension at first, but later on, it provided the Board of Lady Managers tremendous opportunities. They could take their projects into uncharted waters, since the boundaries of their work were not well defined.

However, the Board of Lady Managers first had to come to grips with rancor among its members. One question raised early on was whether the lady managers had to get permission to act from the all-male executive committee of the World's Columbian Commission. Meredith had critically read the World's Fair Bill, trying to glean from it what authority, if any, Congress intended to give the Board of Lady Managers. Her conclusion was ominous: the board lacked funding and authority. Based on her interpretation of the World's Fair Bill, Meredith realized that the World's Columbian Commission had significant control over the women's board. This view was not shared equally by all of the lady managers. Some believed that the lady managers could decide for themselves what they needed to do, in spite of what the law said or left to interpretation.

After some debate, the lady managers voted to discuss with the commissioners the financial status and responsibilities of the women's board. Bertha Palmer then appointed five lady managers—Meredith among them—to the Committee of Conference, which subsequently met with a subcommittee of the commission to discuss the matter further.[33]

The report from the women's Committee of Conference indicated that the meeting was productive. Although the commissioners felt they could not delegate any authority to the Board of Lady Managers, because Congress had not done so in the World's Fair Bill, the commissioners were willing to review the lady managers' requests. The women's report implied that the commissioners would also consider paying the salaries of the president and secretary of the Board of Lady Managers as long as they were not exorbitant.[34]

After the report was presented, Palmer turned to Meredith for her suggestions for formulating the written requests to present to the commissioners.[35] Meredith listed four issues to be clearly addressed by the commission's subcommittee:

First—Ask the Commission to create the Office of Secretary of the Board of Lady Managers with a salary. Our Secretary at this moment has no legal status.

Second—Ask for a specific statement with every exhibit, whether it be in whole or in part produced by female labor.

Third—Ask that all work of women shall be entered with the general exhibit and permit this Board to designate by some device every article that is the product of women's labor.

Fourth—Ask that this Board may in some way have control of space.[36]

Her recommendations found strong support among the lady managers. Meredith had included two of the main points discussed by the lady managers in attendance: the need for their own building and that the general exhibits produced by women be judged alongside those produced by men. There remained a small contingent that wanted women's exhibits to be judged only against other women. It was with this group that Meredith encountered some resistance. Palmer wrote about the hotly contested debate on whether a separate building was needed and if competition solely based on gender was the appropriate course of action to take:

> This [the use of a women's building] was a burning question for upon this subject everyone had strong opinions and there was a great feeling on both sides, those who favored a separate exhibit believing that the extent and variety of the valuable work done by women would not be appreciated or comprehended unless shown in a building separate from the work of men. On the other hand, the most advanced and radical thinkers felt that the exhibit should not be one of sex, but of merit, and that women had reached a point where they could afford to compete side by side with men, with a fair chance of success, and that they would not value prizes given upon the sentimental basis of sex.[37]

Meredith looked for support from the suffragists' camp. Dr. Frances Dickinson, a well-respected medical doctor from Illinois who had aligned herself with the suffragist movement, believed "that there should not be erected a building for the purpose of displaying woman's work separately from the general exhibit."[38] Meredith agreed, noting:

> We speak also of the Woman's Department. Now, there is no Woman's Department in the Columbian Exhibition, excepting that it is all Woman's Department—women are eligible to every department.[39]

In preparing their letter to the commissioners, the women simply requested what they wanted rather than asking the commissioners for permission. The lady managers were walking a fine line between showing deference to the commissioners and retaining control over matters relating to their own board. This would establish the tone for future conversations between the lady managers and the commissioners.

The lady managers' first request clearly expressed to the commissioners that the women should be allowed to manage their own affairs:

1. We request a liberal construction of the Act of Congress which erected this Board of Lady Managers and leaves its duties to be prescribed by your Commission.
2. We do not request a separate building for woman's work.
3. That the Columbian Commission fix the salaries of the Chairman [Bertha Palmer] and Secretary of the Board of Lady Managers.
4. We request that a suitable building be provided and placed under the control of the Board of Lady Managers for official and other purposes.
5. That this Board be allowed to work in conjunction with your Commission in efforts to interest the people of the respective States and Territories in the success of the Columbian Exposition.
6. We further request that the Executive Committee [of the World's Columbian Commission] formulate their instructions to the Board of Lady Managers so explicitly that there may be no misunderstanding of them. Signed: Mrs. Wm. H. Felton, Mrs. John Logan, Mrs. Virginia Meredith, Mrs. John Briggs, Miss Mary Busselle.[40]

The board received a reply from the men's subcommittee near the end of the November 1890 meeting. R. W. Furnas, a commissioner from Nebraska, conveyed to the lady managers that the secretary of the Board of Lady Managers should be paid a stipend of $2,000—though the commissioners would eventually provide $5,000—a year with an additional commitment of $500 to cover postage, printing, and other operational expenses. The subcommittee would also recommend that the commission recognize Bertha Palmer as the presiding officer of both the board and of its executive committee.[41] This latter recommendation was unanticipated, but apparently Palmer—or someone representing her—pushed for its inclusion in the subcommittee's response to the lady managers.

The lady managers were delighted when Furnas told them that their executive committee would be given control of a building on the exposition grounds.[42] Up to that point, the spokesperson for the commission's subcommittee had said everything that the lady managers had hoped to hear and more.

However, another aspect of Furnas's reply was not well received. His subcommittee requested that the women's executive committee be composed of twelve lady managers, with three representatives for each of the four geographical divisions of the United States. Within minutes, loud murmurs abounded throughout the assembly. The women were unhappy about this, as they had already voted for an executive committee of twenty-six lady managers. One of the lady managers asked Furnas whether or not this was mandatory. Furnas backpedaled, stating "that he thought it was only suggestive and he believed it good policy to condense the Board into as small a body as possible."[43] As the women continued to challenge him for a clarification, Commissioner Furnas understood that he was getting himself deeper into trouble and advised the women to stay the course on how they had organized their executive committee. He ended up stating that the Executive Committee of the Board of Lady Managers had the "liberty and powers to do about as it pleased, outside of matters of finance."[44]

Meredith directly asked Furnas after his presentation if what he had just reported to them was in response to the letter they had sent to the subcommittee. He politely replied that it was, in fact, the subcommittee's response to the board's letter.[45] In addition, he mentioned that his statements were merely recommendations from the subcommittee—recommendations that would be presented to the commission at their upcoming meeting in April. At that time, the commissioners could act to accept, deny, or modify those recommendations.

The Board of Lady Managers ended its first meeting on November 25, 1890. The meeting had been an uphill battle for control—both by Bertha Palmer within the group and by the lady managers as they established their place beside the commissioners. But the focus on administrative matters meant that little was decided about how exhibits were to be managed and judged. Meredith was disappointed that "during the first session of the Board of Lady Managers no definite action was taken in regard to the appointment of women judges."[46] Palmer also expressed annoyance with how little the group accomplished in Chicago that November:

> When our Board adjourned in the autumn, we were not in a position to go before the country with our plans. The fear of antagonistic legislation, and the vagueness of the powers given us by the Commission, had caused us to be very conservative in our actions, so much so that while in session we did not decide definitely as to our future work, and this has been the cause of

great embarrassment. I was met constantly with the inquiry "What do the ladies propose to do? There was a very successful fair in Paris without the aid of women. What is there that you can do to add to that success?"[47]

This lack of progress was especially troubling given that future meetings of the full Board of Lady Managers were not assured. The board did not have the funds to pay members' travel expenses for subsequent meetings. Consequently, the executive committee under Palmer's control became an important means of moving the work of the board forward. This committee would act when the full board did not or could not agree on what needed to be done at the exposition. As the lady managers boarded carriages and trains for home, they departed knowing that whatever action needed to be taken was left to those serving on the executive committee. It would thus be the case even as additional meetings with the full board were made possible by generous grants from the United States Congress.

Indiana had formed its own fair commission to raise public awareness on the benefits of attending and displaying products at the World's Columbian Exposition. Late in 1890, Judge Elijah Martindale was speaking with the press, trying to interest both Indiana citizens and businesses to take full advantage of the exposition, which was being held so close to Indiana. He hoped to have a beautiful Indiana building on the Jackson Park grounds, the area in Chicago where the exposition would be located. He believed this could be paid for by public funds provided by the Indiana General Assembly and supplemented by public donations in cash and materials.

Martindale was interested in showing exhibits that highlighted Indiana's natural resources and Hoosier-made products. He had to convince the state's elected officials that public funding to support the state's presence at the exposition was in everyone's best interest. With a little bit of coaxing, the Indiana General Assembly on March 1891 passed a state version of the World's Fair Bill. The state bill created the Indiana Board of World's Fair Managers and charged it with planning and directing the state's commitment to the World's Columbian Exposition. The legislature provided $75,000 to support this work.

Indiana Governor Alvin Hovey was given the authority to appoint twenty-six citizens to Indiana's fair board. He selected a Republican and a Democrat from each of the twelve Indiana congressional districts. To round out his appointments, Hovey added two prominent names to the Board of World's Fair

Managers: Professor John Campbell from Wabash College in Crawfordsville and May Wright Sewall from Indianapolis. Campbell had been secretary to the 1876 Centennial Exposition in Philadelphia —the first so-called world's fair held in the United States—and so seemed a perfect fit for the board. Sewall, "a major national figure in women's education, suffrage, and club movements" who was organizing a women's international congress at the World's Columbian Exposition, was also a logical selection.[48]

In addition to the twenty-six governor-appointed positions, the state legislature required that Indiana's representatives to the World's Columbian Commission and the Board of Lady Managers also be members. To this already long and growing list of committee members were added the governor, president of the Indiana State Board of Agriculture, state geologist, and chief of the Indiana Bureau of Statistics, for a grand total of thirty-eight board members.[49] Each member would be paid for expenses while doing state work.[50]

Moving quickly, Governor Hovey called the Indiana Board of World's Fair Managers to a meeting in early 1891. The representatives decided to showcase the state's natural resources, progressive citizenry, and strong manufacturing base by focusing on exhibits in agriculture, livestock, machinery and manufacturing, building materials, mines and mining, education, and women's work.

Indiana's inclusion of women on the fair board and their placement on committees received national attention through an article in the *Chicago Daily Tribune:* ". . . but Indiana has been in all other respects as generous in official recognition of women as Illinois. They are members of five out of the seven committees, and two ladies, Mrs. Meredith and Mrs. [Laura] Worley, are upon the Executive Committee, which is, of course, the most important."[51] Indiana, the article noted, was "the first State to organize the State Commission, and the advanced stage of World's Fair matters in the State is owing chiefly to the influence and personal effort of Mrs. Virginia Meredith, Vice-Chairman of the Executive Committee of the Board of Lady Managers."[52]

A year later, Meredith spoke about Hovey's wisdom in selecting women to serve on the Indiana world's fair board when she addressed the all-male Indiana State Board of Agriculture. This was the same board to which her husband had been elected president just before his untimely death. She commented:

> [Indiana] Governor Hovey had the intelligence to construe the word *citizen* to mean women as well as men. Governor Hovey construed the word *citizen* to mean women and appointed a woman. We are coming step by

step as women, and I don't doubt but that after awhile we will have women on the State Board of Agriculture; that may be a way off, but we will come to that after awhile. I think it is worth thinking about.[53]

The committees of the Indiana world's fair board worked nonstop to entice people from Indiana to place quality exhibits in the state's building. There were two committees—Women's Work and Education—that were singled out as being very active and extremely creative. Sewall, as chairperson of the Committee on Women's Work, vigorously engaged the women of the state to participate at varying levels, from providing money to furnishing exhibits for the Women's Building and the Indiana Building. Sewall and her committee members used their connections with civic clubs and literary organizations to get their message out to the women of the state.

One of the more significant contributions by the Committee on Women's Work was a survey of working women in Indiana. The *Chicago Daily Tribune* wrote in 1891 that "Mrs. Virginia C. Meredith and Miss Wilhelmina Reitz, the Indiana Lady Managers of the World's Fair, have begun a systematic inquiry relative to the line of industries in which women are employed in this State, with a view to securing a State exhibit by the women."[54]

Good leadership on the Indiana world's fair board helped the state to move forward throughout 1892. Palmer was especially pleased with Meredith's work in engaging the women of Indiana. Palmer even asked Meredith to send her a report outlining how Indiana had achieved so much in so little time. Palmer thought Indiana's approach to the state's role at the exposition could serve as a model and be duplicated in other states where the work was slow, languishing, or nonexistent. Her request to Meredith noted: "I am very anxious for you to commence sending reports to the office, so that we can forward them to the other women, to encourage them in making a beginning, which almost all seem afraid to attempt."[55]

But Meredith could and would criticize the Indiana world's fair board when she felt that the women were not getting their fair share of the money. The *Chicago Daily Tribune* printed some of Meredith's criticism: "Mrs. Meredith is trying to arouse interest in the proposed children's building at the World's Fair among Indiana women. 'Indiana's quota of the expense,' said she today, 'is only $1,000, and if our Indiana Commission would only allow us women of the commission means to hold meetings through the State, the amount could be easily raised, but as yet the commission holds the purse strings tightly against us.'"[56]

Meredith outlined two general thoughts to the Indiana State Board of Agriculture on what the Indiana world's fair board could do to help generate tourist dollars, sell agricultural products, and raise business capital.[57]

> Now, perhaps you will be more interested and will want to know what Indiana is going to do. We have two plans I think that will be of great benefit to the State. One of them is that our Indiana Board shall organize a system of itineraries, which, in my mind, will be of most practical benefit to us. There are many people who will come to Chicago who will not want to stay in that city over Sunday. They will become tired of sight-seeing. It is not a very quiet place to spend Sunday anyway, and we have three or four great lines of railroad coming down into Indiana. Now, why couldn't we have them leave Chicago over Sunday and come down over the Big Four [Railroad]? They can see the broad fields and the great stock interests of our State, and come to Indianapolis and spend the Sunday, and return over the Monon on Monday, and then they will see another lot of good country; or perhaps they can come over the Illinois Central, and can see the great flocks and herds of stock as they pass over this country. There may be some of these men that will become interested and perhaps they may want to buy; they may want to buy some of our coal mines and develop them. There will be great opportunities come to this section. Those towns that are on the lines of these railroads can easily get up a plan by which the people will leave Chicago and spend Sunday in these towns with great profit to the towns and the whole State.

> Right in connection with this plan of itineraries I then have a plan for improving the face of Indiana. It has been said that Indiana is the filthiest point of any State in the Union. I know you would think it was bad enough, for as you travel over the lines of railroad you can see rubbish and old tin cans and stuff in the door-yards, especially in the rear of the buildings fronting these lines of road. Now, I want to reach the women of the State and form them into local improvement clubs. The business of these clubs, as indicated by the name, is to improve the localities. I believe that the women of the State will be equal to this undertaking, for they can have the small boy for their ally in this work. I think the people should see to it that our towns are cleaned up.

> Now, if the people who founded these towns, about fifty years ago, would go to work and clean up these towns—clean up these places so these back yards would present a clean, neat appearance it would make our State a wonderfully fine State in appearance.

Some times I wonder why we do not learn a lesson of cleanliness and neat-
ness from the railroads. The railroads are really models of cleanliness. If
you stand on the rear platform of a train the receding view is one of pleasing appearance—neatly laid ties, perfectly laid and ballasted, a clean grade
and plowed across to the line of fence and the whole length of these lines
you will find no weeds growing. Now, you will find this with all the lines of
railroads throughout the State.

Now, why can not the people make their yards presentable as much so as
the railroads do their right-of-way.[58]

At the first meeting of the Indiana world's fair board, it was agreed that
the state would construct a building at Jackson Park that every Hoosier would
be proud to claim. Indiana received, some time later, a coveted piece of ground
at Jackson Park near the Palace of Fine Arts on which to locate its building.
Indiana's acquisition of this specific piece of ground despite the demands for it
by other states was not too surprising, given that Judge Elijah Martindale had
used his influence as a member of the commission's executive committee to
help secure it. It also didn't hurt Indiana's cause at all that he was the chairman
of the Building and Grounds Committee.

The Indiana Building was officially dedicated on June 15, 1893, and cost the
state $57,162 in public funds.[59] In addition, approximately twenty companies,
mainly representing stone and forestry businesses within the state, donated
$10,206 in materials to the building project.[60] The building was 102 feet wide
by 142 feet long and characterized by some as French Gothic in design. Benjamin F. Havens, the executive commissioner of the Indiana world's fair board, in
his final state report described the building and its use in detail:

Indiana lying adjacent to Illinois, it was taken for granted that large numbers of our people would visit the Exposition. This made the matter of
having a State Building which would be in keeping with the character and
standing of our State, and the accommodation of our people and visitors,
a matter of the highest and greatest importance. The Board early decided
that our State Building should be creditable to our State, and suited to the
purpose for which it was designed, as headquarters for our citizens and
visitors. The Board also decided that the building should display as far as
practicable Indiana building material. The stone steps and door ways from
the oolitic stone fields of our State were the best exhibits of stone in any
building at Jackson Park.

The floors and mantel, in lower story of our building, showed the excellence of our tile industry. The interior hard-wood finish of quartered oak, throughout the building, and parquetry floors in the ladies' parlors, well displayed our hard woods. The brick mantel on the second floor was a very fine display of our clay industry, and the mantel in the lower hall, showed the great capability of the new oolitic stone for carved work. The plate glass in doors and windows was an excellent display of our glass industries.[61]

In addition, the Indiana Building included a large library that contained 600 volumes written by authors from the state.

September 27, 1893, was proclaimed Indiana Day at the World's Columbian Exposition. Along with U.S. President Benjamin Harrison, the speakers that day were Indiana Governor Claude Matthews; Benjamin Havens, executive director of the Indiana world's fair board; John Campbell, executive committee member of the Indiana world's fair board; Clement Studebaker of Studebaker Brothers Manufacturing Company located in South Bend, Indiana; and Virginia Meredith. Estimates indicate 100,000 Hoosiers attended the special one-day event. Throughout the six months that the exposition was open, it drew approximately 300,000 Hoosiers to Chicago.[62]

Indiana exhibitors were well represented by 400 individuals, 200 companies, and 120 school districts. Visitors looking for Indiana exhibits would have to visit the Indiana Building as well as all of the buildings at Jackson Park. Some of the displays in the Manufactures and Liberal Arts Building included "washing machines from Evansville, plate glass from Kokomo, refrigerators from Michigan City, oil tanks from Fort Wayne, and blankets from Seymour. . . . In and around the Agriculture Building . . . contained large pyramids of glass jars filled with samples of corn, wheat, rye, and other cereal grains. There was also a twenty-five-foot-high pyramid of corn in stalk . . . displays of Indiana's wool and honey industries . . . Plows from factories in Indianapolis . . . cultivators made in Brookston and grinding mills from a plant in Crown Point . . . hardwood . . . butter sculpting . . . hundreds of horses, sheep, pigs, and cows."[63]

The rich tradition of Indiana's agricultural community received special recognition. Robert Mitchell, who judged the agricultural exhibition, penned the following comments:

> I report this exhibit was examined by me. The exhibit was not so elaborate as some of the State exhibits, but was so arranged to display the cereals of Indiana and Indiana's productive qualities. . . . The exhibit was excellent in quality, and all the grain plump, and fine in color, fully complying with all

the rules, giving data as to growing and cultivation of the grain on exhibition. I recommend an award.[64]

At the conclusion of the exposition in 1893, the Indiana Building would be sold and all of the exhibits shipped back to Indiana. Unfortunately, the Indiana Building along with other exposition buildings were destroyed when fires devastated most of the structures in January and July of 1894.

᠙᠙᠙

The second meeting of the Board of Lady Managers occurred in September 1891 at Apollo Hall in Chicago.[65] Meredith and Susan Ball, who served as the alternate to Wilhelmina Reitz, represented Indiana at this conference.[66]

The lady managers had a great deal to discuss, given that one year had already elapsed since their first meeting. The fact that the exposition was less than two years away created pressure to develop specific plans for their work. The second summit, unfortunately, produced much of the same political infighting as the first one, and President Bertha Palmer spent her time defending her actions of the previous year.

Palmer, Meredith, and other members of the executive committee came to the meeting upset because they believed that a few disgruntled lady managers had leaked false and incendiary information to local newspapers. Some had claimed that Palmer had acquiesced to the male commissioners by giving away the board's power. Then there was the controversy surrounding the removal of the board's elected secretary, Phoebe Couzins, by the executive committee. Everyone in the room knew that Palmer would defend her leadership skills, and once completed, the sordid and messy gossip surrounding Couzins's dismissal would have to be discussed in detail.

Palmer and Meredith had done their homework. They were working as a well-informed and highly coordinated team during the second conference. But first, Palmer had to deliver a knockout blow to those who had chosen to use the press to personally attack her and the members of the executive committee. Illinois Congressman William Springer opened the session with a short speech, but the applause was short-lived as Palmer approached the podium.[67] A hush settled over the crowd as Palmer began to speak, presenting her achievements in such a way as to defuse the challenges to her leadership.[68]

It didn't take long for Palmer's audience to realize that she had more than readied herself for the challenges. She was conversant on the issues, meticulously organized, methodical in her approach, and firm in response. She began by stating that the commissioners had passed several measures on April 3, 1891, granting specific authority to the Board of Lady Managers.[69]

First and foremost, the lady managers would appoint a percentage of the judges for exhibits that included contributions by women. In addition, the commissioners gave the women their own building to manage as well as the "general charge and management of all the interests of women in connection with the Exposition." Palmer also pointed out that the men's board recognized her presidential powers to manage the women's funds, though this would later be a point of contention between the men and women. And finally, the commissioners had granted salary allowances of $5,000 and $3,000 to the president and secretary for the lady managers, respectively.[70]

Palmer separately addressed each of these points in her speech. As she made her presentation, she must have looked across the audience, making eye contact with those she believed had spread false rumors and caused so much dissension among the rank and file. She added that the Woman's Building ". . . is the only Building over which the Commission has given up its jurisdiction" as proof that the executive committee had become an effective lobbying group for the Board of Lady Managers.[71] She did not relinquish the podium until she had thoroughly discussed and repudiated what her adversaries were telling others about her. The speech was so rich in detail that the written transcript filled thirty-four pages in the board's minutes.[72]

Slowly but surely, Palmer reasserted herself as the leader of the lady managers. She went on to decline the $5,000 salary—except for secretarial expenses—that the men had allotted to the president.[73] This was probably a calculated strategy to strengthen the loyalty of her supporters and win over those who opposed her.

One of the criticisms faced by Palmer, Meredith, and the other members of the executive committee centered around their agreeing to the commissioners' demands that fewer women judges were needed on certain committees, which some believed had weakened the cause of women at the exposition. Palmer conceded that argument but turned the tide on her opponents when she informed the lady managers why she had agreed with the commissioners on this one point. The commissioners were concerned that women who lacked the requisite expertise to properly evaluate displays might judge some exhibits. For instance, the commissioners had asked whether women should be allowed to judge horse-drawn carriages if the only part made by a woman was the curtains? Palmer agreed with the commission on this point but thought she had balanced her position by having the men agree to reduce the number of men judging products primarily built by women.[74]

She finished her lengthy speech and waited for the response. The date was September 2, 1891, a defining moment for Bertha Palmer and the Board of Lady Managers. Isabella Beecher Hooker, one of Palmer's staunch critics, stood up to announce publicly, "Friends, I think you will all join me in saying that our first duty is to thank God for this magnificent report and next, to thank Mrs. Palmer."[75] Palmer had demonstrated that the Board of Lady Managers was on solid footing, in good hands, and moving forward in spite of what others might be saying privately or publicly. She had solidified her existing support and gained new backing.

The controversy over the dismissal of Phoebe Couzins, secretary to the Board of Lady Managers, was then brought to the forefront. Couzins, among other things, had accused members of the executive committee of tampering with a portion of the minutes from their November 1890 meeting. According to Couzins, it wasn't just any part of the official minutes that someone had changed; it was the paragraph describing the executive committee that, when the changes were read, gave Palmer the power to appoint the committee members. When Couzins couldn't get anyone to admit to the altered books, she then took it upon herself to work around Palmer, Meredith, and other committee members. She wrote to the commissioners, the lady managers, and Congress as she tried to draw attention to what she thought were illegal and unethical acts by the Executive Committee of the Board of Lady Managers. After her dismissal from the board, Couzins hired an attorney to support her as she tried to get reinstated.

Couzins's ouster infuriated her supporters, who began sending protest letters to their colleagues around the country, basically indicating that the executive committee's decision to remove Couzins from her elected office was illegal. These lady managers argued that only the full board had the authority to remove Couzins since she was duly elected by all of them.

Palmer was irritated that some of the lady managers had made such an issue of the Couzins affair. She expressed herself candidly in a letter to Meredith and the others on the executive committee, writing, "The Commissioners also understand our position with reference to Miss Couzins better than our members (except the Executive Committee) because they were in Chicago when she made her protest etc. and consequently their information and influence would be serviceable."[76]

Meredith shared Palmer's frustrations about the conflict and expressed her views in a letter to a lady manager who had complained about the way Couzins was being treated: "To my mind the worst offense of the Secretary was disrespectful letters she wrote to members about other members."[77]

With the controversy still swirling a month prior to the April 1891 conference, Palmer wrote to Meredith to address Couzins's removal as secretary, the rumors it had generated, and how to deal with them at the upcoming meeting. At one point, Palmer consulted with Meredith in order to verify background information concerning the matter:

> Can you tell me who took the stenographic report of Mr. Walker's argument in Miss Couzins's case? She has been quoted by Frances Dickinson as saying, "Remember that there is no assurance, no certainty, not even a probability, that the Board of Lady Managers will even convene again," and I wish to know his exact words. How shall I find out? A prompt reply will greatly oblige.[78]

But when it came time to discuss the matter at the conference on September 3, 1891, it was Meredith who was prepared to defend the executive committee's controversial decision to the group. It appeared that, in an effort to stay out of the fray, Palmer had asked Meredith to lead the discussion. What occurred then was further evidence of the close working relationship between Meredith and Palmer. As was customary, Palmer asked that the executive committee's report be read out loud, sentence by sentence. Meredith, as the vice chairman of the executive committee, suggested that since the ". . . report was a lengthy one, it might be better to have it printed rather than read at the present meeting," which would help to better utilize their time planning.[79]

The assembly agreed, allowing Meredith to summarize the details in open discussion. Meredith purposefully read portions that she had previously selected from the minutes to make her points regarding the Couzins's affair. Her strategy was to piggyback on Palmer's successful opening speech by focusing on the accomplishments made by the executive committee. Meredith, in an effort to convince the lady managers that Couzins's dismissal was legal and proper, reminded them that they had given the executive committee the power to act on their behalf. The executive committee had acted and now wanted the full board to approve the action to remove Couzins from her elected office.

Meredith got to the heart of the matter when she said that the World's Columbian Commission at its April 1891 meeting had "empowered the Executive Committee to manage the affairs of the Board of Lady Managers."[80] Meredith further argued her case by saying that "[o]f the Executive Committee, twelve of whom voted for Miss Couzins when she was elected, not one approved her conduct; the twenty-three ladies present at the session were unanimous in the vote upon the resolution of removal."[81] Meredith made the connection that both friends and foes of Couzins agreed that her censure and removal were in the best interest of the Board of Lady Managers. When the discussion subsided, Meredith asked the lady managers to affirm the executive committee's decision to remove Couzins from office. The vote tally favored Couzins's removal.

The only business that remained in the matter was for the board to vote on naming acting secretary Susan Gale Cooke permanently to the post. Hooker, Frances Dickinson, and thirteen other supporters of Couzins abstained from the vote, but Cooke was named as the new secretary. Palmer and Meredith had emerged unscathed.[82]

While the second seven-day conference probably resulted in a more cohesive group than the first conference, the time could have been better spent planning for the future than squandering it on past issues. As the meeting drew to a close, the lady managers found themselves once again failing to progress on their assigned work for the exposition. The *Chicago Daily Tribune* reported this state of affairs in a less than complimentary article about the board. A quote from Meredith in that article clearly reveals her frustration with the slow progress that the women were making toward meeting their goals:

> The Board of Lady Managers held a lively meeting yesterday morning in Apollo Hall. The entire session was devoted to the consideration of the report of the Executive committee showing the work done since its first meeting, April 8, 1891. As soon as the clerk had finished reading the printed report Mrs. Isabella Beecher Hooker took the floor and made violent objections to Art.[icle]1, which gave the Executive committee the power to amend the by-laws of the Board of Lady Managers. Mrs. Hooker declared that only idiots would think of allowing such a clause to stand. This sally called forth a storm of discussion, in which Mrs. Virginia C. Meredith of Indiana, Mrs. Trautman of New York, Mrs. Brayton of South Carolina, and others spoke in favor of the article, and Mrs. Hooker, almost without support, maintained her opposition. Mrs. Meredith said: "The question before the meeting is the approval of the report of the committee. This question should be settled without delay, as still more important business is before us. Do not think that the Executive committee is the end of all things. Remember that the Board of Lady Managers has been vested by an act of Congress with important duties in connections with the Fair. Remember

that in our hands rests the right of women to exhibit side by side and on an equality with men. If we succeeded in nothing else than this one thing we could feel that our time has been well spent. We are trusted with the charge of protecting women against unjust discrimination. Let us make good use of our time while it is ours. Upon our industry now will depend the action of Congress at its next session. If we do well they may give us still further power and responsibility; if we waste our time in idle discussion Congress may abolish our body altogether. We are only just getting down to our real duties in connection with the Fair. Twelve great committees are to be appointed to carry on the real work of our body. These, and not the Executive committee, will have to do the real work of our commission." After considerable discussion the report of the Executive committee was adopted without amendment.[83]

By the time Meredith joined the lady managers, she had spent many hours honing her public speaking skills in front of audiences at Farmers' Institutes and women's clubs in Indiana. So when she was called upon to make presentations about the World's Columbian Exposition, she was equal to the challenge. Women's clubs and professional associations would often invite Meredith's colleague, Bertha Palmer, to speak about the role women were expected to play at the exposition, but Palmer's busy schedule didn't always allow her to accept. Palmer frequently asked Meredith to stand in for her:

> I have had several letters from Mrs. Julia Ward Howe asking me to address the "Society for the Advancement of Women" (of which she is President) at a convention which is to be held at Grand Rapids on Oct. 13th to 17th [1891], on the subject of the Col[umbian] Exposition.

> I shall be unable to attend as I expect to be away from home on those dates, and I have written [the association] . . . asking that space be reserved for us, and saying that one of our members would answer to the subject if possible. . . . I write to ask if you will let me send your name in case I receive a favorable reply . . . as I consider this a most important organization and I want our Board ably represented. I do not want to lose this opportunity, and would be glad to say a few words myself if possible, as I wrote Mrs. Howe.[84]

In some cases, Palmer and Meredith would both be asked to speak. In February 1891, Palmer and Meredith went to Washington, D.C., to address the Women's National Council. It was an audience made up of the movers and shakers in the suffrage movement, including Susan B. Anthony and Julia Ward Howe. Palmer was the featured speaker, with Meredith ". . . given a brief time to describe the industrial relations of women to the Fair."[85]

Meredith also described the work of the Board of Lady Managers in a speech delivered in May 1892 to the Indiana Union of Literary Clubs, an organization for which she had served as president.[86] Meredith titled the presentation "The Relation of Women to the Columbian Exposition." Her speech (see appendix 3 for full text) was one of several presentations in a symposium titled "Woman as a Factor in the World's Progress." It provided an up-to-date overview of what the Board of Lady Managers had accomplished by 1892. Meredith's speech, however, went further than a mere update of accomplishments. In it, she focused on her strong support for the traditional roles of women as mother, wife, and homemaker. She noted, "Personally I wish that every woman might have the supreme good, which is a sheltered life in her husband's home, the contented wife of a noble man." But this time, she also spoke of the value and contributions that women added to jobs and industries outside the home. She included one message that she would repeatedly communicate throughout her life: "It is not likely that there will ever again be any distinction so artificial as that of sex between the skill of men and women—unlikely that there will ever again be a woman's department in any World's Fair."[87]

When Bertha Palmer was asked to develop a report on what the Board of Lady Managers intended to do in the way of agricultural exhibits at the World's Columbian Exposition, she naturally turned to Virginia Meredith. While Palmer had no agriculture experience, Meredith had been managing her own successful livestock operation for nearly a decade. Palmer asked Meredith to write about how women benefited from a rural upbringing and even prospered when they focused on an agricultural profession as their chosen career:

> I think you will know about what I want—a general resume of the advantages to women of an agricultural life from both a practical and an aesthetic stand-point, and the consequent interest taken in this department and its exhibit by the B.L.M. [Board of Lady Managers]. You might mention the opportunity it affords of an honorable livelihood and speak of farming as a science, bringing in the subject of the Agricultural Colleges. . . .

Feeling sure that you will help me out in this with your familiarity with the subject, as well as your valuable experience, and awaiting your reply with the greatest interest and eagerness.[88]

Certainly, Meredith was capable of writing such a report, but when it came to agriculture and the World's Columbian Exposition, she had loftier ambitions than merely writing reports about women in agriculture. She had her sights set on being named chief of the Department of Livestock at the exposition, which was not a department associated with the Board of Lady Managers. Meredith campaigned many months to secure this important agricultural position at the exposition. The *Chicago Daily Tribune* reported in August 1891, "Mrs. Virginia C. Meredith, it is said, would like to be the Chief of the Department of Live Stock, and her friends are quietly working in her favor."[89] A week later, the same newspaper confirmed that Meredith was, indeed, a candidate.[90]

Bertha Palmer asserted her own influence to try to sway the commission's decision:

I had a letter from Judge Martindale last night suggesting that I see the Director-General which I tried to do this morning, but found that he was out of the city for the day. It is my duty to try and advance the interests of women in connection with the Exposition and in your case, it is performed with the utmost zeal and pleasure because I know that your administration of the Livestock Department will reflect credit on all of us. I think Mr. Kerfoot—Chief of the Agricultural Committee is out of the city, but I will see the other members of the Directory who may have influence as soon as possible.[91]

The director-general of the World's Columbian Exposition, George Davis, soon became the focus of a campaign on Meredith's behalf. The *Chicago Daily Tribune* reported, "[Y]esterday there was a score of people in and out of Director-General Davis' office asking him to appoint [Meredith]."[92]

The loud chorus of those wishing to see Meredith become the chief of the Department of Livestock did not impress Davis. He told the press that "he couldn't use a live-stock chief now if he had one, since the work has been completely covered by W. I. Buchanan, Chief of the Department of Agriculture."[93] Davis's statement was probably less than truthful, as it raises the question of why Meredith and her supporters would have spent so much time campaigning for a position unless one existed.

Davis really did have a need for this new livestock department at the exposition, but he faced a rebellion if he appointed a woman to head it up. The secretary of the Live-Stock Breeders' Association, T. B. Sotham of Pontiac, Michigan, lodged a complaint with Davis, protesting Meredith's appointment. It appears from newspaper accounts that while Meredith had proven herself as a capable livestock producer, Davis had received letters from "a number of live-stock men objecting to a woman for the Department of Live Stock."[94] Meredith may have been qualified for the position, but she was facing opposition based on her gender.

Less than a week after saying he didn't need a Department of Livestock, Davis did an about-face and named Eber Ward Cottrell of Detroit as chief of the newly developed department.[95] Cottrell was the land commissioner for the Detroit, Mackinac, and Marquette Railroad, which indicated that Davis's pick was political. After several months, the competition for the position was over, and much to the disappointment of Meredith and her friends, her bid was unsuccessful.[96] Even support from very influential individuals such as Commissioner Elijah Martindale could not ensure that a highly qualified livestock woman such as Meredith would be appointed as chief of the Department of Livestock.

Meredith's failure to secure the chief of the Department of Livestock was, by all accounts, a personal setback for her, but this disappointment was more than offset by her appointment as chairman of the Committee on Awards of the Board of Lady Managers on October 26, 1892. While the work of the livestock department chief has faded with time, Meredith's work as the chairman of the Committee on Awards brought her national recognition during her lifetime and for a century after.

Being the chairman of this committee was one of the most important assignments that Palmer could bestow on a lady manager. Conferring recognition on women exhibitors was the only real activity that Congress had authorized the Board of Lady Managers to do. This person would have the opportunity to meet and interact with other women at a national and international level.

Meredith described her activities in the following manner:

> The work entrusted to myself falls naturally into three periods. The first period being the twelve months of 1893 devoted to active work pertaining to awards, and the selection of judges. . . . The second period, from January 1, 1894, to September 1, 1895, was devoted to the active execution of the resolution of Congress approved December 15, 1893, authorizing the Diploma of Honorable Mention. The time from September 1, 1895, to June 1896 was devoted to the closing of the business in an orderly way . . . completion of the reports upon awards, . . . final reports etc.[97]

While the work of the position seemed to be clear-cut, it would prove to be anything but that.

One challenge facing Meredith was the previous inaction by the Board of Lady Managers. It was not until their October 1892 gathering—the women's third meeting—that they even began discussing in any detail how the displays produced by women would be judged, who would judge them, and how the judges would be selected. This did not leave much time to act, since opening day of the World's Columbian Exposition with the public display of exhibits was slated for May 1, 1893, just six short months away.

To get the work done on time, the awards committee would be one of the board's most active committees and require full-time leadership. Meredith would need to stay in Chicago, "assuming charge of the interests of women exhibitors, their space, location, etc."[98] She would require a salary to allow for this, since her farming operations did not generate the kind of income to make her independently wealthy. The Board of Lady Managers agreed and authorized her to receive $3,500 per year. This allowed Meredith to reside in Chicago, though she still returned to Oakland Farm every two weeks to manage her business affairs there.[99]

Another and perhaps larger challenge facing Meredith was the conflict with the commissioners about the role of the lady managers in the awards process. The men's commission had been establishing its own policy on awards from October 1890 to the spring of 1892, and having already fought with the commission on a variety of issues during this time, Meredith knew that her awards committee would face an uphill battle to complete the tasks assigned to them.

As early as the fall of 1890, the Executive Committee of the World's Columbian Commission had charged its own awards committee with deciding "whether awards shall be granted and what character of awards shall be made, if any."[100] The commissioners ultimately agreed that exhibits would be judged against a standard, rather than competing against similar entries; expert judges would be used to evaluate exhibits individually; and the awards bestowed would include "parchment certificates accompanied by bronze medals."[101] The commissioners also specified in October 1890 that they would select and appoint all judges.[102] This specific policy would draw hostile fire from the women as they began their work and would eventually lead the commissioners to back off of that position.

The lady managers had been led to believe that their board—and not the commission—would have the authority to identify qualified women judges. This was supported by the first half of one of the primary resolutions passed by the World's Columbian Commission, which seemed unambiguous: "Resolved by this Commission, First: That the Board of Lady Managers be and they are hereby directed and empowered to appoint one or more members of all committees authorized to award prizes for exhibits which may be produced in whole or in part by female labor."[103] The second half of the same resolution stated, "and the number of such women members so to be appointed shall be in proportion to the percentage of female labor performed in the production of such exhibits," which left open the question of who would determine that number.[104] The second part of the resolution was modified a year later by the insertion of "such number [of women judges] to be determined by the Standing Committee on Awards of the Commission."[105]

Meredith mistakenly believed that the clarification of the original resolution was inconsequential, because the original wording of the amendment still remained. Therefore, Meredith and the board interpreted the modification to mean that the commission's Committee on Awards would make the final decision regarding percent of female labor in cases where there was uncertainty.[106] To the women, it seemed straightforward: the commission would tell the board how many women were needed, and in turn, the women would appoint female judges to fill those slots. Meredith was comfortable that the commissioners were the ones who had to determine the number of women judges needed. She assumed that they would quickly generate the number so each department could then select the appropriate number of women judges to meet those needs. Yet nothing would be easy for Meredith and her awards committee when it came to the selection, appointment, and placement of judges.

With so little finalized regarding judging matters, Meredith had asked Palmer at the conclusion of the fall 1890 meeting to see if they could both meet with the director-general of the World's Columbian Exposition, George Davis.

Meredith wanted an understanding on how the percentage of women's work contributed to each exhibit would be determined. Meredith concluded "that as all information in regard to female labor must come primarily from the exhibitor, the most effective means to be used in securing the information in an official form would be through the initial applications made for space to exhibit in the Columbian Exposition."[107]

At their meeting, Meredith, Palmer, and Davis struggled to resolve this seemingly simple issue, and though the wording of the inquiry would cause its own set of problems, Davis agreed that the forms filled out by potential exhibitors would contain a statement asking them the percentage of time that females contributed to the exhibit. Meredith and Palmer knew that identifying this percentage of work would be the prelude to determining how many women judges would be appointed to the committees to evaluate each entry.[108]

Meredith was led to believe that the World's Columbian Commission would calculate the number of women judges needed based on a review of each exhibitor's entry form. From this information, Meredith thought the Board of Lady Managers would identify women with the required expertise, secure their appointment, and then assign the judges to the proper departments and exhibits. Neither Meredith nor the Board of Lady Managers could have foreseen that, by early 1892, they would literally have to fight the commissioners tooth and nail—even past the opening ceremonies in 1893—on who had the authority to select, appoint, and place women judges. It became a battle of wills between Meredith and the chairman of the commission's awards committee, John Boyd Thacher. The exchange of caustic words between them would create friction that would last well past the closing of the World's Columbian Exposition.

On January 11, 1893, Meredith convened the first meeting of her committee, which included four lady managers in addition to herself. President Palmer left the workings of the committee to Meredith. The awards committee would establish an office for its work in Chicago, first in the Rand McNally Building in January 1893, then moving in April to the Woman's Building in Jackson Park on the exposition grounds.[109]

Meredith's awards committee had been given the following orders from a special committee of the Executive Committee of the Board of Lady Managers:

> The duties of the Committee had been prescribed by the [sub-executive] Committee of the Board of Lady Managers in a series of resolutions which were as follows: First: . . . to ascertain definitely, in regard to every exhibit in the Exposition, whether or not the labor of women was employed in its

production. Second: . . . duty of the Chairman of the Committee to have properly attached to . . . the official device that designates woman's work in the Exposition. Third: . . . Committee to take any and all action that may be necessary to secure and appoint competent jurors of Award in every class and group of the classification where woman's labor has been engaged. . . . Fourth: . . . Committee may appoint men jurors, wherever in its discretion the best interests of women will be served by such appointment. Fifth: The sum of $10,000.00 . . . is hereby set aside and appropriated for the use of this Committee in carrying forward its work.[110]

The women were under pressure to act quickly, yet many questions about assigning judges and evaluating exhibits still lingered. Meredith was concerned that the number of entries "as foreshadowed by the great number of applications for space filed by proposed exhibitors" would require more judges than what had been anticipated.[111] In fact, 160,000 exhibits were entered, and the commission predicted that 659 judges would be needed to evaluate them all.[112] This presented a real problem for Meredith, who was unsure about how her committee would operate within the commission's anticipated system of judging. To further complicate matters, she thought that identifying competent women judges would be made more difficult if they were not paid for their services while in Chicago.[113]

Some decisions were already set in stone. For instance, the commissioners had resolved not to issue awards based on an exhibition winning over its competitors. Instead, the commissioners decided to employ the same procedures used in 1876 at the Centennial Exposition in Philadelphia. Meredith was familiar with the Philadelphia exposition because she had attended it with her husband, Henry Clay Meredith, who had served as a member of the awards committee there.[114] The managers of that exposition had followed a new system that judged exhibits against a "standard of excellence" rather than against other exhibits.[115] Unfortunately, Meredith's committee was created so late in the planning process that its members were constantly reacting to decisions such as these that had already been made by their counterparts on the commission's award committee.

One particularly upsetting decision had been made only weeks before the women's award committee met for the first time. On December 13, 1892, the Committee on Awards of the World's Columbian Commission had met to discuss the selection of judges and to clarify the presentation of awards. At that meeting, the members developed a set of rules that, Meredith would complain, "proved the source of long and tiresome contention, as indeed might have been foreseen."[116] The lady managers filed a formal protest that they were not given the authority to choose the women judges as part of the new regulations.[117]

But Meredith was not about to accept this decision quietly. In fact, she caused quite a stir when she indicated to the commissioners that, according to her interpretation of the proposed regulations, 100 percent of the judges would be women. The commissioners were probably embarrassed as she presented the reasoning behind her surprising remark. She started off by asking them whether their awards committee had actually read what the commissioners themselves had already adopted as policy in 1891.

Meredith quickly pointed out that "the proposed rules were found to contain no reference whatever to the Board of Lady Managers and its right to appoint Judges of Award," which was in direct contradiction to the resolution adopted by the commissioners themselves in April of 1891 that had assigned this role to the women. Furthermore, Meredith reminded the commissioners that Congress had given the Board of Lady Managers the authority "to award prizes for exhibits which may be produced in whole or in part by female labor." Since the commissioners were planning to use "the Expert Judge System," which required that a single expert judge evaluate exhibits for awards, Meredith concluded that "the examination and the award would have to be made by a committee of one, and that one necessarily a woman. In Shoe and Leather Department, by way of illustration, it may be stated, that every exhibit catalogued contained a per cent of female labor."[118]

This was a perplexing development indeed, but Meredith was ready with a solution: simply include the women in the decision-making process. Meredith asked that the rules be amended to allow representatives from her Committee on Awards to work with the commission's awards committee to determine the number and the selection of women judges.[119]

The commissioners created a special committee to consider the problems raised by Meredith and Palmer. By this time, the commissioners were quite sensitive to congressional criticism, which made Meredith's remarks about them ignoring Congress a rather persuasive ploy. They did not want to stand accused of disregarding the World's Fair Bill, which, of course, they had been doing for quite some time when it came to issues involving the Board of Lady Managers. Nor could they have their own awards committee ignoring policies that they themselves had previously established. The findings from the special committee were forwarded to the commission around Christmas 1892.

In view of the manifest intention of Congress, as disclosed by the provisions of the Act of Congress approved April 25, 1890, that the agency and co-operation of women in the Exposition should be recognized and utilized it seemed essentially proper to your committee [the commission's special committee] that there should be in the fundamental regulations a distinct recognition of woman's relation to the matter of awards. In accordance with this the rules were amended by inserting the following clause: "On each of said [judging] Boards there shall be a number of competent women to be hereafter determined, and on each of the several committees of the Board of Judges having to do with the examination and consideration of exhibits produced in whole or in part by female labor and awards predicated thereon, there shall be one or more competent women."[120]

While Meredith thought the wording proposed in the report advanced their cause, she still was not totally pleased with what she felt were important omissions. She believed that the report "was not adequate, because there was no specific reference to the Board of Lady Managers and its right to appoint Judges of Award, nor was there a definition of the word 'committee.'"[121]

At the January 1893 commissioners' meeting, Palmer, Meredith, and all of the lady managers who had been appointed to the women's Committee on Awards "were unremitting in their efforts to secure such further amendment for the general rules and regulations governing awards, as would explicitly provide for the adequate participation of women judges, as well as a recognition of the right of the Committee on Awards of the Board of Lady Managers to guide and protect the work of women judges."[122] Simply put, they wanted to find their own experts and to appoint them to the appropriate departments.

Meredith wrote a terse letter to the commission on January 12, 1893, reiterating the need for a decision on the matter:

Gentlemen:—

The National Commission has directed and empowered the Board of Lady Managers to appoint one or more members of certain committees, such number to be determined by the Committee on Awards of the National [World's Columbian] Commission. In view of this fact will you kindly direct an early conference between the Committee on Awards of the Commission and that of the Board of Lady Managers?

It is evident that arbitrary rules must be adopted for some of the groups and classes, and looking to the accomplishment of this end, it is the desire of this committee that a conference of the two committees be held, in order to arrive at a just basis for computing the percentage of woman's work in these groups and classes.

It is of the utmost importance that this Committee on Awards should know at the earliest time possible how many women jurors will be required to examine and consider the exhibits produced in whole or in part by female labor.

It is very important that these jurors should have superior qualifications, otherwise the wisdom of Congress in providing for, and the judgment of the Commission in appointing, a Board of Lady Managers will be open to criticism.

To select competent jurors will require diligent investigation; therefore, this committee requests prompt decision in order that it may have time and opportunity to intelligently discharge its duty.

You will remember that the following is a part of a resolution adopted by the Board of Lady Managers, and referred to your body at its December meeting, with a request for definite instructions: "In what manner do you propose that the Committee on Awards of the Board of Lady Managers shall co-operate with your Committee on Awards in obeying the law of Congress in regard to appointing members of the Juries of Award?"[123]

Meredith realized that many questions about dealing with women judges were not going to be seriously addressed by the commissioners. She noted, "This letter was inspired by the conviction that no adequate provisions would be embodied in the general rules governing awards; in view of the amendment of the resolution of the Commission already referred to, by which the number of women judges was to be determined by the Committee on Awards of the World's Columbian Commission, it seemed imperative to reach some understanding in regard to the meaning of the rules as they affected women judges."[124]

As requested, Meredith's awards committee and its counterpart from the commission met to iron out their differences and, the women hoped, to arrive at some understanding. This brought Meredith face-to-face with her adversary, John Boyd Thacher, chairman of the commission's awards committee. As a result of the meeting, the rules were changed on January 16, 1893, with Meredith summarizing the outcome:

First. That, in order to determine the number of women judges that would be required for jury service, he [Thacher] would, in conjunction with the Chairman of the Committee on Awards of the Board of Lady Managers, examine the records in the several departments, and endeavor equitably to make assignments to such groups and classes as the proportion of female labor therein would suggest representation.

Second. Mr. Thacher stated that not only would the percent of female labor involved in the production of the exhibit influence the apportionment of women judges, but the fact that the exhibit was one wholly consumed by women would have much weight and influence in making such apportionment. . . . In consideration of these statements made by the Chairman of the Executive Committee on Awards of the Commission, and regarding them as official interpretations of the rules submitted by the Committee on Awards, we are willing that they should stand in lieu of any explicit utterances in these rules of the rights and privileges of the Board of Lady Managers.[125]

Thacher's remarks seemed to favor Meredith and her awards committee, but in the long run, Thacher would not uphold his end of any bargain he and Meredith had previously agreed to at that meeting. Meredith quickly lost patience with Chairman Thacher, as it seemed every discussion with him quickly descended into arguments and accusations. Meredith just found him difficult to work with, and she was tired of the constant rule making that seemed to exclude any input from the Board of Lady Managers or its committees.

The final award and judging regulations were printed on June 8, 1893, fully one month after the exposition had opened its doors to the public. Meredith was perturbed that the final rules were not to her liking but realized that she was not in a position to ask for more from the commission. Time had run out for her and the Board of Lady Managers.[126]

While the number of women judges that would be needed remained unknown, Meredith's awards committee had to establish how women judges would be selected from a larger pool of applicants who had expressed a desire to participate.[127] They noted that "special aptitude and judicial temperament would be the governing factors, while geographical situation should not limit the choice of the Committee."[128] Not allowing location to determine a judge's appointment was contrary to how the Board of Lady Managers filled vacancies on other committees. Eventually, the methods used to select the women judges would result in a rather heated argument among the full Board of Lady Managers.

Meredith developed a flyer that outlined specific qualities the awards committee was looking for in the selection of a competent judge. The circular also
depicted the type of work that a judge would be expected to perform:

> The Board of Lady Managers of the World's Columbian Commission.
> Concerning the Appointment of Women Judges.
>
> Awards will be granted upon specific points of excellence or advancement.
> When assigned to the examination of an exhibit, the judge must make
> a report in writing of the result of the examination. When the exhibit is
> deemed worthy of an award, then the judge must formulate in written
> words the specific points of excellence or advancement which renders it
> worthy of an award. . . .
>
> To appoint women judges who are competent to render intelligent judg-
> ment, make intelligible reports, and sustain themselves creditably upon the
> Board of Judges, is one of the most important duties entrusted to the Board
> of Lady Managers. Even in the usual and ordinary employments of women,
> it is desired to appoint women of superior abilities with trained and alert
> faculties for observation and expression. While in the comparatively new,
> unusual, and higher callings it is imperative that the women judges should
> possess technical knowledge and broad comprehension of the particular
> line of service they undertake. . . . it therefore invites suggestions and infor-
> mation in regard to women who are eminent and accomplished critics in a
> particular line of industry, education, ethics, or art.
>
> Congress has made an appropriation of $100,000 for the payment of judges,
> examiners, and members of committees to be appointed by the Board of
> Lady Managers in connection with the granting of awards in the World's
> Columbian Exposition.
>
> All communications should be addressed to Mrs. Virginia C. Meredith.[129]

To get the $100,000 for judges' stipends, Palmer and Meredith had traveled
to Washington in February 1893 to address the House and Senate Committees
on Appropriations.[130] This appropriation from Congress to the Board of
Lady Managers became another contentious issue that drove a deeper wedge
between the men's and women's Committees on Awards. George Davis, director-
general of the World's Columbian Exposition, had estimated that his Committee
on Awards needed 659 judges to review all of the anticipated exhibits and had
asked Congress in November 1891 for $570,880 to cover judges' expenses, such
as salary and transportation costs.[131] This request "contained no reference

to the participation of the Board of Lady Managers in appointing Judges of Award," an omission that was all too commonplace and likely intentional.[132]

Using Meredith's figures, Palmer estimated that the Board of Lady Managers needed 130 women judges. In March 1893, when Meredith and Palmer convinced Congress to award $100,000 to the Board of Lady Managers to cover the cost of hiring women judges, the appropriation was not new money. Instead, this earmark came directly out of the $570,880 that had been granted to the commission. But now this $100,000 could only be spent under signature of Palmer as president of the board and of Meredith as chairman of the Committee on Awards.[133]

At last, the lady managers had gained some measure of control over money pertaining to their own work. But while the women's award committee finally had money to work with, the commission still had not told Meredith the number of women judges to secure. Meredith was deluged with requests from women wanting to be hired as judges. However, she found "much attention was demanded by investigations to ascertain the per cent of woman's work involved in the production of exhibits. . . ."[134] Director-General George Davis wrote to the chiefs of the thirteen commission departments on April 15, 1893, ordering them to transmit to Virginia Meredith ". . . lists of exhibits in your respective departments which have been produced in whole or in part by the labor of women. . . . On these lists should be noted the percentage of the labor of women as indicated by the applications."[135] Meredith seemed pleased to get the information from all of the departments, with the only holdout being the Department of Fine Arts.

Meredith knew this information would help her fulfill one of the duties that the board's executive committee had placed on her, which was to ". . . make apparent to all students of the Columbian Exposition the important participation of women in the production and perfection of exhibits."[136]

To highlight the work by women, a card attached to each exhibit would either say "Made in whole by female labor" or "Made in part by female labor."[137] Meredith viewed the wording as "being unostentatious, could not be objected to by an exhibitor, and yet would be easily noticed by any one seeking the information it conveyed."[138]

Palmer, on April 14, 1893, sent a letter to the commissioners asking them to clarify whether the Board of Lady Managers had the authority to develop such a card. In quick order she was told that "the Board of Lady Managers had full power to design the device" but that the commission would need to give its final approval.[139] Thus, their idea was submitted to the commissioners with full expectation that this simple request would receive approval.

Commissioner J. W. St. Clair from West Virginia was assigned to review the Board of Lady Managers' request regarding the card. To the utter disbelief of Meredith, St. Clair found her card to be highly objectionable. His investigation and report of April 24, 1893, formed the basis by which the Commission declined to authorize the Board of Lady Managers' request to place the educational cards on any exhibit.[140] St. Clair wrote:

> ... it would not only be wrong and unjust to placard any of the exhibits in the manner indicated without the consent of the exhibitors, but in my opinion, it would be out of taste, contrary to experience, and would very likely militate against the artistic appearance of the exhibits themselves.
>
> I am satisfied from conversations held with various exhibitors that they will not consent, as a rule, to any such announcement by way of placards as is proposed to be made by the Board of Lady Managers, and unless an arbitrary rule were made requiring all exhibitors whose exhibits were produced in whole or in part by female labor to submit to having them placarded, it would be very unfair to women, because it would show a disparagement of their labor and deceive the public, because it would only be in that case a partial advertisement of the extent of women's work in the production of the articles themselves on exhibition, that the genius and labor of women ought to be advertised in some more dignified form than that imparted by a placard.
>
> I am clearly of the opinion that it would be the grossest error to adopt any system of placarding the exhibits, and it ought not to be done.[141]

With a vote that backed St. Clair's recommendation, the commission nixed the board's idea of highlighting the role that women played in producing the exhibits. Meredith indicated that this vote made it "impossible for the Chairman of the Committee on Awards to discharge this particular duty imposed upon her by the sub-executive committee of the Board of Lady Managers."[142]

Just days before the exposition opened on May 1, 1893, Meredith was ready to move her office to the Jackson Park location. Thacher offered to share space in his office with her, but Meredith quickly and flatly turned him down. She felt that the "... fact that our Committee had not been admitted to any official participation in the general administration of awards rendered it undignified that we should seem to participate by sufferance only, or in a subordinate capacity; it was therefore decided by the Committee on Awards of the Board of Lady Managers that it would maintain an independent office, giving undivided attention to that phase of the work explicitly defined as its own."[143] It was a clear indication that she and Thacher were not seeing eye-to-eye on most matters and that they were barely speaking to each other by the time the exposition opened.

Palmer assigned Meredith a suite of offices on the first floor of Pavilion A, near her office. Soon Meredith's office was inundated with "a steady stream of visitors, including the foreign Commissioners, with inquiries and recommendations in reference to the appointment of judges. The several members of our Committee were necessarily engaged much of the time in the reception of visitors and attention to inquiries for information."[144]

While she had an office and countless guests to deal with, everything else relating to awards and judges was still undecided, even though the exposition had already opened its gates for the public to view all of the wondrous exhibits from around the world. The women had the money to hire the best judges, "[b]ut the sense of security, which all these favorable conditions might naturally be expected to create, was dispelled by the menacing fact that the Standing Committee on Awards of the Commission, whose duty it was to determine the number of women judges that might serve in the Columbian Exposition, could not be induced to take any action whatever."[145]

Still, when members of Meredith's awards committee reconvened on May 3, 1893, they had to make decisions as best they could, given the lack of information available to them. The members agreed to pay women judges from the United States $6 for each day they worked as a judge. Transportation expenses would be paid in addition to the daily stipend. Foreign judges would receive $750 for their efforts, with transportation expenses included in that amount. Later, the commission required the Board of Lady Managers to amend the pay scale of the American women who judged exhibits in the Department of Fine Arts to $750 as well.[146]

The committee members also would have to prepare the actual slate of women judges. Meredith told the group that she ". . . believed the responsibility of selecting competent women to act as judges was so great that it should be shared by the entire Committee."[147] Meredith's decision to have the entire awards committee participate in nominating judges was a perceptive one. She understood that the slate of judges prepared by her committee would have to be approved by the entire Board of Lady Managers. Therefore, it would be better if the recommendations came from the entire committee instead of being left to her sole discretion.

With Thacher's committee continuing to give Meredith's committee the cold shoulder, Meredith lacked crucial information for the process. She still did not know how many women judges the commission would allow her to hire. And even if she were given the long-sought-after number, she had not ever been told which exhibits they would judge. Consequently, Meredith faced the dilemma of selecting the most competent women to judge exhibits without knowing what expertise to look for in those judges.

> Efforts were unceasing, by personal interview and otherwise, to secure a decision from the Committee on Awards of the Commission in reference to the number of women to be appointed as judges. After five months of such effort, and the Exposition being already in progress, it seemed apparent that the resolution of the World's Columbian Commission, directing that the number of judges to be appointed by the Board of Lady Managers should be determined by the per cent of female labor engaged in producing exhibits, was to be ignored.[148]

On May 26, 1893, John Thacher committed a serious blunder when he bypassed Meredith and asked board president Bertha Palmer if she would agree to pay for forty international judges out of the funds that Congress had provided to the Board of Lady Managers. Palmer passed Thacher's letter on to Meredith for her response. Palmer would force him to deal with Meredith, who by this time had her hackles up and was ready for a fight.

> Replying to your letter of the 26th addressed to Mrs. Palmer, and which has been referred to the Committee on Awards for consideration, I am instructed to say that the law of Congress seems plain and explicit in regard to the use of the funds appropriated for the expenses incident to the granting of awards.
>
> If your proposition contemplates that the additional forty judges to be apportioned in a certain contingency, to foreign nations, shall be appointed by the Board of Lady Managers before considering the proposition, we shall have to be informed as to what proportion of the two hundred and thirty-three judges already apportioned to foreign nations are to be women and whose compensation, consequently, is justly a charge against the $100,000 appropriated by Congress for payment of judges, examiners and members of the Committee to be appointed by the Board of Lady Managers. An early reply will greatly oblige the Committee.[149]

Meredith's reply elicited no response from Thacher.

Meredith and her committee continued selecting judges based on their review of the exhibits and using information provided to them by the chiefs of the commission's departments. The committee prepared its list of potential judges and submitted them to President Palmer for consideration by the Board of Lady Managers. While Meredith's committee members had their own opinions about how many women judges would be required, Meredith realized that there would be no final decision about the final number of women judges unless she initiated some drastic measure to shake up Thacher and his committee. Now it was time for Meredith to put Thacher on the defensive. On June 27, 1893, she sent a letter to Thacher about her committee's plans:

> The Committee on Awards of the Board of Lady Managers is about ready to make a public announcement of the judges appointed. The number determined upon is one hundred and thirty. This is in harmony with statements made [by representatives of the Board of Lady Managers] before the Congressional Committee in January last. With the hope that it may meet with your views, and that we may be favored with an immediate answer, I have the honor to remain, Yours very truly . . . [150]

It appears that her letter was leaked to the *Chicago Daily Tribune*. This finally forced Thacher to respond, since the newspaper reported the disagreement on June 29, 1893:

> John Boyd Thacher, having ended his troubles with the foreign Commissioners, may be plunged into others, but of more delicate and somewhat different character. For several months the lady managers have been carefully selecting the list of expert women judges whom they wish to have appointed upon the various examining boards. It is a pretty large list, for it numbers 140. The entire number of judges which Mr. Thacher expects to appoint will be about 650, so that the lady managers will ask for more than one-fifth of the number. Then, too, Mr. Thacher has calculated that at the outside there will be not more than 300 domestic judges. The lady managers are figuring on about twenty-five of their judges being foreign women, so that 115 will be domestic, giving them, if their wishes are carried out, one-third of the American judges. Mr. Thacher has not yet informed Mrs. Virginia Meredith, the Chairman of the Woman's Committee on Awards, what number of judges he will fix upon for the lady managers. He will hold a conference today and may then reach a conclusion." [151]

With a news conference scheduled to address the matter, Thacher called his committee into session, with Meredith and Palmer in attendance representing the Board of Lady Managers. While Meredith was pleased to finally be getting attention, she must have turned red with anger when Thacher said he was willing to give the board "thirty-six women judges from the entire quota of six hundred and fifty-nine."[152] But Meredith and Palmer stood their ground.[153] Both sides reconvened that afternoon, but the *Chicago Daily Tribune* reported that the "[w]oman's committee was unwilling to materially reduce the number of judges requested."[154] The time for breaking the logjam was at hand.

Meredith received a letter from William F. King, vice chairman of the men's award committee:

> Replying to yours of June 27, 1893, the Committee on Awards of the World's Columbian Exposition are of the opinion that the Act of Congress of March 3, 1893, in appropriating $570,000.00 for the payment of committees, judges & examiners of award, and in giving $100,000.00 thereof to the Board of Lady Managers, practically determined that the number of men to women for the American appointments should be in the proportion of one woman to five and seven-tenths men. You are advised that we are ready to accept the proportion of women appointments which would aggregate fifty-seven.[155]

Thacher must have thought that he would have a better chance of Meredith taking the deal if someone else sent the letter to her. He had, once again, changed the rules by disregarding a previous agreement where female judges would be appointed based on the percent of female work. Instead, the number would now be determined by the proportion of funds distributed by Congress to each of the awards committees.

Meredith seemed dejected as she considered her position. She knew that Thacher and his fellow commissioners held the upper hand. Still, she wrote back to King on July 1, 1893, to apply what pressure she could:

> . . . and in reply am pleased to say that the decision of your committee eminently satisfactory, in so far as it accepts the action of Congress as having practically determined that in appointing American judges in the Columbian Exposition the proportion of men to women shall be as one to five and seven-tenths.
>
> May I inquire if there is anything in the action of Congress to indicate that the same proportion is not practically determined in regard to the

number of foreign judges to be appointed, and was it not the duty of your committee to take care of this point in your negotiation with the foreign commissioners?[156]

She raised the obvious question: Why wasn't the same proportion of men to women judges considered for hiring foreign judges? The reply came not from Thacher or King, but from Oscar R. Hundley, secretary to the men's award committee:

> No proportionment of women judges was fixed by the Act of Congress. The agreement was only that "one or more" should be appointed upon the committees of those Departments into which women's work in whole or in part entered.[157]

Hundley went on to add:

> The intent of our further proposition was to reserve to this committee the adjudgment of women judges to their usual class when advised of their names and qualifications. We would not, for instance, consent that all your appointments should be made in any one committee; nor should we be willing to accept in any committee one who was obviously without qualifications. This committee does not, however, wish to be understood as assuming that you will tender any appointments who are not qualified. No difficulty is anticipated in the practical conduct of the matter in co-operation with the Board of Lady Managers.[158]

Hundley's letter referenced Congress's World's Fair Bill of 1890 but not what his own commission had agreed to with respect to women judges. He also failed to address other points that Meredith had included in the letter.

Meredith wrote back, asking more questions, but with no time left, Meredith and the other lady managers were forced to accept the commissioners' terms. Meredith's committee would develop its list of nearly five dozen expert judges and place its full slate of candidates before the Board of Lady Managers for approval. The men's awards committee would then review the final list of women judges and assign them to the appropriate departments and exhibits. Meredith continued to place blame squarely on the shoulders of the commissioners, who had failed to uphold their word or enforce their own policies:

> The system of awards adopted for the Columbian Exposition, while ideally perfect in theory, was in administration incredibly crude. . . . Under the rules adopted the position of the Committee on Awards of the Board

of Lady Managers was particularly unfavorable for the reason that the Committee found itself with authority to select judges, but without authority to guide or guard their services, or even to place them where they might participate in deciding methods to be pursued in making examinations for awards, by formulating a standard of excellence which would insure a degree of uniformity in awards.[159]

The Board of Lady Managers met again in Chicago on July 7, 1893, for a work session that would last more than a month. Virginia Meredith submitted for the full board's review the names of the fifty-seven women judges chosen unanimously by her awards committee.[160] Meredith included information about how each was selected and to which department each might be assigned, noting:

> It was the firm policy of the Committee to make selection wholly on the basis of qualification, due regard being shown when possible to geographical lines. The Board [of Lady Managers] had, whenever the subject was under discussion, shown a high conception of the importance of choosing judges upon the highest considerations, even going so far as to formally declare, that its Committee on Awards should select men, if competent women were not available; and it adopted with enthusiasm the first report of the Committee, in which it was announced that the Committee would not in its selection of judges be bound by geographical lines.[161]

Deliberations by the Board of Lady Managers on whether to accept or reject the nominees consisted of several weeks of off-and-on debate and produced one of the last major battles that the lady managers would have among themselves. As if having to deal with Thacher wasn't enough, now Meredith had to defend her committee's choices to her own colleagues. Meredith noted that there were many objections to how the list was developed and that consensus "was not reached without a long and serious contest, to which much publicity was given by the newspapers," though she went on to state that "the real point at issue was at the time entirely misapprehended by the press and the public generally."[162]

This fight reverted back to arguments based on geographical lines. Some states lacked a single judge on the list. Meredith countered that the board had directed her committee to select the most qualified women as judges. She tried to explain why some states were not represented: "[F]irst, from some States there had been no person recommended for appointment; second, from other States, those recommended were not suggested because of any expert knowledge or peculiar fitness, but simply on account of superior literary education and high social standing; third, from some States there were almost no exhibits, and therefore little interest in awards."[163]

Meredith described the debate and its outcome:

> The contest was gradually defined, until for the Board the choice lay between either confirming nominations already made by the Committee on Awards—nominations made presumably on account of fitness, irrespective of locality—or forcing their withdrawal in order to make places for others for whom it was not claimed they were better fitted to be judges, but only that they were residents of certain States or Territories. This contest extending over several weeks was characterized by every species of tactics known to parliamentary usage, and every possible influence of press, politics, and personal entreaty. It deserves to be recorded that the outcome of this contention brilliantly marked the ability and rectitude of the Board of Lady Managers. The majority of the members by their daily attendance and undaunted courage in standing for a principle, in the face of a bitter fight (than which nothing could be more hideous to each personally) vindicated the integrity of the Board in its high aim to do the best possible for women, regardless of considerations of policy or compromise.[164]

While Meredith presented this sanitized version of the events, other accounts dealing with the selection of judges were more personal. Florida Cunningham of South Carolina "charged that her state had been left out of the awards jury through Mrs. Meredith's 'malice.'"[165] As the arguments reached a heightened pitch, "[a]nger and bitterness broke to the surface again: Mrs. Meredith made a 'scathing arraignment' of Mrs. [Ida] Ball, and Mrs. Ball retaliated with a severe attack on Mrs. Meredith. The [Phoebe] Couzins factions vocally supported Miss Cunningham; the Palmer followers grouped under the Meredith banner."[166] Even the *New York Times* found the confrontation worth reporting on August 6, 1893:

> The Board of Lady Managers indulged in another decidedly unpleasant wrangle today. It lasted about two hours, and in that time many unpleasant and disagreeable things were said, tears were shed, and many of the ladies gave vent to their feelings by hissing and uttering strange noises.
>
> Mrs. [Ida] Ball of Delaware, Secretary of the Committee on Awards, read a long complaint of Mrs. Meredith, Chairman of the committee. She frequently referred to Mrs. Meredith as the "arrogant Chairman of the committee," and said that when she could not attend she sent her sister

to act as overseer, when the sister had no right to a seat in the committee. At frequent intervals the women expressed their surprise loudly.

But the sensation came last when Mrs. Ball said: "And now, in conclusion, I desire to say that Mrs. Meredith is an arrogant, malicious, ungenerous, vindictive woman."

Before she had finished these expletives half the women in the house were on their feet, many shrieking wildly. Others hissed and stamped their feet, and some wrung their hands in despair. Mrs. Palmer used her gavel vigorously and called in vain for order, but the excited females paid no heed to her. . . .

During all the uproar Mrs. Ball, who is a pretty, black-eyed little woman, stood perfectly calm and smiled sweetly on the turbulent women who surrounded her. When, at length, order was restored, Mrs. Ball repeated the sentence. The uproar was renewed and continued for some time.

Mrs. Ball then took her seat and in an instant Mrs. Meredith was on the floor.

"So far as any difference that exists between Mrs. Ball and myself is concerned," she began in a tremulous voice, "we can settle it ourselves. But when she says I sent my sister to preside over the committee she tells that which is absolutely false."

Here the speaker [Meredith] broke down and began to sob hysterically. Then there came another scene of wild confusion. Everyone wanted to talk at once. Motions were made by the dozen, but nothing was done until Mrs. [Bertha] Palmer, who was pale with excitement, succeeded in restoring the meeting to order.

Mrs. Ball got the floor again and said she would retract the word "malicious."

There was loud applause. Some one moved that the entire proceedings be expunged from the records, and that the matter be laid on the table. The motion prevailed, and the meeting adjourned.[167]

Meredith suggested, "Mrs. Ball had persistently worked in the interests of the awards committee of the commission and against those of the board. Her partiality for the commission had from the first placed the committee in an embarrassing position."[168] Meredith was accusing Ball of leaking information about discussions and strategies being tossed about by the women's committee back to the men's award committee. It was a strong condemnation on Meredith's part of one of her colleagues on the Board of Lady Managers.

Meredith stated that every committee member had signed a statement asking that Ida Ball be removed from "further service on the Committee on Awards."[169] The Board of Lady Managers voted to remove Ball from the committee, though many qualified their vote with expressions of the type: "I felt that it was my duty to the Board to vote against her, while I was sorry to do so...."[170]

On August 14, 1893, the Board of Lady Managers ended its marathon session. Despite all of the uproar, the women had finally accomplished their goal of hiring female judges based on experience and expertise.

The Board of Lady Managers was allowed to hire fifty-nine foreign judges in addition to the fifty-seven domestic judges they had named.[171] The board appointed the chosen judges, but Meredith would note that "by declination, resignation, and ineligibility the number in active service at any one time never exceeded ninety-six."[172] The women judges were assigned in due course to the following commission departments: Agriculture, 7; Horticulture, 5; Liberal Arts, 27; Manufacturer, 45; Ethnology and Archaeology, 9; Fine Arts, 5; and Mines and Mining, 1.[173]

Meredith was blunt in her remarks that the commission's lack of timely decisions cost her committee and the World's Columbian Exposition many well-qualified women judges. She indicated, "It was a source of regret that a number of women of signal ability and great reputation were obliged to decline appointments as judges of awards, for the reason that at the late date when a definite agreement was reached with the Executive Committee on Awards of the Commission, these had already made plans for the summer which precluded acceptance."[174]

The panel included three Hoosier judges: Eliza A. Blaker, Indianapolis, Department of Liberal Arts; Louise W. Boisen, Bloomington, Department of Horticulture; and Laura D. Worley, Ellettsville, Department of Agriculture.[175] Each woman judge received an intricately engraved certificate of appointment signed by Bertha Palmer as the president of the Board of Lady Managers and by Meredith as the chairman of its Committee on Awards.[176]

On July 15, 1893, Meredith called a meeting of the women judges in her office in the Woman's Building.[177] She spoke to them about their responsibilities, "giving in detail an interpretation of the rules governing awards, emphasizing the responsibility devolving upon each judge in her individual capacity in her relation to exhibitors, as well as in her responsibility in upholding and justifying the action of Congress, which provided for the participation of women judges in the Columbian Exposition."[178]

With so much going on, Meredith was repeatedly asked by Palmer to take care of many details, including the foreign exhibits and reports updating Palmer on the status of the women judges:

> I beg that you will have the porcelain exhibit in the Danish case in the Woman's Building entered for award. It is really fine, and should be entered as soon as possible. We wish to have as many medals awarded for exhibits in the Woman's Building as possible, and trusting that you will attend to this at once.[179]

> I enclose herewith a letter from Miss Cassgemat of Spain, which will explain itself. I beg you will do what you can toward having her opera favorably brought to the notice of the jury, and ask that you return her letter with report as soon as convenient.[180]

> I telephoned you this morning, asking for a report as to the number and individual names of the women who have received medals, and I now want to know the proportion of jury service performed by the women and men. That means the number of days on which service has been performed, as the women have, generally, worked more days than the men. They have been kept on duty longer. I think the result will show a very large proportion in our favor, especially if the service is counted by days. Trusting that you may be able to give this information as soon as possible, . . .[181]

The women judges made a good account of themselves. The lady managers had great pride when "Mrs. Cornelius Stevenson was elected Vice President of the Board of Ethnology and Archaeology [of the men's award committee]."[182] While the initial response to having an exhibit judged by a competent woman was less than enthusiastically endorsed, Meredith noted that once the "women were allowed an opportunity to demonstrate their ability, there was a marked demand for their services."[183] Meredith also observed that "in many cases exhibitors requested that women judges should be sent to examine their exhibits."[184]

Meredith's Committee on Awards received numerous compliments about the positive contributions made by women judges, who were said to be "especially strong in those Departments where scholarship and special training was demanded."[185] An example from the commission's Department of Agriculture clearly shows the goodwill that one such highly qualified judge generated by her efforts:

> ... in the group including cereals there was but one woman judge detailed to make examination therein. The appreciation of her work was conveyed by a special resolution, and also by a personal letter addressed to herself from the President of the Board of Judges in that group of agriculture, in which he said, "I express the sentiment of this entire committee, when I say that the efficiency of your work, and the dispatch with which it was performed, proved to any one who may have been skeptical, that even in agriculture, woman, who at the first was appointed to the place of helper, is fully competent to lead, and that there is no field of activity open to man, into which woman may not successfully enter."[186]

On August 23, 1893, the Board of Lady Managers held a special ceremony in the Woman's Building in honor of the women judges.[187] Meredith opened the ceremony with a short speech and was soon followed to the podium by international speakers from England, Germany, Italy, and Sweden.[188]

The Board of Lady Managers offered praise for and congratulations to the women judges who had demonstrated their professionalism in carrying out their duties at the World's Columbian Exposition. The board gave each judge an Isabella coin "as an expression of our appreciation of the manner in which their work has put forward the cause of women throughout the world."[189] The Isabella coin, named after the Queen of Spain, had been issued by the U.S. Mint in 1893 at the request of the Board of Lady Managers. It was the first U.S. commemorative quarter ever made and only the second commemorative coin ever issued, the first being the Christopher Columbus coin minted in 1892.[190]

In turn, the women judges presented Meredith with a diamond-studded gold watch and chain in October 1893, just before the judges departed for home.[191] The hostess that night was Countess Zampini Salazar of Italy, who "gave some very warm tributes to the Indiana commissioner."[192]

As Meredith accepted her gift, she must have felt a large measure of satisfaction at having successfully stood up to Commissioner John Boyd Thacher on the issue of naming women judges. Through her determination, the lady managers had carried out the mandate given to them by Congress: that their board appoint women judges to evaluate exposition exhibits that included work by women. The fact that the women judges had proven themselves as competent professionals and excelled in their work made this a significant victory indeed for the lady managers.

But Meredith had another, very important reason to celebrate that evening. Just one month earlier, in September 1893, she and Palmer had successfully petitioned the secretary of the U.S. Treasury to grant the lady managers financial freedom from the commissioners. A *Chicago Daily Tribune* headline said it all: "Lady Managers Are Emancipated. Their Vouchers No Longer Need Review by the National Commissioner Thacher."[193] The newspaper article stated:

> Mrs. Potter [Bertha] Palmer and Mrs. Virginia C. Meredith, Chairman of the Committee on Awards of the Lady Managers, have turned the tables on the National Commission, its Auditing committee, John Boyd Thacher, and every other person, and freed themselves from all restraint in the spending of their money. A letter received yesterday from Assistant Secretary [Charles] Hamlin of the Treasury Department at Washington completely emancipates the Board of Lady Managers from the control of the National Commission, and hereafter the women will spend the appropriations from Congress without the intervening signature of any commission officers. . . . [T]he lady managers will pay all their own bills, including the woman judges of awards. . . . Mrs. Palmer and Mrs. Meredith asked Secretary [John] Carlisle to relieve them from the supervision of this same [commission] Auditing committee. Mr. Thacher is also relieved of signing the vouchers for the woman judges. He thought he was best qualified to do that, inasmuch as he appointed them, but Mr. Carlisle seems to think differently, so Mr. Thacher's signature is no longer necessary.[194]

It had been a long time in coming, but the lady managers had, at last, gained the right to control their own budgets and expenditures.

Meredith's lasting legacy from the World's Columbian Exposition was her work with the Diploma of Honorable Mention, an honor bestowed upon both men and women. Where the Diploma of Award given by the commission recognized exhibits, the Diploma of Honorable Mention recognized the people behind the exhibits: "inventors, designers, and artisans assisting in the production of exhibits that received awards."[195] This type of award had been given at the Paris exposition in 1889, but the awards given by the lady managers marked the "first time that a Government, through its legislative branch, has thus definitely directed an official and honorary recognition of the artisan."[196]

The Committee on Awards of the Board of Lady Managers discussed the Diploma of Honorable Mention in January 1893 at its very first meeting.[197] But it was in September of 1893 that Meredith and Palmer—fresh from the rare but exhilarating victory that had given them financial freedom from the commission—pitched their ideas on issuing these diplomas before a special session of Congress.[198]

True to form, Thacher was quick to argue that if Congress agreed to sponsor the Diplomas of Honorable Mention, then the commission should issue them. The commissioners believed they were better suited to carry out the wishes of Congress, since they had administered the Diplomas of Awards. But the commission had played hardball with the Board of Lady Managers in the past, and now it was time for the lady managers to reciprocate.

Meredith and Palmer went before a Conference Committee on Appropriations, which granted their request to fund the diploma project. Unfortunately, the allocation of funds came "without any specific mention or authorization of the Diploma of Honorable Mention." Meredith ascribed Congress's reluctance to support the Board of Lady Managers' administration of the diploma as an instance where men ". . . objected to so important a duty being delegated to a Board composed of women."[199] It was the second time that Meredith blamed gender discrimination as a barrier to her interests—the first being her failure to get the job of chief of the Department of Livestock.

Part of the failure to secure the diplomas was that the commissioners were actively engaged in defeating any bill that gave the Board of Lady Managers the authority to administer a diplomas program. The commissioners, who were politically connected at all levels of government, sent telegrams to ". . . the President of the Senate and Speaker of the House of Representatives, asking that no action be taken, until the World's Columbian Commission could formulate objections."[200] A September 25, 1893, letter summed up the commissioners' objections, saying, "[T]he resolution is dangerous to the interest of exhibitors and utterly inadequate for a proper recognition of the worth of the artisan. We, therefore, most respectfully remonstrate against its passage."[201] The commissioners' tactics worked well enough that even though the bill favoring the women passed the special session, it did not reach the president's desk in time. Thacher and the commissioners won the first skirmish, but they would soon feel the sting of defeat.

Meredith and Palmer had become seasoned politicians and skilled tacticians in their own right. They redoubled their efforts, knowing that a legislative snafu had prevented their bill from becoming law. On October 17, 1893, the headlines described the political strategy implemented by the Board of Lady Managers and Thacher's unwillingness to have them issue the diplomas:

> LADY MANAGERS' PLAN TO OUTWIT JOHN BOYD THACHER. Mrs. Potter [Bertha] Palmer . . . and Mrs. Virginia C. Meredith . . . think they have outwitted John Boyd Thacher's scheme to prevent the lady managers from being authorized by Congress to grant honorable mention to experts who have contributed to the production of exhibits which have received medals and diplomas at the Exposition. They have drawn up a new joint resolution, which Congressman [Allen] Durborow received yesterday and which he is asked to present at once. The lady managers think it will go through, for it is approved by Director-General [George] Davis and the Board of Directors of the Association of American Exhibitors. It was upon the strong protests by the American exhibitors to the lady managers' original plan that Mr. Thacher hoped to defeat the entire project. When the American exhibitors learned just what was proposed by the lady managers, they fell in with the idea.[202]

Meredith and Palmer had to wait until December 1893 for Congress to return from its recess.[203] The Association of American Exhibitors had done an about-face, and the *Chicago Daily Tribune* reported that "a large number . . . telegraphed Congressmen from their several States to aid in the passage of the new Durborow resolution."[204] Congress passed a joint resolution stating: "[t]hat a diploma of honorable mention may be conferred upon designers, inventors, and expert artisans who have assisted in the production and perfection of such exhibits as are awarded diplomas in the World's Columbian Exposition or are formally commended by the Director-General thereof; and authority is hereby given to the Board of Lady Managers of the World's Columbian Commission, to present said diplomas. . . ."[205] Soon after, President Grover Cleveland made it official when he signed the joint resolution into law.[206]

Palmer gave credit to her old friend, Congressman William Springer of Illinois, for assisting the lady managers in their successful efforts.[207] Newspaper accounts were brutally honest about what actually transpired in getting the resolution passed on December 8, 1893:

> When the measure was first introduced in Congress, it was in the hands of Representative Durborow. He mixed the matter, and a new resolution was introduced, which Congressman Springer undertook to carry through. . . . Mr. Thacher has a strong lobby at Washington, which defeated the measure until the last moment, when it was placed in the urgency deficiency bill.

Seeing that bill was about to fail it was taken from it and presented as a joint resolution during the closing hours of Congress. It was passed in the House, and then went to the Senate, where it was adopted in Executive Session. Meanwhile Mr. Thacher received notice from Washington that the resolution was dead, and he was congratulating himself accordingly. It was passed at too late an hour for the Speaker of the House and President of the Senate to sign it, and it laid over until Thursday afternoon, when Speaker [Charles] Crisp and Vice-President [Adlai] Stevenson attached their signatures. Yesterday it went to President Cleveland, and he did not hesitate to make it a final act of Congress.[208]

Meredith wrote that this "resolution, honoring the brain and the hand of the laborer, is unprecedented in the United States, if not in the world, in its quality of dignifying and emphasizing the worth of the individual to the State."[209] It would fall to Meredith to decide how to confer the diplomas on the appropriate persons.[210]

In January 1894, the Board of Lady Managers moved its offices from the Woman's Building at Jackson Park to a suite of rooms at 701 Masonic Temple in Chicago.[211] While the exposition had ended on October 30, 1893, Meredith's work on awarding Diplomas of Honorable Mention had just begun.

She hired a large staff of sixteen people—all females except for one male accountant—to tackle this enormous task.[212] To start with, Meredith needed an official list of exhibits that had been issued a Diploma of Award. She hired a clerk to create this list from the records of the Executive Committee on Awards of the World's Columbian Commission, which by this time had moved its offices to Washington, D.C.[213] Once the list was assembled, Meredith and her staff began tracking down exhibitors in the United States and abroad.[214] Each exhibitor would receive a letter explaining the new award and requesting information about those who had worked on the display, including designers, inventors, and expert artisans. Exhibitors were required to certify that each person named to receive the diploma had "assisted in the production and perfection of the exhibit."[215]

Meredith had great difficulty getting the foreign commissioners to provide her with current addresses for their exhibitors who had excelled at the exposition. This lack of response led Meredith to ask Palmer, who had a friendly working relationship with many of the foreign dignitaries, to use her political connections to get them to cooperate with Meredith. Eventually, most countries assisted Meredith with her request, though there were a few exceptions. Germany refused to do so, which, according to Meredith, was "[a] decision doubtless influenced by the unsatisfactory status of the medals and diplomas of award."[216] Great Britain asked that she contact the exhibitors directly.[217]

The one country that Meredith was very pleased with was Japan. She found that Japan's report was "complete and exact . . . a completeness very pleasing to the office force, and in contrast to the carelessness of many domestic exhibitors, with whom it was only necessary to conduct an extensive correspondence, devoted mainly to a repetition of the initial letter of explanation."[218] Japanese officials must have been very pleased with Meredith as well, for they gave her one of her most cherished gifts, described by one reporter as "an exquisite Japanese picture, a painting on silk, presented to her by the Imperial Japanese Commissioner, the picture set in an effective lacquer frame."[219] Given on behalf of the Japanese government to Meredith for her work with representatives of Japan at the exposition, this painting would adorn the walls of Meredith's homes in Cambridge City as well as her home in West Lafayette.

Meredith was a diligent organizer who kept meticulous records, a skill she had undoubtedly honed on her Indiana farm. Meredith's staff members recorded the letters they sent out in the Exhibitors' Book, including the address, mailing date, and department the exhibit had been assigned to. As the responses were returned, the information from the exhibitors was entered in the Artisans' Book, which held the names and addresses of those being nominated for a Diploma of Honorable Mention.[220] Names returned by the exhibitors automatically were awarded the diploma.

Toward the end of 1894, after four years in Chicago, Meredith began refocusing her thoughts on Oakland Farm, which she had neglected during the previous couple of years. She decided to scale back her work in order to spend more time managing the affairs of her Cambridge City farm. Working part-time on the awards project slowed the processing for thousands of diplomas that would be awarded. Palmer urged Meredith to quicken the pace and, on more than one occasion, asked about the status of the program:

> In our hurried conversation a few days since you said that the sending out of the Diplomas of Honorable Mention would require six months' time from the first of October and at that time you had not included in the estimate Diplomas to be sent to certain countries from which you have not yet received a favorable response. You and I agree that it would be well not to send the report of the Board of Lady Managers to Congress until our work

is finished. The coming session of Congress is a short one and the report must consequently be handed in about the first of March.

I am writing to call your attention to the fact and to see if you can arrange to have the Diplomas of Honorable Mention finished before that time. . . .[221]

Meredith and her staff would not meet Palmer's deadline. Instead, they completed most of the work by August 5, 1895, "about eighteen months after correspondence upon the subject was begun with exhibitors in every part of the world."[222] In November 1895, Meredith's office was the last from the exposition to close.[223]

The response to the diplomas was best summarized by Meredith, who indicated ". . . the letters of appreciation received by the chairman were of all degrees of appreciation, often touching in their acknowledgment of indebtedness to the Board of Lady Managers for securing from Congress legislation that permitted an official recognition of labor, and thereby especially identifying the recipient with the great Columbian Exposition."[224]

In the end, the *Chicago Daily Tribune* stated that "nearly every country in Europe has supplied applicants for diplomas, and, in addition to this, diplomas have been sent to Japan, Ceylon, and India."[225] All totaled, Meredith's Committee on Awards issued 11,702 diplomas at a cost of $25,000.[226] Each engraved and embossed diploma was signed by Bertha Palmer as the president of the Board of Lady Managers, Meredith as the chairman of the awards committee, and George Davis, director-general of the World's Columbian Commission.[227] Even at the end, Meredith continued to compete with John Boyd Thacher of the men's awards committee by noting that she had completed mailing the diplomas before "the medals of award came from the mints."[228]

Many of the lady managers were invited to attend important social events within their home states and across the country during the exposition and for many years afterward. They were treated as celebrities. Meredith was no exception, and she was often introduced as the "Lady Manager from Indiana" when she attended social functions. The details of one such event—a reception to honor Meredith that included 150 guests—made the social column in the *Chicago Daily Tribune,* which described Meredith's dress as a "[c]ostume of blue-gray brocaded moiré, on train, and finished with costly lace and jewels."[229]

Virginia Meredith became the fodder of articles in leading newspapers and important magazines of the day. In 1893, a *Harper's Bazaar* article profiled Meredith along with three other lady managers. In many ways, the magazine article reflected the celebrity status that women such as Meredith achieved through their involvement with the Board of Lady Managers and the World's Columbian Exposition. Nancy Huston Banks, who wrote the article titled "World's Fair Women," stated, "The *personnel* [italics in original] of the Board of Lady Managers of the Columbian Exposition is singularly representative of the advancement of American women. This is, indeed, so generally true that no detailed individual description of all or even a majority of the more striking instances is possible within the limits of the present paper. But the fact may perhaps be made sufficiently clear by the presentation of a brilliant group of four women pre-eminently distinguished in their several lines."[230]

Meredith's rise among the socialites of Chicago was mentioned in the *Chicago Daily Tribune* during the spring of 1895. Mary Ford, a speaker on arts, had been invited by the Arche Club, an art appreciation organization, to give a series of presentations about Chicago's best painters and sculptors.[231] One thousand guests attended the event on March 29, 1895. The guests could listen to Ford's presentations as well as view a display of 100 paintings and 25 sculptures. Meredith was listed as a patroness for the event.[232]

Around that time, Meredith was one of three lady managers highlighted in the *Atlanta Journal* column "In the Social World." While the *Journal* article noted her business skills, livestock interests, and work on the exposition, it included other attributes, which helped Meredith to further enhance her position among the wealthy, the connected, and the social elites of the country:

> Personally, Mrs. Meredith is a woman of culture and elegance. Her manner, which, in business is positive and reserved, becomes cordial in social life. She is handsome, especially in evening dress, and possesses an air both impressive and influential. She has blue eyes, brown hair, touched with gray, and the brilliant color and general bearing of the cultivated English woman.

> It will interest Atlanta people to know that Mrs. Meredith will probably spend a part of the winter in the south, accompanied by her younger sister, Mrs. Earl, and may be expected to visit this city on her tour. A number of Atlanta ladies met Mrs. Meredith in Chicago and they will be pleased to renew their acquaintance with her here and give her a taste of southern hospitality.[233]

Cleary, Meredith's name was firmly associated with the exposition, elevating her stature among women of influence in this country. One history of Wayne County, Indiana, noted:

> No name figures more conspicuously or is mentioned with greater honor on the pages of the history concerning the connection of women with the great World's Columbian Exposition, held in Chicago in 1893, than that of Mrs. Virginia Claypool Meredith, yet her wide and brilliant reputation comes not alone from her association with that triumph of American skill and ingenuity. She is always found taking an advanced stand in favor of higher and broader education and of great business possibilities for women, and is to-day one of the most competent authorities on agricultural, and especially stock-raising, interests in the entire country. Thus leading an advance movement that cannot fail to prove of permanent benefit to the race, she may well be termed a public benefactor, for her broad missionary spirit and her splendid intellectual attainments have combined to engrave her name enduringly on the history of the world's progress.[234]

Meredith was one of many men and women invited back to Chicago in January 1923 to a special meeting hosted by the Chicago Woman's Club. The audience listened to Lorado Taft, a sculptor, who spoke on the beautiful buildings that once stood in Jackson Park. The lone surviving building was the Palace of Fine Arts, for which the city was soliciting bids for demolition. Taft commented, "We must not permit it. We must rise in protest."[235] In the end, efforts to save the building were successful, and today it is known as Chicago's Museum of Science and Industry.

Ten years later, Meredith would return to Chicago once again for a weeklong celebration of the fortieth anniversary of the World's Columbian Exposition. This was held during the 1933 Chicago World's Fair, which was called the Century of Progress International Exposition. As one of the last surviving representatives from the original Board of Lady Managers, Meredith was an honored guest. The *Richmond (Ind.) Palladium and Sun-Telegram* reported:

> But few of the members of Mrs. Potter [Bertha] Palmer's board of lady managers of the fair of 1893 still survive and Mrs. Meredith is the only one to date to have attended this year's exposition. An exposition automobile conveyed Mrs. Meredith and her party, which included her daughter, Dean Mary L. Matthews of Purdue University, and Mrs. Maurice Murphy [a newspaper reporter], of Indianapolis, from her hotel to the fair grounds, where

after she had been taken on a tour of the grounds she was received by Rufus C. Dawes, president of the exposition, in the administration building.[236]

Meredith was given a dignitary's tour of the grounds and buildings. Her comments were brief, but she seemed impressed with the event, stating:

> Wonderful as was the World's Columbian exposition of 1893, more wonderful still is a Century of Progress exposition of 1933. I came to Chicago feeling that I would see an interesting and different world's fair, but not one comparable with that of 1893. But I was greatly surprised. This fair is so different in architecture and color and it also is a greater fair. More marvelous is the fact that it was produced and opened in these times of economic stress [the Great Depression].[237]

The United States Congress and the city of Chicago expended large sums of money and much effort to make the six-month World's Columbian Exposition an event that would be remembered long into the future. The Board of Lady Managers played a major role in this international exposition. These women had their own building and administrators at a time when women were still striving for more rights in U.S. society. In fact, the World's Columbian Exposition would be the first international exposition to feature such an extensive display recognizing women's creative and intellectual accomplishments.

While the World's Columbian Exposition placed the work of women in the spotlight, it also gave Virginia Meredith a national stage. With her successful work at the exposition, her reputation grew well beyond the confines of Cambridge City and her native state of Indiana to one of national prominence.

During the forty years following the 1893 exposition, Meredith would continue her successful livestock breeding business, help establish groundbreaking departments for women at two prominent universities, become a well-known speaker promoting women's issues and their contributions to society, travel extensively throughout the United States and Europe, and even begin serving as a university trustee at an age when most people have already retired. While it is difficult to pinpoint a single event as having more importance than others in her life, there is little doubt that her work on the Board of Lady Managers at the World's Columbian Exposition was a watershed moment in her future career, reputation, and legacy.

1890. ✳ ✳ ✳ PROGRAM. ✳ ✳ ✳ 1891.

SEPTEMBER 8.—With Mrs. Meredith.

Responses Relating to Womanhood.
Author's Object in Ramona..Alice H. Reese
Principal Characters and Pen Pictures..............................Katharine Callaway
Conversation : Ramona ....Virginia C. Meredith, Leader

SEPTEMBER 15—With Miss Overbeck.

Responses relating to Autumn.
Composite Photography..Hettie Overbeck
How to Converse Well..Lena L. Doney
Conversation : What Books Have Influenced Me..............Sue Logan Marson, Leader

SEPTEMBER 22—With Miss Wheeler.

Responses relating to Music.
Music: Instrumental...Minnie Wheeler
Chopin...Alice Swain
Conversation : Margaret E. Sangster....................................Ophelia G. Shults, Leader

SEPTEMBER 29—With Mrs. Marson.

Responses relating to Friendship.
The Silver Question..Virginia C. Meredith
Coins and Paper Money..Sue Logan Marson
Conversation : Afternoon Topics..Della W. Davis, Leader

(3)

The Helen Hunt Club routinely held educational programs in members' homes.
Virginia Meredith hosted one such meeting at Oakland Farm on 8 September 1890.
Courtesy of Cambridge City Public Library, Cambridge City, Ind.

Virginia Meredith's presidential ribbon from the seventeenth annual convention of the Indiana Union of Literary Clubs held in 1906 at Winona Lake, Ind.
Courtesy of Indiana State Library, Indianapolis.

Virginia Meredith's program guide for the 1913 Indiana Federation of Clubs meeting at the Claypool Hotel, Indianapolis, Ind. Courtesy of Indiana State Library, Indianapolis.

In 1938, the Indiana Federation of Clubs, in cooperation with the United States Department of Agriculture Forest Service, dedicated the Virginia Claypool Meredith Memorial Forest in Shoals, Ind., in honor of their two-term president and active club member. Courtesy of Indiana State Library, Indianapolis.

Virginia Meredith at the time of the World's Columbian Exposition, circa 1893.
Courtesy of the Robert Miller Family.

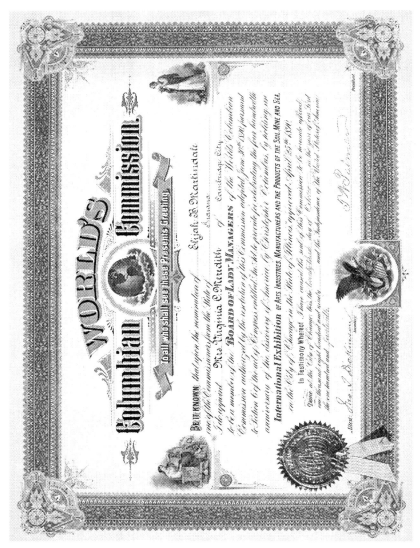

Virginia Meredith's ornate certificate of appointment to the Board of Lady Managers of the World's Columbian Commission. Courtesy of Indiana Historical Society, Indianapolis.

Board of Lady Managers medal belonging to Virginia Meredith, front (left) and back (right).
Courtesy of the Robert Miller Family.

An invitation for Virginia Meredith to attend the dedication of the buildings for the World's Columbian Exposition in Chicago in October 1892. Courtesy of Indiana Historical Society, Indianapolis.

The honor of your presence is requested
at the Opening Ceremonies of the

World's Columbian Exposition

in Chicago,
at ten o'clock Monday Morning May First,
Eighteen Hundred and Ninety Three.

Joint Committee on Ceremonies.

World's Columbian Commission.	World's Columbian Exposition.
P. A. B. Widener, Chairman.	Edward F. Lawrence, Chairman.
Bradley B. Smalley,	Charles T. Yerkes,
V. Drispaux Greener,	Charles H. Wacker,
Gorton W. Allen,	James W. Ellsworth,
George H. Barbour,	William D. Kerfoot,
Thomas B. Keogh,	Charles H. Schwab,
Arthur I. Ewing,	Alexander H. Revell,
Thomas W. Palmer,	Charles Henrotin,
John T. Dickinson,	Thomas B. Bryan,
James Hodges,	William P. Ketcham.

Edward C. Culp, Secretary.

To Mrs. Virginia C. Meredith
Cambridge City, Indiana.

Virginia Meredith's personal invitation to attend the opening ceremonies of the World's Columbian Exposition on 1 May 1893. Courtesy of Indiana Historical Society, Indianapolis.

Board of Lady Managers
of the
World's Columbian Commission.

Mrs. Bertha Honoré Palmer, President
Mrs. Susan S. Cooke, Secretary.

Committee on Awards.
Mrs. Virginia C. Meredith, Chairman.

Room 708 Masonic Temple.

Chicago, July 25, 1895.

Miss Frances M. Goodwin,

Dear Madam:-

I have pleasure in handing you herewith, the Diploma
of Honorable Mention to which you are entitled under a resolution
of the Congress of the United States, directing that such a Diploma
may be conferred upon those who assisted in an important way in the
production and perfection of an exhibit which received the formal
commendation of the Director-General of the Columbian Exposition.
This action by Congress was not taken until after the close of the
Exposition.

A certificate is now on file in this office, declar-
ing that you were connected with the exhibit as indicated in the
Diploma and which received the formal commendation of Director-General Davis.

With congratulations, I am,

Yours very truly,

Virginia C. Meredith

Chairman, Committee on Awards,

Board of Lady Managers.

A July 1895 letter from Virginia Meredith (above) and a Diploma of Honorable Mention (right) given to a participant at the World's Columbian Exposition. Courtesy of Indiana Historical Society, Indianapolis.

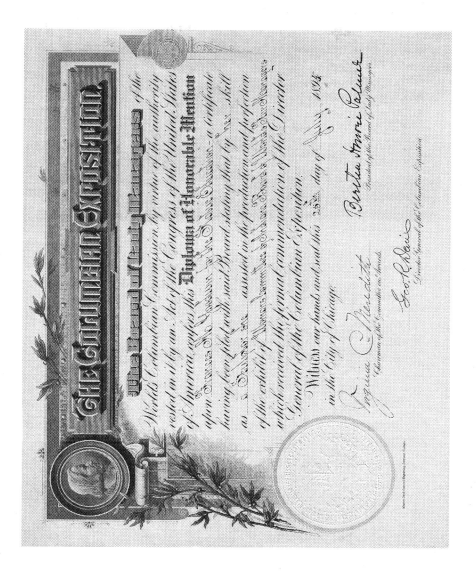

199

An 1893 letter of appreciation from the Imperial Japanese Commission to Virginia Meredith expressing gratitude for her assistance at the World's Columbian Exposition in Chicago.
Courtesy of the Robert Miller Family.

Virginia Meredith loved this screen painting (on silk), a gift she received from the Imperial Japanese Commission. She proudly displayed it at Oakland Farm, Norborough Farm, and in her West Lafayette home. Courtesy of R. Cameron Miller.

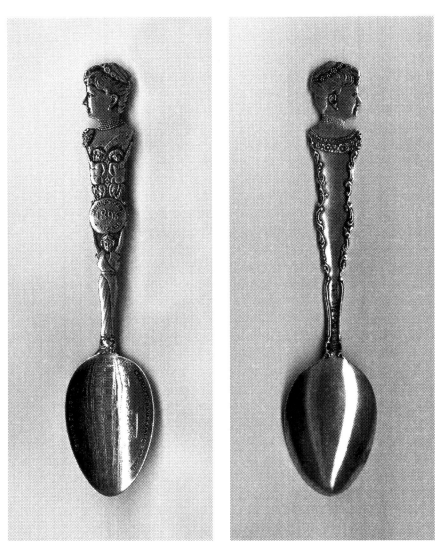

**Virginia Meredith's commemorative spoon from the World's Columbian Exposition,
view of front (left) and back (right).** Courtesy of the Robert Miller Family.

Purdue University had a display at the World's Columbian Exposition in Chicago.
Courtesy of Archives and Special Collections, Purdue University Libraries.

William J. Wedekind, a blacksmith from Hagerstown, Ind., received recognition for displaying his tools and horseshoes in a beautiful, handmade wooden cabinet.
Courtesy of Wayne County Historical Society, Richmond, Ind.

Educator and Advocate

Advancing the Science
of Home Life

CHAPTER 7

Farming cannot go on prosperously unless the farm home is
maintained in its integrity—the abode of intelligence and earnest living.
Such a home is maintained only when the woman who is its center
loves the farm for itself and what it can do in developing those whom she loves.
What will help her more in gaining an intelligent grasp of the situation than
an education acquired where the conditions are in sympathy with,
are in line with the farm?

—Virginia Meredith, *Breeder's Gazette,* 4 August 1897

THE AGRICULTURAL PRESS regarded Meredith, first and foremost, as an agriculturist. As a livestock breeder of registered Shorthorn cattle and Southdown sheep, and sole owner of Oakland Farm, Meredith's reputation attracted livestock breeders, university agriculturists, and trade magazine writers to her home. To agriculture, she was a farmer first, a woman second.

Meredith's upward rise among the male-dominated agricultural community brought her to the attention of influential women, who saw her as a business-woman first, agriculturist second.[1] As one Cambridge City, Indiana, writer noted, "[W]omen distinguished in educational and cultural life, from this country and abroad began visiting her home at Cambridge City to discuss her opinions of country life, the education of college-aged women, and other issues important to women."[2] Meredith was important to them precisely because she was a well-educated woman who was accomplished and independent.

Some knew Meredith from speeches she gave to state, national, and inter-national audiences. Others became familiar with her through the numerous articles that appeared in the *Breeder's Gazette.* One newspaper article stated, "[A]s a lecturer and writer upon agricultural and household subjects, her home has been the resort for years of leaders in such lines of thought."[3] It is not surprising, then, that Meredith tirelessly spoke out on issues she felt strongly about: managing a home, educating rural women, and farming as a career for women. At a time when the roles of women in society were evolving, Meredith was an active participant in the evolution, speaking out for change and even helping to pioneer its progress.

Home economics and domestic science programs were new curricula offered in the late 1890s on college campuses. Land-grant institutions such as the University of Illinois, Iowa State University, and Kansas State University were among the first to offer these fields of study.[4] Virginia Meredith would figure prominently in efforts to establish and promote home economics education at Purdue University and at the University of Minnesota, while her adopted daughter, Mary Matthews, would later make her own contributions to these efforts.

In the book *A History: Fifty Years of Cooperative Extension Service in Indiana,* author Dave Thompson Sr. acknowledged Meredith's pioneering efforts, noting: "[I]t will be well to tell a few items about the beginnings of Home Economics Demonstrations which go back to Farmers' Institutes and its two great leaders, Prof. W. C. Latta, and Mrs. Virginia C. Meredith."[5]

Meredith herself credited Farmers' Institutes for educating women across Indiana:

> Long before Home Economics became a subject of instruction, farm women attended institutes and appropriated whatever pertained to the farm home, the farm family and farm income, so they were ready and eager to hear those speakers who came later to discuss, first, Domestic Science and afterward, Home Economics.[6]

Farmers' Institutes were the local educational programs that came under the direction of Purdue University's professor of agriculture, William Carroll Latta, in 1889. The Indiana Farmers' Institutes, the largest educational program of their day, were the predecessors of today's Purdue University Cooperative Extension Service. Farmers' Institutes meetings were held annually in late fall and winter in each of Indiana's ninety-two counties. During Latta's tenure, more than 5 million men, women, and children were given instruction at these gatherings.

As director of the institutes, Latta was the driving force behind delivering Purdue's latest farm production research information to growers and ranchers, but as he developed programs for farmers, he quickly recognized a need to offer programs for farm women as well, so he soon insisted that county educational programs include subjects of interest to women taught by women speakers. By as early as 1891, Latta's strategy to include educational topics of interest to women began to attract attention. When Virginia Meredith addressed the Elkhart County meeting that year, a program attendee later recalled, "Mrs. Virginia C. Meredith['s] . . . eloquent pleas for special training for homemaking and her characterizing it as a profession was a revelation to the majority of the farmers' wives who had thought of their work as mere toil."[7]

In the spring of 1894, just two months after Meredith's last "Women and the Farm" article appeared in the *Breeder's Gazette,* Latta enlisted Meredith's support for developing a course in home economics at Purdue University. He discussed using the Farmers' Institutes as a means to promote development of the curriculum:

> If your judgment approves it, would it not be well to make a plea for much the same kind of education for the girl as for the boy in order, first, that husbands and wives may be in the highest sense helpful to each other in their life upon the farm, and second, in order that the wife, when left alone, may be able to successfully conduct the business? We would like to develop a course of study in the school of agriculture for the girls parallel to that given to boys as we believe it would be greatly helpful, but as present there is practically no call for anything of the kind. I have been hopeful, however, that the Institute work would, in the near future, create a call for something of this kind.[8]

Latta was betting that, with enough time, Meredith and the other women speakers he had recruited would convince the women of the state that taking either Purdue's regular (four-year) farm course or one modified to include home economics would be a worthwhile investment. Latta knew the first hurdle to overcome was getting educational topics of interest to women placed on Farmers' Institute programs throughout the state.[9]

By 1894, Meredith was commuting between her job for the Board of Lady Managers of the World's Columbian Exposition in Chicago and Oakland Farm in Cambridge City, Indiana, so she could only make time for a few speaking assignments for the winter Farmers' Institutes.[10] With Meredith spending more time in Chicago, Latta began recruiting additional women speakers for the upcoming 1894 institutes. In addition to Meredith, two other women figured prominently in the early years of institute work. They were Kate Mount, the wife of Indiana Governor James Mount, and Mrs. W. W. Stevens of Salem.[11]

Local female workers also contributed much to the early institutes. As was the case with all speakers, Latta handpicked each of them. He looked for good speakers with a wealth of experience.[12]

Latta encouraged chairmen around the state to schedule women speakers in order to boost attendance at the meetings and generate interest in women's programs.[13] As Latta attended institute programs around the state, he noted the number of women that made up the audiences and was always pleased when the turnout of women was greater than anticipated.[14] By 1895, Latta was describing the institutes as friendly to farm families. And by 1896, he was consistently asking his speakers to offer presentations about the importance of a college-level agricultural education for women.[15] Working together and independently, Meredith and Latta both contributed to the early start of home economics at the Farmers' Institutes, but it would take many more years before domestic science would be considered a legitimate field of study at the Purdue University campus.

By November 1895, Virginia Meredith had sent out the last honorable mention awards for the World's Columbian Exposition and finished the final reports for the Board of Lady Managers. At the Chicago railroad station, she handed the agent her one-way ticket back to Cambridge City. The long train ride to Indiana gave her time to reflect back on the past few years of service as the chairman of the Board of Lady Managers' awards committee. She had accepted that position never realizing that the job would monopolize her time to the extent that it had.

Sitting in the seat and staring out the window, Meredith anticipated her return to Oakland Farm, the fresh country air, and the work that comes with raising livestock. She looked forward to planting crops and the presence of new calves, lambs, foals, and pigs. She stepped off the train at Cambridge City and walked across the platform, eager to get home. However, events taking place in Minnesota would interfere with her intentions of returning to full-time farming.

In 1895, the Minnesota legislature passed a bill that gave women an opportunity to attend the School of Agriculture at the University of Minnesota. It was described as "neither a high school or a college" but rather more in line with a trade school, where young men and women could focus on hands-on application of knowledge in farming and homemaking.[16] Those wanting to earn a college degree could instead enter into the University of Minnesota College of Agriculture.

In early 1897, university administrators were "casting about for someone of taste, education and understanding to organize the [women's] department in the school of agriculture."[17] Virginia Meredith topped their list to become the school's first preceptress of women, or department head, who would help guide the initial class of women beginning in October 1897. Meredith was the leading candidate for obvious reasons. She was a successful farmer who understood the practical relationship between a farm home and farm field. She had the practical rural background to readily connect with female students who had similar interests and experiences. She had, for a decade, written extensively about the importance of women owning their own farms and managing their own homes.[18] And she had established quite a reputation as one of the more visible lady managers at the World's Columbian Exposition in Chicago.[19] William M. Liggett, the dean of the University of Minnesota College of Agriculture, knew Meredith could bring credibility to the fledgling Minnesota program and, in time, turn it into a nationally recognized program.

The Liggett family had come to know Virginia Meredith through mutual farming interests. Dean Liggett previously had managed the Wilcox and Liggett farm in Swift County, Minnesota, breeding and handling livestock similar to Meredith's.[20] In fact, Liggett had attended the June 18, 1895, Shorthorn sale that Meredith held at Oakland Farm, paying $1,710 for ten cows and heifers, and $290 for one bull that day.[21]

Liggett was familiar with Meredith's views on women's education and home economics as a legitimate field of study.[22] He had confidence that she could help the university recruit women for the agricultural program, so he contacted Meredith to see if she had any interest in becoming the preceptress of the new program.[23]

Liggett at first was disappointed when Meredith flatly turned down his offer, simply saying, "Impossible."[24] According to a friend of hers, Meredith may have declined the first offer because of concerns about her ability to "measure up to the responsibility."[25] Even though she turned down the original request, Dean Liggett would not take "no" for an answer. He asked her what stood in the way of her accepting the position. Meredith surely told him what she really wanted to do was to farm. But another major concern of hers was, Who would set the rules for women students to follow?

Once Liggett understood this, he made Meredith a counteroffer that addressed those concerns, and she ultimately accepted. First, because the school year consisted of two terms of three months each, arrangements were made for Meredith to teach in St. Paul during the school year, then be allowed to return to Cambridge City in late March or early April to manage her own farm during the growing season.[26] Second, Liggett gave Meredith full authority for the women, though this provision would later be challenged. As preceptress, she would set the rules the women would have to follow. This accommodating offer convinced Meredith to take charge of the women's program in the School of Agriculture.[27] Meredith officially accepted the position on July 19, 1897, agreeing to an annual salary of $1,800.

When the university hired Meredith, it was newsworthy enough to make the August 4, 1897, *Breeder's Gazette*. This was exactly what Liggett had envisioned by selecting Meredith as the first preceptress in the University of Minnesota School of Agriculture.

> Mrs. Virginia C. Meredith, Cambridge City, Ind., has been elected Preceptress of the Minnesota Girl's School of Agriculture. A woman fitter for this work could not be found. Dean Liggett has high ambitions for the Minnesota College of Agriculture, proof enough of which is found in this selection of a head for the girl's school. That Mrs. Meredith should devote herself to such work is not surprising to those who have noted the trend of her writings in this journal on home life on the farm and agricultural education.... Indiana will be greatly loathe to lose her from the institute and other farm educational work with which she has been so prominently identified, but the field afforded at the Minnesota College for giving effective shape to her educational ideals is doubtless too inviting to be declined. It would seem that a new departure in the education of young women on the farm is about to be inaugurated under a conduct that will afford it a thorough test.[28]

Meredith decided to sell her Shorthorns and Southdown sheep before leaving for Minnesota in the fall of 1897.[29] She knew that constant travel between Minnesota and Indiana— similar to what she had done while working on the World's Columbian Exposition in Chicago—was not an option. Except for holidays, she would live in the dormitory in St. Anthony's Park along with fifteen-year-old Mary and ten-year-old Meredith.[30]

As Virginia Meredith arrived that October, a brand-new women's dormitory was opening its doors to coincide with the beginning of the new term. The dormitory was built on the campus near the other agricultural buildings. It was an impressive and elaborately designed structure that could house 120 students.[31] There "the girls were firmly established under ... [her] strict surveillance...."[32]

Meredith's authority over the women was, in many respects, one of her more important contributions to the school. Many thought that men and women living in such close proximity to each other was a bad idea and opposed making the school coeducational. Meredith acted quickly to dispel these concerns. One history of the school stated, "Holding high ideals of social behavior, she quickly set up rules of conduct and established regulations governing the dormitories which proved highly effective in controlling student behavior and educational to both girls and boys in attendance at the School, much to the relief of Dean Liggett and to the satisfaction of the Board of Regents."[33]

One student, Adel Thompson Peck, reflected back on her years as a student under Meredith, writing in 1923:

> Mrs. Meredith always impressed me as being about ideal for a first preceptress. She had a stateliness of bearing and an innate dignity which was very necessary. Farm girls in those early days were farther from the center of culture than they are today, public schools were not as closely connected with the city school curriculum, and she seemed to bear those things in mind, endeavoring constantly to bring out the best in each girl under her charge. I believe now that her culture and womanliness had a direct effect on the girls in her charge. She too had a splendid knowledge of Animal Husbandry, Agriculture as well as Home Economy, and she did much to dignify the early efforts of the School of Agriculture along those lines. Her high ideals and standards of living were made a part of our dormitory life and three years of such teachings could not help but have a marked effect on the lives of girls under her charge. I really think that Mrs. Meredith had a very large place in the hearts of Minnesota mothers and girls for they had every confidence in her.[34]

The women lived in a dormitory that was more like a large home, finely furnished and containing many amenities:

> The building is handsomely furnished and is equipped with all modern conveniences. As one enters the large sitting-room with its hardwood floors, covered with rich rugs; its delicately tinted walls, with the ceiling divided by heavy beams; its finely carved furniture and piano, the impression given by the artistic, home-like room is pleasing.

> The students' apartments are arranged in suites of three rooms, each suite being occupied by two girls. Each girl has a bedroom and the two have a small sitting-room in common. There is an abundance of bathrooms and

closets and in all ways the building takes rank with the halls for women in other large universities.

The dining hall, which is a commodious building, lighted from two sides, each having a semicircular succession of windows, is used in common by the young men and young women, who are seated together at tables accommodating eight persons each. This room has a balcony for musicians and is used for dancing parties and other large social functions, which are given several times in each school year. The food served is plain, but excellent in quality and admirably cooked.

For board, room and laundry each student pays $3 a week. Those who do not care to buy text books can rent them at a cost of $2 a year. The entire expense of the student for the school year, which begins when thrashing is done in October and closes before seeding time in April, is $85.[35]

Meredith was expected "to organize and inaugurate the [women's education and home economics] plan" for the School of Agriculture.[36] She had a good foundation on which to build her program, because "... summer courses in Cookery and Sewing had [already] been given for two years."[37]

The forty-eight-year-old Meredith understood her charge.

It was the expressed desire of the Board of Regents that the course of study arranged for the young women should be suited to farm life both in the industries pursued and the social life developed. The long established departments in agriculture like Dairy, Animal Husbandry, Horticulture and Gardening promptly organized classes adapted to the needs of farmwomen. Some of these courses were strongly specialized for practical instruction with others to teach in an elementary way the history and the scientific aspects of farming in order to create in the minds of young women an understanding and sympathy with farm life. . . .[38]

Meredith organized the educational courses into three branches: domestic economy, domestic science, and domestic art. Meredith took charge of domestic economy, while the other two branches were assigned to two other faculty members, Juniata L. Shepperd and Margaret J. Blair, respectively.[39] Meredith had the female students attend many of the same classes as the men, except the women took courses relating to the management of the home rather than blacksmithing and carpentry.[40] In all, the course would take the women three years to complete:

Course of Study for 1897–1898
(October 1897 to April 1898)

FIRST YEAR—First Term
Common Classes: Agriculture, Botany, Drawing [farm houses], Music or Athletics, Physiology, Study of Breeds
Male Students: Agriculture, Blacksmithing, Carpentry, Military Drill, Study of Breeds
Female Students: Laundering, Physical Culture, Sewing, Social Culture

FIRST YEAR—Second Term
Common Classes: Botany, Farm Accounts, Music or Athletics, Physiology, Algebra
Male Students: Carpentry, Blacksmithing, Military Drill
Female Students: Cooking, Drawing, Home Management, Physical Culture

SECOND YEAR—First Term
Common Classes: Dairy Chemistry, Dairy Husbandry, Fruit Growing, Music or Athletics, Zoology, and Entomology or Algebra
Male Students: Breeding, Military Drill, Physics
Female Students: Cooking, Household Art, Physical Culture, Sewing

SECOND YEAR—Second Term
Common Classes: Agricultural Chemistry, Dairy Husbandry, Music or Athletics, Physics, Vegetable Gardening, Algebra
Male Students: Field Crops, Military Drill
Female Students: Cooking, Home Economy, Physical Culture

THIRD YEAR—First Term
Common Classes: Agricultural Chemistry, Forestry, Music or Athletics, Plane Geometry
Male Students: Handling Grain and Machinery, Veterinary Science
Female Students: Sewing

THIRD YEAR—Second Term
Common Classes: Civics or Geometry, Dressing and Curing Meats, Green Houses and Hot Beds
Male Students: Feeding, Soils and Fertilizers, Veterinary Science
Female Students: Domestic Economy, Hygiene, Sanitation [41]

Grace B. Andrews offered a first-hand account of what it was like to be one
of the first women graduates of the School of Agriculture in 1898:

> Co-education in the Minn. S[chool] of A[griculture] meant the material-
> izing of the plans and hopes of a great many. Minnesota had the first
> Agricultural School in the world for boys, and was also first in allowing
> girls to attend, and in having a special curriculum for them.
>
> A summer school for girls was held for four years before they were admit-
> ted to the regular school. The first one was held in the spring of 1894. Prof.
> [Theophilus] Haecker [professor of dairy husbandry] was much interested
> in the idea of a short course for girls from the farms, and he got out a folder in
> favor of a summer school. This was distributed by the Farmers Institute
> speakers at their meetings.
>
> The summer schools were so well attended, people began to consider
> the advisability of a longer course for the girls. The Woman's Auxiliary of the
> State Grange was especially interested in a girls' school. They knew, perhaps
> better than any other organization, the need for one and the great good that
> might come from it. . . .
>
> The opposition to the girls coming was rather strong. Some were skeptical
> and argued that the mothers could teach them, or that Home Econom-
> ics and the agricultural subjects such as the girls would want to take, could
> be had at the Summer School of five or six weeks—and the other branches
> of the course in the high schools. . . .
>
> The work on the new building was commenced at once, and in the fall of
> 1897 was ready for use. There were 34 girls who registered in the fall—only
> 18 of them living in the dormitory, the others coming from near-by homes.
>
> To be sure, we felt rather lost in the classrooms at first. The boys had
> become somewhat resigned, as there had been two girls here the year
> before, taking the subjects the boys had, as there was no Home Economics
> course at the time.
>
> In the dining room there was a mere sprinkling of girls. Two girls were put
> at a table with six boys. Some of the boys were fortunate enough to escape
> this infliction as there were so few of us.
>
> The school was especially fortunate in having such a woman as Mrs.
> Virginia C. Meredith as preceptress. She was a woman of refinement and
> culture and at the same time a practical farmer. She had great faith in a

school of this kind and it was she who had to lay the foundation for this course.

During the first two years Mrs. Meredith was often called upon to speak at agricultural conventions and meetings, and the topic given her was always the work the girls were doing at the school....

The curriculum was much the same as it is now. Some of the subjects have been sub-divided. We were not expected to take Blacksmithing, Carpentry or Vet.[erinary] Science, though I believe some of the girls did persuade Mr. [James] Drew to let them take a few lessons in blacksmithing, and after much hard work evolved something by courtesy called a barn door hook, but it really looked more like a warped skewer. Then too, we have some in our ranks who aspired to painting barns.[42]

In addition to her role as preceptress, Meredith was the instructor for a number of courses during the six-month school year. Her teaching schedule for October to December 1898 was to teach two morning classes: Household Art and Social Culture; and Social Culture. From January to March 1899, she taught Home Economy, Domestic Hygiene, and Home Management.[43]

The catalogs from the School of Agriculture describe in detail what Meredith covered in her courses:

Home Economy. Is taught as the just proportion between income and expenditure: the distinction of economy, frugality and parsimony are considered with reference to a definite proportion in the expenditures which are made for existence, comfort, culture and philanthropy. A study is made of the sources of income, especially of the income from the farm in the form of house, food and luxuries. The purchase of clothing, household stores and furnishings is considered from the standpoint of the suitable. The relation of cash and credit to cost is also considered. Attention is given to savings and forms of investment, a bank account and the use of a check book. Each student in this class is required to submit at the close of the term a paper setting forth in detail the use of a certain named income for one year, embracing not only every item of necessary home expense but also an outlay made for travel, luxuries, accident, sickness and other emergencies. The habit of keeping a household account is calculated to strengthen the judgment in making a wise use of money, therefore an analysis and study of expenditures as here indicated serves to bring clearly before the student's mind the relative importance of the different things which money will procure.[44]

Home Management. Includes both housekeeping and home making and the teaching of the subject naturally falls into three divisions, household work, sanitation and family life. The instruction is based upon the belief that housekeeping is as important as it is difficult—and that home making is the noblest form of human endeavor. The points in detail in the preparation of food, the making of clothing, the care of the house and household belongings, and the ordering of the family life are considered in their relation to an adequate plan for home management. To start the student in the correct way of becoming mistress of the business of housekeeping is the end sought. It is believed that for one who knows the reason for the doing there is no drudgery, therefore students are taught the specific danger that lurks in dust and dirt, in order that they may understand the dignity of the unceasing war which the housekeeper makes upon those forces. The practical benefit to be derived from the knowledge students have gained in the cooking, sewing, laundering and dairy class is emphasized and shown its relation to an adequate plan for the daily program for the home. While the science of family life has not been formulated yet some of its fundamental principles are recognized and may be taught.[45]

Household Art. Is taught by a series of lectures treating of the adornment of the house and grounds, noting the distinctive character of the country home and the opportunity for embellishment found in the surroundings. The intention is to show that thought and energy can accomplish as much or more than money in making a farm home attractive; also to show the importance of acquiring correct knowledge and correct taste in order to secure every possible convenience, combined with harmonious forms, colors and styles in walls, draperies and furniture. The true relation of beauty and use and the influence of surroundings upon life and character are considered in connection with the possibilities for improvement that may be found in simple and inexpensive methods.[46]

[Domestic] Hygiene. As a special study for women, considers the health of the family as dependent upon pure food, pure water, personal cleanliness and proper habits, as well as upon heredity. The aim is to show how a correct knowledge of the laws of nature is essential not only to the restoration but to the preservation of health. Several lectures by a physician will be given upon maidenhood, maternity, motherhood, infancy and related subjects. These special lectures will be supplemented by the regular lectures in class, thus extending and simplifying the subjects in plain and easily understood terms.[47]

Social Culture. A course of lectures is given on the usages of good society, including manners, behavior, the voice, conversation, forms of address, invitations, etc. Attention is directed to the fact that all approved etiquette rests upon the great law of kindness. The importance is shown of personal fitness for society through attention to the laws of health and to personal habits, as well as through the refinement of a cultivated mind and sympathetic spirit. Suggestions are made in reference to reading, literary taste and the choice of books. Especial stress is put on the thought that the family life ought to be the highest expression of good society, and therefore the manners and conversation in the home should be the very best of which one is capable. Next in importance to the power of thinking correctly is the power of approaching others with ease and speaking with tactful directness, and consequently any study or practice intended to cultivate the social nature deserves earnest attention. Some instruction is given in the elementary principles of parliamentary usage.[48]

As part of their Social Culture class, the women students practiced their skills "in meeting and entertaining people as a step in Community development. . . .[49] Within a month of arriving, "Mrs. Meredith and the young ladies of the school entertained the members of the faculty on the evening of Nov. 15th [1897]."[50] This practice continued throughout Meredith's tenure at the University of Minnesota.

After the first year, Meredith was receiving rave reviews from the editors of *Farm, Stock and Home,* a popular regional farm paper:

This brief notice can not be closed, however, without referring to the part that the girls' preceptress, Mrs. Virginia Meredith, took in accomplishing the results we are proud of. She provided to be just the woman for the place. Her womanly grace, her ability, culture, instinct and sympathy admirably qualified her to discharge the duties and carry the responsibilities of her position. To the girls she was at once teacher, friend and mother. She inspired the love and confidence of her pupils, making them ready and eager to follow her precepts and examples, and convinced every one with whom she came in contact that the girls were not only safe in her keeping, but would leave the school with larger, higher and better views of life and living because of their association with her. It is most fortunate that such a preceptress was secured to aid in the inauguration of co-education at the School of Agriculture; and it is a pleasure to announce that she has been engaged to continue the work grandly begun.[51]

Within two years, Meredith's program was being covered by some of the leading papers of the day, including the *Chicago Daily Tribune,* which had this to say: "The aim being to make women not only intelligent as farmers' wives but also to make them capable of conducting a farm."[52] She was invited to speak at numerous events, which gave even more credibility to her program at Minnesota. One such occasion was in 1900 at the national conference of the General Federation of Women's Clubs in St. Paul, Minnesota, where she spoke on "The Power of Initiative in Home Making."[53]

Virginia Meredith enjoyed teaching home economics and interacting with the young women. Once, Meredith was appointed as "God-parent of the class," which meant that she served as counselor to both the male and female students for the 1901–02 school year.[54]

She found teaching to be personally satisfying and professionally reward-ing, writing:

> This I consider the finest work I have done, though far from being as pleasant as farming. There are now sixty young women enrolled, with 230 men. The course is unique—broad enough to embrace home science in all its phases, including the study of horticulture, gardening, elementary agri-culture, poultry and breeds of live stock. In fact, this is the one school in the world, so far as I know, where women are fitted for the life they will lead."[55]

In addition to teaching her students, Meredith continued to promote the work of the school beyond the campus. In July 1900, she delivered a speech titled "What Agricultural Colleges May Do for the Farmer's Daughter" at a national conference designed to help establish home economics as a legitimate field of study.[56] This conference—one of a series that came to be known as the Lake Placid Conferences—were instrumental in encouraging more colleges to offer programs in domestic science.

Meredith's speech at the conference drew attention from the *Massachusetts Ploughman and New England Journal of Agriculture,* which noted:

> Occasionally, in the hundreds of "conferences" which assemble during the summer, one finds one which has something worth while to say. Such seems to have been the Home Economics Convention at the Lake Placid Club, New York. Here was ably presented by Mrs. Virginia C. Meredith, a farmer herself, the work of the Government to the farm home. Mrs. Meredith is in charge of the girls at the Minnesota Agricultural School, which is a unique institu-tion, standing, like the high school, between the farm and the college. Here, with a few hundred boys, some ninety girls are now being educated. The

girls, it seems, were admitted about three years ago in response to a request from some boys who wanted their sisters to have a better chance. The aim is to give the girls instruction that will make them sympathetic with the life of the farm. It has at last been recognized that it is the girl and not the boy who is the disintegrating factor in farm communities. The reason why people do not stay on the farm is not because the boy wants to leave it, but because the girl is not satisfied there. So at this unique Minnesota school the girl is trained six months in school and six months at home. Thus the country born maiden is weaned *to* and never *from* her home life, and much good to the community results. [italics in original][57]

Later that same year, the University of Minnesota marked the first time that students could work toward a bachelor's degree in home economics.[58] Two of three women who had completed the School of Agriculture curriculum chose to pursue bachelor's degrees through this new College of Agriculture program.[59] On May 5, 1900, the university made Meredith a professor of home economics—the college's first—to teach these two aspiring women.[60]

Her teaching duties as a professor of home economics were in addition to continuing her duties as an instructor and preceptress for the School of Agriculture. By teaching in both the school and the college, she joined the ranks of many professors in the agricultural courses who taught in both institutions.

Meredith established the following description for her college-level courses:

Home Economics. This course is intended to give breadth, strength and thoroughness to the concept of home, and also an appreciation of its privileges as a career for educated women.

Course I. Lectures once a week during the second term of the junior year. The evolution of the home; the family as a social and economic institution; the relation of the home to civic life; the home as a place and an opportunity for the right development of the physical and spiritual natures.

Course II. Lectures once a week during the second term of the senior year; home administration; the organization of a home; generic lines of expenditure; domestic service; and disposition of waste.[61]

With 100 women enrolled in the School of Agriculture program by 1901, the University of Minnesota received plenty of attention from the press for the work being done to educate women in domestic science and farm production. The papers wrote about where Meredith went, what she did, and what she said. One publication noted that:

[f]or three years she has been acting in that capacity [of preceptress] and
the success of the school is greatly beyond the provision made for it by the
projectors. Many representatives from educational institutes in various
sections of the country have been sent to Minneapolis to investigate Mrs.
Meredith's work, and without a single exception favorable reports have
been made concerning the system and methods.[62]

Soon others would begin to emulate Meredith's work and model their own
university programs after what they had observed at the University of Minnesota.

Even with all of her duties at the University of Minnesota and Oakland Farm,
Meredith still found the time to speak and write about the importance of the
home. In 1901, Meredith spoke at the summer meeting of the Indiana Horticultural Society. According to the *Indiana Farmer's Guide* report on Meredith's
speech, she defined "the home as a place and an opportunity for the right
development of physical and spiritual natures. She also said it is one of the most
expensive institutions we have anywhere, and that this vast expenditure of
money for the maintenance of the homes could be justified on no other ground
than that they [homemakers] have a work to do which can not be done successfully anywhere else."[63]

Expanding on this theme, Meredith addressed the National Household
Economics Association meeting in Milwaukee, Wisconsin, before the start of the
1902 fall term. She titled her presentation "The Home as a Factor in Civil Life."

> The home is the most expensive institution in existence. We have a right to
> demand much of it before we justify its existence. It would be far cheaper
> to have people live in large communities, hotels, and asylums, catered to
> by one cook, warmed by one central plant, furniture, clothing, and books by
> one buyer; cheaper but not economical, if my definition of home is correct.
> Mrs. [Ellen] Richards [a highly regarded university chemist and a pioneer
> in home economics] says: "The home exists for the protection of child life."
> I say the same thing in other words when I say that home is a place and an
> opportunity for the right development of the physical and spiritual natures.
> All money is spent in four generic lines—for existence, comfort, culture,
> and philanthropy.[64]

What Meredith was trying to impress on her audiences was the need for women
to better understand money management and how to spend money wisely.

Virginia Meredith's reputation grew as she wrote articles for the farm press and textbooks for university classes, and addressed audiences numbering in the thousands. The accolades for her work on behalf of farm women drew praise in 1902 from the *Ohio Farmer,* a midwestern agricultural newspaper:

> Among the women who first advanced the idea of education for women along practical lines was Mrs. Virginia C. Meredith of Oakland Farm, Cambridge City, Indiana. No woman in the country has done so much to advance the interests of farm women as has Mrs. Meredith, yet she is by no means of that large class who pose as reformers. She is essentially a worker who believes in illustrating her ideas, and the success with which she has accomplished the thing she set out to do proves beyond question the practical character of her theory. . . .
>
> It was her example and her dauntless energy and enthusiasm that caused the introduction of subjects concerning woman's interests into farmers' institutes. An institute that now fails to discuss topics of interest to the farm woman is unique in Indiana. The woman's department has come to stay and its practical value is no longer questioned.
>
> Countless thousands of farm women have been cheered, soothed and sustained by Mrs. Meredith's brave and enlightened utterances. She speaks as one having authority, for it is not by precept alone that she teaches, but furnishes in her own work and experience an example that any woman may study with profit.[65]

Meredith returned to the Minnesota campus in the fall of 1902, anticipating the upcoming year. Her time there, so far, had been professionally and personally rewarding, and she looked forward to meeting the incoming class of women. But the year, begun with excitement, would end disastrously for her.

Meredith had always understood that, as preceptress, she was in charge of the women at the School of Agriculture. But by the winter of 1902, Meredith and Frederick D. Tucker, the newly appointed principal of the School of Agriculture, began arguing about who had the last word about the women at the school. Tucker maintained that "he had jurisdiction over the girls as well as the boys," while Meredith insisted that she had authority over the women students.[66]

The editors of *Farm, Stock and Home* clearly blamed Meredith for the disagreement: "[T]here was a brief conflict of authority between Mrs. Meredith and Mr. Tucker, brought about by the former's desire or determination to make

the girls in the School of Agriculture a student body by themselves, over which
Mr. Tucker was to have no jurisdiction."[67] This was the same publication that,
at the beginning of Meredith's tenure at the School of Agriculture, had praised
her work. The two could not resolve their difference of opinion, and Tucker took
his concerns to Dean William Liggett, who sided with Meredith.

Tucker became angry with Liggett and Meredith, and decided to bring
the matter to the attention of the University of Minnesota Board of Regents.
By the time the board heard the complaint, Meredith had already completed
her six-month term on April 4, 1903, and was headed back to Indiana.[68] The
board formed a special committee to look into the validity of Tucker's differences with Meredith and Liggett, which reported its findings back to the board
on June 3, 1903[69]:

> After visiting the School of Agri.[culture] and taking counsel with other
> persons than those who were parties to the difficulty in question, your
> committee would report that, in their opinion, the interests of the school
> would be promoted by the resignations of Mr. Tucker, Mrs. Meredith, . . . [70]

Newspaper accounts were decidedly against Meredith. At least, that is the
position that *Farm, Stock and Home* took as it reported what others were saying: "It seems to be the feeling of those who know the facts and are in position
to give an unprejudiced opinion, that the blame for all friction between principal and preceptress is because the last repeatedly exceeded her authority and
rights, and made things very uncomfortable for Mr. Tucker, who has faithfully
tried to do his duty."[71]

One headline read: "Is It a 'School For Scandal'?"[72] In another account,
Tucker's resignation was called "A Loss to the State."[73] Frederick Tucker went
from being a principal earning $1,800 a year to president of the Memorial
College at Mason City, Iowa, earning $5,000 a year.[74]

The minutes of the University of Minnesota Board of Regents did not
elaborate any more than to say that the report was filed and the offered recommendations were accepted. In August 1903, just months before the start of the
new school year, Meredith sent her resignation to the board, abruptly terminat-
ing her tenure as preceptress and professor.[75]

Once Meredith left the University of Minnesota, her invitations to speak
about the home and women's education increased significantly. Teaching young
women at the university had solidified her view that home economics was as
important as any other field of study. For Meredith, though, home economics

was more than cooking and sewing. She consistently believed that farm women should receive an agricultural education about the business side of farming as well as the personal side of the home.[76]

Meredith traveled across the country and even internationally, speaking to various organizations on the home and sometimes on agriculture. According to one reporter's account, she "visit[ed] every state in the Union and was invited to address national councils of women in England and France."[77] She may have also addressed gatherings of the National Council of Women in Berlin, Germany, and London, England.[78]

Meredith spoke before the General Federation of Women's Clubs in St. Paul, Minnesota, in 1906. A newspaper account noted, "Mrs. Meredith presented her thoughts in a clear, forceful manner, as one who has a vital message to deliver. It was one of the fine addresses of the convention."[79] She also spoke to the Richmond (Ind.) Chautauqua on domestic science on September 1, 1906, where she received this flattering write-up in the program: "Mrs. Virginia Meredith needs no words from us, as she is so well and favorably known. but all are looking forward with delight to the address of this wonderfully gifted lady, who can run a farm or make a speech."[80]

While Meredith had become a popular speaker, she remained close to the Helen Hunt Club in Cambridge City. In 1910, Meredith addressed the club on "Elimination and Elaboration in Home Making." The local paper wrote the following paragraph on the presentation she made that day:

> She strongly advocates the elimination from the home of everything that fosters mental and physical unrest, the elaboration of whatever tends toward correct and sane living. The necessity in the housekeeper for ability to control herself and the situation whatever it might be, was discussed in its various phases. Mrs. Meredith believes that the young people should have a place of their own in the home, and emphasized the necessity and discussed the difficulty of providing suitable amusements. It is of vital importance that boys and girls are trained in the home to a realization of what is good taste in home furnishings. Some practical suggestions in the matter of elimination were banishment of all heavy upholstery and draperies from sleeping rooms, and the discountenance of the elaborate Sunday dinner custom. The second item especially gave rise to an animate discussion pro and con. The points made by Mrs. Meredith were discussed with much practical benefit to the members.[81]

From her early years as a speaker at the Farmers' Institutes, Meredith had included topics of interest to women, trying to help Professor William Latta build support for a home economics curriculum and, later, a School of Home Economics at Purdue University. Though her time became more limited for this work during her involvement at the World's Columbian Exposition and even more so during her tenure at the University of Minnesota, she still participated occasionally in an attempt to support Latta in his efforts toward this important goal.

Latta had witnessed an increase in women attending Farmers' Institutes in Indiana due, in a large part, to women speakers such as Meredith, and he wanted to parlay this increased interest into support for a home economics course at Purdue. Without an established college course to promote, Latta decided to try to draw more women to Purdue's Winter Short Courses, an intensive program typically held between January and March that allowed attendees to earn a certificate of completion. Latta had developed this program in 1888 as a way to provide college-level instruction to farmers of all ages who could not be full-time students. It took awhile, but the winter courses had become immensely popular with the state's farmers and their sons.

Just before Meredith committed to the University of Minnesota position, Latta hired her to present two sets of lectures—including some designed specifically for women—at the January 1897 program. Her courses were described in the catalog:

> Special Lecturers. Mrs. Virginia C. Meredith, Cambridge City, Ind. (Jan. 25-29). Six lectures on cattle, for men and women: The care of the calf; the development of the cow; early maturity; feeding—aids to digestion; relation of cattle to general farming in the Middle States; breeds and pedigree.
>
> Five lectures for women: Farming as a career for women; the business relation of housekeeping to farming; attractive and profitable avocations for home-makers; the social life practicable and necessary on the farm; how an education can help those who live in the country.[82]

Unfortunately, despite Latta's continued efforts to provide programs of interest to women, the women's enrollment at the Winter Short Courses failed to increase. As a result, President Winthrop Stone of Purdue University was very hesitant to create a home economics department at the university.

With Meredith at Minnesota, Latta had lost one of his chief allies, and despite his tireless efforts to promote women's programs at the Winter Short Courses and the Farmers' Institutes, popular interest in a four-year college course was still lacking. In 1901, Latta requested Meredith's help in trying a new approach: engaging homemakers associations to unite in their support for a home economics college course. Though Latta and Meredith had not corresponded much during the previous few years, the letters between them increased as Latta sought to have Meredith participate at the Women's Conference he was organizing for leaders of these associations:

> We are, also, planning to have a conference of twenty, or more, women, who are interested in the Farmers' Institute work. . . . The suggestion of a conference, which is my own, grows out of a desire to interest the Farmers' wives and daughters, largely, and cultivate a sentiment which will insure patronage of the work in Domestic Economy at Purdue, as well as to look after the interests of the women of the farm at Farmers' Institutes. . . . Can you come and present, informally, "The Needs of the Daughters"?[83]

The timing of the Women's Conference in August worked well for Meredith. She would be in Indiana managing the affairs of her farm in Cambridge City and would not leave for the University of Minnesota until six weeks after the conference.

Latta wrote to Meredith, letting her know what he wanted her to address in her speech at the conference:

> With reference to the conference. There are several things that I want to accomplish, but I am not yet clear as to the method of procedure. I want, *1st.*—To have the women who come, realize the importance of organization in their interest. *2nd.*—To effect both a State and County Organization that shall have for their purpose the betterment of the condition of the women of the country. *3rd.*—To carry home and fix the truth that the farmers' daughters need a liberal education which shall include a thorough training for home-making and house-keeping. *4th.*—To show those who come that the Agricultural college is the place where this training should be secured. *5th.*—To have them realize that the Agricultural College must have both financial support and patronage in order to do the kinds of work for which it was established.[84]

A few weeks later, Latta confided to Meredith the challenges they were facing and asked her to keep their communications in strict confidence:

> Since first writing you, I have advised with President Stone with reference to what we should undertake at the [Women's] Conference. While he and I do not view the work for women from exactly the same standpoint, yet we are agreed on the main essentials. In his letter he says he thinks we ought to

emphasize what can be done for women at the Farmers' Institutes. He feels just as I do that there is a restlessness and irrational expectancy as to what the Agricultural College should do for the farmers. I presume you have felt it. We have most painfully. Too many farmers are ready to complain and too few are ready to lend support, and only now and then one is ready to give his son, or daughter, the education which the Agricultural College is established to impart. Doctor Stone would emphasize what we are now doing . . . rather than lay stress upon other things that we might do. Eager as I am to have additional provision for farmers' daughters at Purdue, I believe Dr. Stone is substantially right. By substituting a few subjects that may be grouped under "Home Economics" for certain technical subjects of the Agricultural Course, I believe our course here would be well suited to the needs of farmers' daughters. For some years, in our Winter Course circulars, we have advertised instruction in Domestic Economy (cooking), House-hold Chemistry, House Sanitation, Horticulture, Floriculture, Botany, Dairying, English and Art. The response thus far has been very meager. The result is depressing to Dr. Stone, and it would be discouraging to me if I were disposed to be discouraged. I have, however, made up my mind not to be discouraged, but "Fight it out on this line." . . . In writing you thus I am speaking in confidence and trust you will so regard it.[85]

The Women's Conference, held on August 16, 1901, brought more than two dozen women by special invitation to the Purdue Agricultural Experiment Station.[86] The public was invited to attend Meredith's evening keynote presentation.[87] However, the Women's Conference produced little in the way of support for a home economics program.

By 1902, Latta had tried every trick in the book to create a home economics curriculum at the university, including contacting a state representative in an effort to enlist political support, but the farming community seemed unwilling to send its daughters to Purdue. Based on the women's lack of support, President Stone remained firm in his opposition, and within months, Latta learned that home economics courses would be dropped from the 1903 Winter Short Courses.[88]

With Meredith's resignation from the University of Minnesota, she quickly resumed her speaking engagements at the Indiana Farmers' Institutes and her work with Latta to drum up support for a Purdue home economics program. The 1903 season was her busiest yet, and this time, she would concentrate on issues that related directly to the home.

In addition, she used her influence as a past university professor to lobby Purdue President Winthrop Stone to establish a home economics program.[89] However, she wanted much more than just a home economics program; she wanted more equal representation for women in agricultural programs. Mrs. Lewis Taylor "recalled going to President Stone's office with Virginia Meredith to 'demand something for the womenfolk' at the all-men's agricultural meetings."[90]

Meredith also wielded her political leverage, speaking to the influential representatives on the Indiana State Board of Agriculture. In 1904, Meredith told these male delegates that Purdue needed to establish a home economics course. Her talk was aptly named "The Need of Special Training for Agricultural Pursuits" (see appendix 4 for full text):

> I will refer only to those means that could be met by the Agricultural College, as I understand what can be or ought to be done by an Agricultural College. And by agricultural pursuits I am going to include not only those things that have to do with plant and animal life, but I will also include a very important part of agriculture, and that is the home and the farm, and the need for special training for the one who makes that home. . . .
>
> People are all the time saying that people are discontented on the farm, usually because the women on the farm are not happy and contented. I believe that there is need of special training of the farmers' daughters along these lines. They should be trained along the point of animal life, for that is such a large part of farming. Not that we want the girl to be a farmer, but we want her to be in sympathy with the life on the farm—with the father and brother—and with the husband. She should understand plant and animal life as taught in the classes by teachers of enthusiasm. If this is done she will see so much more in the farm than before. This special training will also aid them in designing houses and barns which are fit for farmers to live in. This is something that will make their lives more comfortable. This is much nicer than being compelled to live in a house which a carpenter will put up for you. The home is the place where the opportunity is given for right development of the physical and spiritual natures, and the girl who is in school is taught about cookery, about sewing, and the elementary principles of hygiene. The girl who is specially trained will make a better housekeeper, a better wife, a finer woman, and a greater factor in the social life of the country. So, then, we have the greatest need of this special training for women who are going to live in the country. There is a great need of this. There is a great need everywhere.[91]

While President Stone had resisted creating a home economics department at Purdue for many years, he eventually relented and together with the university trustees created a new Department of Household Economics within the School of Science in the fall of 1905.[92] Completing the four-year program allowed students to receive a bachelor of science designation on their diplomas.[93]

What convinced Stone to change his mind? That is unknown, but perhaps he faced political pressures within the state to create such a program, since many of the nation's land-grant universities had followed the recommendations of the Lake Placid Conferences and created departments of home economics within their own colleges. Stone noted that "Purdue should offer to women opportunities comparable in scientific and technical value with those enjoyed by men," but not to the point of creating a School of Domestic Science as other Midwest colleges had done and not by placing the program in the School of Agriculture.[94] Purdue University historians William Hepburn and Louis Sears rather bluntly stated, "The action of Purdue in 1905 was considerably belated. The University deserves no credit as a pioneer."[95]

To head up the new Department of Household Economics, Stone hired Ivy Frances Harner, an experienced home economics teacher from Kansas State Agricultural College. Her office and classrooms were in Ladies Hall on the southwestern part of campus. While the building was not in the best condition, Harner did manage to teach courses on foods, sewing, and chemistry.[96]

With Harner's resignation in 1908, the management of the program was turned over to Henrietta W. Calvin, also of the Kansas State Agricultural College, for four years. In 1912, Professor Mary L. Matthews, Virginia Meredith's adopted daughter, took charge of the department.[97]

Matthews had graduated in 1900 from the University of Minnesota School of Agriculture, where she had enrolled upon arriving with Virginia Meredith in 1897. When Matthews graduated from the school, she received a certificate offering admission into the College of Agriculture, where she began her studies that same year. At the time, there were only two faculty members teaching home economics: Virginia Meredith and Juniata Shepperd. When Matthews took to the stage at the 1904 commencement exercise, "she received more applause upon accepting her diploma than did any other graduate in the entire class. This was because she was the first woman to whom the University had ever granted the degree of Bachelor of Science in Home Economics. . . ."[98]

Matthews lived at Norborough Farm in Cambridge City for two years before pursuing her career in 1907, when she moved to Lafayette, Indiana, to teach clothing at the Lafayette Industrial School.[99] After a brief stint as an instructor of clothing in the University of Minnesota School of Agriculture from 1908 to 1909, Purdue offered Matthews the position of instructor in extension home economics in 1910.[100] Her first task at Purdue was to organize the household economics courses offered at university's first summer term.[101]

It was under Matthews's tenure as head of the department that home economics at Purdue University emerged as a legitimate science with far-reaching implications that went well beyond the home.[102] Matthews's impact was evident as the program flourished under her tutelage. By 1926, President Edward Elliott and the Purdue Board of Trustees transferred the Department of Household Economics from the School of Science into the newly created School of Home Economics.[103] All seven Purdue trustees—including Virginia Meredith, who had joined the board in 1921—voted to support the new school.[104]

Meredith was present when Elliott named Mary Matthews as the first dean of the school.[105] Matthews was also listed among the faculty of the Agricultural Experiment Station, which gave her status in the School of Agriculture.[106]

Purdue established the School of Home Economics because the program had begun drawing more students than the traditional agriculture programs in the School of Agriculture. During the 1924–25 school year, the Department of Household Economics in the School of Science had an enrollment of 300 students, only slightly behind the 354 students in the School of Agriculture. By the following school year, the number of students enrolled in the Department of Household Economics surpassed the School of Agriculture by 33.[107] By 1927, one year after the School of Home Economics was established, enrollment had grown to 426 students, far outpacing the 354 students enrolled in the agricultural programs.[108]

The School of Home Economics took a major leap forward when the Home Economics Building—today known as Matthews Hall—was dedicated in 1923.[109] The building cost the university $200,000 and was approved for construction by the board of trustees at its July 1921 meeting. The vote would have been one of Virginia Meredith's first official acts as a trustee.[110]

Dean Matthews had free rein to organize the school as she saw fit. She settled on five separate departments: applied design, clothing and textiles, foods and nutrition, home administration, and industrial management.[111] Even though she was now dean, Matthews also remained the head of the Department of Home Administration.[112]

The first bachelor's degrees were conferred by President Elliott at the June 1927 graduation ceremonies. Those first students could choose either a bachelor's degree in home economics or in science. Forty-nine students out of the fifty-four scheduled for graduation selected the bachelor of home economics degree. One year later, the entire class opted for the home economics degree.[113] Matthews moved quickly to build the program, creating a master of science degree in home economics by 1928.[114]

One of the key strengths that Matthews brought to the job was an understanding that home economics was much like agriculture, encompassing many different areas of study. The school's curriculum, under Matthews's leadership, changed as society required more graduates trained in child development, housing and household equipment, textile technology, food research, foods in business, home economics extension, commercial design, interior design, and arts and crafts teaching.[115]

A report filed by Matthews to the board of trustees clearly indicated an upward trend in graduation numbers in the School of Home Economics. More importantly, graduates were getting jobs. Dean Matthews's success in increasing enrollments meant that she was running out of room in the Home Economics Building. On October 21, 1931, Matthews asked the trustees to approve another home economics building within ten years.[116] Her request would not be fulfilled until 1957, when the Home Economics Administration Building—now called Stone Hall—was constructed just east of the original building.

Matthews continued to lead the School of Home Economics until her retirement in 1952, when she was named dean emeritus. In 1968 Mary Matthews died at her home located just off the western edge of Purdue University's West Lafayette campus.

In 1905, when Purdue University established its Department of Household Economics, no statewide home economics organization existed.[117] Credit for creating interest in a state organization goes to Gertrude McCheyne Phillips in 1909. McCheyne Phillips earned a home economics degree from Kansas State Agricultural College and joined the Department of Household Economics at

Purdue University. Her responsibilities at Purdue included speaking at Farmers' Institutes and Winter Short Courses. McCheyne Phillips developed the first three-day short course that focused on domestic economics as its central theme. Her work was so appreciated that a network of clubs was formed across the state.[118] These Home Economics Clubs—later renamed Home Demonstration Clubs— were actually the women's auxiliaries to the Farmers' Institutes. In 1960, Neva Smith wrote about the early days with the Tipton County Women's Auxiliaries:

> Very few know that the very first meeting held in regard to the Home Economics Association was in kind Professor Latta's office at Purdue. The Indiana Corn Growers Association sent 'Little Miss Smith' as I was known to many, and three other girls to the short course at Purdue. At the first public mass meeting, when they were discussing ways and means, I asked the question, "How can we in Tipton County secure funds from the state to begin the Auxiliary?" Some person laughed, and I was crushed and could say no more. Professor Latta came up to me, tapped me on the shoulder, and said, "Little girl, come to my office at 8 o'clock in the morning and we will discuss plans."[119]

Both Virginia Meredith and Mary Matthews clearly understood that creating an active state organization would be a tremendous asset in moving the fledgling home economics program forward, and furthermore, an association would give its members political strength as they dealt with issues important to women in the state. So, with interest in a statewide organization increasing, the mother-daughter team organized a meeting to discuss the feasibility of creating an umbrella organization that would unite those who were interested in the study of home economics.

Matthews called the meeting to order on January 17, 1913, on Purdue University's West Lafayette campus.[120] Many of the women in attendance that day were already on campus attending festivities associated with Farmers' Week.[121] Mrs. Oliver Kline from Huntington, Indiana, opened the discussion by presenting her reasons for supporting a statewide organization. Kline suggested that a rough draft of a constitution be drawn up. Meredith had come prepared and presented a "skeleton" constitution that she had crafted prior to the meeting.[122] The first constitution stated that the purpose of the organization was "to promote the general knowledge of home economics; to bring into affiliation all organizations dealing with this subject; to secure the teaching of home economics in the [high] schools of the state."[123]

Fifty-eight individuals and ten clubs signed on as charter members of the Indiana Home Economics Association.[124] Many of the women who joined that day were or had previously been local speakers at Farmers' Institutes.[125]

Meredith was elected president, and Matthews and Professor G. I. Christie of the Purdue School of Agriculture were chosen for the executive committee. Flora Meeks of Parker and Mrs. Lewis Taylor of Newburgh rounded out the officers' slate as vice president and secretary, respectively.

During the association's second meeting on January 15, 1914, Meredith was reelected president. She said, "Every community needs organized groups of women to guide, in a common sense way, spirited discussion about whatever will make Indiana homes better homes."[126] Her old friend, Professor William C. Latta, was added to the association's executive committee. However, in 1917 the association barred men from serving on the executive committee.[127]

Meredith was elected president for a third consecutive term in 1915. It was during this term that she convinced President Winthrop Stone to speak at the association's meeting. His topic was "The Future of Home Economics at Purdue."[128] What must have gone through Meredith's mind as she listened to Stone give his speech? Her discussions with Professor Latta meant she was well aware that, in the past, Stone was anything but a friend of home economics at Purdue University.

At the association's first statewide meeting, held in 1916, approximately forty local clubs had signed up as state-affiliated clubs. By 1938, there were 733 affiliated clubs with a combined membership of 21,461 women.[129] In 1916, Virginia Meredith yielded the presidency to Mary Matthews, who was elected twice and served in that capacity until 1919.

The death of a friend, a painting, an essay contest, and a donation to the School of Home Economics played an important role in Meredith's later life. The story begins with Lucy Wallace Wade, a popular instructor of home economics at Purdue University. In 1924, Wade entered St. Elizabeth Hospital in Lafayette, Indiana, for an appendectomy.[130] To the surprise of her close friends, Wade did not recover. She died on October 22, 1924.[131] Three days later, home economics classes were cancelled to allow students to attend her funeral.[132]

The Purdue faculty passed the following resolution on November 27, 1924, honoring Wade:

In the tragically sudden death on October 22, 1924, of Miss Lucy Wallace Wade, instructor in Textiles in the department of Home Economics, Purdue University has suffered a great loss.

A graduate of Purdue University, an experienced and successful teacher, of fine culture and enthusiasm, of a gracious and sympathetic spirit, Miss Wade won the respect and affection of both her pupils and colleagues.

She was thoroughly in touch with the educational, social and civic movements of the day, that her influence extended far beyond the confines of the class room and the University.

In every undertaking for the betterment of social conditions, or in the inspiration of individual lives of higher ideals and finer achievements her sympathy and enthusiasm and service could be confidently relied upon. Very quietly, yet very surely she moved among us making beautiful her daily duties by the loyalty and courage, and joyousness she brought to them; touching lives helpfully through her gracious, unselfish eagerness to serve.

The faculty of Purdue University, recognizing the abiding influence of the work and life of Miss Wade, record this testimony of their respect and affection. Carolyn E. Shoemaker, T. F. Moran, and Stanley Coulter, Chairman.[133]

Several years later, the Hoosier Salon, an art association, held a show in Chicago. One of the paintings in the exhibition was called *An Old Red Dress,* painted by Indiana artist John Millikin King (1897–1977). This painting was awarded the George T. Buckingham Prize, which recognized the best work of the exhibition by an artist under the age of thirty-five.[134]

Officials from the Purdue Memorial Union and the Lafayette Artists' Association brought the Hoosier Salon show to campus on March 3, 1928.[135] To help members of the community better understand what they were seeing, tour guides led the public throughout the gallery, giving a brief introduction to each painting.[136]

Meredith wanted the students on campus to view the exhibition of Indiana artists. She created a contest with a cash prize for the best essays submitted by the students on what they observed from viewing the paintings. The first-place winner would receive $10, with second prize receiving $5. The students had to limit their essays to a thousand words or less. The nearly 60 essays submitted for Meredith's contest would be judged by faculty in the Purdue University English Department.[137]

On the evening of March 29, 1928, a closing banquet was held in the Purdue Memorial Union in honor of the Hoosier Salon. Professor Thomas F. Moran was the master of ceremonies. Others on the podium included Robert Grafton, a Michigan City painter representing Indiana's artists; David Ross, chairman of the Purdue Board of Trustees; A. R. Ross, the mayor of Lafayette; and Mrs. J. F. Morrison of the Lafayette Artists' Association.[138]

Meredith took to the podium to name the first- and second-place winners of her essay contest. She awarded first place to Dorothy Puckett for her essay "An Old Red Dress"; second place went to R. S. Goodnow for "The Morning Shift."

An Old Red Dress would leave for other showings, but the painting returned soon thereafter to stay forever at Purdue University. Many had viewed the painting that reminded them of their friend, Lucy Wallace Wade. Meredith wanted to buy that specific painting to honor Wade. Approximately 70 people donated money toward King's $450 asking price. Meredith had agreed to make up the difference between the donations and the actual cost of the painting. She ended up giving the largest donation, $50.[139] On April 21, 1928, the painting purchased by the friends of Lucy Wallace Wade was presented to the School of Home Economics. It is still displayed today in Matthews Hall on Purdue's West Lafayette, Ind., campus.[140]

Virginia Claypool Meredith received many honors late in life relating to her work in home economics. Recognition of Meredith's work began when the Home Economics Society, organized in 1919 at Purdue University, changed its name in 1926 to the Virginia C. Meredith Club.[141] New members were voted into the club based on their grade point average.[142] Meredith spoke "at many meetings during the early years of the Club, and once each year at the open meeting she occupied the principal place on the program."[143] In 1927, she addressed a joint audience of the Virginia C. Meredith Club and Omicron Nu, the national honor society for home economics, in the auditorium of Purdue's Home Economics Building—today's Matthews Hall. On that occasion, she reminisced about the struggle that took place to develop the field of home economics as a true science.

In 1928, Meredith received another honor in the form of an educational loan fund named for her. Back in 1912, Meredith had steered the Indiana Federation of Clubs to establish a loan program for women at a number of state universities. She was pleased to have had a part in the loan process for "the lasting good it will do many young women who need financial help in getting through college."[144] In a fitting tribute, the Tippecanoe County Federation of Clubs, in turn, honored Meredith by establishing a similar college loan fund for women at Purdue University in her name.[145] The university trustees officially recognized the Virginia C. Meredith Fund on June 11, 1928. Mrs. Floyd T. Jones from West Lafayette provided the first donation of $32 to the fund.[146] Additional gifts from five more women would bring the total amount of money in the fund to $227.[147]

In 1930, Meredith was invited to attend a ceremony at the University of Wisconsin, where she would receive an award of recognition for her work as a "pioneer in the science of homemaking."[148] On February 3, Meredith found herself mingling with a large agricultural crowd, which had gathered as part of an ongoing celebration called Farm Folks Week, a popular annual event sponsored by the university's School of Agriculture in Madison, Wisconsin. During the preceding twenty-five years, seventy-eight individuals had been recognized as significant contributors to that state's agriculture.[149]

The award Meredith received that night was the "Award of Eminent Service."[150] In addition to Meredith, four others, all from Wisconsin, were recognized that evening.[151] Meredith's award was unusual in that few individuals living outside of the Badger State had ever been recognized in such a manner.

Glenn M. Frank, president of the University of Wisconsin, presided over the ceremonies that February evening. Speaking to the gathered audience, Frank read the inscription on Meredith's award: "Virginia Claypool Meredith, working alone, won success in farming, and later working with others pioneered effectively in the science of home making."[152] In a single sentence, Frank captured Meredith's life and work in agriculture and home economics. She listened to the president's words with pride. It was a special day in her life.

One of the more important tributes that a university can confer on an individual is to name a distinguished professorship in honor of that person. The

Purdue University School of Home Economics designated a distinguished
chair in Meredith's name nearly forty years after her death. In 1974, Helen E.
Clark was the first recipient of the Meredith Distinguished Professor of Home
Economics.[153] Later, when the school changed its name to the School of
Consumer and Family Sciences, the award was renamed the Meredith Distinguished Professor of Foods and Nutrition. In 1984, Avanelle Kirksey was the
second professor to be granted the title. Making the award extra special was
that Clark and Kirksey were the first women in the entire history of the university to ever hold distinguished chairs.[154]

Purdue University honored Virginia Meredith again in 2006 when it named
her as one of its women pioneers.[155] The first fifteen women inductees were
selected from a list of ninety submissions.[156] Among the group were many
notable firsts for the university: first trustee, first full professor in the Purdue
Department of Statistics, first professor of agriculture, first African-American
professor, and first director of the women's residence halls. The Council on the
Status of Women held the award ceremony on August 30, 2006, at Westwood,
the university home of Purdue President Martin Jischke.

In 2000, the University of Minnesota bestowed a similar honor on Virginia
Meredith and Mary Matthews when they were among a hundred people identified on a list called the "Centennial 100," which recognized the important
contributors to home economics at the university. This list was part of the university's celebration of the 100-year anniversary of the founding of the home
economics department.[157]

While Meredith pushed her agenda for expanding the role of women in
American society, it was her moderate views that allowed her to hold broader
and somewhat more controversial positions. While it is true that she wanted a
better future for women, she never once gave up on her past: a rural heritage
that hinged on the indispensable role of a woman raising a family and managing the home. She always promoted a woman's right to work outside of the
home but, at the same time, strongly acknowledged the important work performed by women at home. For her, it was not an either-or position. Meredith
staked her claim that both positions were compatible, legitimate, and important
for women. Her basic premise was that every woman should be appreciated, no
matter what her chosen role in life.

In many aspects, Meredith was walking a difficult line as she advanced women in society and the woman at home. Her pursuit of home economics as a legitimate area of study in college was one way to reconcile both causes.

*Purdue University's First
Woman Trustee*

୭ ୬୧ CHAPTER 8 ୬୨ ୭

Indeed a very modern definition of education is that it consists
of the development of intelligence, a training in skill, and
"the learning of how to live agreeably with our fellowmen."

—Virginia Meredith, *The Purdue Agriculturist*, March 1924

VIRGINIA C. MEREDITH MOVED to West Lafayette, Indiana, in 1916, leaving her rural home for a life in town. She was sixty-seven when she left her eastern Indiana farm to move into her daughter's home at 356 West State Street.[1] Her adopted daughter, Mary Matthews, had, by this time, risen through the ranks at the university to become professor and head of the Department of Household Economics.[2]

Meredith spent time writing on agriculture and women's issues, and she maintained an active calendar of speaking engagements. She also remained involved in women's groups, participating in the recently established Indiana Home Economics Association and attending the annual meeting of the Indiana Federation of Clubs. Through it all, she continued to address the virtues of farm life and the heightened need for the nation to educate its women. But just five years after her arrival in West Lafayette, a change to Indiana state law would open the door to a whole new career for Meredith.

On March 9, 1921, the Indiana General Assembly passed a bill requiring that more alumni be appointed to the Purdue University Board of Trustees. Just prior to this, the board had consisted of nine members, all appointed by the governor, with three drawn from the Indiana State Board of Agriculture. Under the new law, the Purdue University Alumni Association was granted authority to nominate three alumni trustees, with one a School of Agriculture graduate. The governor still controlled the remaining six appointments, but he was somewhat constrained by the Indiana General Assembly to select two in each of the following areas: agriculture, manufacturing sector, and "citizens of character and distinction."[3]

The new law also required the governor to select at least one woman among those six appointments. This was due, in part, to the women's suffrage movement, which put pressure on all public institutions to appoint qualified women when board positions became available. To meet this obligation, Indiana Governor Warren T. McCray chose Virginia C. Meredith as the first female member of the Purdue Board of Trustees.[4] She was well qualified to serve, having spent many years as a speaker at the Farmers' Institutes, a noted agricultural writer and lecturer, a renowned livestock breeder, a university professor, and an advocate for women's education at the university level.

At one time, the offices of the Purdue University president and board of trustees were housed in Eliza Fowler Hall, a building that once stood where today's Stewart Center is located. Here, the president and his advisors on the board discussed university business and policies. And it was here, on July 1, 1921, that Virginia Claypool Meredith attended her first board of trustees meeting. The seventy-two-year-old Meredith looked around the table, comfortable with the fact that she knew many of her male colleagues. In addition to Meredith, the trustees attending the July 1921 meeting included Franklin F. Chandler, Perry H. Crane, John Hillenbrand, Cyrus M. Hobbs, Henry W. Marshall, James W. Noel, Joseph D. Oliver, and David E. Ross.[5]

The actual agenda discussed at her first board meeting included awarding a coal contract; the purchase of a 120-acre farm a little more than two miles west of Purdue for horticultural experiments; approving an addition to the Dairy Barn; renewing farm leases; and updates on the transfer of the Davis Forestry Farm to Purdue University.[6] One agenda item in particular must have been a dream come true for Meredith. At her first meeting, she would vote with the board to authorize the construction of the Home Economics Building.

Meredith and her fellow trustees were also assigned duty on the board's standing committees.[7] Each trustee normally chaired a three-person standing committee in addition to serving on other standing committees. Meredith was assigned to chair the Science and Technology Committee and appointed to serve on the Agriculture Committee. Eventually, she also served on the Committee on Technology and Engineering and the Committee on Science and Industrial Arts.[8]

Assignments to standing committees were augmented by service on numerous ad hoc committees formed to resolve problems that arose during the year. Committee work was vital to the success of the larger board. Issues were debated and agreed to in committee. Consequently, committee reports presented to the full board normally were unanimously accepted when voted upon.

With her talent for writing, the trustees often turned to Meredith to write special messages on behalf of the board. She would pen words of appreciation when significant persons retired from campus, when an expression of condolence was in order, or when a commemorative plaque needed the proper inscription.[9]

Meredith generally voted with the board's majority. However, on rare occasions—perhaps four times—she dissented. In 1930, she was the only one of the trustees to vote "no" on a motion to reaffirm the board's position that the university would not hire relatives of current Purdue employees.[10] In another case, the Purdue University president wanted to dispense with reading the minutes at the beginning of each board meeting, arguing that it was a waste of time to read them "as each member of the Board received from the Secretary soon after each meeting a complete mimeographed copy of the minutes."[11] The motion passed, but Meredith, Joseph Lilly, and James Noel voted against changing the long-standing procedure.

Seldom would Meredith express anger, though one time she voiced her displeasure with performance arrangements for the military band:

> Mrs. Meredith also stated her objection to the Purdue Military Band's playing at the Speed-way Races at Indianapolis, last Memorial Day, because she felt they should be present at the Memorial Day services at the University. The members of the Board concurred in this opinion.[12]

Throughout her fifteen years as a trustee, Meredith's style was to listen more than to speak up during board meetings, unless the subject involved women or agriculture. From the start, she was an advocate for campus housing for women, home economics as a career for women, and women's physical education.

Meredith took her appointment seriously, faithfully attending meetings and executing her duties. Between July 1, 1921, and December 21, 1935, the board called 106 meetings to order. During that fourteen-year span, Meredith only missed two meetings: one on January 4, 1927, and the one on December 21, 1935. The board members must have been shocked to learn that "Mrs. Meredith was prevented by illness from attending the meeting" in 1927.[13] Her nearly perfect attendance ended in 1936, when she suffered health problems.

At the age of eighty-seven, her good health for so many years started failing her, and she would miss all but one meeting in 1936.

The trustees found it rather amusing when Purdue President Winthrop Stone asked them for permission to take a July vacation in 1921. James Noel made the following motion "tongue in cheek" after the president asked for time off: "I move that the President be granted such vacation as he desires to take."[14] Little did the trustees know when they laughed about the president's request that it would be their last—and Meredith's only—meeting with him.

Stone and his wife enjoyed mountain climbing as a recreational pastime. Shortly after the July board meeting, the Stones traveled to Canada to climb Eon Mountain in the Canadian Rockies. The peak of Eon Mountain soars 10,860 feet above sea level and lies along the Alberta and British Columbia border. Dr. Stone would be the first person credited with climbing the peak.

It was strenuous work to reach the summit that July 17 afternoon. The Stones stayed with the climb until around six o'clock that evening, when they had nearly reached the summit. President Stone left his wife on a ledge that was forty feet below the actual summit and continued climbing. His wife remained behind, waiting until he had explored the peak. Tragically, as Stone completed the climb, the rocks gave way, and he fell 1,000 feet to his death. It would take search-and-rescue teams many days to recover Stone's body.[15]

Obviously, the Purdue University community was in shock over the sudden death of President Stone. It was especially difficult for the trustees, many of whom had longstanding relationships with the president. At the September 4, 1921, board meeting, Meredith read the memorial that she and fellow trustees Joseph Oliver and David Ross had written for Stone:

MEMORIAL

The Board of Trustees of Purdue University hereby orders entered in its records this expression of its deep feeling of loss in the death of President Winthrop Ellsworth Stone whose life ended on July 17, 1921, with appalling suddenness near Banff, in Alberta, Canada, when, with his wife, he was engaged in his chosen summer recreation of mountain climbing.

Elected president of Purdue University in 1900 he has since that time with untiring energy been organizing plans to perfect the departments, and devising ways to meet the needs of a technical institution whose opportunity for service was always expanding far beyond its resources and whose student enrollment during his administration increased from 800 to 3,100. Steadfast in purpose, quiet in manner and without ostentation he has accomplished here a great and permanent piece of work. When we were seeing his work as parts and pieces of a particular year, or plan, we could not truly appraise it but now when he has left his work it stands revealed in its entirety and we are able to perceive clearly the proportions and dimensions of the great and permanent values wrought by President Stone in Purdue University.

His organization of the University has been so thorough and comprehensive that even the grave emergency due to his appallingly sudden removal has made no confusion. We find each Department fully prepared for the coming college year so that students and faculty can go forward with assurance and in the accustomed way.

To name the list of President Stone's activities would be to indicate in some degree the nobility of ideals and energy of will of one richly endowed with the spirit of service, with a discernment of human needs, with an understanding of the obligations of patriotism and of high scholarship. In many contacts with important and serious interests he has been a trusted counselor and effective executive. He was intimately associated with numerous national movements, notably serving the Association of Land Grant Colleges. He made signal contributions to the advancement of the educational interests of Indiana through his long connection with its State Board of Education. During the Great War [World War I] when the resources of Purdue University were tendered to the Federal Government he worked with unflagging energy while 5,000 enlisted men were housed, fed and given technical training in 1918 on its campus, when 2,500 were enrolled in its Student Army Training Corps, when University Departments were stimulating agricultural production and promoting food conservation.

To the faculty, the alumni and the students of Purdue University as well as to its Board of Trustees, President Stone has left an example of thoroughness in work, of patience, courage, fairness and steadfast loyalty to the institution which they may wisely emulate in all their relations to the University.

We extend profound sympathy to President Stone's family, to the father, the brothers, the sister, his two sons and to his devoted wife who has for years shared the high adventure of his mountain climbing, an endeavor that has been called the recreation of men of learning and which he has himself described as an approach to the Empyrean heights. We would commend to them, if it may be done without intrusion, the comfort there is in

contemplating his achievements and his character, the consolations there
are in a trust in that Divine Providence by which he charted his life.[16]

While Purdue University staff and students mourned their loss, behind-
the-scenes action to fill the void left by Stone's death was already underway. The
president of the board of trustees, Joseph Oliver, believed chaos would descend
on Purdue University unless he acted quickly and decisively. He took swift and
immediate action to ensure the continued smooth operation of the university.

It was not until the board meeting on August 4, 1921, just weeks after
Stone's death, that the trustees were fully informed of the unilateral action
taken by Oliver to fill the vacancy caused by the president's death. Oliver had
made an executive decision to place Henry W. Marshall, who was at the time the
chairman of the board's executive committee, to become interim president of
the university.[17] When the matter was presented to the full board for open discussion and approval, the trustees supported Oliver's actions, wholeheartedly
agreeing with his decision.[18]

Meredith voted favorably when the trustees made an unusual move to
modify the board's bylaws and create the position of vice president, a new
administrative position. Once modified, the trustees approved the motion that
said: "BE IT RESOLVED: That Henry W. Marshall be and is hereby elected Vice-
President of the University with power to perform all the duties and exercise the
powers of the President until further order of the Board. . . ."[19]

Marshall was a well-known local businessman in and around Lafayette
who was, at the time of his appointment, the publisher and editor-in-chief
of the *Lafayette Journal and Courier*.[20] He adamantly refused payment for his
work and only reluctantly agreed to have the university cover half of the thirty-
dollar weekly salary paid to his personal stenographer.[21]

During his time in office, Marshall worked closely with Dean Stanley
Coulter, the chairman of the faculty.[22] Together, Marshall and Coulter would
lead Purdue University through a stressful year, allowing the board time to
thoroughly review qualified presidential candidates.

Meredith listened as Marshall made it very clear to the board that any
issues other than routine matters would be brought before the trustees for
their consideration. Marshall, for the most part, remained out of the public eye.
Behind the scenes, however, he was a tireless worker who balanced the budget
and still found money to complete projects around campus that Stone had
started or promised to start.[23] Marshall remained at Purdue's helm for thirteen
months.

During that time, the trustees focused on the lengthy and complicated process of picking the successor to the immensely popular Stone. The hiring of the top administrative official at Purdue University was made more difficult because none of the trustees had ever participated in interviewing and selecting a university president. Each of the current trustees had been appointed to the board while Stone was president.

Names were bantered about as to who the next president might be. After interviewing several candidates, the board unanimously decided to invite Dr. Edward C. Elliott to campus for an interview and, if terms could be arranged, offer him the position.

Elliott was a young administrator who had received his doctorate from Columbia University and had been a professor at the University of Wisconsin before becoming the chancellor of the University of Montana.[24] He knew university administration and was keenly aware of the challenges that faced the president of a land-grant university.[25]

The board met in special session on May 16, 1922, to discuss making Elliott the successor to Stone. Dr. Elliott attended the meeting, where he engaged in an informal discussion on Purdue policies and the duties and powers assigned to the president. Elliott was asked about any conditions he would have for accepting the position, if it were, in fact, offered to him.[26] He presented a detailed list of requirements outlining what he expected from the board before he would agree to leave his job in Montana for a new one in Indiana. Some of his stipulations were more or less routine matters common to any job negotiation: he wanted a starting date of September 1, 1922; an annual salary of $10,000; and a one-month vacation annually. He asked that the university pay his moving expenses from Helena, Montana, to West Lafayette, which he estimated to be around $1,800. And Elliott told the trustees that he expected the university to provide him and his wife with a rent-free, university-owned home. The university, he believed, should provide upkeep on the house and property, cover all utilities and taxes, and pay for business-related entertainment expenses.

One additional demand that Elliott placed on the board gave the trustees pause. Elliott wanted the board to relinquish all personnel decisions and day-to-day educational matters to his control. Meredith and the others realized that their choice for the next university president was proposing to divide the responsibility for managing the affairs of Purdue University between himself and the trustees. Meredith heard Elliott propose that the board would be responsible for the university's finances and policies but that the daily management, including personnel, would fall to the president. Elliott made it very clear where the line of demarcation would lie between the president's office and the board of trustees, and the trustees understood that agreeing to this condition would elevate the authority of this president above those of previous administrations.

After Elliott listed his conditions of employment and answered a few more questions, he was asked to wait outside the meeting room. The trustees debated one last time whether or not Elliott was still their top choice. In spite of his demands, it did not take long for Meredith and the others to decide that Elliott had the professional experience and personal demeanor that they were searching for. He was their clear choice to lead the university. They voted, and Elliott received the board's unanimous support.

Elliott was called back into the room at Eliza Fowler Hall. Upon entering, he must have been pleasantly surprised when "the members of the Board rose and greeted him as the President-Elect of Purdue University." In a brief speech to the board, Elliott commented that "Purdue University has honored me. I will endeavor to honor Purdue University."[27] He would do so for the next twenty-three years.

The trustees, pleased with finally getting the president they wanted, announced to the faculty at a special 4 P.M. meeting that same day that Dr. Edward C. Elliott had agreed to become the sixth president of Purdue. At the conclusion of this announcement, the board reconvened in Eliza Fowler Hall, where Indiana Governor Warren T. McCray had arrived to express "his approval of the action of the Board in electing Dr. Elliott President of Purdue University. He also congratulated Dr. Elliott and assured him that he will receive a hearty welcome when he comes to Indiana to make his future home."[28]

The change in leadership from Marshall to Elliott marked a time of transition between Elliott's hiring on May 16, 1922, until he took over the reins that following September. During this three-month period, the board issued several proclamations, praising the gratuitous work and leadership that Marshall had given Purdue University following President Stone's death. At one board meeting, Meredith was asked to read a tribute she had penned that recognized Marshall's extraordinary service to the university. As she finished reading the resolution, the trustees gave Marshall a resounding round of applause in appreciation.

RESOLUTION

This meeting of the Board of Trustees of Purdue University held June 13, 1922, marks the completion of a college year which has been unprecedented in difficulties and in activities, but nevertheless a year of eminent success in all its features under the administration of Acting-President Henry W. Marshall: therefore, it is deemed fitting at this time to express formally and officially, not only our high estimate of the executive force shown by Mr. Marshall, and his masterful grasp of the educational aspects of the University, but also to record our deep sense of the heavy debt of obligation owing to Mr. Marshall on account of his determination not to accept any compensation for his services as Acting-President of Purdue University. The tragic close of President Stone's administration on July 17, 1921, put upon the president of the Board of Trustees a responsibility that has been signally justified in the appointment of Mr. Marshall.

An increased enrollment of students has made increased claims . . . upon the teaching staff as well as upon classrooms and laboratories: outside contacts through the expansion of the Extension services of the University have created conditions requiring the utmost tact and diplomacy to regulate: the year has been filled with the exacting details of an extensive building program: there have been important situations in the Faculty organization brought about through death, resignation and transfer of its members: while overshadowing all else has been the serious seeking and wise selection of a new President for the University.

In these new and difficult circumstances Mr. Marshall has been accessible, patient, fair and firm; he has with rare understanding performed the whole duty of an executive holding in trust the educational and financial interests of a great University.

To grateful appreciation of past services the Board of Trustees adds its sincere wishes for Mr. Marshall's future health and happiness.

Signed—Virginia C. Meredith, James W. Noel, C. M. Hobbs.[29]

Marshall replied, "I want to express my gratitude to the Board for the adoption of the resolutions. I have tried in every way to do what was for the best interests of the University. I may have made mistakes, as we all do, but it has been my constant endeavor to consider first of all the interests of the institution. I wish to thank you again for your favorable expression toward me."[30]

Nearly ten years later, the trustees would accept the faculty's recommendation that Henry Marshall receive an honorary doctor of laws degree.[31]
He would be honored along with his friend, Stanley Coulter, who was dean
emeritus of the School of Science. Coulter received an honorary doctor of science degree. The degrees were fitting tributes for men who had helped steer
Purdue through a turbulent period.

The changing of the guard occurred at the September 2, 1922, board meeting. Marshall tendered his resignation to the trustees, and Dr. Elliott was sworn
in as the new president of Purdue University. He calmly stepped forward, telling
the trustees, "Mr. Chairman and Members of the board of trustees: On the 16th
of May, in this room, I gave you my word. I am here to redeem that word by my
works. That tells the whole story."[32] Elliott's presidency marked not only a new
beginning for Purdue but also the start of a fourteen-year professional relationship between President Elliott and trustee Virginia Meredith.

When the Purdue trustees faced issues affecting women students at the university, Meredith was quick to voice her opinion, often showing tenacity as she
worked to make improvements for the female students. In 1924, she found an
important ally in Purdue President Edward Elliott when the trustees discussed
whether the university should provide physical education for its women students. According to the minutes of the board, President Elliott brought up the
need for an

> ... organized physical education for women students, saying that it was
> earnestly desired by such students, and that Purdue University is the only
> institution of its size which does not provide such a course; that it had been
> suggested that temporary quarters might be arranged in the basement of
> Ladies' Hall; and that he asked the authority of the Board to investigate
> the feasibility of making use of these rooms, and also for making use of
> all facilities afforded on the campus, for the physical welfare of women
> students.[33]

President Elliott read a letter to the board that had been written by Carolyn E.
Shoemaker, Dean of Women, and supported by Wilhelmina Schoenholtz,
president of the Women's Council of Purdue:

My dear President Elliott:

I have recently had several sessions with the Women's Council. This Council, as you may know, is composed of representatives of the Sorority houses, and of Ladies' Hall and of We Girls. Thus you see it is All-University.

The girls are anxious to have compulsory physical education next year. This means that the basement of Ladies' Hall must be put in shape; and, also, that a woman be in charge of athletics. Their arguments are as follows:

(1) Every first-class institution administers such training: (2) Every girl is entitled to such work, much of which will be corrective in nature: and (3) Demands are being made upon Purdue graduates to administer such courses.

In their favor, I may add, that, with one night a week in the [Memorial] gymnasium, with voluntary attendance, we have worked up to a point system for awarding sweaters; we have teams in hiking, volley ball, basketball, etc; and we have membership in the National Woman's Athletic Association. Then, too, this would place our sports upon a much safer basis, including regular training, medical examination, etc.

Furthermore, I am crowded for space in Ladies' Hall during the opening week of School. If the basement could be finished off it would give me much needed room.[34]

After a lengthy discussion, Meredith offered the following well-scripted and apparently threatening resolution:

The Board of Trustees hereby authorizes and directs that there shall be established at the beginning of the college year 1924-1925 a course in physical training for women students in the University. Said course to be in charge of a competent and experienced woman Director, and there shall be provided in the Memorial Gymnasium such times and places as may be satisfactory to the said Director for the administration of the courses, together with suitable and adequate equipment that may be required.

Proper academic credits shall be given for the work and it shall be required of all women students except in cases where the Director in charge and the University Physician shall decide that a student may be excused.

Said Director of Physical training for women shall be chosen by and be directly responsible to the President of the University for the faithful performance of the duties of the position—and she shall be paid a salary the same as that paid to men for similar service.[35]

It was quite a remarkable statement for the 1920s that a woman should be paid the same as her male counterpart, but perhaps it was too boldly worded, because not a single trustee offered to second the motion. Apparently, the board wanted more details before supporting Meredith's resolution. Instead, David Ross, a trustee and close friend of Meredith's, got the board to agree to the following motion: "I move that President Elliott be requested to submit plans at the next meeting of the Board for the physical education of women."[36]

Time would drag on as information was gathered. In the fall of 1924, President Elliott asked the trustees whether they thought that a soon-to-be-vacated part of the Electrical Engineering Building, constructed in 1889, could be converted to a women's gymnasium. He had devised two plans based on whether the building would be completely overhauled or just partially remodeled. Remodeling was a less expensive approach that would allow the project to be completed quickly.[37] Turning the entire building into a women's gymnasium was a bolder proposition that Meredith herself preferred over remodeling.

President Elliott and Meredith were serious about supporting a women's physical education program and gymnasium at Purdue University. Elliott even went so far as to invite Elsa Sameth, professor and head of the Women's Physical Education Department at the University of Nevada, to come to Purdue in 1924 to review the plans. Professor Sameth indicated that "these plans, if carried to completion, would provide facilities and space, in proportion to the number of students, not exceeded in any institution with which she was acquainted."[38]

Meredith took advantage of the momentum in October 1924, when she introduced a new motion to turn the Electrical Engineering Building into a gymnasium for women:

> The Board of Trustees approves the plan outlined by President Elliott for establishing and developing a department for the Physical Education of Woman students, and hereby authorizes him to proceed in converting the present Electrical Engineering Building to that use and to secure instructors and equipment.[39]

The Board unanimously voted in favor of this motion, and by May 8, 1925, the board "approved the reconstruction of the old Electrical Engineering Building into a Woman's Gymnasium at an approximate cost of $16,050.00."[40] On January 5, 1926, the board asked President Elliott to obtain the require bids.[41]

In June 1926, Meredith's excitement over the prospect of a women's gymnasium was dashed when the sealed bids were opened. The contractors' bids were much higher than what the trustees had anticipated. John Hillenbrand moved to reject all of the bids "on account of the excessive total cost involved."[42] Only one trustee did not consider the bids unreasonable. Meredith stood firm that a gymnasium and a physical education program for women students was more important that the $21,000 price tag it would take to turn it into a reality. In her opinion, Purdue University had done little to date to help its women students and the need for such a program outweighed the extra cost. She believed that, for a change, it was time to invest in the women.[43]

Meredith was not able to convince the other trustees of her views. The outright rejection of the bids soured the trustees on spending any money to create the gymnasium. When all was said and done, the trustees would only spend $3,649 to do slight touch-ups and repairs by installing new wiring and plumbing, and adding some partitions throughout the structure.

The repairs were completed in 1927, but in 1929 the building was demolished to make room for the Wetherill Laboratory of Chemistry. While Meredith had tried to get a modern gymnasium for the women, in the long run, her efforts were unsuccessful. However, the fight she put up marked her as a strong advocate for women and their right to a university education equal to that of the men.

In 1924, Purdue University marked fifty years as an educational institution. Dean Andrey A. Potter of the School of Engineering, Professor Thomas Moran of the Department of History, and Professor William Hepburn, university librarian, were appointed by the executive committee of the faculty to put together a semicentennial celebration. The faculty then turned to the trustees to see if they were willing to help with planning the program.

The president of the board of trustees, John Oliver, told faculty members that the trustees would cooperate with them in any manner the faculty wished.[44] Meredith was one of three trustees assigned in late 1923 to work with the faculty on the planning efforts.[45]

Meredith wanted to do something special for this once-in-a-lifetime event. She asked the board to approve the following resolution that she had written:

> WHEREAS, It is desirable and fitting that the University should have at the time of its Fiftieth Anniversary, a portrait of President Stone, whose twenty-one years of administration were eminently influential in the development

of the Institution during that period: therefore be it RESOLVED, That a Committee of three be appointed, of which President Oliver shall be one, to obtain
the necessary information about a suitable artist and also to confer with
Mrs. Stone, and to report at the next meeting of the Board of Trustees.[46]

The board passed the measure, and Meredith began the process of trying to find a suitable artist to paint Stone's portrait.[47] She wrote to Wayman
Adams (1883–1959) at his New York studio about the possibility.[48] Adams was a
Hoosier by birth, having been born in Muncie, Indiana. In addition, he received
his training at the John Herron Art Institute in Indianapolis and was a nationally recognized portrait painter. Meredith told the trustees that Mrs. Stone had
"expressed appreciation of the action of the Board of Trustees and very particular satisfaction in having an artist of the distinction of Mr. Wayman Adams
considered in connection with the commission for the portrait."[49]

On December 14, 1923, Adams replied from New York:

My dear Mrs. Meredith:—

I have received the book and your letter with regard to painting a portrait
of Doctor Stone, the late President of Purdue University, and feel compli-
mented that you have written to me.

Most painters make a reduction in price when a portrait is to hang in a
public place and I am glad to do it in this case.

My price for portraits are:
    Bust $1,000.00
    Two-thirds length...................1,500.00
    Full length 2,000.00

I am willing to paint the bust size (25 x 30) for $650.00 and the two-thirds
size (40 x 50) for $1,000.00.

I would paint the portrait to be approved by Mrs. Stone and Dean Stone
[President Stone's son] of Columbia University.

Hoping these terms meet with your approval I am,

Sincerely yours,
Wayman Adams

Meredith replied, instructing Adams that the bust-size portrait must be delivered to Purdue University no later than April 20, 1924, so as to be part of the
semicentennial celebrations.[50]

Adams completed the portrait and delivered it a few weeks earlier than the April 20 deadline.[51] The painting was exhibited on campus on April 8 and was well received by Mrs. Stone and President Stone's brother, Harlan F. Stone. The semicentennial celebration took place on May 2, 1924.

The trustees agreed to pay for the publication of 1,000 copies each of two books that would commemorate the fifty-year celebration: *Purdue University: Fifty Years of Progress,* which was co-authored by librarian William M. Hepburn and history professor Louis M. Sears, and *Proceedings of the Semi-Centennial Observance,* written by English professor Robert W. Babcock.[52]

In 1928, Meredith's fellow trustees were determined to commission a portrait of her in honor of her selfless service to the university. She may have been the only trustee to receive such an honor. John Millikin King, a thirty-two-year-old Indiana artist known for his portraiture, painted Meredith's likeness. Coincidentally, King had also painted *An Old Red Dress,* the painting acquired for the Purdue School of Home Economics in April 1928. King's portrait of Meredith was the feature painting during the spring exhibition of the Richmond (Ind.) Palette Club during May of 1929.[53] Local stories indicated that "Mr. King has painted an admirable portrait of Mrs. Meredith and gives the Wayne county public an opportunity of seeing it before it is sent to Lafayette."[54]

The painting was unveiled on May 21, 1929, and the trustees encouraged Meredith to select a location on campus for displaying it. She chose the Home Economics Building. Her portrait has since looked out on the university that she loved. The portrait's various locations through the years reflect Meredith's accomplishments in connection with Purdue. It was placed first in the Home Economics Building, central to women's education in which she firmly believed. The portrait was later moved to the Purdue Memorial Union, which reflected Meredith's patriotic contribution to the men and women who served their country in time of war (see Chapter 9).[55] Today, it occupies a prominent location in a women's residence hall named in her honor.

No issue was too small to be ignored by Meredith and her fellow trustees. John Purdue (1802–76) had died in Lafayette, Indiana, on September 12, 1876. He had asked to be buried on campus. His wishes were honored, and his grave was placed directly east of University Hall.

By 1923, nearly fifty years after John Purdue's death, the board of trustees became embarrassed by the state of the hedge around his gravesite, which had grown unsightly. Meredith, the chairperson of the committee in charge, advised "that it be replaced as soon as practicable by another hedge, to be of a variety of dwarf evergreen that requires neither trimming or clipping."[56]

They would ask Cyrus Hobbs, a fellow trustee and one of the most respected horticulturists in the state, to help with the beautification project around the grave. Hobbs agreed that the current hedge would be "removed and the entire surface planted with juniper, either in the fall or next spring."[57] Hobbs informed the trustees when the planting of shrubs was completed and that "the plants gave every promise of excellent growth."[58]

The trustees generally discussed a variety of routine topics at their meetings. But in the spring of 1934, they were presented with a unique agenda item. Meredith and the other trustees learned from President Elliott that an individual wanted to donate a mold that had been used to make brick for the first two buildings built at Purdue University.

> The mold was made under the instructions of John Purdue, late in the year 1873, by Phillip Miller of Lafayette, and was presented to the University by his son, Michael Miller of Lafayette (now 72 years of age), who assisted both in making the brick and in erecting the buildings. The letter accompanying the mold was written by Mrs. A. O. Lee, daughter of Michael Miller [as follows]:
>
> *Original Mold of Bricks in first 2 buildings of Purdue*
>
> Late in year 1873—John Purdue ordered Phillip Miller to manufactor a special brick mold—for bricks to be used in first two buildings built at Purdue University. The size of these bricks were [sic] 1¾ in. thick—3¾ in. wide by 8 in. long.
>
> The Molds hold 3 bricks and there is [sic] 3 molds to a set.
>
> The brickyard that manufactored these bricks was located on Moorehouse gravel road above Littleton hill. Three years later it moved to Owen & Holloway Strs. in LaFayette. Contractor who built the two buildings was Joshua Chew and was built in 1874.
>
> Donator of special mold is Mr. Michael Miller, 524 S. 4th St., Lafayette, Indiana (age 72 yrs.) son of the deceased Phillip Miller owner and manufactor of molds and bricks. Don[o]r helped manufactor and build the two buildings.[59]

Professor William Hepburn, a university librarian, picked up the donations and brought them before the board for inspection.[60] The molds were placed in the John Purdue Room in the library.

By the time Meredith was appointed as a trustee, her direct involvement with agriculture was well in her past, but her reputation as a noted livestock producer followed her wherever she went. That she was well known within agricultural circles made her appointment to the Purdue Board of Trustees' influential Committee on Agriculture an easy choice for Joseph Oliver, president of the board. Between 1921 and 1930, the Committee on Agriculture was the most active board committee.

Membership on this committee was an important assignment. President Edward Elliott directed the committee to do more in the way of making the Purdue agricultural programs more successful, sustainable, cooperative, and accountable. Through President Elliott, this committee influenced how agriculture was taught, what research was conducted, and how the campus farm was staffed and equipped. Committee members found themselves immersed in the details of agricultural enrollments, extension programs, and farm construction projects.

The agriculture committee also invested a great deal of time in off-campus issues, such as accepting donations of farm properties, building barns, constructing or repairing residences for employees, and stocking livestock on Purdue's outlying network of farms. The committee would have to offer recommendations to the full board on whether leases should be renewed, whether farms donated to Purdue should be kept or sold, and even whether to allow the mining of limestone at the Moses Fell Dunn Farm in Lawrence County, Indiana.

While Meredith's work on building projects at Purdue thrust her into the public view (see Chapter 9), her effort on the Committee on Agriculture did not bring the same degree of public attention. But through it, Meredith would have a long-lasting impact on Indiana agriculture well into the future.

Meredith was a member of the Committee on Agriculture from her first day on the board, serving for fifteen years. She was never appointed as committee chairperson, and there are no explanations as to why members with less seniority were appointed as chair while she was not. Perhaps she didn't want the responsibilities that came with the position, or maybe she felt that she had been away from farming for too long. It is also possible that the trustees of the 1920s felt more comfortable with a man heading up this committee. Committee chair or not, Meredith fully participated in the work of the agriculture committee. She took every opportunity to promote agricultural education, research, and extension at Purdue University.

Some of Meredith's most rewarding moments as a trustee came from her involvement with students in the Purdue School of Agriculture. She must have beamed with pride when the board members learned that students from the animal sciences department won several prestigious awards at the 1930 International Live Stock Exposition.[61]

> President Elliott presented to each member of the Board a report prepared by Dean Skinner, giving a detailed list of the honors and prizes awarded Purdue University at the 1930 International Live Stock Exposition. The prizes won amounted to $2,230 and the sale of show stock to $2,894.88, while the expenses in connection with the exhibit were only $944.79.

> The members of the Board of Trustees expressed their gratification at the splendid showing made by the University; and upon motion of Mrs. Meredith, carried unanimously, the Secretary was directed to convey to Director Skinner and through him to the members of his staff assisting in the exhibit, their sincere and hearty congratulations upon the high standing accorded Purdue University as well as upon the exceptionally numerous and large prizes received, and upon the proportionately small expense connected with the exhibit.[62]

Meredith also undoubtedly enjoyed working with School of Agriculture donors. Two special gifts came from her board colleague, Henry Marshall. In 1928, President Elliott notified the board that Marshall had donated a herd of registered Herefords to Purdue. Meredith's experience raising some of the finest Shorthorn cattle in the country gave her a keen appreciation for the importance of Marshall's gift to Purdue students learning about livestock evaluation, judging, and production. A few years later, the trustees received another livestock gift from Henry Marshall. In 1933, he donated a "Belgian stallion, Baron de Dottignies No. 14450, valued at $500 to Purdue University."[63]

Sometimes Meredith's duties as a trustee were bittersweet. In 1923, William Carroll Latta, one of her oldest and closest friends, was nearing retirement, and the director of the extension service, George Christie, asked the trustees to relieve the seventy-four-year-old of his responsibilities for the immensely popular Farmers' Institutes. Now Meredith and the board would return a small favor to Latta, who had served Purdue University for forty-one years. The trustees would provide Latta, who at the time did not have a retirement plan, with a stipend for the remainder of his life.

> THAT, On the recommendation of the President, and the Director of Agricultural Extension, Professor W. C. Latta, who has served the University for forty-one years, be relieved of the strenuous work that his position as Farmer's Institute Specialist demands, and be appointed Consulting Specialist in the Department of Agricultural Extension at his present salary ($1,600), and that at the same time he retain his present position and salary in the School of Agriculture ($400).[64]

Occasionally, Meredith must have found some of the agricultural issues decidedly humorous. One such episode occurred in the spring of 1931. A Purdue truck loaded with cows was heading east toward Lafayette when it wrecked on the Main Street Bridge. Damages to the vehicle amounted to $100. After rounding up the animals, the driver found that one steer had mysteriously disappeared into the countryside. As it turned out, the missing steer "was picked up by a nearby farmer who sent it to an Indianapolis market."[65]

Purdue University was able to identify the farmer by tracing the sales receipts. Caught red-handed selling a steer that didn't belong to him, the farmer agreed to pay the university the amount that he had received from selling the cow.[66] The farmer never made good on that promise.

Slightly more than a year later, the case of the steer and the unpaid bill reappeared before the board. Controller Robert B. Stewart admitted that the steer incident actually saved Purdue University money when workers building the campus airport accidentally cut trees on property that did not belong to the university:

> When the airport was started, some cherry trees on Mrs. Burns' land were cut down without authority. As you know, there is always an argument as to the value of growing trees, and Mrs. Burns presented to us the opinion that the trees were of considerable value to her property if for no other reason than for shade for her livestock. Knowing this situation, I have finally adjudicated Mrs. Burns' claim against the University by agreeing to offset with her our claim for the balance due on the steer. The amounts involved for the steer and a small amount at the Creamery represent a balance of $33.75, which is the amount which we may say is the Airport cost for removing trees along the boundary line.[67]

Coincidentally, the man who had sold the Purdue steer lived on the farm where the cherry trees were accidentally cut. Stewart's report alludes to the fact that justice was finally served for $33.75, and the airport construction continued unabated.

From the beginning, the School of Agriculture was quite different from the other schools on campus. Its charge was unique: teaching students, conducting research, and educating Indiana's citizens. In order to accomplish its mission, the university owned and leased thousands of acres near campus and around the state for growing crops and raising livestock to use in its various programs.

During Meredith's time, Purdue University already owned three farms that donors had deeded to the agriculture programs at Purdue University: Moses Fell Dunn Farm in Lawrence County donated in 1914; Davis Forestry Farm in Randolph County donated in 1917; and the Pinney Farm in Porter and LaPorte Counties donated in 1919. By 1925, Purdue University agricultural programs had 2,865 acres of land under production. In 1933, Purdue University accepted 300 more acres of farm ground that George Throckmorton donated in memory of his father, "who was a pioneer farmer in Tippecanoe County...."[68]

The trustees always seemed perplexed about how to run Purdue's extensive farm holdings. Having so much land under production meant constantly spending money on personnel, building construction and repairs, improved roads, newer equipment, and improved livestock needed to manage all of the university's agricultural lands. Periodically, the trustees paid visits to the farms to see for themselves what projects were deemed important by Purdue staff.[69]

After just a few years at the helm, President Elliott began looking seriously at the cost of running the agricultural programs at Purdue. By 1925, the university was experiencing tremendous growth, as undergraduate enrollments topped the 3,000 mark and the beginnings of a graduate program were evident in the 76 students pursuing advanced degrees. The faculty had also been increased to more than 300 to meet the demands of both the graduate and undergraduate programs.[70]

However, the School of Agriculture was unable to achieve enrollment numbers comparable to the other schools across campus.

> President Elliott called the attention of the Board to a statement of comparative enrollments for first semesters for the five [inclusive] years

1922–1926 . . . and pointed out numerous important deductions drawn therefrom, particularly the fluctuation in the enrollment in the School of Agriculture and the greatly increased enrollment in the School of Home Economics and in the Schools of Engineering, especially the School of Electrical Engineering.[71]

What seemed to really irk Elliott was that the School of Agriculture's enrollment was less than stellar in spite of all the attention and money it was receiving from the university. Even the relatively new School of Home Economics was outpacing the School of Agriculture, whose existence went back to the founding days of campus.

This was the second year in a row that Elliott had pointed out to the board the enrollment problems in the School of Agriculture.[72] To address concerns about increasing the enrollment in the School of Agriculture, Meredith and the other trustees hired a full-time recruiter in 1926.[73] President Elliott was so pleased with the efforts of the recruiter that, in October 1928, he finally mentioned the enrollment figures for the School of Agriculture in a more positive light to the trustees.[74] In 1930, with agriculture enrollment continuing to increase, Elliott informed the trustees that the recruiter would be retained as the field representative for the School of Agriculture.[75]

But it wasn't just low enrollments in the agricultural program that frustrated the president. Elliott was tired of what he thought was too much duplication of programs, too much infighting among the agriculture faculty, and too little cooperation between the three main agricultural programs: teaching, research, and extension. There was a need to address the fact that these three prominent but equal programs were managed by two strong-willed men, John Skinner and George Christie.

Teaching agriculture courses, managing the teaching faculty, and operating the Purdue University Farm and Creamery were the responsibility of John Skinner, dean of the School of Agriculture. George I. Christie managed the Department of Agricultural Extension and all of the field agents. The Indiana Agricultural Experiment Station, with its research programs and federal funding, was also under Christie's control.

President Elliott felt that these men did little in the way of working cooperatively. Elliott conveyed to the board on numerous occasions that "plans for placing the School of Agriculture on a more economical basis, was far from satisfactory; and that whole-hearted cooperation on the part of the School of Agriculture, the Agricultural Experiment Station and Department of

Agricultural Extension, which is essential if these plans are to be carried out, is not forthcoming."[76]

Meredith and her fellow Committee on Agriculture members reported on their review of the agricultural programs to the full board on October 14 and 15, 1925.[77] A careful reading of their report—especially of item four—shows there was a concern for getting the programs to work effectively and efficiently together, regardless of who managed them:

> The Committee [on Agriculture] was in session from 10:00 A.M. until noon, and from 1:45 P.M. until 3:45 P.M. [on September 22, 1925] the following actions were taken by the Committee:
>
> 1. That the Board of Trustees reaffirm the existing policy of granting collegiate degrees in Agriculture only on the basis of four years of study.
> 2. That further consideration of the proposal for the establishment of a two-year course in agriculture be postponed indefinitely by reason of the estimated increased expenditure involved thereby.
> 3. That the University should give further immediate attention as to ways and means for bringing the School of Agriculture and its work more effectively to the attention of those whose positions enable them to exert influence upon farmers, in particular the bankers of the state. There should also be closer contact with the staff extension service for this purpose.
> 4. That there should be a joint conference of the Faculty of the School of Agriculture, the staff of the Agricultural Experiment Station and the staff of the Agricultural Extension Department for the purpose of devising more effective cooperative methods for promoting the interests of the School of Agriculture.
> 5. That the President of the University request the Dean and Faculty of the School of Agriculture and the Director and staffs of the Agricultural Experiment Station and the Agricultural Extension Service to consider and to report upon the desirability, the utility and the probable expense of a type farm (this term to include not only agriculture as a productive and economic activity, but also normal home life and the influences contributing to such) as an integral part of the instructional plan of the University for training in agriculture.
> 6. That this Committee approved the recommendation submitted by Dean Skinner that the present eight weeks' winter course in agriculture be extended so as to contain two terms of eight weeks each—one in the autumn and one in the winter.[78]

Meredith would have played an active role in preparing the review and all of the resulting recommendations, but her influence can clearly be seen in the request to include farm production and the accompanying home life as part of the Purdue agriculture curriculum.

Elliott turned to Meredith and the Committee on Agriculture to help him increase student enrollment in agriculture, reduce duplication of effort, make program administrators more accountable, and reign in program costs.

This was a tall order. It would take the Committee on Agriculture the better part of five years to unify the School of Agriculture. Change was often slow as the board tried to consolidate multiple programs with similar activities into a single program administered by one individual. These changes were significant as Meredith and her fellow trustees began the process of breaking down institutional barriers among the School of Agriculture, Agricultural Experiment Station, and Agricultural Extension Department:

> On the recommendation of the President [with the agreement of the Committee on Agriculture], the name of "Department of Farm Mechanics," as used in the School of Agriculture, and "Rural Engineering," as used in the Agricultural Experiment Station, be changed to the "Department of Agricultural Engineering," both in the School of Agriculture and in the Agricultural Experiment Station.[79]

And:

> On the recommendation of the President, the following joint recommendations in regard to the Department of Agronomy from Dean J. H. Skinner, of the School of Agriculture, and Director G. I. Christie, of the Agricultural Experiment Station and Agricultural Extension Department, effective September 1, 1926, be approved:

1. That the present Department of Agronomy, in the School of Agriculture, and the Department of Soils and Crops, in the Agricultural Experiment Station and the Agricultural Extension Department be consolidated into one Department to be known as the Department of Agronomy.
2. That Professor A. T. Wiancko be designated as the Head of the newly constituted Department of Agronomy, at a salary of $4,000.
3. That Professor M. L. Fisher, upon the assumption of his new duties as Dean of Men, retain his title of Professor of Agronomy in the School of Agriculture and also be designated as Associate in Agronomy in the Agricultural Experiment Station, at a salary of $1,000.[80]

The trustees on the Committee on Agriculture left no stone unturned as they dug into the affairs of the School of Agriculture. The committee members requested that Dean Skinner explain why it cost so much to run the Department of Dairy Husbandry, the Dairy Farm, and the Creamery.[81]

The board also directed Elliott to forward the following questions to Dean Skinner; Director Christie; Professor Howard W. Gregory, who was in charge of dairy husbandry; Professor Luzerne H. Fairchild, an associate professor of dairy husbandry; and Ralph E. Roberts, instructor in dairying:

> Conforming to the mutual understanding had at the conference on Tuesday afternoon, March 30 [1926], held for the purpose of examining into the finances and present operation of the Dairy Farm, the Dairy Herd and the Purdue Creamery, and of considering the possibility of devising more definite policies for the conduct and regular support of these University enterprises, you are requested to prepare proper statements concerning the following proposals:
>
> 1. Is it not possible so to increase the volume of business of the Purdue Creamery as to provide a safer margin of annual profit, thereby enabling the Creamery to be maintained on a self-supporting basis, including the expenditures for the replacement and the obsolescence of equipment?
> 2. Are the conditions surrounding the conduct of the Purdue Creamery as an educational enterprise such as to make absolutely necessary the adoption, by the Board of Trustees, of a policy whereby funds for the annual replacements and improvement of the equipment of the Creamery should be provided from sources other than the revenues derived from the commercial operation of the Creamery?
> 3. Under the existing student situation in the School of Agriculture, is not the Board of Trustees, in the interests of reasonable economy, justified in revising the report adopted in 1921 relative to the maximum numbers of livestock to be maintained on the Purdue University Farm so that these numbers will be reduced by at least one-third; such reduction also to apply to the number of the Dairy Herd?
> 4. Should not steps be taken by the University to dispose of the present Dairy Farm as such? If not, what plans should be adopted for the proper support and development of this farm?
> 5. Should not the amount of time devoted by students to livestock judging courses be substantially reduced?
>
> It will be appreciated, I hope, that these proposals are presented not from any hyper-critical standpoint. Rather from a desire that there may be a clearer

understanding by the Board of Trustees of the financial and educational responsibilities involved in the undertakings here under consideration.[82]

Skinner answered on behalf of his colleagues. He was, no doubt, annoyed at being questioned in this manner.

Some reasons why report on numbers of livestock to be kept on the farm should not be revised and the number reduced one-third.

1. The number of animals now on the farm is necessary to meet the requirements of the laboratory instruction and for demonstration purposes. In some classes, as for instance horses, the number is not adequate for instruction and farm work. In hogs the number is below requirements due to lack of housing.
2. The number of animals of breeding age on the farm has never exceeded standard and at present is 20 to 45 per cent below the standard set.
3. Representative herds of the more important breeds must be kept up to a certain minimum in order—
   a. To supply the needs for instruction and make possible successful practical breeding and management.
   b. To maintain breeding males in good condition and secure greatest value from them.
   c. To make necessary replacements and develop and improve the quality of the herd.
4. Young stock must be grown out so as to determine their value for replacement in the herds.
5. The capacity of available equipment for livestock on the University Farm is suited to the handling of numbers of animals set as a standard in the report.
6. To set a lower standard would mean that it would be necessary to maintain at all times the number of animals set by the standard and to do this would mean interference with practical management and the constant tendency to exceed it wheras the present standard makes it easy to hold down the number below the standard and does not handicap management.
7. To reduce the numbers one-third would not reduce the overhead costs to any large extent with the exception of cost of feed. This reduction in cost would probably be more than offset in sales due to the inability to make desirable improvements and necessity for elimination of animals before their value is demonstrated.

Reasons Why Time Given to Livestock Judging Should Not Be Reduced

1 — Ability to select suitable animals for different purposes is one of the
     big factors in profitable farming.
2 — The freshman course lays a broad foundation upon which students
     can build.
3 — The minimum of time is now required.
4 — Less time to judging would make the courses of little value.
5 — Many students and alumni want more livestock judging.

Skinner failed to answer many of the questions posed to him in the president's letter, so with a partial response in hand, Elliott then asked that the whole
matter of farm policy be referred to the Committee on Agriculture: Meredith,
Palmer Edgerton, and David Ross. On June 5, 1926, Meredith and the two other
trustees questioned Dean Skinner, Director Christie, and Professors Gregory
and Fairchild—all of whom understood that the committee had the full backing of President Elliott and were intent on getting answers to their questions.

> The morning session, which continued until noon, was devoted to a thor-
> ough discussion of the several issues relating to the Purdue Creamery,
> the livestock policy of the Purdue University Farm and the conduct of the
> Dairy Farm, as presented in the communication of the President of the Uni-
> versity dated March 31, 1926 and addressed to Dean Skinner, Director
> Christie, Professor Gregory, Professor Fairchild, Mr. R. E. Roberts.[83]

Following the morning meeting, the committee spent the entire afternoon
of June 5 touring the farm and inspecting the livestock. Meredith and her colleagues made the following report:

> Special attention was given to the development of the so-called Dairy Farm
> and to the condition of the equipment of the Purdue University Creamery.
> Before ending the session of the Committee at five o'clock, a visit was made
> to the lots which it is proposed to purchase for the use of the Horticul-
> ture Department of the Agricultural Experiment Station, said lots lying
> at the south end of Marsteller Street and adjoining the property now held
> by the University.

> As a result of the inspection of the farms, livestock, etc., the Committee
> makes the following additional recommendations to the Board of Trustees:

> 1. That while substantial progress has been made in the matter of the
>   utilization of the Dairy Farm for the purposes of providing forage crops

for the Dairy herd, those in charge of this Farm should each year present a detailed report setting forth the costs of the operation of this Farm.

2. That immediate steps be taken to provide funds for the repair of the refrigerating rooms of the Purdue University Creamery ($2,500); and that provision be made in the next legislative budget for the replacement of the present obsolete equipment of the Creamery and the installation of needed modern equipment such to cost approximately $25,000.

3. That a careful study be made to the present policy of purchasing feeding stuffs for both the Purdue University Farm and the several farms of the Agricultural Experiment Station with a view of discovering possible greater economies.

4. That the Committee recommend to the Board of Trustees that the twelve lots lying in the region of the south end of Marsteller Street be purchased from the funds of the Agricultural Experiment Station at an approximate cost of $7,000, such purchase to be made subject to the approval of the Governor.

5. That the Committee on Agriculture be instructed to continue its activities for the development, economy and efficiency of the agricultural instruction in the University.[84]

The Committee on Agriculture voted favorably on the following recommendations at the June 14, 1926, board meeting:

1. That the Committee on Agriculture recommends to the Board of Trustees the continuance at least until June 30, 1927, of the general policy for the operation of the Purdue University Farm, with special reference to the number of livestock maintained for the purposes of instruction, as set forth in the report approved by the Board of Trustees on June 7, 1921.

2. That the Controller of the University, with the active assistance of the Dean of the School of Agriculture, be instructed to secure, as far as may be economical and expedient, the necessary data for the fiscal year beginning October 1, 1926, relative to the gross and net costs of maintaining the Purdue University farm, including all livestock thereon, and to report the same to the President of the University for transmission to the Board of Trustees. And further, that said Controller, with the active assistance of the special committee now in charge of the Dairy Herd and Farm, be instructed to report in a similar way upon the cost of maintaining the Dairy Herd and Farm.

3. That on the basis of the foregoing data, there be devised a plan for allocating the cost of maintaining the Farm and herds as between use for the instruction of students and use for general public purposes.[85]

The first break for President Elliott to reorganize the School of Agriculture occurred when Professor Fairchild resigned from the Dairy Department in 1926. Elliott and his agricultural committee saw an opportunity to make drastic management changes for the creamery and for the dairy farms and livestock.[86]

Another break for Elliott came two years later in the form of George Christie's resignation. Christie told the president he intended to resign as director of the Agricultural Experiment Station and the Department of Agricultural Extension on September 1, 1928, to accept the position of president of Ontario Agricultural College in Guelph, Ontario, in Canada.

The board received notice of Christie's resignation at its June 11, 1928, meeting.[87] President Elliott and the trustees quickly consolidated the management of all of the agricultural programs under Dean John Skinner with a view toward streamlining all operations and cutting costs.[88]

Elliott and the trustees were quick to grab full control of the flow of money into and out of the Agricultural Experiment Station and the Department of Agricultural Extension, something they seemed unable to do when Christie was director of both programs. Meredith and her colleagues debated the matter of consolidation at length, finally voting in favor of the proposal to give Skinner full control of all of the agriculture programs.[89]

Once Skinner took over all of Purdue's agricultural operations, the Committee on Agriculture ceased playing a major role in the management of the School of Agriculture.[90] Meredith and the other committee members had done much of the unpleasant work in the consolidation that took place. By April 1931, Elliott and Skinner were working well together.

Today Purdue University's West Lafayette campus includes dozens of state-of-the-art buildings and thousands of professors, instructors, and other professionals teaching more than 39,000 students from around the country and the world. Systemwide, Purdue University enrolls more than 70,000 students from across Indiana, the nation, and the world. It is a world-class institution of higher learning, meeting tomorrow's challenges through its up-to-date education curriculum in the classroom, extension outreach to Indiana communities, and research programs that advance science by unlocking unsolved mysteries. The Purdue University Board of Trustees still plays an important role in the overall management of the university.

Nearly fifty years after Austin Claypool was named a trustee, his daughter, Virginia Claypool Meredith, followed in her father's footsteps as a Purdue University trustee, becoming the first woman to serve the university in that capacity. Meredith was a trustee at a time when women were demanding more from public officials and public institutions. During her fifteen-year tenure, she would be appointed five times by governors from different parties, different ideologies, and broad political spectrums.

She strongly believed in the mission and the work of the Purdue trustees. Even when her health required her to resign from duties and responsibilities to other groups, she still continued to attend trustee meetings on a regular basis.

Past writers have superficially examined her role as a trustee by focusing on her as the first woman to serve in that position. While this was, no doubt, an important historical distinction, her real work went way beyond the title. She stayed true to her convictions that women were an important part of Purdue University and that, in return, the university needed to do more for the women of the campus.

She would spend countless hours working on behalf of the School of Agriculture and the university as a whole to ensure that its students were receiving the best education. Her role may have gone largely unnoticed by the public, but it was significant, nonetheless. Those who benefited in the past and those who are still benefiting today from the work that she accomplished as a trustee may never realize the extent of her impact and the value that it has added to their lives.

A Landmark for Veterans
and a Home for Women

Today, on this May morning, wherever our flag flies there are roads of remembrance—
roads of remembrance *that lead to some consecrated place—*
roads of remembrance perhaps to the stately tomb dedicated to the unknown soldier,
or to the rows of soldiers' graves in the big cemeteries, perchance to the crosses
on Flanders Field, or to a long grave in a remote country graveyard.
Everywhere flowers are borne, beautiful flowers that speak a language
of remembrance and forget the ugly scars of war. . . .

—Virginia Meredith, from a speech given at the Purdue University
Memorial Day Exercises, West Lafayette, Ind., 13 May 1933

THE PURDUE MEMORIAL UNION STANDS at the eastern edge of Purdue University's West Lafayette, Indiana, campus, serving as a meeting place where students, faculty, staff, alumni, and the community can gather in a relaxed atmosphere. When traveling west on Indiana's State Highway 26 toward Purdue, the Union, as it is commonly known, is one of the first buildings visitors see on campus.

Each day thousands of people walk by a distinctive bronze plaque hanging on the first floor of the Union. This plaque is inscribed with hundreds of names of individual donors who financially supported the construction of this architecturally unique building. Little do people passing by know, however, that this impressive building has one of the most interesting and colorful histories of any building on the West Lafayette campus.

Virginia Meredith was heavily involved with the design, construction, financing, and management of the Purdue Memorial Union. However, she didn't start the process. Her efforts in the early 1920s to get the Union built were preceded by those of George O. Hays, a graduate of the Class of 1912, who had pushed for a student union a decade earlier. Hays successfully convinced the student council in 1912 to support a fund-raising drive to build a student union on campus, just like other midwestern universities had done. The members of the 1912 senior class and the seniors that followed them were each asked to donate five dollars to help finance this student union. These funds were turned over to Purdue's board of trustees for safekeeping until enough money was collected to support construction.[1]

World War I put the fund-raising campaign on hold. As Americans were focused on the hostilities in Europe, private donations for a student union nearly came to a complete standstill. The signing of the armistice on November 11, 1918, brought an end to the war and awakened in Americans the desire to honor those who had served in it. As a result, the initial concept of a gathering place for students that Hays had proposed years before evolved into a building memorializing Purdue's veterans.

Meredith became a strong proponent of the idea that Purdue University should erect a building dedicated to the 4,013 alumni who had served and especially for the 67 who gave their lives as the ultimate sacrifice.[2] In her notes, Mary Matthews, Meredith's daughter, demonstrated her mother's commitment to war-related efforts, noting that Meredith "[d]id much lecturing on behalf of various causes sponsored by the Council of Defense."[3] Meredith had lived through the horrors of both the Civil War and World War I, and now she had an opportunity to recognize the men and women who gave so much for the freedom of her country.

The memorial building project needed leadership and committees to work out many of the details during its construction. Organizers formed an unincorporated association, called the Purdue Memorial Union Association, complete with a leadership body known as the board of governors. The governors initially would oversee the financial campaign, the development and drawing of the building's design, and all aspects of the construction project. The organizers of the newly formed association asked the Purdue trustees to select three of its members to serve on this governing board. On September 2, 1921, the trustees chose Virginia Meredith, Joseph Oliver, and David Ross for this task.[4]

Meredith was a logical choice to represent the trustees since she was already an outspoken supporter for a memorial building. Five weeks later, the seventy-two-year-old Meredith—a novice trustee for just over three months—presented this resolution to the board of trustees:

> WHEREAS, It is the intention of the Purdue Memorial Union as an association to celebrate Armistice Day, Nov. 11, 1921, with formal ceremonies:

THEREFORE BE IT RESOLVED, by the Board of Trustees of Purdue University that its Building Committee is hereby authorized to invite the Building Committee of the Board of Governors of the Purdue Memorial Union to a conference and, if it is found desirable in order to promote the success of the Armistice Day ceremonies, the two committees shall jointly select, locate and mark on the campus as approximately as it can be done at this time, the southwest corner of the proposed Memorial building.[5]

Raising money for the construction of the Purdue Memorial Union would take center stage throughout the 1920s. Those paying a pledge of $100 or more toward the building fund would hold a special distinction at Purdue University. Not only would their charitable contribution allow them to become life members of the Purdue Memorial Union Association, but their names would also be "permanently inscribed in bronze in a display on the main floor of the building."[6] Pledges of monetary support from students, alumni, and others poured in from around the country.

Before long, Meredith had been named as the president of the Board of Governors of the Purdue Memorial Union. She would direct both the trustees and governors in the financing and construction of the building. Serving as a Purdue trustee and as president of the board of governors would be difficult. Meredith would have to make sure that each organization's interests were compatible with those of the other.

Meredith assumed this leadership position with the full expectation that this would be a quick construction project. The initial plans called for the building to be financed by private donations and placed on state-owned, university-controlled property. She couldn't foresee at the outset the problems that would arise when the Board of Governors of the Purdue Memorial Union Association eventually failed to meet their financial commitments. And she couldn't have realized that the odd combination of a privately supported building on a parcel of public land would ultimately force the trustees to take over the financing and management of the project.

So in early 1922, when Meredith, as president of the board of governors, and David Ross, representing the governors' building committee, came before the trustees to present their construction plans for the Purdue Memorial Union, they portrayed a rosy scenario regarding the amount of money that donors had pledged toward the project. Meredith told the trustees that the governors had approved a set of blueprints, which outlined the design and scope of the building project as well as the following:

> A financial statement from the Purdue Memorial Union [Association]
> shows total pledges for the Memorial Building $865,236.75
> Cash and bonds on deposit   126,467.69
> Estimated receipts by July 1, 1923   419,864.62
> Estimated receipts by July 1, 1924   531,529.43
>
> Pond & Pond estimate that the main section of the Memorial building can
> be erected and put in usable shape for $403,000.00, and its construction
> financed through the funds of the Union.[7]

Meredith's report referenced the architectural firm of Pond and Pond. Irving Pond (1857–1939) and Allen Pond (1858–1929) were prominent Chicago architects who were well known for their designs of student unions at the University of Kansas, University of Michigan, and Michigan State University.[8] Many of their buildings are still considered important for their historical architectural significance.

The financial plan indicated that the board of governors had an impressive sum of $865,236 worth of pledges. No one seemed too concerned at the time that the governors only had about ten percent of the total amount of cash actually in hand. However, the unpaid pledges would hamper the construction of the project for years to come.[9]

The board of trustees agreed in principle with the board of governors, and the trustees released the funds being held in escrow to start the project. The trustees also gave their approval of the architectural plans drafted by Pond and Pond, while retaining final approval for the building's location.[10]

The board of trustees agreed to let its own building committee enter into the contract for and generally supervise the construction of the Purdue Memorial Building. The control was such that the chairman of the Purdue Memorial Union Building Committee had to approve all fees and charges. The chairman would then submit his authorized expenditures to the secretary of the board of trustees, who would pass them along to the university treasurer for payment.[11] The trustees were now invested with the board of governors in the project. There was no turning back, as the trustees would find out in the near future.

The trustees debated for quite some time before deciding where to locate the building. They finally decided that it should be built on the southeastern edge of the campus, to give it a prominent and highly visible location.[12] And so on June 13, 1922, with her hopes running high, Meredith chaired the groundbreaking for the building. She introduced fellow trustee David Ross, who turned over the first spade of dirt, while the project contractor, A. E. Kemmer, laid the first furrow.[13]

Construction began in earnest on July 5, 1922, but less than a year later, excitement turned to disappointment as the board of governors ran out of money. To everyone's surprise, the donors were not honoring their commitment to pay off their pledges.

By the fall of 1923, the trustees knew that the project was in serious trouble. It became apparent that they might have to find the funds for the building's construction. If the project were left incomplete, the Purdue Memorial Union would be little more than an eyesore. Yet, the trustees did not want to assume full financial responsibility for the project. They released a veiled threat as a means of encouraging payment on delinquent pledges:

> THAT if possible, the Purdue Union Memorial Building should be made available for use. Otherwise it must be boarded up and remain in that condition until sufficient money can be collected on delinquent and maturing pledges to meet the bills for building and equipment. It is estimated that $300,000.00 will be required to complete and equip the building, including the cafeteria.[14]

The trustees were trying their best not to intercede beyond their initial commitments. David Ross, head of the Purdue Memorial Union Building Committee, spoke at the October 10, 1923, board of trustees meeting, stating that the "funds were exhausted for the present, as pledges had not been paid when due."[15] In fact, trustee David Ross, one of Purdue's all-time greatest benefactors, and fellow trustee Henry Marshall had borrowed a sizable amount of money from the First Merchants National Bank to roof the building before winter set in.[16] Without their beneficence, the building would have been left to deteriorate from that winter's wind, rain, and snow.

The news on the status of the Purdue Memorial Union had not improved when the trustees reconvened on December 21, 1923. Thus far, $350,000 had been spent on the partially completed building, but more than $500,000 remained uncollected from the now $969,615 in pledges. Marshall and the trustees agreed that the best avenue for financing the project was to have the Purdue Memorial Union Association incorporate as a legal entity. The association could then borrow $200,000 to "complete the essential features of the Building."[17]

Within days of the trustees' meeting, President Edward Elliott requested a meeting with members of the Purdue Memorial Union Association.[18] Elliott wanted the project completed to avoid any embarrassment to the university. He asked the association to incorporate and then issue $200,000 worth of bonds in denominations of $1,000 each, with the proceeds used to complete the building. In a bold move, the Purdue University trustees authorized Elliott to "guarantee the payment of said notes, both as to principal and interest and to endorse such guarantee on said notes."[19]

The agreements entered into that day between the president—who was representing the trustees—and the Purdue Memorial Union Association were written down into a memorandum of agreement, binding on both parties. Naively, the trustees clung to the notion that the university stood to lose little by backing the bonds. They believed that the individuals who had pledged their support were honor-bound to pay their pledged amounts.

By early April 1924, the Purdue Memorial Union Association had borrowed the necessary $200,000 to continue the start-and-stop construction project.[20] Everything seemed promising at first, but the cash-strapped project stalled again by July. Once again, the promised pledges had failed to materialize.[21]

The trustees, for the first time, chose to use university funds to bail out the project. They agreed to spend up to $30,000 to buy equipment for the building. For the short term, however, all equipment purchased by Purdue would remain the property of the university until such time as the association repaid the debt.[22]

The Purdue Memorial Union was still not finished when the doors first opened on September 9, 1924; however, a premature grand opening would allow the Purdue Memorial Union Association to quickly begin generating its own revenues.[23]

> The main floor had temporary pine floors, and the walls and ceilings had not yet been plastered. The second floor was not sufficiently finished in order to be available for use. . . . The ground floor of the original building housed the cafeteria, located on the southwest corner. . . . It contained two sets of serving counters designed to serve 1,000 people per meal. Weekly meal tickets were sold to students for $4.50, and the cafeteria served 240,000 in its first year.[24]

To raise cash, Meredith and her fellow trustees restructured the fees paid by students. Starting with the 1924–25 academic year, each student would pay an additional activity fee of five dollars per semester, with four dollars for the Purdue Memorial Union and one dollar to help pay for lectures and concerts.[25]

President Elliott was a stickler for keeping the university's financial affairs in order. At a meeting with the trustees on October 8, 1924, he voiced his displeasure about the methods used by the Purdue Memorial Union Association to manage and monitor expenditures. Because Purdue University and the trustees were now in a financial relationship with the association, Elliott had authorized the university controller, William Middlebrook, to oversee the association's finances.[26]

Middlebrook's findings led the university to assume the management of the Purdue Memorial Union Association's accounts. From that point forward, the accounting process used by the association's board of governors would have to conform to the standards that Purdue University used to run the campus.[27] Ever so slowly, control of the Purdue Memorial Union was shifting from the association to the university trustees.

If the association failed to repay the bonds when due, then Purdue University was on the hook for $200,000. The trustees realized that the only way they could avoid using university funds to complete the project was to make an all-out effort to collect the thousands of dollars in unpaid pledges.[28] They were ready to apply pressure on those who had, thus far, failed to pay. A letter sent out in 1925 by Purdue University politely but firmly requested that those who had not yet paid honor their commitment to the university:

Dear Sir:

At a special meeting of the Board of Trustees of Purdue University held December 31, 1923, the Board seriously considered the matter of the unfinished condition of the Purdue Memorial Union Building. At that time, owing to the delay in the payment of pledges, the building was in such a state of partial construction that rapid deterioration would ensue. Also the appearance of the building and grounds was most unsightly, producing a bad public impression of this most prominent portion of the Campus.

In view of the fact that all the pledges for the Purdue Memorial Union were in the form of legal obligations to the Board of Trustees of the University, the University itself was placed in a most difficult position. In order to relieve this situation and to proceed with the necessary minimum construction, the Board deposited your pledge along with others as collateral for a $200,000 gold note issue, guaranteeing the issue as the principal and interest. This gold note issue was effected through the Lafayette Loan and Trust Company of Lafayette.

The Lafayette Loan and Trust Company reports that to date payments on your note are delinquent. We do not wish any action taken which would cause you embarrassment, but we must call your attention to the fact that there are no funds other than the funds accruing from subscription pledges to meet these maturing gold notes.

Pending further action on the collection of overdue subscription notes, the Board of Trustees of the University at a meeting held April 8, 1925, instructed

the President and the Secretary of the Board of Trustees to communicate
with you and to report when you expect to discharge your obligation.

May we not receive a prompt reply from you concerning this matter so
important to the welfare of the University?[29]

The trustees were pleased by the initial responses. Some sent payment for
the full amount. Many others indicated their willingness to make partial payments over time. The letter garnered enough positive reaction that members
of the board decided to trust the sincerity of the donors and take no further
action at that time.[30] The trustees still believed that the subscribers who were
in arrears would soon make good on their promises.

On December 31, 1926, Meredith's term as a member of the Board of
Governors of the Purdue Memorial Union Association expired, but her fellow
trustees nominated her to serve another three-year term to represent their
views.[31] Apparently, even her involvement with this financial disaster had not
lessened the other trustees' opinion of her. She would finally see the Purdue
Memorial Union completed during this new term, but it would take another
three years of setbacks, compromises, and, finally, a takeover by the trustees to
bring her dream fully to life.

By January 1927, the hopes of the trustees were dashed when pledge
payments did not fully materialize. The trustees were not at all pleased. In fact,
in the weeks just prior to the January board meeting, President Elliott sent a
letter to the university's legal counsel, Allison E. Stuart, suggesting the need for
serious action:

... [I]t appears that the number of delinquent subscribers to the Purdue
Memorial Union Fund is too great to permit the payment of interest and
the serial redemption of the gold notes. In view of this contingency, the
officers of the Purdue Union Association some time ago sought the co-
operation of the alumni leaders, especially in the metropolitan areas,
to bring such personal and sentimental pressure upon the delinquents
as might result in the increase of funds available to the Purdue Union
Association. In a number of instances, the alumni leaders advised that
in all probability collection can only be secured through legal action and
advised that the necessary legal steps be taken to this end....

Will you please advise the Board of Trustees whether or not legal action
can be taken by the Lafayette Loan and Trust Company in the name of that
company, or must legal action be brought in the name of the Trustees of
Purdue University?[32]

Elliott was inclined to take those who hadn't paid to court, with the lawsuit brought in the name of the bank holding the loan. Stuart counseled otherwise, saying, "[W]e think, where it is necessary to sue on pledges to the Memorial Union Fund suit should be brought in the corporate name of the University as trustee for the Purdue Memorial Union Building."[33] Stuart estimated the cost at $10 to $50 per lawsuit.[34]

The cost to recover the money and the bad press it would generate among the Purdue alumni made this an unacceptable option for President Elliott and the trustees. So, once again, the trustees wrote to those who had not fulfilled their pledges, this time threatening to pursue legal action and strip them of life membership in the Purdue Memorial Union Association. The trustees even devised a plan to obtain partial collection of the funds.[35]

By 1929 it was clear that any further attempt to collect on back pledges was futile, and the trustees agreed to finance the remainder of the project.[36] They estimated that a bond issue for $410,000 would cover the cost of completing the design of the original building along with the new residence wing that they wanted to add.[37]

On May 14, 1929, members of the Purdue Memorial Union Association Board of Governors and Board of Directors met with members of the Purdue University Board of Trustees to discuss President Elliott's plans for completing the building. David Ross, who happened at that time to be the president of all three boards, called the meeting to order. When all was said and done, there was unanimous agreement to allow the board of trustees full control of the project.[38] By July 1, Elliott named Lloyd M. Vallely as the manager of the Purdue Memorial Union (1929–60), firmly transferring permanent control of the building to the university.[39]

It would take eight years from start to finish, but at the January 8, 1930, board meeting, the trustees were informed that the Purdue Memorial Union was finally complete and operational.

Purdue University did make a last-ditch effort to collect the unpaid subscriptions. The university was serious about this, even hiring a graduate of the 1930 class, Orval J. Martin, to help in the collection process. Martin, an outstanding former student athlete, visited alumni centers around the state, reminding people that Purdue still needed payment on the pledges to meet its obligation on the outstanding gold notes that were coming due.[40] But even this effort failed, and eventually, much would be written off as bad debt. The gold notes were retired in 1930.[41]

Meredith would offer her own words on both the difficulties and successes incurred by those wanting to see a memorial union on the Purdue campus. In a 1929 university pamphlet, Meredith wrote:

> The constitution which was to become the rule of action in all things pertaining to the Purdue Memorial Union was written with careful thought and had careful criticism. This constitution placed all administrative authority in a Board of Governors whose membership would include representation from students and faculty as well as from the Board of Trustees of Purdue.
>
> When the Board of Governors of the Purdue Memorial Union was organized there was given to me the distinguished honor of being elected its first president, having been previously appointed one of the representatives from the Board of Trustees. The memory of those early days is the memory of earnest men dedicating time, thought, and financial credit to a great purpose. Especially clear emerges the memory of two aspects of the undertaking—the ever widening vision of the social values involved—and the ever growing appraisal of the financial responsibility.
>
> In the afternoon of June 13th, 1922, amid the beauty of the campus in summer time, a goodly company assembled upon invitation of the Board of Governors to witness the significant ceremony of turning the first sod and running the initial furrow for the foundation of the stately edifice that was to be. The turning of that little spadeful of soil was followed by a stupendous effort to carry forward the memorial to commemorate a noble section in the history of Purdue University.
>
> On the morning of November 25th, 1922, in the presence of the Governor of the state, University officials and students, there occurred the classical ceremony of "laying the corner stone." The most interesting document deposited therein was the list of 7,020 persons whose subscriptions had made possible the beginning of the memorial. From this date until the completion in 1929 was a long road where disappointments and discouragements darkened the way, a time when only the persistent efforts of a few stalwart minds with fine courage kept the way open. This loyal group was inspired and sustained by a masterful conviction that here was a contribution of value to future generations of Purdue students—a contribution that would in some way promote the fellowship and the friendly virtues which are conceived to be a heritage from the noble 4,000 we commemorate in this Memorial Union.[42]

Meredith took on the Purdue Memorial Union construction project in September 1921—just two short months after becoming a Purdue University trustee—and saw the project through to completion in January 1930. History has long forgotten the difficulties associated with the funding and construction of the Union and even the names of those such as Meredith who were instrumental in bringing this extensive project to fruition. What does remain, though, is a well-known building that has long been the hub of the West Lafayette campus. Under its roof are the 192-room Union Club Hotel, ten retail restaurants, a bank, an art gallery, a full-service copy center, meeting rooms, ballrooms, and a recreational area offering bowling and billiards. Thanks to the perseverance of Virginia Meredith and others, the Union has provided lasting recognition for veterans and is a well-known campus landmark.

Meredith's work on the Purdue Memorial Union was accomplished as a member of the Purdue Memorial Union Association Board of Governors, which meant that she still had separate and ongoing responsibilities as a member of the Purdue University Board of Trustees during the Union's construction. When Meredith had become a trustee in July of 1921, she brought to the position a desire to see the university do more for women than what the trustees had done during the past fifty years. Simply put, Meredith focused her attention on redirecting university resources toward issues of importance to women.

Meredith's interest in women's issues was recognized and, for the most part, appreciated by her fellow board members. She was asked on numerous occasions to represent Purdue University at various conferences that dealt with women's issues. For instance, Stella Fox, president of the Lafayette branch of the American Association of University Women, wanted Meredith at her conference. Fox wrote to the trustees asking that Meredith be appointed to represent Purdue University at the 1924 convention in Washington, D.C. The association was offering a special session for women who were university trustees.[43]

Meredith convinced the board to accept membership in the American Association of University Women. It was a symbolic gesture in that Indianapolis was the host city for the group's upcoming national convention in the spring of 1925.[44] Meredith was asked to deliver a presentation at the convention, which she did on April 9, 1925. She also helped organize a conference for women university trustees to be held in the fall of 1925 at Bloomington, Indiana.[45]

There were occasions throughout the years when women's issues were very personal to Meredith. Early in her career as a Purdue trustee, the name of her adopted daughter, Mary Matthews, was brought up at a September 10,

1921, board meeting.[46] The death of Professor A. M. Kenyon, head of the Department of Mathematics, had left an opening on the faculty's executive committee. Dean of Men Stanley Coulter gave acting President Henry Marshall a list of five names from which to select Kenyon's replacement.[47] These names included Matthews from the Department of Household Economics, as well as Herbert L. Creek, head of the Department of English; Richard G. Dukes, head of the Department of Applied Mechanics; Martin L. Fisher, assistant dean of the School of Agriculture; and William Marshall, acting head of the Department of Mathematics.

Dean Coulter's list included candidates that he knew could ably serve on the committee, but he left it to the wisdom of the acting president to make the final selection. Coulter declined to recommend a specific candidate, saying, "I do not feel that you would make a mistake in naming any one of these."[48] Marshall decided to appoint Matthews to fill the vacancy:

> . . . because the Home [Household] Economics Department has no direct representation in the Executive Committee as now organized. As a further reason for this appointment, there has been but one woman member of the Committee and fourteen men. I feel that because of the large number of women students, there should be two women on the Executive Committee.[49]

Meredith was surely pleased for her daughter. Meredith had long fought for equal representation for women, and this decision highlighted the growing importance of women students and professors to Purdue University.

Given her commitment to women's concerns, it is not surprising that Meredith took up the cause of inadequate housing for female students at Purdue University. Meredith frequently brought up the need for Purdue University to spend more time and money addressing the needs of its women students. She was keenly aware of the inequities that existed between men and women on campus.

Campus housing for women became Meredith's leading cause as a trustee. Her goal was to keep President Elliott, other top university administrators, and the board of trustees focused on this one important issue. She pushed this agenda throughout her fifteen years as a trustee, and it took nearly all that time to see her dream of a new women's dormitory come to fruition.

When Purdue University offered courses to its first official class in 1874, it had but six faculty members, four dozen students, a 100-acre farm, and five buildings. Ladies Hall (1874–1927) and Purdue Hall (1874–1961) were two of those original buildings. Ladies Hall was the women's dormitory and Purdue Hall was the men's dormitory. Before it was demolished, Ladies Hall stood near the site that Stone Hall occupies today.

By 1921, Ladies Hall was a forty-seven-year-old, dilapidated building that no longer served as a dormitory. Just months after becoming a trustee, Meredith discussed the awful condition of the structure, the need to quickly rectify unsafe conditions, and the value of modernizing the building.

Meredith recognized that the board moved forward on agenda items and solved problems through committee work. If she wanted to get attention focused on Ladies Hall, she would have to get the president of the board to form a committee to investigate the issue. In 1921, Meredith, made a motion "that a special committee be appointed to investigate the condition of Ladies' Hall and report a plan for its future use."[50] She already had a plan. She wanted to reinstate Ladies Hall, at least for the short term, as a women's dormitory.

During the early 1920s, there were several hundred women attending Purdue. A large percentage of those women found housing through their association with campus sororities. Others lived at home with their parents or relatives. Some were fortunate enough to live in cooperative houses that Purdue rented from local residents. The women that Meredith was most interested in helping were students who secured room and board by hiring themselves out as cooks, maids, and servants in the community.

For Meredith, the availability and affordability of student housing for women was a glaring inequity that the university needed to set right. Meredith agreed to chair the committee on the future of Ladies Hall. It took her committee months to gather all of the information needed to discuss the options intelligently.

On March 14, 1922, Meredith presented to the full board her committee's findings and recommendations:[51]

To the Board of Trustees: Your committee appointed to investigate the condition of Ladies Hall and to report a plan for its future use, beg leave to report as follows: 1st. We found that the building generally needs extensive repairs and that a part is past repair. 2—We found that the main structure as originally built, when it shall have been vacated by the Home Economics Department, can be repaired at a comparatively moderate cost and arranged to meet the social needs of the women students in the University until such time as an adequate Woman's Building may be erected on the campus.

Therefore we recommend; (1) That the wing which was built as an addition to the main structure, at the northwest corner, be entirely removed, thereby restoring the original plan and proportions, and further, that the Building Committee be instructed to contract for this removal at the earliest time possible after the present equipment of the Home Economics Department shall have been removed to the new Home Economics Building [known today as Matthews Hall]; and at the same time to put the exterior of the building in complete repair, including a new porch and an approach on the south. (2) That authority be given this committee to employ a competent contractor to estimate the approximate cost of putting the interior of Ladies Hall in repair and equipped to meet the present social needs of women students; namely, substituting electric lighting for gas now in use, thoroughly overhauling or replacing the present heating apparatus, new flooring on the main floor, some replastering, a large opening with doors between the two large rooms on the main floor, the placing of suitable lavatories, closets and lockers on the second floor, redecorating the walls, painting wood work and such minor repairs as are necessary.[52]

Meredith was subtly suggesting to the trustees that they consider repairing and restoring Ladies Hall as a temporary measure until such time as a new women's dormitory could be secured on campus, which she believed the women really deserved.

An issue related to the renovation project came before the board a month later. Purdue University was asked to renew its lease for a home at 527 State Street that had housed a few of Purdue's female students.[53] Dean of Women Carolyn Shoemaker wrote to the Purdue president suggesting that the trustees should not renew the lease if, in fact, Ladies Hall would once again become a dormitory for women.[54] The trustees referred the matter to the Ladies Hall committee and made Dean Shoemaker an advisory member of the committee.[55]

It took the committee three fact-finding meetings over six weeks to file a final report on the future use of Ladies Hall.[56] The board received three recommendations: (1) to convert the building into a dormitory for women students; (2) to convert it into a social headquarters for women students; or (3) to repair the ex-terior, as already ordered, and postpone for one year any repairs to the interior.

Meredith indicated that she and most of her committee favored the first option, turning the Ladies Hall into a dormitory for women. Meredith asked the architectural firm of Nicol, Scholer, and Hoffman to develop a cost estimate for converting Ladies Hall into a dormitory. The architects estimated that the repairs and alterations—minus the purchase of furniture—would cost the university nearly $28,000.[57]

The board agreed with this proposition. They authorized the Building Committee to request construction bids for the project. Understanding that special equipment, furniture, wall coverings, and more were needed, the board formed yet another committee chaired by Meredith—this time with Ross and John Hillenbrand as members—to look into the purchase of these extra items.[58]

The trustees and the architects were astounded by the submitted bids, which were "so greatly in excess of the architect's estimates that none were accepted."[59] The trustees decided to scale back the work so that the cost of limited repairs, replacing the roof, and the purchase of furniture would only run between $5,000 and $6,000. In the fall of 1922, plans were scaled back, and the construction was completed by the start of the upcoming semester. Ladies Hall would now accommodate just fewer than fifty women.[60]

The board put just enough money into the project to keep the building useful. It was nothing more than a stopgap measure to get a few more years out of the structure. Only five years later, in 1927, President Edward Elliott and the trustees deemed that the cost of repairs for Ladies Hall—estimated to be $22,000—exceeded what they were willing to spend. The building had outlived its usefulness.

> [F]or repairing Ladies' Hall, one of the oldest buildings on the campus, or to cease using the building. The roof and the heating facilities should have been replaced this fall. The building, which is used as a woman's dormitory, accommodates only about fifty girls and is not suitable for this purpose. The matter was carefully considered, and the Board decided that because of its dilapidated condition and its unsuitability for use as a dormitory, it would be unwise to attempt to repair it or to make any further expenditures.[61]

Ladies Hall was torn down late in the summer of 1927, removing one of the last of Purdue's five original buildings.

While the building was razed, the water pump from Ladies Hall was left standing. The Physical Plant removed the old hand pump the following year, but it wasn't destined for the trash heap.[62] The pump had been in the same location—the southeastern corner of Ladies Hall—even before the building was constructed in 1874. Many of the alumni had fond memories of the pump, and it was said that "resourceful coeds used the pretense of getting water to supplement their dating with 'chance meetings' by the old pump."[63]

President Elliott, no doubt at the suggestion of some alumni, had the pump redone from top to bottom and relocated it south of University Hall. In 1958, the Purdue Reamer Club had the pump moved to the southeast corner of Stone Hall, where it remains today as a tribute to Ladies Hall and as a reminder of an era long gone.[64]

By all accounts, Meredith was pleased that removing Ladies Hall meant replacing the structure with a new women's dormitory. Tearing down Ladies Hall made Meredith's message about the need for adequate housing for women students even more pertinent. She continued to point out that most of the land-grant schools in the Midwest had already built modern dormitories for women.

As the last of the debris was being cleared away, Purdue University administrators renewed their practice of leasing space in local homes for women students. They were obligated to do so, because the destruction of Ladies Hall displaced approximately fifty women.[65]

Within a few months, the Vater house at 415 West State Street in West Lafayette was rented by Purdue University at a cost of $1,000 a year. It was referred to as a housing annex for women students. Apparently, it was a break-even proposition for Purdue. The rent paid by students covered the lease and other associated expenses.[66]

Another home—the George Dexter house located at 116 Marsteller Street—was rented to twenty women. The home was probably where today's Marsteller Parking Garage stands. Not only did it provide housing for women, but it also became the official office and home of Dean of Women Carolyn Shoemaker.

Meredith and Elliott clearly knew that renting homes for students was nothing more than a temporary fix for the problem at hand, which was a shortage of affordable housing for women. With Ladies Hall gone and more homes being rented to women, Meredith was able to convince the remainder of the board in the fall of 1927 that long-term housing for women needed to be provided sooner rather than later.

She was assigned to chair another committee to "investigate the matter of residence halls for women students, and to report upon the comparative value of the systems in use in other educational institutions."[67] It was the first time that Meredith was directly asked to explore the possibility of building a women's dormitory. In addition to Meredith, the committee included Purdue Controller Robert B. Stewart; Dean Shoemaker; Dean Mary L. Matthews; Professor Gertrude Bilhuber, head of the Department of Physical Education for Women; and Lella Gaddis, state leader of extension home economics. Purdue President Elliott and David Ross, president of the board of trustees, were *ex officio* members.

Meredith's committee met several times in the fall of 1927 to establish policies and begin the work.[68] Meredith suggested visiting the women's residence halls at the University of Illinois to get a better perspective on what it took to house large numbers of women on campus.

Meredith was pleased to learn that a reliable donor, well known to the board, wanted to support the construction of the dormitory. Frank M. Cary (1858–1936) and his wife, Jessie Levering Cary (1865–1927), had previously donated $50,000 to support a men's dormitory in memory of their son, Franklin Levering Cary. The younger Cary had been preparing to enter Purdue University when he died at the age of eighteen. The donation made by the Carys was combined with $180,000 that the university had borrowed and used to build the men a modern dormitory on property donated by Professor George Spitzer and Belle R. Spitzer.[69]

While the men's dormitory was nearing completion in 1928, Frank Cary approached the trustees to express "his satisfaction and pleasure in the Franklin Levering Cary Memorial Hall now being constructed as a Residence Hall for men students."[70] Cary then offered another $60,000 to erect a residence hall for women. He informed the trustees that he had originally made this request as part of his will, but because Controller Stewart had told him that the university was in desperate need for additional housing for women, he decided to move forward with the gift.[71]

Cary placed two conditions on the trustees: (1) that the architect who had designed the men's dormitory, Walter Scholer of Lafayette, be hired to prepare plans for the women's dormitory, and (2) that the dormitory be named in honor of his wife, who had died recently.[72]

Meredith personally thanked Purdue's benefactor for his generous and kind contribution by offering the following resolution:

> The Board of Trustees of Purdue University accepts with profound appreciation Mr. Cary's offer of $60,000.00 to be used in the erection of a Residence Hall for Women at the University. In his wish that the gift may serve as a memorial to his wife, the late Jessie Levering Cary, this Board promises cordial cooperation not only as a worthy memorial to a fine woman but also as an expression of the consideration and respect due to Mr. Cary on account of his friendly goodwill to Purdue University, which has been shown in repeated benefactions. By this gift, inaugurating an important development in education for women in Purdue University, Mr. Cary's foresight and understanding are destined to have a very great value, and merit the deep feelings of esteem and gratitude which we hereby express to him.[73]

The announcement of the gift coincided with the report that Meredith was preparing to deliver to the board of trustees. Her committee filed a partial report with the board, leaving for a later date the question of how a new women's dormitory would be operated.[74] The report provided some very specific design recommendations for the building. The proposed women's dormitory would have a capacity of 150 residents, which was about the same capacity as the newly constructed Cary Hall for men. In addition, the committee requested that the architect take note of residence halls at the University of Illinois, Indiana University, and Kansas State University.[75]

Frank Cary and the trustees signed a contract that identified each other's obligations, and the trustees assured Cary that they would borrow sufficient money to complete the women's residence hall.

Meredith and the other trustees were so confident that the project would go through that they decided they would no longer lease the home at 116 Marsteller Street.[76] As a result, Dean Shoemaker lost her office again and was given temporary quarters in the Engineering Administration Building.[77]

The committee reconvened to discuss the construction details with the architect. Walter Scholer drafted several plans, incorporating the wishes of Cary and the trustees. After some discussion, they all decided on a "group of four buildings with a central kitchen." They chose to locate the women's dormitory north of State Street on property known as the Russell land. Purdue University did not own this property at that time but expected to acquire it.[78]

Unfortunately, after what seemed to be a promising start, the project would soon face one roadblock after another, including a lengthy legal battle. In the fall of 1929, nearly two years after Cary had stepped forward with his $60,000, all planning progress came to a near standstill. Property owner Phillip Russell was unwilling to sell his land to the university because he believed that Purdue's offer was too low. Years before, his father and mother, Hiram and Rachel Russell, had donated to John Purdue property on which to build the university. The younger Russell, however, was not inclined to treat the university with the same generosity. Suits and countersuits ensued as Purdue tried to gain control of the Russell property by condemnation through eminent domain. The issue slowly wound its way through the legal system and would ultimately end up before the Indiana Supreme Court.

After nearly two years, Frank Cary grew tired of waiting and considered transferring his $60,000 toward building another men's dormitory or withdrawing it completely.[79] In an effort to avoid losing the donation, the trustees decided that "the President of the University, the President of the Board and

Mrs. Meredith be appointed a special committee, with power to act, to confer with Mr. Cary regarding his gift of $60,000, should any emergency arise."[80]

An initial ruling by the Indiana Supreme Court was in Purdue's favor, but it only addressed part of the land that Purdue University wanted to appropriate and not the tract on which the university wanted to build the women's residence hall. However, it was cause for optimism, and President Elliott asked Stewart to present the findings from his study to estimate the number of women who would eventually live in the university residence hall.[81] Stewart's report depicts the importance of sorority housing at Purdue University during the first quarter of the twentieth century:

> Controller Stewart stated that of the six-hundred and three undergraduate women now enrolled, one-hundred and thirty-five were residents of Lafayette; that reports from the sororities show that in order to maintain their houses two-hundred and twenty-five members are required; that approximately seventy-five girls are working for room and board; and about the same number work as much as possible. There are many girls who cannot afford to pay as much as $40.00 a month for shelter and subsistence.

> A general discussion followed from which it appeared: (1) That to insure enough occupants to place a women's residence hall on a paying basis, freshmen girls must be required to live there; (2) That such a regulation would seriously affect the finances of the sororities and could not be put into operation without due and sufficient notice; (3) That parents would probably approve the regulation as a protective measure for their daughters; and (4) That the plans and specifications previously presented must be modified in order to bring the cost within the sum which can wisely be expended for the construction and equipment of the building.[82]

Ultimately, Stewart predicted 118 freshmen women would occupy the new dormitory, but Meredith was not convinced that Stewart's estimate was accurate. She suspected that Stewart was trying to scale back the project.

Meredith asked Mildred Beisel, instructor in foods, to do another estimate on the number of women who needed housing on campus. Beisel believed that 254 women could reside in the hall but that many of them would not be able to afford the $375 to $405 annual rate contemplated by the committee. Meredith and the other committee members then agreed to create a financial revenue plan based on a minimum of 140 women and a maximum of 175 women. Beisel's numbers had helped Meredith to expand the project to accomodate more women.[83]

Stewart "... suggested that the Committee, in the light of this report, determine recommendations upon the following problems: (1) the size (capacity) of the proposed hall, (2) the rate to be charged for occupancy, (3) the financial plan to be followed, (4) the location of the building, (5) the matter of a name for the hall and (6) certain details of construction."[84] Ultimately, the committee members would recommend building a dormitory that would be rented to 159 women students at an individual cost of $375 per year.[85] The committee members also agreed to construct the south building of the group of four buildings first.

By this time, however, Frank Cary had found another venue to honor his wife. He had helped to build a new children's home in Tippecanoe County that had been named the Jessie Levering Cary Home for Children, so he no longer wished to name the women's dormitory in his wife's memory.

Everyone believed that, with a little bit of luck, the new women's residence hall would be opened by September 1, 1930.[86] Lack of a women's dormitory had, by now, begun to limit enrollment. President Elliott attributed fewer women students enrolling in 1930 to this stumbling block.[87] But the Purdue trustees' optimism about the construction of a women's dormitory would soon turn sour when they learned that Phillip Russell had again filed a legal action against Purdue University.[88] This bit of bad news was the last that Cary would tolerate; he wanted out of the deal.

Fortunately for Purdue University, Cary agreed to donate toward building another men's dormitory instead, to which the board—including a reluctant Meredith—agreed in April of 1930.[89]

By June 1930, arrangements for securing a residence hall for women were falling apart. Meredith must have been frustrated, having spent the better part of nine years working to improve campus housing for women with nothing tangible to show for her efforts. Purdue was so close to construction, but the feud between Russell and the university appeared to be intractable.

Stewart was unable to answer Meredith's questions about how long it would take to settle the litigation. However, he restored some hope to Meredith when he crafted a clever plan that not only made Cary happy but kept his donation committed to building a women's dormitory.[90] Stewart wrote:

> There is now a reasonable demand for another men's residence hall evidenced by the number of applicants who cannot be accommodated in Cary Hall and by the fact that our men students are willing to pay as much as $125 per semester for rooms in the Memorial Union. Since the opening of Cary Hall two years ago the enrollment in the University has increased by

some 400 students most of whom are men. Another hall housing about 125 would not absorb the increase and therefore would not disturb the fraternity system since that has not expanded during the interval considered. . . .

Since providing for the women's residence is most important, it is proposed that we proceed to build a new men's hall by issuing bonds for at least $185,000 as permitted by law, name this new hall to please the donor, take the donor's gift and apply it to the new men's hall. This would be effected as follows:

Mr. Donor gives us	$50,000. Cash
We sell bonds for approximately	$185,000. Cash
We then have	$235,000. Cash

We pay the cost of the new men's hall, approximately, $185,000. We retain for future use, $50,000, which is the remainder left from the bond issue to be used for "other dormitory construction purposes."

When we come to build the women's hall, we will have a sum of $50,000.00 and need sell bonds only for the balance needed. The men's hall of proved earning capacity will carry its cost, the donor will have his building and we will have assured safe financing for the women's hall which can be built then upon settlement of the present litigation. Meeting of Committee on Physical Plant and Equipment, May 15, 1930.[91]

During the summer of 1930, Stewart worked with Cary to broker a new deal for a men's dormitory to be called Franklin Levering Cary North Hall.[92] Purdue, with a now $190,000 bond in hand, was ready to begin building the additional men's dormitory, with rooms at Cary Hall North available near the end of January 1931.[93]

In July the state Supreme Court found in favor of Purdue's bid to appropriate the tract of Russell's land where the university proposed to build the women's dormitory. The court appointed a board of appraisers to establish a fair value on the property. The trustees were chagrined to learn that the appraised value was $1,000 an acre—Russell's original asking price. Purdue University officials thought the land was overvalued and chose to contest the appraisal.[94] While the legal proceedings continued, the board continued exploring ways to fund construction of the women's dormitory, estimated to cost $250,000. The trustees still had $50,000 of Cary's money that had not been spent on preliminary costs such as planning and architectural fees. Fortunately, a new potential source of funding presented itself when the National Industrial Recovery Act, administered by the federal Public Works Administration, was instituted in June of 1933 to create public construction jobs.[95]

Purdue University surveyed its female students to see how many of them would actually rent rooms in the dormitory if it were built within the next year.[96] Dorothy C. Stratton, who had replaced Carolyn Shoemaker as the dean of women, wrote up the results:

My dear President Elliott:

Dr. [Harriet] O'Shea [of the Educational Psychology and Nursery School Administration and in charge of personnel work for women] and I finished yesterday the survey of a representative cross section of women students on the matter of residence in the proposed dormitory next year. The enclosed card was used. Some students were interviewed personally, others were reached through the Physical Education and Home Economics classes. There was no selection—sorority and local women were included. The total number included in the survey was 296. Of this number there were 143 Freshmen; 56 Sophomores; 75 Juniors; 21 Seniors, and 1 Special.

In answer to the question, "If a dormitory for women similar to Cary Hall for men were available at $40 a month, would you choose that in preference to your present living arrangements?":
    69 answered Yes
    9 were doubtful
    218 answered No

The percentage of "Yes" answers was 23. That was nearly one-fourth of the entire group. The number of "Yes" answers may be somewhat increased by the optimism of youth.

On the basis of this sampling of the "climate of opinion" of the women students, and assuming that we shall have 450 Sophomore, Junior, and Senior women next year, which is our approximate enrollment of these groups now, slightly over one hundred women now in school should be available for dormitory residence next fall. If one adds to this number the incoming Freshmen and the additional students who might be attracted to Purdue by a residence hall it seems that we should have no difficulty filling the 115 spaces available.

Twenty-three women indicated that they prefer a single room, 27 prefer the double room where both sleep in the room, 12 prefer the double room with one sleeping in the room and one on the sleeping porch, 6 did not answer the question.

Of those 218 students who answered "No":
  88 live at home
  60 live in sororities
  43 find the cost too high
  27 indicate no reason

The nine women classified as "doubtful" are mostly those who cannot afford $40 a month. Of the 27 who indicate no reason, it is probable that lack of money is the cause. There seems to be general enthusiasm for the dormitory, but widespread disappointment at the cost. We should not fail to recognize that the construction of the proposed unit, desirable as it is, does not touch the housing problem of a great many of our women who want group life and University supervision but who cannot afford the price. They are now existing on $20–25 a month.[97]

Purdue's protracted legal proceedings against Phillip Russell ended anticlimactically in 1934 with an Indiana Supreme Court decision transferring title on 32.45 acres of Russell's property to Purdue University for $32,002, which included the land for the women's dormitory along with an intramural field.[98] Real cost to Purdue amounted to nearly $1,100 an acre when interest, legal services, briefs, and abstracts were added to the calculation.[99]

Controller Stewart gave the trustees the green light, saying that this, "under the judgment referred to, finally ends all litigation and legal entanglements pertaining to this land and the University may henceforth enjoy it in any manner which the Trustees may direct."[100]

With the legal wrangling finally finished, the project was put on the fast track. A revised construction cost was estimated at $255,000, and the funds to pay off the building loans would come from the anticipated 125 students paying $225 a year for rent and board.[101]

In the spring of 1934, the Purdue trustees learned that the Public Works Administration would grant the university funds to cover thirty percent of the cost of labor and materials on the women's dormitory as well as provide a loan of $115,000. The trustees unanimously approved the federal government's terms.[102] Purdue also tapped additional university funds to build the dormitory at a final cost of $259,000.[103]

On April 25, 1934, the efforts by Meredith and, indeed, of her entire committee came to fruition when the trustees convened to receive bids for building and equipping the long-awaited women's dormitory.[104] The board accepted the lowest bids that same day, and work on the women's dormitory started soon thereafter.[105]

After securing the necessary funds and accepting the construction bids, the university made sure that the dormitory was a wise investment by requiring that all freshmen women not living at home reside in the new women's residence hall. Only the dean of women had the authority to waive the housing requirement for these students.[106]

The university prepared an information pamphlet called "Women at Purdue University," which described educational opportunities for women at Purdue and announced the opening of the new dormitory, now officially called Women's Residence Hall. The pamphlet was sent to all women graduating from Indiana high schools at that time along with a card for requesting information regarding the hall.[107]

Less than six months later, the trustees toured the newly completed Women's Residence Hall. They were even served lunch in the dining hall.[108] An official dedication in the large living room of the hall took place as part of the homecoming events on October 20, 1934.[109] Approximately 150 people attended the opening and listened to Virginia Meredith as she presided over the events. President Elliott; David Ross, president of the board of trustees; Bess Sheehan of the Indiana Federation of Clubs; and Inez Canan, a 1916 home economics graduate, all spoke during the ceremonies.[110]

In addition to the speakers, the event included a cornerstone ceremony, which included a time capsule of sorts.[111] According to the *Purdue Exponent,* "the contents of the box placed in the cornerstone were various pamphlets on the activities and curriculum for women, a memorial to Dean Carolyn Shoemaker, copies of the *Exponent,* plans and photographs of the hall, a Bible, and records of the organization of the institution's [Purdue's] administration."[112] Meredith gave the closing address, which she kept very brief by dedicating the building "to the happy and useful living of Purdue women students."[113]

Meredith's dream of a women's dormitory had become a reality. Built to accommodate 119 women, 112 applications were received when it opened in September 1934. Just one year later, there were 189 applications for housing there.[114]

Getting Women's Residence Hall built had taken nearly thirteen years, but Meredith knew she had contributed to a better learning environment for women students at Purdue. Touring the dormitory early in the fall of 1934, she could sense the impact that the building would have on the women who would call this place home. The building, today named Duhme Residence Hall, stands several blocks west of the Purdue Memorial Mall and still serves as a women's residence hall.

Even though Meredith was, by this time, eighty-five years old, she was still up to the challenge to do more when Dean of Women Dorothy Stratton called for yet more housing for women students the following year.[115] Stratton had conducted another survey, concluding, "private homes are still housing as many women as the University and the sororities combined" and noting, "The impossibility of achieving any kind of uniformity of supervision in this number of houses is apparent."[116]

Stratton also noted that she was placed in an awkward position when parents asked her to recommend off-campus housing for women students. She identified a serious problem to the trustees:

> The University prints in its catalog the statement that "women students may live only in houses approved by the Dean of Women." I am thus placed in the position of recommending to students and to parents houses which I know and which they soon learn are not desirable and, in some instances, not even safe places for their daughters to live.[117]

Meredith saw a new opportunity to erect yet another dormitory for the women students.[118] Controller Stewart, who had a knack for getting outside donors to help with Purdue projects, explored funding possibilities for an expansion of Women's Residence Hall. He contacted Frances M. Shealy, who, in 1935, had created the Joanna Barry Shealy Fund as a loan program to assist deserving women students in the university.[119]

Stewart convinced her to use $70,000 of this fund toward the construction of an addition to the women's residential hall. Shealy indicated to the trustees that she would "appreciate it if the new facilities provided a room and bath for my use if required. Such a provision, with the annuity provided, would then more completely assure my security during my remaining lifetime."[120]

Meredith surprised everyone when she cast the only vote against the motion. She did so because she felt that simply building an addition to the existing structure trivialized women's needs on campus and that a second women's dormitory was in order. When the board then expressed its interest to prepare the plans for the "addition to the Women's Residence Hall, to provide accommodations for approximately 72 additional women students at an estimated cost of $95,000," Meredith again cast a "no" vote.[121]

Meredith's last meeting as a trustee was on April 15, 1936. But she continued to work hard, questioning Stewart's justification for planning an addition to the current women's dormitory instead of building another one. Eventually, Meredith convinced the board to change their plans from building an addition

to constructing a new women's dormitory. The board passed the following resolution at that meeting:

> Mrs. Meredith raised the question of the adequacy of the plans for an
> addition to the present Women's Residence Hall and asked the Controller
> to state the financing problems involved if an approximate duplicate of the
> present Women's Residence Hall were to be constructed instead of the addi-
> tion formerly contemplated. The Controller stated that bonds could be sold
> at the present time on a 3¼% basis. If the proceeds of the Shealy gift, as
> well as a 45% grant from the Public Works Administration, were available
> for the project, a new building similar to the present structure might be
> undertaken safely by the University, without increasing further the rates for
> board and room for women students. However, if a grant from the Public
> Works Administration were not available, it would be necessary to increase
> the cost of room and board for women students in the residence halls if an
> additional similar building were to be erected. Thereupon, Mrs. Meredith
> presented the following resolution and moved its adoption:
>
> WHEREAS, pursuant to a certain resolution adopted by this Board on
> December 21, 1935, an application has been submitted to the Federal
> Emergency Administration of Public Works for a grant ($61,875) in aid
> of financing the cost ($137,500) of additions to the present Women's
> Residence Hall on the campus of Purdue University, and
>
> WHEREAS, to more adequately meet the needs of residence facilities for
> women at the University, it is now the desire of this board to erect a
> separate, additional women's residence, similar to the present Women's
> Residence Hall on the campus of Purdue University; now, therefore,
>
> BE IT RESOLVED that the officers of the University be and they are hereby
> authorized and empowered to file an amendment or supplement to the
> application now pending before the Federal Emergency Administration of
> Public Works for aid in financing a new, separate structure similar to (not
> an addition thereto) the existing Women's Residence Hall, and
>
> BE IT FURTHER RESOLVED that David E. Ross, A. B. Gray, and F. C. Hockema,
> respectively President, Treasurer, and Secretary of said corporation, and
> Edward C. Elliott, as President of said University, and each of such officers,
> be and they are hereby authorized and empowered to execute any and all
> applications, amendments or supplements to applications and other neces-
> sary or proper instruments required by said Public Works Administration

in connection with its consideration of the construction of said building as a Public Works Administration project.[122]

Stewart had already made an application to the Federal Emergency Administration of Public Works for a smaller grant for the addition. The board, agreeing with Meredith, redirected him to amend the application to include a proposal for erecting a women's dormitory similar to Women's Residence Hall.[123]

Purdue, consequently, received another sizable grant from the Federal Emergency Administration of Public Works. The federal government agreed to fund 45 percent of the projected expenses up to $142,200.[124] In addition, the university would sell $125,000 worth of bonds, and Frances Shealy's contribution would add another $63,000 toward the construction expenses.[125]

During this time, Meredith's health deteriorated, confining her to her home and causing her to miss the trustee meetings after that April 1936 meeting. Her colleagues on the board sent a card, letting her know that her presence was missed and including a special message from the secretary of the board of trustees: "[We] are happy to inform you that your dream regarding a second Women's Residence Hall has come true."[126] Virginia Meredith would not live to see Women's Residence Hall–North open in September of 1937. Today, Shealy Residence Hall—named for Frances Shealy—stands just north of Duhme Residence Hall.

In 1952, sixteen years after Virginia Meredith's death, Purdue University honored her by naming a brand-new women's residence hall as Meredith Hall. It was a fitting tribute to her work to secure safe and affordable housing for the women students of Purdue University.

Meredith's efforts in the 1920s led to the building of two dormitories for women students, who made up a relatively small percentage of the student body at that time. Today, Purdue's West Lafayette campus has more than 16,000 women students, comprising 42 percent of the university's enrollment. One-fourth of the women live in university-managed residence halls—nearly all of which are coeducational. Though many changes have occurred since Meredith's days as a trustee, the legacy of her accomplishments on behalf of women students still remains more than seventy years later.

Farewell to the
Grand Lady of Agriculture

⚬ ☙ CHAPTER 10 ❧ ⚬

With the wisdom that comes by experience
we may learn that here and now dwells happiness
if we have a mind to discern it.

—Virginia Meredith, from a speech given at the Annual Conference
of Farmers' Institute Workers, West Lafayette, Ind., October 1910

THROUGH HER WORK IN MANY AREAS, Virginia Meredith had become an elder statesperson on farming, rural life, family, education, and women. Her common sense approach to life, her unwavering belief in people, and a pleasant personality led to numerous invitations to social clubs and professional functions. People wanted her at their programs, sometimes as a speaker, but more often than not, just for her presence. Meredith's counsel was sought out by other university trustees, college professors, teachers, and students at Purdue University.

Her personal presence was such that it left a lasting impression:

> One recognized in Mrs. Meredith the best in womanhood,—a friendly and delightful personality, versatile in her tastes and talents, courageous and frank in supporting worthy causes, tireless in her own quest for knowledge, fearless in her championing of careers for women, and always a loyal exponent of public education. She was possessed of a wonderful sense of humor, sympathetic understanding and staunch integrity, and retained a remarkable alertness of mind throughout her entire life.[1]

Both Meredith at age seventy-five and Latta at age seventy-three must have been pleased to make the cover of the 1923 *Indiana Farmer's Guide,* one of Indiana's leading agricultural papers. The accompanying tribute describes their contributions to the betterment of the rural Hoosiers:

Two of Purdue's veteran agricultural workers, Prof. W. C. Latta and Mrs. Virginia C. Meredith, are paid the tribute of having their picture on the cover page of the last issue of the *Indiana Farmer's Guide*. The picture was taken at the recent county agent conference where both were in attendance. . . . The editorial page of the *Farmer's Guide* gives an explanation of the picture and pays the following tribute to the two: "The cover page picture this week is one of unusual interest to Indiana farmers. It shows two of the oldest and best known agricultural workers in the state, Professor W. C. Latta and Mrs. Virginia C. Meredith. Professor Latta has long been in charge of the farmer's institute work and is a professor of agriculture at Purdue University. The development of agriculture of Indiana is in no small measure due to the untiring efforts of this grand old man. Mrs. Meredith has had a wide experience as a practical Shorthorn breeder, and a speaker and writer on agriculture. She is now one of the trustees of Purdue University and edits a department in a leading livestock journal. Few women of Indiana have reached a higher place in the prospect of the public than Mrs. Meredith.[2]

Professor William Carroll Latta's last years were spent writing a book titled *Outline History of Indiana Agriculture*. He placed Virginia Meredith in select company when he listed her among the leaders who he thought were instrumental in bringing about meaningful change to the lives of Hoosier farmers and their families. Meredith was the only woman on Latta's list of historically important agriculturists in the state. She would take her place alongside her father-in-law, Solomon Meredith, who also made Latta's list.

Leaders of Progress—We thus see that such aggressive apostles of progress as John H. Farnum, the Owens, John McClure, Caleb Mills, Henry Ward Beecher, W. H. Ragan, H. M. Simpson, Joe A. Burton, C. M. Hobbs, E. Y. Teas, Sylvester Johnson, I. D. G. Nelson, Dr. A. C. Stevenson, J. D. Williams, Sol[omon] Meredith, Joseph A. Wright, Dr. R. T. Brown, Adams Earl, James Riley, I. N. Barker, James A. Mount, H. F. McMahan, J. G. Kingsbury, J. J. W. Billingsley, John B. Conner, Ben F. Biliter, L. B. Clore, Mrs. Virginia C. Meredith, and many others, at different periods and in their several spheres of influence, were getting in their good work. By precept and example they were injecting the ferment of new thought which was slowly but surely leavening public sentiment in favor of wider intelligence and higher standards of living on the farm and making possible a more scientific, more practical, and more successful pursuit of agriculture.[3]

In 1931, the *Christian Science Monitor* recognized the eighty-three-year-old Meredith as a woman who stood out in agriculture. The headlines read: "Write Their Names High on Agriculture's Roll of Honor."[4] The subtitles to the article read: "Women Become Full Farmers in Activities of Agriculture" and "The Effect of Women in Business." This article brought national prominence to her and six other women not only for breaking down gender barriers but also for becoming accepted among the agriculturists of the day. It described the important role women played on the farm and noted their contributions to agricultural associations:

> Farm business woman, she is called, and it is no contradiction of terms in the year 1931. Thousands of her kind, good homemakers all, are also full partners in the agricultural enterprise of their men folks. Not only do they bring in much needed cash by raising poultry, eggs and vegetables and selling them with other products of their skill in their own roadside or town markets, but they keep the books for the farm business, study cooperative marketing and speak up in organization meetings of the great benefit of the industry, say its leaders.

> The city woman who would seek to take part and even hold office in her husbands' trade association would be something of a novelty, but farm women are active participants in both the National Grange and the American Farm Bureau Federation, two leading organizations of American farmers, and no one thinks of criticizing.

> So general, indeed, is the partnership of man and woman in the farm economy that the individual cases of women who have succeeded in running farms of their own have come in for little notice.[5]

Meredith must have smiled as she sat in her rocker in front of the fireplace on that chilly November day, reading the last paragraph of the article. In her younger days, great notice and much attention was given to women such as herself who managed the entire farming operation. Fifty years later, the *Christian Science Monitor* stated that "900,000 women were gainfully employed in agriculture, while 257,000 women owned farms or were tenants. Nearly ten thousand were farm managers and foremen."[6] The barrier had not only fallen, but the notion that gender made a difference in agriculture had been shattered forever. She knew that, in a small way, she had helped to create this drastic change within the agricultural profession and among women in general. As she folded up the paper, she must have leaned back in her chair and breathed a deep, satisfied sigh of happiness.

Meredith's last major address was at the Purdue University Memorial Day Exercises held in Eliza Fowler Hall on May 30, 1933. Titled "Roads of Remembrance," this speech has been cited as an important presentation that she made to the faculty and students as a Purdue University trustee (see appendix 5 for full text):

> Today, on this May morning, wherever our flag flies there are *roads of remembrance* [italics in original]—roads of remembrance that lead to some consecrated place—roads of remembrance perhaps to the stately tomb dedicated to the unknown soldier, or to the rows of soldiers' graves in the big cemeteries, perchance to the crosses on Flanders Field, or to a long grave in a remote country graveyard. Everywhere flowers are borne, beautiful flowers that speak a language of remembrance and forget the ugly scars of war. . . .

> One never ceases to wonder, to speculate, about the world war—was it a rendezvous of youth? I have a fantastic notion that there was held a conclave of the spirit of youth. Did they, the youth from every nation, find that they were speaking the same language—a language not understood by their elders? Did they, in that strange language, in some mysterious mood, in some strange place—high Olympus or deep cave of the gods— did they say to each other that they would bring to pass a new order? That they would take apart the old world and put it together again after a new pattern? Is this chaos that is now so confusing, so perplexing, that one cannot discern whether it is the trumpet call of the new order or the wail of farewell to the age—is it the old hope of a time when war drums should throb no more? . . .

> The past is safe—let us cherish it. Always there will be open roads of remembrance whereon shall crowd those who seek a lost love and others looking for courage glorified, for sacrifice sanctified by faith. Wherever they may be, these hallowed places known to each heart, we would invoke for them the benign mood of Nature. . . .[7]

Meredith continued working right up until her death. She made her last presentation in 1936, on the occasion of the tenth anniversary of the Purdue School of Home Economics. She must have felt a sense of pride as she looked across the audience, thinking back to a time when women were not given such career opportunities.

One of her last writing assignments was to pen the introduction to a book published in 1936 called *Stories and Sketches of Elkhart County* written by Henry Bartholomew, who was the president of the historical society in Elkhart County, Indiana. As it was throughout Meredith's life, agriculture was the central theme:

> Truly many have perished unknown to fame. So it comes to pass that we should honor the writers who are willing to patiently explore the story of the past, in order to discover the beginnings—to trace the way to fine things.
>
> One who would write history needs not only discernment in aptitudes and activities of individuals and groups of individuals but needs to have an understanding of the fertility of the soil in giving opportunities to these to develop. A great English Statesman has said that "Livestock is the prop of great agriculture" and it remains undetermined whether the Briton created roast beef or whether the roast beef created the Briton! And who shall say just how much the fertility of the corn-belt has contributed to the perfections of homes and highways which now are accepted as the high mark of accomplishment in a century's influence of the Indiana pioneer. And too, there must be a discriminating look at the emigration of the early days—did any very considerable number come from barren soil of mountain or hill countries—or did the traditions of better things come with those who came from the fertile soil, where had been established the better ideals of living. Whatever angle may be followed it is the beginnings that hold unfailing interest and we are forever the debtors of those who have the taste for this study, who have the patience that will not stop short of the ultimate truth, who preserve the careful restraints of truth and at the same time preserve a readable story. Let us thank the one who like this author is willing to work faithfully in recording the story of early pioneer life when trends were established because ideals were created and nurtured with integrity of soul and vision of a good life in a fair country.[8]

In the last years of her life, Meredith's path would cross with that of the famous young pilot, Amelia Earhart, who was hired by Purdue University in the fall of 1935. Purdue President Edward Elliott had convinced Earhart to join the Purdue staff to assist young women students in choosing their career paths. Earhart became an important symbol for Purdue University and would stay at the campus until 1937, when she embarked on her around-the-world flight that ended in her mysterious disappearance in the Pacific Ocean.

Earhart's love of flying took her away from campus for most of the year, but for about six weeks each year she lived on campus working with the students. Her time at Purdue was spent giving presentations on opportunities for women and leading classroom discussions on aeronautical science. It must have pleased Meredith to hear Earhart and others of that generation promoting the idea that educated women with skills and talents could perform any job that the workplace offered.

In 1934, Meredith sat at the speaker's table as Amelia Earhart spoke to an audience of 500 people at Purdue University.[9] Meredith had introduced the aviator to the crowd and would do so again the following year, when Earhart was formally introduced to faculty and students as a member of Purdue's faculty.[10] On November 11, 1935, Meredith provided the opening remarks when Earhart spoke to a crowd estimated at 3,500 in the Purdue Memorial Gymnasium. Meredith praised Earhart, saying she was very courageous in her work, "breaking down the competitive struggle for social advantage between men and women."[11] The idea of equal opportunity for women formed the basis for an important bond between the two women whose generational differences and personal backgrounds were remarkably different.

During her introductions for Earhart, Meredith sometimes "took the occasion to recall some of her own pioneering work."[12] It must have been exhilarating to listen to Meredith talk of a past where she had to break down barriers facing women and moments later hear Amelia Earhart talk of a future where women could go wherever their aspirations and training would take them.

Meredith had enjoyed good health most of her life. However, in September 1936, she suffered a debilitating heart attack that left her bedridden.[13] President Elliott and her fellow trustees were worried about her declining health and discouraged by her absence at trustee meetings. To bolster her spirits, they sent her flowers and a get-well note:

> On behalf of the members of the Board of Trustees and the President of Purdue University, I [Frank Hockema, secretary to the trustees] have been instructed to express to you their deep sympathy on account of your inability to be present at the special meeting today....
>
> The roses sent to you with this are messengers of cheer and friendliness. If wishes were effective, you would soon be enjoying buoyant good health and your usual busy days.[14]

No one knew at that time that Meredith's health would not improve. Within three months, she would die from complications arising from the heart attack (see appendix 6 for full details found in her published obituary). On December 10, 1936, Virginia Claypool Meredith, the woman who had been called "the most remarkable woman in Indiana" and "Indiana's most widely known farmer," died at 4:30 P.M. in her home on Waldron Street. She was eighty-eight years old.[15]

The *Lafayette Journal and Courier* reported, "Messages of sympathy poured into the household from over the state and nation, attesting widespread interest in the aged woman, her life work covering a span of more than three quarters of a century."[16] It was obvious that Meredith had had a profound impact on many people through her articles and speeches around the country, and numerous personal connections.

Newspapers from around the country announced her death, often adding editorials further noting her accomplishments.[17] The *Indianapolis Star* wrote: "The activities she sponsored are now familiar in all state and university departments of physical education, home economics and farming, yet her memory deserves lasting honor throughout the years as one of Indiana's galaxy of outstanding women."[18] The *Purdue Alumnus* noted, "Yet that keen-eyed, intensely active pioneer, Mrs. Virginia Claypool Meredith, honorary member of Lafayette Altrusa, is not only keeping her pace with the world today—she is watching the world catch up with her."[19]

The *Lafayette Journal and Courier* extolled Meredith and her accomplishments (see appendix 7 for full text of article):

The spirit of Mrs. Virginia Claypool Meredith, her glowing faith, her pioneer personality, her abiding Americanism, her sane and sound wholesomeness, envigored and expressed with the true orator's force and clarity, will continue for many years to influence the lives and careers of her friends and associates left behind.

Mrs. Meredith was remarkable in so many ways it is difficult to appraise her services without appearing to exaggerate. To rhapsodize, or wax fulsome in her praise would be to risk feeling in imagination the frank displeasure of a plain-thinking, plain-speaking spirit, one of whose most charming characteristics was a sense of humor....

Whether as an aggressive, successful stock-raiser, carrying on the large business of a departed husband; as a messenger to farmers' institutes, passing on her own experiences to men and women; as an orator contacting groups in many other states; as an educator establishing new ideas and

modern methods, or as the distinguished trustee of a university, working with extraordinary energy and loyalty for progress and soundness
in teaching Americanism and wholesome, common sense doctrines and
homely living to the young, Mrs. Meredith was ever a valued contributor to
the general good. She had very definite fundamental ideas as to the aims
and functions of Purdue university as a sound factor in the education of
young womanhood for home-making.

Keen of wit, zestful, humorous, understanding, sympathetic, widely read,
quick at repartee, sure in decision as between right and wrong; courageous and frank in support of her convictions, Mrs. Meredith combined in
one vibrant and friendly personality those myriad qualities that make for
leadership.

Neither titles nor medals of precious worth, nor the applause of thrilled multitudes may express with any measure of adequacy the significance or extent
of the great service she rendered to her state, to Purdue university and to
those who were fortunate enough to know her as friend and counsellor.[20]

President Edward Elliott provided a tribute on behalf of her friends on the
Purdue University Board of Trustees and her university family:

Thus comes to an end a brilliant career of devoted service to the nation,
the state, the University and above all to the advancement of the place of
women in our civilization. All who had the privilege of working with her
were constantly the beneficiaries of her kindly and farsighted wisdom.
She was an ideal University trustee. The best of her life was built into the
University she loved so much and served so well. This is indeed a time of
sadness and grief for all of us.[21]

Services for Meredith were held the following Saturday at her Waldron
Street home, presided over by the Reverend Dr. W. R. Graham, minister at
Central Presbyterian Church in Lafayette. The School of Home Economics
cancelled classes that morning to allow students and faculty to attend the
services.[22] Her family honored Meredith's request to keep the service a simple
affair. The *Journal and Courier* noted that "the funeral of the distinguished rural
welfare leader . . . was free of all ostentation, its simplicity reflecting the gentle
nature of the woman who had earned a state's gratitude for outstanding civic
service."[23]

At 9:30 that Saturday morning, "buglers at different stations on the campus
sounded taps while all activities ceased. Home economics classes were dis-
missed for the entire morning. The campus flag was at half staff."[24]

The pallbearers included Purdue President Edward C. Elliott, Robert A. Simpson of the Purdue University Board of Trustees, and Dean Andrey A. Potter of the engineering school. After the service, many of those in attendance departed West Lafayette for Cambridge City. As they passed through Indianapolis, the funeral procession was provided with a police escort through the city. Virginia Claypool Meredith was laid to rest next to her husband, Henry Clay Meredith, in the Riverside Cemetery in Cambridge City.[25]

Meredith's will was executed on December 31, 1936, by Judge John B. Hudson.[26] Written nearly ten years before her death, the will was a brief half-page note—single-spaced and handwritten—that stated:

> On this second day of May 1927—I, Virginia C. Meredith, do make this my last will—I give and bequeath to Mary Lockwood Matthews my household goods, furniture and silver—Also give and bequeath to her any and all property of any description that I may have at the time of my death—I do this in recognition of the affection and care which she has given to me, and trusting her to give to Meredith Matthews [Meredith's adopted son and brother to Mary Matthews], to Virginia C. Miller [Meredith's niece] and Austin B. Claypool [Meredith's nephew] some suitable memento or remembrance from me.

On January 12, 1937, a month after her death, Purdue University paid homage to Virginia Meredith by holding a memorial for her at Eliza Fowler Hall. The special memorial service was, according to President Elliott, "a fitting part of the program of the annual Agricultural Conference and Farm Bureau Day."[27]

President Elliott presided over the service, while Meredith's pastor, the Reverend Graham, conducted the invocation and closing benediction. The Purdue University Concert Choir led by A. P. Stewart, the music director, provided a warm setting for the ceremonies.[28]

Addressing the audience were individuals who had personally known Meredith and had interacted with her through many of the organizations that comprised so much of her life's work. Meredith's agricultural ties were honored by Earl Robbins from Centerville, representing the Indiana Livestock Breeders Association, and by Albert Ferris from Milton, representing the Indiana Farmers' Institutes, where Meredith had participated for more than two decades as a speaker.

Two groups that Meredith had helped to organize and had served as president for sent representatives as well. Mrs. George W. Jaqua represented the

Indiana Federation of Clubs, while Mrs. Elmer Waters spoke for the Indiana Home Economics Association.

Mary E. Tyler, a Purdue senior, represented Omicron Nu, the national honorary society for home economics, of which Meredith was a member. Another Purdue senior, Lillian A. Murphy, spoke on behalf of the Virginia Meredith Club at Purdue.

David E. Ross, a longtime friend and colleague of Meredith, spoke on behalf of the Purdue University Board of Trustees, a group that Meredith had served for the last fifteen years of her life. The Purdue University trustees provided this written tribute to Meredith as well:

> With sincere sorrow this Board records the death of Mrs. Virginia Claypool Meredith at her home in West Lafayette, December 10, 1936, at the age of eighty-eight years. This tribute to one who was a valued friend and colleague for the past fifteen years comes not alone from the Trustees, as an official Board, but also from them as individuals.
>
> Mrs. Meredith was a woman of rare qualities, of great intellectual strength, of highest ideals, of gracious personality. She was meticulous in the discharge of all her duties as a Trustee, and while her special interest was in the women of the University—for whom many of her dreams and aspirations were realized—the problems of the University as a whole engaged her mind to an extent and with a completeness that was indeed remarkable.
>
> Mrs. Meredith was not only a brilliant woman, of wide interests, with a comprehensive grasp of the many difficulties that beset the Board, but she was also a loyal and understanding friend, wise in her counsels, keen but kindly in her criticisms. She was ever alive to world conditions and world problems, yet vitally interested in the home and its influence. She was a delightful hostess in a home which one entered with joy and left with a consciousness of uplift and of blessing.
>
> Words, no matter with what depth of sincerity they are spoken, are after all an evanescent tribute. In the work she did, in the lives she helped, in the inspiration she gave, Mrs. Meredith created her own enduring memorial.
> Signed: Edward C. Elliott
>   James W. Noel
>   Robert A. Simpson
>   David E. Ross, Chairman[29]

But it was a moving piece written by Esther Marguerite Hall Albjerg, a history instructor at Purdue, that captured the meaning of Virginia Meredith's life to all, reflecting on how a farmer's daughter had touched so many people during her long and productive life:

> Two generations ago an English statesman wrote Lady Beaconsfield, "There are things in the world which one not only enjoys at the time but which one remembers always." An acquaintance with Mrs. Meredith was just such an experience. In some ways, she personified the pioneer woman at her very best; that is, she was versatile in her tastes and talents; she was courageous in her championing of worthy but still unpopular causes; she was tireless in her own quest for knowledge and in her advocacy of public education; she was a practical states-woman who wanted to translate the theory of popular democracy into a workable reality; she was an ardent idealist who always thought life an occasion for the rendering of creative service.

> There were at least three qualities which Mrs. Meredith always revealed whether she was entertaining her club with her inimitable reminiscences or introducing Amelia Earhart in an incomparable manner to a vast student audience or directing the thoughtful attention of those attending a Memorial Day service. These attributes were: a remarkable intellectual alertness that had survived the physical disabilities of increasing years and had withstood the mental inertia of comfortable middle age; a glorious sense of humor which enlivened all she said and invariably added memorable wit and epigram to the occasion which her presence graced; an unfailing evidence of sterling integrity which unconsciously gave moral dignity to what she said and enhanced the influence of both her deeds and her words. You might not always find yourself in agreement with her but invariably you honored her for her sturdy and well-defended argument. She could advocate her viewpoint with disconcerting directness, but throughout her long life-time, she remained a stranger to malice and pettiness.

> The extraordinary fullness of her life, the wide extent of her beneficent influence, and the singularly arresting quality of her personal character remind one of those great American women of whom Edwin Mims has said: "They have lighted fires on the altars of human souls; they have made the light to shine in the dark corners. Their children have been incarnate ideas in the lives of others. They have done for the State and for the communities what others have done in the homes."

> Even during the past decade, Mrs. Meredith remained a remarkable woman who at four score years had won a moral triumph over the infirmities of advancing age, who continued to pioneer in the realm of ideas even if no longer able to do so in deeds, who could still move with distinction and

converse with brilliance in company with the keenest minds of her day. Furthermore, to know her was to feel the chastening inspiration that can come only from contact with a truly great and noble gentlewoman.[30]

It was a fitting tribute to Virginia Claypool Meredith, whose mark on Purdue University, women's education, and American agriculture would, indeed, be a lasting one.

This dormitory was constructed to accommodate the 1897 arrival of the first women students to attend the University of Minnesota's School of Agriculture, some of whom are pictured here. Courtesy of the University of Minnesota Archives.

An interior view of a room within the women's dormitory. Courtesy of the University of Minnesota Archives.

Virginia Meredith as pictured along with another staff member in a 1900 University of Minnesota brochure. Courtesy of the University of Minnesota Archives.

The dining room at mealtime. Virginia Meredith is pictured just to the right of the pillar, facing the camera. Courtesy of the University of Minnesota Archives.

Mary L. Matthews at
graduation from the
University of Minnesota's
School of Agriculture in 1900.
Courtesy of the University
of Minnesota Archives.

Mary L. Matthews, circa 1918.
Courtesy of the Robert Miller
Family.

A course description for Meredith's classes at the 1897 Purdue University Winter School of Agriculture, also known as the Winter Short Courses. Courtesy of Archives and Special Collections, Purdue University Libraries.

Virginia Meredith in her mid- to late forties, circa 1895.
Courtesy of Indiana Historical Society, Indianapolis.

The Breeder's Gazette

Vol. LXVIII. CHICAGO, JULY 8, 1915. No. 2. 1,754.

MRS. VIRGINIA C. MEREDITH, A "GAZETTE" CONTRIBUTOR AND AN EMINENT LEADER IN THE
ADVANCEMENT OF FARM WOMEN.

Virginia Meredith was featured on the cover of the *Breeder's Gazette* on 8 July 1915.
The photo was taken in 1895, when Meredith was forty-six. Courtesy of the Robert Miller Family.
Reproduced from the *Breeder's Gazette*.

THE VIRGINIA C. MEREDITH PAGE

One of "The Gazette's" Most-Esteemed Contributors This Week Assumes
Editorial Charge of a Page to Be Devoted to the Women and
the Boys and Girls of the Stock-Farm Home

VIRGINIA C. MEREDITH'S PAGE

Lessons From the Life of Trees—An Ancient Elm in Indiana—The Appearance and Falling
of Leaves—"What An Old Tree Says to the Young"

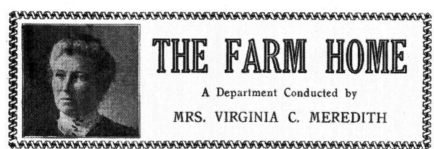

THE FARM HOME

A Department Conducted by

MRS. VIRGINIA C. MEREDITH

The Home

Conducted by

MRS. VIRGINIA C. MEREDITH

The name of Meredith's *Breeder's Gazette* column changed several times from 1921 to 1924,
but she retained editorial control. Reproduced from the *Breeder's Gazette*.

Virginia Meredith helped purchase the painting *An Old Red Dress* by John Millikin King to honor the memory of Lucy Wallace Wade, an instructor of home economics at Purdue. Today the painting hangs in Matthews Hall on the West Lafayette, Ind., campus. Reproduced with permission from *The Scrivener Magazine.*

Virginia Meredith, age seventy-five, in 1924. Courtesy of Archives and Special Collections, Purdue University Libraries.

In 1916, Virginia Meredith moved to West Lafayette, Ind., to live with her daughter, Mary Matthews. The two eventually moved into this home at 629 Waldron Street in 1927. Courtesy of the Robert Miller Family.

Virginia Meredith sitting in her Waldron Street home, circa 1930.
Courtesy of the Robert Miller Family.

The Purdue University trustees were photographed at Eliza Fowler Hall during Meredith's first year as a board member in 1921. Front row (left to right): Henry Marshall, John Hillenbrand, Meredith, Joseph Oliver, and David Ross. Back row (left to right): Purdue President Winthrop Stone, Cyrus Hobbs, James Noel, Andrew Reynolds, Franklin Chandler, and Perry Crane.
Courtesy of Archives and Special Collections, Purdue University Libraries.

The Purdue University Board of Trustees held most of its regular meetings on the West Lafayette, Ind., campus at Eliza Fowler Hall, shown here circa 1929. Courtesy of Archives and Special Collections, Purdue University Libraries.

The Purdue University trustees pose on the steps of Eliza Fowler Hall on 4 January 1928. Front row (left to right): Mary Williams (board secretary), Virginia Meredith, David Ross, John Hillenbrand, and Joseph Lilly. Back row (left to right): James Noel, Palmer Edgerton, Robert Simpson, Purdue President Edward Elliott, and J. E. Hall. Courtesy of Archives and Special Collections, Purdue University Libraries.

Virginia Meredith's last board meeting, 15 April 1936. Seated clockwise around main table, from left: Purdue President Edward Elliott, Purdue Controller Robert Stewart, and trustees Palmer Edgerton, Robert Simpson, Meredith, James Kimbrough, David Ross, J. E. Hall, Joseph Lilly, John Hillenbrand, and James Noel. At back table: F. Hockema, secretary of the Purdue Board of Trustees (left), and Jean Harvey, title unknown. Courtesy of Archives and Special Collections, Purdue University Libraries.

John Millikin King's 1929 portrait of Virginia Meredith (right) hangs in Meredith Hall, a women's residence hall, on the Purdue University campus in West Lafayette, Ind. *Reprinted with permission from the* Richmond (Ind.) Palladium-Item.

The south side of Ladies Hall (below), facing State Street on the Purdue University campus, West Lafayette, Ind. One of Meredith's first projects as a trustee was to work for improvements to this building, which was eventually torn down in 1927. It stood near the present-day site of Stone Hall. *Courtesy of Archives and Special Collections, Purdue University Libraries.*

Laying the cornerstone of Franklin Cary Memorial Hall, 5 November 1927. Pictured are (left to right): Russell Gray, title unknown; Purdue President Edward Elliott; Virginia Meredith; Purdue trustee Henry Marshall; donor Frank M. Cary; Purdue trustee E. Perry; and P. Judah, title unknown. Courtesy of Archives and Special Collections, Purdue University Libraries.

Purdue University honored Virginia Meredith in 1952 by renaming this women's residence hall as Meredith Hall. Courtesy of Arlene Blessing.

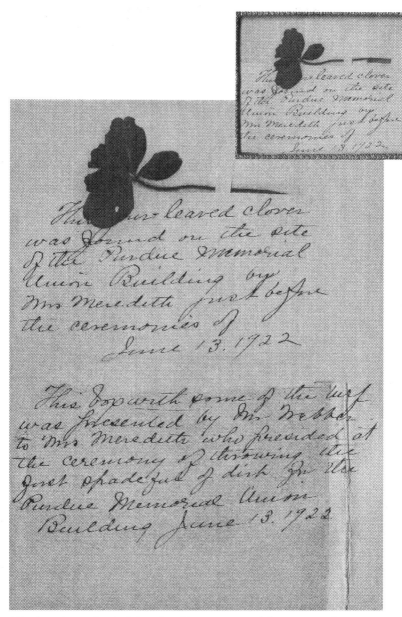

This photo shows a four-leaf clover found by Virginia Meredith just prior to the groundbreaking ceremonies for the Purdue Memorial Union on 13 June 1922.
Courtesy of Archives and Special Collections, Purdue University Libraries.

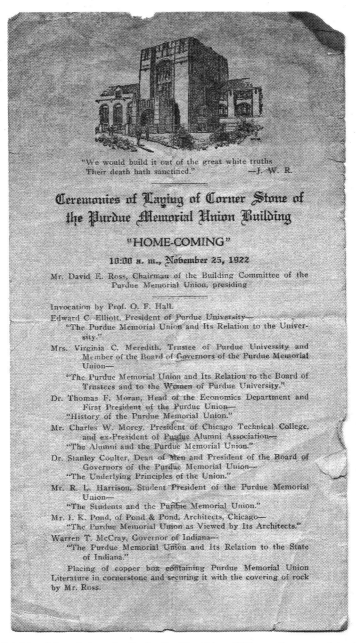

"We would build it out of the great white truths
Their death hath sanctified." —J. W. R.

Ceremonies of Laying of Corner Stone of the Purdue Memorial Union Building

"HOME-COMING"

10:00 a. m., November 25, 1922

Mr. David E. Ross, Chairman of the Building Committee of the
Purdue Memorial Union, presiding

Invocation by Prof. O. F. Hall.

Edward C. Elliott, President of Purdue University—
"The Purdue Memorial Union and Its Relation to the University."

Mrs. Virginia C. Meredith, Trustee of Purdue University and
Member of the Board of Governors of the Purdue Memorial
Union—
"The Purdue Memorial Union and Its Relation to the Board of
Trustees and to the Women of Purdue University."

Dr. Thomas F. Moran, Head of the Economics Department and
First President of the Purdue Union—
"History of the Purdue Memorial Union."

Mr. Charles W. Morey, President of Chicago Technical College,
and ex-President of Purdue Alumni Association—
"The Alumni and the Purdue Memorial Union."

Dr. Stanley Coulter, Dean of Men and President of the Board of
Governors of the Purdue Memorial Union—
"The Underlying Principles of the Union."

Mr. R. L. Harrison, Student President of the Purdue Memorial
Union—
"The Students and the Purdue Memorial Union."

Mr. I. K. Pond, of Pond & Pond, Architects, Chicago—
"The Purdue Memorial Union as Viewed by Its Architects."

Warren T. McCray, Governor of Indiana—
"The Purdue Memorial Union and Its Relation to the State
of Indiana."

Placing of copper box containing Purdue Memorial Union
Literature in cornerstone and securing it with the covering of rock
by Mr. Ross.

**Virginia Meredith spoke just after Purdue President Edward Elliott at the ceremonies to lay
the cornerstone of the Purdue Memorial Union, held 25 November 1922 during Homecoming.**
Courtesy of Archives and Special Collections, Purdue University Libraries.

326

Indiana Governor Warren McCray provided the closing remarks at the Purdue Memorial Union cornerstone ceremony, 25 November 1922. Virginia Meredith (wearing a black hat) is seated at the far left of the raised platform. Courtesy of Archives and Special Collections, Purdue University Libraries.

An early photograph of the Purdue University Memorial Union, circa 1935.
Courtesy of Archives and Special Collections, Purdue University Libraries.

President Edward Elliott places a flower on the grave of John Purdue while Virginia Meredith (fourth from right) and David Ross (third from right) look on during the 1933 Memorial Day Exercises on the Purdue University campus in West Lafayette, Ind. Courtesy of Archives and Special Collections, Purdue University Libraries.

Virginia Meredith (first row, second from left) was joined by daughter Mary Matthews, dean of the Purdue School of Home Economics (back row, fifth from right), and Purdue trustee David Ross (first row, first from left) at the dedication of the Women's Residence Hall at Purdue University in West Lafayette, Ind., on 20 October 1934. Others pictured include staff members from the new dormitory and representatives from several midwestern universities and women's groups. Courtesy of Archives and Special Collections, Purdue University Libraries.

Ceremony marking the opening of Women's Residence Hall in West Lafayette, Ind., 20 October 1934. Virginia Meredith (standing holding cane) dedicated much of her fifteen-year tenure as a trustee to improving living arrangements for the women students at the university. Courtesy of Archives and Special Collections, Purdue University Libraries.

Virginia Meredith (center) at her last public speech, given in 1936 on the occasion of the tenth anniversary of the Purdue University School of Home Economics. Standing (left to right): Mary Beeman, assistant in the Home Administration section of the school; Elizabeth Elliott, wife of Purdue President Edward Elliott; David Ross, trustee; Meredith; Inex Canan, of the Women's Residence Hall; Mary Matthews, dean of School of Home Economics; and Dorothy Stratton, dean of women at Purdue. Courtesy of Archives and Special Collections, Purdue University Libraries.

Virginia Meredith in her early seventies, circa 1920.
Courtesy of the Robert Miller Family.

The Order of the Exercises Held in Memory of

Mrs. Virginia Claypool Meredith

at

Eliza Fowler Hall

on

January the Twelfth
Nineteen Hundred and Thirty-seven

•

Presiding
PRESIDENT EDWARD C. ELLIOTT

Organ Prelude
H. I. METZGER

Invocation
The REVEREND W. R. GRAHAM
Central Presbyterian Church

Purdue University Concert Choir
A. P. STEWART, Music Director

Addresses
MARY E. TYLER, Omicron Nu.
    National Honorary Home Economics Society.
LILLIAN A. MURPHY, Virginia C. Meredith Club.
MRS. GEORGE W. JAQUA, Indiana Federation of Clubs.
MRS. ELMER WATERS, Indiana Home Economics Association.
EARL ROBBINS, Indiana Livestock Breeders' Association.
ALBERT FERRIS, Indiana Farmers' Institutes.
DAVID E. ROSS, Board of Trustees, Purdue University.

Benediction
The REVEREND W. R. GRAHAM.

Organ Postlude
H. I. METZGER

Purdue University issued a memorial booklet and held a campuswide memorial service for Virginia Meredith on 12 January 1937. Pictured here is the order of the service and names of participants as included in the booklet. Courtesy of Archives and Special Collections, Purdue University Libraries.

Epilogue

❦ EPILOGUE ❦

VIRGINIA MEREDITH WAS BREAKING NEW GROUND in the 1880s, just as women around the country were asking and demanding to be heard. With each passing year and each new achievement, her fame and influence grew, making her contributions complex and nuanced. She was one of the first women to manage a large farming operation, to stand on a podium addressing men on livestock production, and to promote equal opportunities in agriculture for women.

Meredith grew up with wealth in a family that broke from the tradition that a woman's place was only in the home. Her parents believed that Virginia should be free to choose a life that matched her talents. Austin and Hannah Claypool also knew that Virginia's success would depend upon her having a well-rounded education. A formal education, a love of reading, and a desire to continue learning throughout life were her parents' greatest gifts to her.

Her mother taught her about the science of managing a home and the art of entertaining guests, while her father taught her to understand the business of farming—what worked and what didn't. She also learned the importance of local and national politics. Family, education, farming, business, and politics were the foundations of her childhood. She had at her disposal all of the advantages that an influential family could offer a child, and she used them well.

As Virginia Meredith came of age, she was a well-read, college-educated woman who held strong opinions about the world around her. She rarely backed down from a challenge, always putting up a good fight on causes she deemed important. She was eloquent in her arguments and forceful when persuasion was needed. Even though she professed strong opinions, she made friends easily and retained their lifelong loyalty.

Her life and education took on new meaning when she married into the famous Meredith family from Cambridge City, Indiana. Overnight, she was thrust into the political world of her father-in-law, General Solomon Meredith, and her husband, Henry Clay Meredith. Her connections with the general allowed her to dine with presidents and mingle with those who were at the upper levels of power in American society in the late nineteenth century.

Many descriptions have been used to identify the complex woman named Virginia C. Meredith: farmer, speaker, writer, club woman, lady manager, professor, trustee, and pioneer. While her accomplishments are diverse, Meredith was most proud of being a farmer. It was her passion for agriculture that allowed her success in managing Oakland Farm and Norborough Farm at Cambridge City.

All in all, her experiences with the Claypool and Meredith families gave her the technical training and the personal confidence necessary to manage Oakland Farm when her husband unexpectedly died early in their marriage. Virginia not only successfully managed the farm but also kept it prosperous by producing Shorthorn cattle and Southdown sheep that breeders from around the country wanted for their own herds. It was at Oakland Farm that she honed her skills from a young woman with an agricultural background into an experienced farm manager with an aptitude for the male-dominated business. Over time, her novelty as a woman farm manager gave way to an appreciation of her worth as a livestock expert who knew how to raise quality animals. It was a slow transition, but men eventually came to recognize her as an astute livestock breeder and shrewd businessperson, and accept her as a knowledgeable colleague.

Whether or not Virginia Meredith wanted the spotlight, she readily became a symbol to others that women could achieve success in vocations traditionally held by men. The farm gave Meredith independence and security, which was something that women of that day found difficult to achieve on their own. Along the way she developed a talent for observation that continued to add more meaning to her experiences of what did and did not work at her farm.

In the late 1880s, Professor William Carroll Latta of Purdue University clearly understood that this woman rancher from eastern Indiana was, first and foremost, a very knowledgeable livestock breeder. He soon hired her to discuss the importance of purebred livestock at Farmers' Institutes. It would take time, but the men to whom she was speaking forgot that she was a woman and listened intently to her practical advice on raising purebred livestock.

As a paid lecturer for Purdue University's Farmers' Institutes, Meredith crisscrossed the state on trains and in horse-drawn carriages in the winter, talking about livestock management, the farm home, and education for women. She was a deliberate speaker, with words used eloquently, arguments filled with facts, and points stated intelligently. She became one of the most requested speakers in Indiana and soon began making speeches around the country as one of the first female lecturers on agricultural subjects.

She could and did talk about her success in farming and agricultural production, but in the same conversation, she often spoke out about the home. Meredith wanted women to get a college education on par with men and became an outspoken activist on the significance of the rural farm home as the cornerstone of the farmstead. As Meredith spoke in front of audiences and penned articles that found their way into magazines, journals, and newspapers, she developed a national reputation that eventually opened up many doors for her as her career extended beyond the farm.

At the same time that Meredith was expanding her influence in agricultural circles, she was also helping expand the influence of women in general through her club work, using these groups to further the intellectual and societal interests of the women they served. Meredith believed that effecting social change hinged on changing public sentiment, and she recognized that clubs offered a way for women to bring their collective voice to bear on issues of importance to them. While Meredith and other well-known women of the time may have received credit for this work, Meredith would likely have acknowledged the thousands of women whose names were not written in books but who made it possible for succeeding generations of women to advance the issues important to them.

Meredith's accomplishments and political connections in Indiana helped to secure for her an appointment as one of the state's lady managers to the World's Columbian Exposition in Chicago. In that position, Meredith's leadership skills came to the forefront and she was widely recognized as she successfully handled many of the difficult issues that the Board of Lady Managers faced at the Chicago fair. Becoming a lady manager was a defining moment in the transition of Meredith from a well-known agricultural woman from Indiana to a national spokesperson on women's issues.

Soon, in addition to being a voice for women's education, she became a pioneer, as she was asked to establish a home economics program at the University of Minnesota. Her early efforts in the field of home economics led the way for many of the land-grant universities, such as Purdue University, to establish home economics schools.

After leaving Minnesota, Meredith continued to be a forceful advocate for professional and educational equality for women through her work as a Purdue University trustee. In that capacity, she became a voice for women students and helped shape the policies of the university at a pivotal time in its history. During her time on the Purdue University Board of Trustees, she became known for her work in breaking down the barriers that existed all around her. She was a fighter who never gave up a fight. She might lose a battle or two, but in the end, her views often prevailed.

She stayed true to her belief that issues related to women students needed to be addressed by the university, working even harder to convince others when she failed to advance her position. David E. Ross, a longtime colleague of Meredith's on the Purdue Board of Trustees, wrote about his first-hand experience listening to her discuss her points of view:

> Virginia C. Meredith was a woman of the highest ideals and courage. Her loyalty was unquestioned. She was inflexible in her principles and adherence to conscientious objectives set for herself. Her life was dedicated to the betterment of women, and never did she lose sight of her goal.
>
> She always met discouragement with perseverance and was generous to a fault with those who opposed her, endeavoring to win new converts to her cause by tolerance, understanding, and kindly persuasion where a less brilliant intellect would have failed. It is most gratifying to know that many of her dreams and aspirations for women were realized . . . as an example of what can be done through the resourcefulness, wisdom, energy, and sincere devotion of a great and noble character.[1]

While written in a very polite and respectful manner, Ross's words underscore that Meredith was a woman with grit, fortitude, tenacity, and determination. In essence, she would argue her positions until she persuaded others to align with her views.

Virginia Meredith's legacy is a testament to those who continue to work to improve women's lives, the family, and the rural community today. She had to strike a delicate balance, but she managed to promote women's rights without sacrificing a woman's role in the home. For Meredith, respect and rights for women from work to home were inseparable.

Meredith was a natural leader. People listened to her when she spoke. She moved easily between speaking on a stage in front of hundreds of people and working with people one-on-one to encourage them to do better. She was a believable person in what she said and in how she expressed herself to others. Her involvement in agriculture, business, education, and administration modeled success for many younger women. She inspired other women to believe in themselves, helping them break down the stereotypes of women that surrounded them in their own lives. Many women witnessed Meredith's courage to go forward when others stopped, her stamina to pursue a cause while others quit, and her tenacity to believe that she could cross the finish line when others had come up short.

Managing her own farm had given Meredith the opportunity to hone her skills and to express herself in all that the production of livestock and crops involves. Her successes over a long period of time spent farming gave her the basis to move upward and outward, tackling issues outside the farm fields and within the farm home. She explored the world beyond the farm as a speaker, lady manager, club organizer, and college professor, but the pull of the farm always tugged at her inner being.

While she was many things to many people, ultimately Virginia Claypool Meredith was a farmer who just loved seeing her crops grow and her livestock grazing on her pastures. Farming gave her peace of mind, a purpose in life, and a connection to the natural world around her. As she herself would say, "I am a farmer," which described her as simply as one could do. [2]

Appendix 1

Complete Text of "Farm Life: Its Privileges and Possibilities" by Virginia Meredith*

Dr. Lee, in his eulogy of Henry Grady, said: "The glory of the mind is the possession of two eyes—the eye of sense and the eye of reason. With the former we look upon the world of facts; with the latter we look into the world of ideas. Through the mind commerce is kept up between these two worlds. Over this mental highway facts travel into the world of reason and are changed into ideas. Stars become astronomy; flowers, botany; atoms, chemistry. Ideas travel into the world of sense and are changed into facts. Ideas of beauty are turned into painting; ideas of harmony into music; ideas of form into sculpture." Facts and ideas form the sum of life. Where shall we find the best place for forming a correct estimate of the real and relative value of facts and ideas? Shall we find it in the country? I will not say that the country-bred man is the best type of man, but I will say, that with his opportunities he should be the best type of manhood. The expanse of horizon, the vigor of heaven's own air, the power of pure sunlight, the constant and close exhibition of great forces, these influences should brush away the cobwebs and give him the power of clear vision. I recall a paragraph from *Ramona:* "Nothing is stronger proof of the original intent of Nature to do more for man than the civilization in its arrogance will long permit her to do, than the quick and sure way in which she reclaims his affection, when by weariness, idle chance, or disaster, he is returned, for an interval, to her arms. How soon he rejects the miserable subterfuges of what he had called habits; sheds the still more miserable pretences of superiority, makeshifts of adornment, and the chains of custom! 'Whom the gods love, die young,' has been too long carelessly said. It is not true, in the sense in which men use the words. Whom the gods love, dwell with nature; if they are ever lured away, return to her before they are old. Then, however long they live before they die, they die young. Whom the gods love, live young—forever."

Any civilization is at fault and must fail at the point where it divides or seeks to divide the best of life from the country—where soul and mind growth is made impossible in rural places. That civilization only will endure which discovers how

* Virginia Claypool Meredith, "Farm Life: Its Privileges and Possibilities." Speech delivered at the annual meeting of the Indiana State Board of Agriculture in Indianapolis, Ind., January 1892. Indiana State Board of Agriculture Annual Report, 1892, vol. 33, 540–43.

to make education, in mind and ethics, as easy and accessible for the country boy as for the city lad.

It is said that one can not be a lover of good books unless he is also a lover of the open air—think of that—ponder it well.

If one would study literature, he is bade go study the authors that wrote when the world was young—why? What did they write of? How did they write about the country life and pursuits? Would there were time to read some illustrations of how the great Greek, Homer, adorned his verse; read for yourself the *Iliad,* that fountainhead of poetry, fresh and full of forceful illustrations; bearing the farm in mind, read the description of the Shield of Achilles, that miracle of art, a gift of Vulcan.

As farmers, we need to be practical; to be concerned about *facts.* Our corn is a fact that must be got into a bushel measure and for which we must get dollars. But is that all? We raised lots of good fodder when we raised the bushel of grain—how about ideas? May we not use the corn crop as poets use it? May not our mind have some activity in changing facts into ideas? It was not a farmer, but a woman (Phoebe Cary), who said of corn:

> That precious seed into the furrow cast
> Earliest in spring time crowns the harvest last.

Homer tells of Menelaus, whose "Soul was melted like the dew which glitters on the ears of growing corn that bristles in the plain":

> Cleon true possesseth acres, yet the landscape I,
> And half the charms to me it yieldeth, *money* can not buy;
> Cleon harbors sloth and dullness, freshening vigor I,
> He is velvet, I in fustian, *richer* man am I.
>
> Cleon is a slave to grandeur, free as thought am I;
> Cleon fees a score of doctors, need of none have I;
> Wealth surrounded, care environed, Cleon fears to die,
> Death may come, he'll find me ready, *happier* man am I.
>
> Cleon sees no charms in nature, in a daisy I,
> Cleon hears no anthems ringing in the sea and sky,
> Nature sings to me forever, earnest listener I;
> State for state, with all attendants, who would change? not I.

An intense longing for country life has characterized cultivated natures. Literature abounds with examples. Cicero and Diocletian, Virgil and Cincinnatus, among the ancients celebrated the charms of the agricultural life. Mount Vernon was the poem of Washington's life, and Monticello the delightful retreat about which clustered the dearest and noblest plans of Jefferson. We find these two exchanging letters about crop rotation and soil deterioration in the same spirit of enthusiasm that marks the intelligent farmer of to-day.

What is farming? Its realities assume phases in harmony with one's own nature. One will tell of all its hardships, another of its charm in the lovely June time, "knee deep in clover." City folk will talk of its independence—country folk of its drudgery. What is farming? It is an art, a science and a profession. With such scope, should not privileges and possibilities cluster about the farmer? As a vocation farming allows the widest range for individuality. Here, more than in any other calling, can one have liberty to exercise the *power of choice,* that greatest privilege of existence, and also the greatest responsibility of life, because the power of choice involves the possibility of making a mistake. All conduct, intelligent or otherwise, rests upon the power of choice. We choose high or low thoughts, aims, friends, methods of farming. Choice never denied us. We are sovereigns with our own acre and with our own brains. If we exercise our high privilege and choose knowledge rather than ignorance of breeds and their adoptions; knowledge rather than ignorance of crops, soil and cultivation, we shall get the last ounce of value from our acre.

We are to seek truth—knowledge—in all the lines that center upon the farm. Acquire information, in order to discover what is best for own acre—and our own brain. Our tastes and preferences are to be candidly considered. Patient study is being bestowed upon the problems of soil and heredity, and farmers coming after us are to be congratulated upon the opportunities that will be theirs. Each of a dozen lines of farming appeals to the active and intelligent mind. The farmer may become a manufacturer. Webster's definition of a manufacturer is "one who works raw materials into wares suitable for use." In political economy, that nation is most prosperous and illustrates the best civilization whose exports leave her shores in the form fitted for ultimate consumption. Is not something of the same nature true of the farm? And is it not notably the privilege of the farmer to work the raw material of the soil into food suitable for use? Prof. Roberts says that history does not furnish a single example of a nation rising to any degree of civilization whose food was a few unconcentrated products. Better food makes better men. To produce and improve the food of the world is notably the privilege of farmers in this latitude. Sir Chas. Dilke says: "Self-government, personal independence, true manliness can exist only where the snow will lie on the ground—cringing slavishness and imbecile submission follow the palm belt around the world."

"Books are made where wheat grows." Is it not curious that the grasping intelligence here indicated belongs to the latitude capable of the highest type of farming.

It lies within the province of the farmer to be an artist; his business has to do with life; he makes or brings about the conditions for its creation or development.

We note a great contrast in the laws that govern the reproduction of wheat and those that rule in the animal kingdom. In the wheat we observe an exquisite wonder of nature controlled by an unvarying law. But when we turn to the domestic animals we discover the law of variation which opens a grand domain for the exercise of intelligence. Here the artist may use his creative faculty and we find him molding into beauty, and into value, the "red, white and roan," the Jersey, the thoroughbred horse.

We plant, and sow, and reap. We may also think. Let no one say he must leave the farm in order to be near the great currents of thought. Mental vigor is not denied an outlet on the farm. What are we doing to make girls and boys in love with the farm? Are we forgetful of the graces and accomplishments of life? Do not we on the farm, underestimate those graces and accomplishments? Are they not realities that are important to our pleasure and enjoyment? It has been said so often that the soil holds all the real wealth of the world. So often said that the farmer feeds and clothes the whole world; that the idea of material property has become firmly lodged in all our conceptions of farming, and thus "propputty," as Tennyson's farmer quaintly puts it, becomes the key note to all the music in nature.

James Parton said, "If any young man were to ask me: Shall I become a farmer? I would have to reply by asking him another question: Are you man enough?" Think of that. Recall how from a crude form of farming has been evolved agriculture as a profession, directed by intelligence and sustained by capital. There is too much talk of farming as an exhausted industry, when really we have the most inadequate conception of its possibilities as a profession and an industry. We should distinguish between the farmer and farming—farming goes on forever. Let us dignify our calling, but more than all let us exalt our home on the farm. Let us make much of our farm and our farm life, cherish its privileges and realize its possibilities. We read to the ideal southern home, the home on the plantation. The typical New England home is the one on the farm. The hospitable western home is the home in the country. The family should find nowhere else such favorable conditions for its development. Here there is time for conversation, here there is opportunity to know each other. As an oak grown in free air is stronger, so the boy grown in free air develops more of manliness. He is not dwarfed by the close crowding of other natures.

Appendix 2

Complete Text of "Why Short-horns Are the Best Cattle for Indiana Farms" by Virginia Meredith*

I will name twelve reasons why short-horns are the best cattle for Indiana farms—others may be easily given.

First.—Because the farms are comparatively small, with a rich, fertile soil, well adapted to the heavy beef breeds, and well watered.

Second.—Our farmers are generally engaged in general purpose farming—they are not dairymen nor feeders.

Third.—The best beef markets are near by; Chicago, Louisville, Cincinnati, Pittsburg, Indianapolis.

Fourth.—Many railways render shipping easy.

Fifth.—Better feed for making beef and milk is produced nowhere; bluegrass, corn, oats, clover and—alfalfa, shall we add?

Sixth.—The old time high grade short-horn of Indiana was profitable before the dairy cross was made.

Seventh.—A better farmer's cow does not exist than the short-horn—heifers for milk, steers for beef.

Eighth.—A better steer than the short-horn has never been bred.

Ninth.—High class herds are well established in the State, making breeding stock easily accessible.

Tenth.—Indiana bred prize winners have in every principal exhibition of the country demonstrated that conditions here are favorable to the breed.

Eleventh.—The Indiana farmer lives near the great school of beef production, and may attend the International and learn its lessons.

Twelfth.—The short-horn breeders of the State are liberal in encouraging the local development of the breed by offering special prizes for Indiana bred cattle exhibited at the State Fair.

The business to be profitable requires an investment in courage and patience as well as investment of money in cattle. The cattle must become part of a plan of

---

* *Virginia Claypool Meredith, "Why Short-horns Are the Best Cattle for Indiana Farms." Speech delivered at the annual meeting of the Indiana State Board of Agriculture in Indianapolis, Indiana, January 1905.* Indiana State Board of Agriculture Annual Report, *1905, vol. 46, 317–18.*

farming for a long period of years. One must farm as if one expected to live forever. Farming goes on forever, and our part in it must be carried on with fidelity. I was in a $5,000 home not long ago that had been paid for by the maturing of a 15-year endowment policy in a life insurance company. A comfortable home, but can you not believe that it took courage and fidelity to a purpose to pay those fifteen successive premiums out of a meager salary? An investment in cattle must have the element of time provided for, if success is to come—it is the accumulated benefits that count. Beef breeds of cattle can not be profitable except they have good pasture—and good pasture is itself a matter of years—of a long period of time.

If one asks what is the trend of the beef markets today—asks what is the outstanding point in the situation—the answer comes clearly, unmistakably—the demand for the ripe yearling—and he ought to be profitable, for a penny saved is two pence earned and the steer that does not go to the market until two or three years old often has pounds laid on and then lost. When these pounds are laid on for the second time each pound represents the cost of making two pounds. There is then a practical argument in favor of the ripe yearling pushed from birth to block. Can any animal sell anywhere for six or seven cents, unless he carries the blood of some pure breed? Assuredly not. Can the farmer—should he—raise the calves which later he markets for beef, or would he better allow the man on the ranch to raise the calves, while he feeds and finishes them for market?

Perhaps after all the essential question is—what kind of farmer are we thinking of? One of our agricultural journals recently displayed in its columns this suggestive question: "Are you a farmer or a soil robber?" The answer will be yes or no according to the ratio between the acres and the cows of the farm. But it is not enough merely to keep cows; the kind of cow determines the direct profit—of course the indirect profit of improved soil is important—but we want both the direct and indirect profit.

What does the farmer invest in his cow? Feed, shelter, care and a purchase price. The purchase price usually indicates the quality of the cow, that is, the amount and kind of pure blood she carries. It would be easily demonstrated that the ratio between the purchase price and the amount invested in feed, care and shelter is a shifting one. At the end of five years, ten years, the greater part of the investment is in feed, care and shelter—but unchanging and immutable is the potency of her breeding, her quality as represented in the purchase price, as a factor in profit and loss. Our farmer will find then, if he invests $1,000 in feed, shelter and care, that the supremely important thing in the transaction is the purchase price of his cows; and it is for him imperative that he know positively which breed is best for him on his farm. Quality inheres in breed, and can not be found apart from it. No seven cent beef is sold anywhere except it carries the blood of some pure breed. The margin between the three cent steer and the seven cent steer is wholly a matter of pedigree. The profit which the farmer expects on his investment in feed, shelter and care depends upon his judgment in paying the initial purchase price for his cows and the sire of their calves.

In this connection I recall something I once heard Mr. Billingsley say in an [a farmer's] institute: "Go home, marshal your live stock in a procession, and as it passes before you ask yourself this question, 'Does this live stock represent my intelligence?'"

In order to induce the farmers of Indiana to keep short-horn cows, pure bred or high grade, we must preach the gospel of their quality, their ability to make baby beef of high quality at an economical cost. We must preach the gospel of continuing with the cattle, courage and patience. We must learn and give out generously the truth about feeding and care.

The most practical plan presented in regard to co-operation among farmers was published in the *Breeder's Gazette* of December 7 and proposed by Mr. John Thompson, of Iowa, and I hope that our American Short-Horn Association may find it possible to do some effective work along the line suggested by Mr. Thompson.

Appendix 3

Complete Text of "The Relation of Women to the Columbian Exposition" by Virginia Meredith*

Woman holds a three-fold relation to this great enterprise. She has an official connection with its *administration* and has great interests at stake as an *exhibitor*, but possibly it is in a third relation—as *student* of the exposition—that we may find a cluster of strong influence and important results.

The board of lady managers as a part of the administration of the Columbian Exposition is a startling innovation upon established custom, but when we recall that reliable statistics in many of the eastern states show one-third of those engaged in the industries to be women—and when in Indiana alone there were, so long ago as 1880, fifty-one thousand women who were willing to register as engaged in some wage-earning capacity, (the number is much larger now)—and when we observe, as we must, that women are steadily deserting the lower callings to enter the higher, where more of intelligence and trained skill are required, it does not seem unfitting that they should have a place of authority in an industrial exposition. Personally I wish that every woman might have the supreme good, which is a sheltered life in her husband's home, the contented wife of a noble man. But, as that is not practicable, it is a matter of congratulation that her entrance into man's domain is justified by the fact that she consecrates her money to noble uses. As a wage earner this exposition will enlarge her province, will dignify her life and her pursuits, and so make her an important factor in bringing about easier conditions and helpful surroundings for every creature. The betterment of humanity is the ultimate end, beckoning women into the industrial field. Useful contrivances that help the hand promote mental and soul growth; until physical conditions are easy for a nation, can the people of that nation live grandly or think nobly? It is impossible from this point of view to overestimate the importance of these so called industrial expositions.

Just how the few lines which authorize the formation of *The Board of Lady Managers of the Columbian Commission* ever crept into the congressional act is a mystery, an unfathomable mystery, judging from the atrocious grammar and inelegant diction that are combined in the name alone, one might infer that it was the

---

* Virginia Claypool Meredith, "The Relation of Women to the Columbian Exposition." Speech delivered at the third convention of the Indiana Union of Literary Clubs symposium titled "Women as a Factor in the World's Progress" in May 1892. In "The Bulletin" (detailed summary from conference program), 1892. Located in the General Federation of Women's Clubs, Indiana Federation of Clubs (Collection 29), Indiana State Library, Indianapolis, Ind.

work of a novice—but bad as the name is, we are so glad to be in existence that we bear the name with becoming meekness.

The board has already accomplished some worthy work—first and foremost it has been able to abolish the "Woman's Department," an abolition greatly desired by the most progressive thinkers and leaders. It is not likely that there will ever again be any distinction so artificial as that of sex between the skill of men and women—unlikely that there will ever again be a woman's department in any World's Fair. This advanced and courageous action on the part of the board deserves more commendation than it has received, for you will readily recognize that the board by abolishing the separate exhibition, in competition, of woman's work, deprived itself of an easy opportunity to make a striking display of its own energy and ability. It would have been easily possible to secure a great aggregation of beautiful and useful articles for a strictly woman's department. But when surrendering this tangible proof of its influence and its usefulness, the board took a very advanced stand, believing that what women are doing in conjunction with men needs to be more fully recognized in order to properly accent in public estimation the part women are now taking in the industries and professions; and also believing that the comparison of their work side by side with that of men would not only be helpful to women themselves, but it would be a revelation to the public of the great extent to which women are engaged in remunerative employments.

In the second place, the board has secured the adoption of a plan by the Installation department whereby information will be elicited with every exhibit as to whether or not the work of women was employed in any degree in the production of the article to be exhibited. By this plan will be determined the privilege and authority of the board in naming members of the juries of award. The act of congress says explicitly that the board of lady managers "may appoint one or more members of all committees authorized to award prizes for exhibits which may be produced in whole or in part by female labor."

In the third place the board has secured from the Chicago directory a very great and a graceful concession, a $200,000 building "for administration and other purposes." The Woman's Building afforded an opportunity for women architects to illustrate their ability in that line. I can assure you that it was a proud moment when Miss Hayden had completed working drawings that elicited cordial praise from Supervising Architect Burnham. The exterior decorations have been designed by Miss Rideout, of California, and the caryatides were modeled by Miss Yandell, of Kentucky. The interior decorations, such as woodcarving, brass work, screens, hangings, &c., &c., will be made by women from everywhere. The building with its roof gardens, will be an imposing illustration of woman's brain and hand— architects and artists will through it tell a charming story of aspiration, imagination, sentiment and cunning handiwork.

In the fourth place, through the efforts of Mrs. Palmer, the President of the Board, there has been inaugurated a notable impulse toward co-operation, and to mutual understanding among women the world over—all women of every nation are being made to know of the magnitude of this opportunity, and also of the significance to civilization of the industrial freedom to women.

We expect to have a children's palace where will be illustrated by manikins the peculiarities of every nation in dressing and caring for babies, including a representation of the very best methods that conform to the principles of modern hygiene; here, too, will be all the forms of amusing children, intelligent or otherwise; here, too, it is proposed that for a small fee mothers may leave their little ones in small groups to receive the attention of kindergartners—the older ones being taken to see exhibits which they can understand when explained by the teacher, etc., etc.

It is also proposed to erect, under the auspices of the Board, four women's dormitories near the Fair Grounds, the funds are to be secured by the sale of stock at $10 per share, no one being permitted to take more than ten shares. These dormitories will be under the most careful supervision, and are intended to provide comfortable lodging at a cost of about 35 cents per day. As the stock is transferable, and will be received in payment for lodging, it should not only be a good investment, but a very practical convenience to women who visit the Exposition alone. Mrs. Matilda B. Carse, so well known in connection with the Woman's Temperance Temple, at Chicago, is at the head of this work, and its success is thereby assured. A further enumeration of the purposes of the Board would be tedious, but this much may be helpful in bringing out the comprehensive scheme of the Board embracing, as it does, every field for woman's active brain and quick hand.

In our thinking we should, as women, keep close to the industrial feature of the Columbian Exposition, for there lies a vast and almost unexplored domain peculiarly fitted for the exercise of woman's intelligence.

What have the men of this new world been doing the past four hundred years—since Columbus discovered America? *Producing wealth*—their success has been amazing—almost menacing. But the *consumption of wealth* is now the advancing problem that cries out for an answer. Every economy is practiced in the production of wealth, only to be followed by prodigality in consuming it. This new problem is bringing us to a proper appreciation of what is usually and truly called woman's work. In order to still the spirit of unrest now upon the sex, women do not need so much to change their vocations and avocations as that they need to understand, and to bring men to understand the dignity and important possibilities of what has always conceded to be woman's sphere—home.

One may follow any line of production and certainly find that its ultimate destination—its consumption—intimately concerns woman. To illustrate in a plain way, inventive genius has been taxed to supply economic methods of growing wheat; government has sought to frame wise laws that will open new markets for wheat and protect the home one; great capital and splendid brains have combined to make its transportation rapid and cheap—all the forces of nature and human ingenuity have been strained to the utmost in order to put good flour at a low price into our homes—but there and then co-operation, invention, capital, brains, and even nature itself abandons the precious product to waste and absolute loss. In woman's province—the *consumption* of wealth—there has been no advance in methods that can be compared to that in the *production* of wealth—the two should be equally the field for intelligence. Now that Universities *and Clubs* are teaching women to think, we may confidently expect this great problem which has to do with the consumption of wealth will be solved by woman, especially as it lies so largely in her legitimate domain. Club women, as representative of the highest intelligence of the sex, should bend every energy toward bringing about a radical change in our educational system—there must be devised a system that has to do with the consumption of wealth. We must have in our cook one who has been taught the chemical properties of flour, who has learned the almost infinite edible possibilities of the potato and every other vegetable—we must have a nurse for our children who has herself known the training of the kindergarten. The young girl who will after awhile be the mechanic's wife, has an inalienable right to be taught how to darn and to mend, and what is even more important, she is entitled to be taught a gracious appreciation of the dignity of darning and mending! In this age of civilization it is not right that the laborer's boy should wear clothing so cheap that when the knee is worn and torn the garment is thrown away to be replaced by another as cheap and as worthless. We clamor for cheap sugar—make it an issue in political campaigns— but when we get it for 5 cents per pound, instead of 10, what does it signify if we, at the same time, think it too much trouble to ascertain the limit of liquids to hold it in solution, if we disregard the chemical changes produced by heat? Any line of production followed to its ultimate destination intimately concerns woman—even those twin torments of the sex, whisky and tobacco, are wonderfully wasted in the consumption! It would be vastly more comfortable for everybody if men could be made to understand how to get the most pleasure from these commodities.

How to get the maximum good from every thing produced by labor or thought is the problem now projecting itself upon our times for solution, and women must do some earnest thinking in this line, if they are to bear their share of the work to be done for humanity. This, of course, means a concentration of attention upon educational methods—a study that is no light undertaking if we are ever to arrive at correct conclusions. Women can not afford longer to waste time in *re*form, she must control *formative* processes. She must make of children what she would have men and women to be. The mother in the past has been content with a six years possession of her child, and afterward renounced responsibility by abandoning the child to a system of education and an environment in business and in society, over which she had no control—and over which the child's father seeks to have no determining influence, because he is so absorbed in making money to support the school, to support the legislature that enacts laws, to support the officers who build school houses, to support the city government that builds streets and employs policemen—so engaged in making money to support the State government that builds asylums and prisons, that he really has no time to think about the why and the wherefore—to think about how to make those streets safe for his daughter—to think about how to train a boy that will not need prison or asylum—to think about the kind of school that will help to develop his child, and not to cripple it. It is a positive loss to the state, it is a public disaster, when the children of the state have not every power—physical, mental and spiritual—harmoniously and fully developed.

If careful living, which means plenty and comfort for everybody—if content with one's lot could be made to replace the present *want* and *unrest,* this would be a pleasant world to live in. Who can say how great a factor the new woman—the intelligent woman—will be in making new conditions that will help on mightily the world's progress? George Eliot's expression, is to my mind, the right conception of the function of the feminine character: "The sweet presence of a good diffused, and in diffusion ever more intense."

It is only in the higher realm that diffusion can be the means of intensity— in the material world concentration is the measure of intensity.

The Russian government sent to our Centennial Exposition in 1876 an educational exhibit that is but just beginning to be understood—sloyd—manual training, not for a trade, but as an instrument for mental training, is destined to hold a high place in our educational system. Let us, as Club women, when attending the Columbian Exposition, keep our eyes and our minds open for suggestions, so that it may not take fifteen years for an idea to penetrate our intelligence, but be ready each in her own town to urge better methods, and so help forward the idea that physical conditions must be easy before mental and spiritual progress for humanity is possible.

Appendix 4

Complete Text of "The Need of Special Training for Agricultural Pursuits" by Virginia Meredith*

There is one time when I feel proud, very proud, and it comes once in ten years, and that is when the census taker comes around and says, "What is your occupation?" And I say, "Farmer." And he usually says, "You don't want me to put your name in as a farmer, do you?" I certainly do, for I am a farmer, and I have an opportunity to gratify my pride once in ten years.

I am to talk this evening on "The Need of Special Training for Agricultural Pursuits." I will refer only to those means that could be met by the Agricultural College, as I understand what can be or ought to be done by an Agricultural College. And by agricultural pursuits I am going to include not only those things that have to do with plant and animal life, but I will also include a very important part of agriculture, and that is the home and the farm, and the need for special training for the one who makes that home.

I suppose, like myself, all here are decidedly enthusiastic about forestry. We see great possibilities in this system, and I am sure we have larger and broader views, and certainly a greater fund of knowledge as to that subject. Is there any need for special training in agricultural pursuits? Another way of putting the question is: Are we satisfied with what the acre is doing for us? Are we satisfied the acre is bringing us its very best returns? Do we think we are getting enough wheat, enough corn; are we getting the quality that we want in apples and pears and peaches and strawberries, and are there enough being raised of these different fruits? Does everyone have as many apples as they want, as many strawberries? Are there any needs along this line? Is the acre doing for us all that it should?

I was very much pleased this evening when I was asked to take a drive around Kendallville. I saw the beautiful streets and homes, and then I saw an onion field where they tell me they will raise nine hundred bushels of onions to the acre. Isn't that a great thing? How many are doing that for the acre? And have we any right to expect it from the acre? Down in our county we had a yield of wheat of from five

* *Virginia Claypool Meredith, "The Need of Special Training for Agricultural Pursuits." Speech delivered at the annual meeting of the Indiana State Board of Agriculture in Indianapolis, Ind., January 1905.* Indiana State Board of Agriculture Annual Report, *1905, vol. 46, 566–73.*

to seven bushels average. The people are taking five or six acres to raise what ought to be raised on one acre of ground. Who gets the thirty bushels of wheat to the acre? I have a neighbor—a woman farmer—who got thirty-two and one-half bushels to the acre, instead of five or six? How did she get thirty-two and one-half bushels to the acre? Was it luck, or did she make herself a student of seed vitality and the right kind of seed for her soil? I say she got thirty-two and one-half bushels to the acre because she studied the subject of seed vitality and the amount of seed to be sown on her soil. It was not luck. So, then, there is a way of getting over thirty bushels of wheat to the acre. Then there must be special training.

I was in France a few years ago and they were harvesting what I thought was a good crop of wheat, which was an average of fifty bushels to the acre for all of France. Think of that. The average in England, as you know, is something over thirty bushels. Now France and England were old before the United States of America was discovered, so that there must be something in the tending and studying of the soil, vitality of the seed, choice of variety, etc. We need it. If we had it we would not have to own six acres of land in order to get what we should get from one. I think we have a very interesting department resulting from the study of the seed corn in Indiana within the last few years.

I once heard a young man who had spent four years of time and money in a college say that if he had learned nothing else but what he learned about capillarity he would have been well repaid. He had learned it in college, and he had learned it in connection with the cultivation of corn, etc., and in dry seasons he could raise additional bushels. So, we who are not getting sixty or eighty bushels of corn are in need of special training that will enlighten us about the soil, the acre—about the seed and its vitality, and about its cultivation—knowledge of the principles, which is special training. What do we mean? Simply this. First to observe accurately and to think correctly, and to draw conclusions with sound judgment. A trained mind is able to do that much more readily than a mind which is not trained. I am particularly interested, and anyone who lives in Indiana must be, in live stock, and yet, what do we find? Cattle, sheep, horses, hogs and everything else that have been bred in Indiana the same for years. There are great possibilities in this line, but yet, how many farmers are there who are equipped with cattle that are fit either for meat or beef; sheep that are fit for mutton; horses that are fit for draft or speed horses. There needs to be special training along these lines, because it is most profitable—the most profitable line of husbandry that can be engaged in. I was very much interested a short time ago to hear a friend of mine say that he raised tomatoes because he found he was able to sell more water in that way than any other way, ninety-five per cent. being water, and that took none of the vitality away from the farm. So in the matter of live stock. We are carrying little fertilizer away from the farm. As you know, there is a deep-seated prejudice against pure-breed cattle, the breeds which we call pure breeds. A pure breed makes a much better butter cow, much better beef. We find any amount of cattle that will lay on perhaps as many pounds as the very best pure breeds, but they haven't the quality which, put on the market, brings high prices, so the profit is lost. So we need special training along these lines.

To illustrate: Opportunities often come to people who have this special training. I want to tell you of a young man who knew how to take care of cattle, and his services were engaged by a rich man on a fine farm, and he was very successful. In a short time the interests of the owner were drifted entirely away from the farm, and he could not dispose of it in the way he wanted to. So this young man got an opportunity to buy the pure-bred cattle at a low price, and this was certainly a great opportunity. This was on account of his special training. I fear we neglect our opportunities. You can read in papers and books where someone will tell how he can put on two hundred pounds of beef, and another four hundred pounds of beef from the acre of grass during the season. This, of course, was done by people who had had special training. These things are interesting, and we live in our own possibilities in this State of Indiana.

I want to tell you about a young man who studied in an agricultural school. He was not so very young, for he was about thirty-five years of age. He found that he was getting a good deal from his experience, because it enabled him to cut double. He did not come with the intention of staying the full time, but when he went home and found how much he had really learned he went back to the school for the full course, and graduated when he was thirty-eight or nine. That man is now raising every year four or five thousand range lambs, mostly upon rape, which he plants with his corn. He is doing this year after year, and his lambs top the market in Chicago. Isn't this a wonderful use of the acre—that ability to make an acre bring you the very last dollar of profit? This special training gives additional power, and we all need it. Who has money enough? Certainly no farmer. We want more money from our acre. I know a young man who happened to fall heir to some land that was very thin. It was not a very promising place on which to begin farming. He was a graduate, and of course had this special training, so he thought the matter over carefully and found that his land was well adapted to melon raising, so he began to raise melons. He supplied the market with melons and cabbage. In about six years that man had saved enough money to build him a house, and he now has a more comfortable farm. He has a wife who was instructed in domestic science. This man knew that melons would be profitable and could be raised well, and he knew this on account of his special training—the very training which he got from within the agricultural school—for this training gave him an insight into the subject and an enthusiasm for it, and this, backed by advice and counsel of older people, caused him to make a wonderful success. Now many have the acre and many have the special energy that we can put in these different lines. There is so much to be said along this line of the acre, and that is the point from which we should estimate everything we do on the farm—"the acre."

I wish to speak briefly about some other phases of this subject. People are all the time saying that people are discontented on the farm, usually because the women on the farm are not happy and contented. I believe that there is need of special training of the farmers' daughters along these lines. They should be trained along the point of animal life, for that is such a large part of farming. Not that we want the girl to be a farmer, but we want her to be in sympathy with the life on the farm—with the father and brother—and with the husband. She should understand plant and animal life as taught in the classes by teachers of enthusiasm. If this is done she will see so much more in the farm than before. This special training will also aid them in designing houses and barns which are fit for farmers to live in. This is something that will make their lives more comfortable. This is much nicer than being compelled to live in a house which a carpenter will put up for you. The home is the place where the opportunity is given for right development of the physical and spiritual natures, and the girl who is in school is taught about cookery, about sewing, and the elementary principles of hygiene. The girl who is specially trained will make a better housekeeper, a better wife, a finer woman, and a greater factor in the social life of the country. So, then, we have the greatest need of this special training for women who are going to live in the country. There is a great need of this. There is a great need everywhere. I wonder if you would be shocked if I were to say that I think there is a special need for the training of women to be farmers. I live twelve miles from my father's, and I drive that many, many times in a year, and for six miles on every side of the road every farm is owned by a woman, and only one woman lives on her farm. She is a German woman who was left a widow with several children, and she was enabled by this farm to raise and educate these children. Some of these women who owned these farms longed to live on them, but they didn't know how to manage them. One of the greatest changes which has come to us in the last fifty years has come through the inheritance laws of the United States, which allows a daughter to inherit equally with the sons, and so it has come to pass that girls inherit farms. Sometimes they do not know what to do with them. There are a great many women who never get married for the very best of reasons. May be you don't know what they are. There are not enough good men to go around. This woman would like to live on the farm if they could make things go, and there is no business to my mind so suitable to women as farming. She is removed from competitors. If she undertakes to be a doctor, medical students will not have a woman in the class if they can help themselves. Ministers will not permit women to preach. Men do not want women in the professions, and I for my part, do not want my girl to be a clerk, or do any of the things girls do down town. I would so much rather she would farm, because I know that every good man on a farm will help her if she needs help, and will do it in the very best spirit in the world. We have all seen this many times. If a woman is left a widow every man wants to help her. They do not say: "You shan't farm here in my neighborhood." I know a woman who lives on an eighty-acre farm that has put four children through the University at Bloomington. Wouldn't you rather see your daughter managing a farm, a little one or a big one, than see her working down town? I think it is a fine thing. Since girls can get that sort of an education, why not give it to the girl that wants it?

All along the line I see there is need for special training. We want more from our acre—more dollars. Why? We want the dollars that we may buy culture; that we may buy comfort; that we may exercise philanthropy. The dollar is a beautiful thing when it is correctly used. Anyone can earn a dollar, but so few know how to spend them wisely. So we want more money from our acre; more fruit; better cattle; more butter, more cream, etc. We can do this only by special training. There is no such a thing as luck any more. We used to think that the witches got into the milk and the butter would not come. But since we have got the thermometer we have found that witches did not control the cream. The housewife now knows what she is doing, and the reason for doing what she is doing. She has the special training which gives the reason back of all things, and that gives skill in the art. I think the philosophy of a thing is very important. If we are trained in an agricultural school by a professor who understands what he is doing, we will get the science, art and philosophy, and we will be equipped to live. It is better to learn how to live than to learn how to accumulate dollars. Yet, this special training gives power to get dollars, and the power to use the dollars wisely. I thank you.

Appendix 5

Complete Text of "Roads of Remembrance" by Virginia Meredith*

Today, on this May morning, wherever our flag flies there are *roads of remembrance*— roads of remembrance that lead to some consecrated place—roads of remembrance perhaps to the stately tomb dedicated to the unknown soldier, or to the rows of soldiers' graves in the big cemeteries, perchance to the crosses on Flanders Field, or to a lone grave in a remote country graveyard. Everywhere flowers are borne, beautiful flowers that speak a language of remembrance and forget the ugly scars of ugly war.

I like to read again and again some lines written by an Indiana woman—Susan Perkins.

The Flag
Pray for your flag when it goes forth to war
With courage in cause that is just—
Let anger be slow
Let resentment not grow
Save with knowledge, unbiased, assured.
But where your flag leads
Even though your heart bleeds—
Pray for strength to endure,
Pray for faith that is pure.
Let us lift up our eyes
To where our flag flies—
And again let us pray
That forever and aye
It may stand in its might
For humanity's right
To freedom, to justice,
To peace and to joy—
Pray, pray for your flag.

* Virginia Claypool Meredith, "Roads of Remembrance." Speech delivered at the Purdue University Memorial Day Exercises in West Lafayette, Ind., on 30 May 1933. Original program located in Special Collections and Archives, Purdue University Libraries, Stewart Center, West Lafayette, Ind.

I recall clearly that day when the news came that Fort Sumter had been fired on; I recall how hearts were heavy, and the world looked black. And wherever there were young men—in college, in factory or on farm—patriotic fervor mounted high. It has been said that all wars are fought by boys and that the sorrows of war are borne by women; always, however, there are groups of mature men—patriots—who do the hard thinking and planning that belong to the actualities of war.

I often feel that in Indiana we have not kept glowing as we should the memory of the great war governor, Oliver P. Morton. His task was like that of Lincoln—a heart-breaking, a mind-racking task. Governor Morton was a familiar friend in our home; I heard daily the story of his struggle with a turbulent legislature—the kind of legislature that is a terror to its own constituents and a hindrance to a governor who would loyally serve his country. The support given Governor Morton by wealthy men at home was a splendid patriotic service that helped Morton's "glowing reason" to keep Indiana in loyal line—a much more difficult and hazardous undertaking than our histories record.

It is said that the poet has an insight which gives the gleam of truth to his verse. [William] Dudley Foulke in his life of Morton [book titled *Life of (Oliver P.) Morton*] quotes Riley:

> . . . One whose earthly will wrought every mission well,
> Whose glowing reason towered above the Sea
> Of dark disaster like a beacon-light
> And led the ship of state, unscathed and free, out of the gulf of night.

I like that phrase—"glowing reason." At the time of the War of the Rebellion organization was lacking, pitifully lacking, in the care of our soldiers at the front, and upon home folk fell a heavy burden; there was work for all. I myself, a young girl, rose to heights of heroism—at least I felt that I was rising to such heights. At the time when Morgan's army invaded our state, I loaned my own riding horse to one who was going with the mounted company to repel the invasion. Well, my horse came back safely, as did the gallant volunteer who rode him!

Horses were far more important then than now. We had on our home farm three pensioners, horses that had seen service in the Army of the Potomac. Barney, a gaited saddle horse, shared Indiana honors in the battle of Gettysburg. Barney was one of the noted horses of the Army of the Potomac with speed and endurance; at the battle of Gettysburg Barney was the only horse of the Iron Brigade that escaped with his life. He was then sent to the home farm to end his days in Indiana.

On those historic days of '63—July 1, 2 and 3—the Rebel General [Robert E.] Lee rather surprised the northern army by his rapid advance and it became imperative to "hold" the Rebel army by engaging it in battle until the Union troops could be placed in position. For this duty the "Iron Brigade" was chosen because it had seen service and proved itself; in that brigade, First Division, First Army Corps, was the 19th Regiment Indiana Volunteers. Barney belonged to Lieutenant Samuel Meredith and shared the glory of the day. In the annals of warfare never was there such gallant defense and never was there such dreadful slaughter. "The gallant six hundred" glorified by Tennyson must yield to this record, never surpassed.

A second pensioner was a big roan, Tom, sent home from Gettysburg. In the early days after Appomattox there was a constant stream of soldiers coming to our home in a very active effort to qualify for Government help, and every old soldier wanted to see "old Tom" and stroke his glossy shoulder.

And there was still another pensioner—a handsome bay horse given to General Meredith—Turk. On parade he was so prancingly grand that he justified all the equestrian statues that now adorn the land! These three pensioners had the freedom of the pasture, and when Fourth of July came and when the enthusiasm of a little town fired cannon to celebrate the day, it was most interesting to see these three horses join in a mad gallop to the farthermost point in the pasture. They remembered the cannon's roar—and they wanted no more of it!

Just what is the contribution of these wars that destroy our youth—what is their contribution to the ideals of citizenship? "The best project anywhere," says Dean Bailey, "is a good man or woman working in a program, but unhampered." What is the program?

One never ceases to wonder, to speculate, about the world war—was it a rendezvous of youth? I have a fantastic notion that there was held a conclave of the spirit of youth. Did they, the youth from every nation, find that they were speaking the same language—a language not understood by their elders? Did they, in that strange language, in some mysterious mood, in some strange place—high Olympus or deep cave of the gods—did they say to each other that they would bring to pass a new order? That they would take apart the old world and put it together again after a new pattern? Is this chaos that is now so confusing, so perplexing, that one cannot discern whether it is the trumpet call of the new order or the wail of farewell to the age—is it the old hope of a time when war drums should throb no more?

The past is ours! The past is safe! Columbus found a world, with no science, no art, "save the invincible surmise of his soul"! Can we save our souls, if we travel these roads of remembrance, cherishing glorious memories?

I have seen three "impossible" things come to pass. In the span of one life I have seen slavery abolished in the United States; I have seen the position of Labor changed completely; I have seen Florence Nightingale open to the mothers of men doors that had been closed and sealed through all the centuries! I count it a high point in my life that on a certain Sunday morning, in Edinburg—in old St. Giles Church, the Church of John Knox, the very Gibraltar of what is fixed and finished and unalterable—I there heard Ian McLaren, John Watson, preach from an address to "the weary and heavy laden" made 2,000 years ago by a modern teacher, with a new note—"Come unto *Me*." He of the Bonnie Briar Bush said, "Nothing—nothing—is impossible to a hundred men with pure hearts and strong souls."

The past is safe—let us cherish it. Always there will be open roads of remembrance whereon shall crowd those who seek a lost love and others looking for courage glorified, for sacrifice sanctified by faith. Wherever they may be, these hallowed places known to each heart, we would invoke for them the benign mood of Nature.

On this May Day we would invoke Nature's peace and quiet, and repeat the good lines of Richardson:

> Warm summer sun,
> Shine kindly here;
> Warm southern wind,
> Blow softly here;
> Green sod above,
> Lie light, lie light;
> Good night, dear heart,
> Good night, good night.

Appendix 6

Obituary of Virginia C. Meredith,
Lafayette (Ind.) Journal and Courier, 11 December 1936

MRS. MEREDITH, FAMED HOOSIER LEADER, IS DEAD
Queen of Agriculture and Purdue Trustee for Many Years
Expires at 88 and Leaves Valued Heritage.

Mrs. Virginia Claypool Meredith, 88 years old, one of the most illustrious women in the history of Indiana and long prominent in national farm and home affairs, many years ago called "The Queen of American Agriculture," and the only woman who ever served on the board of trustees of Purdue university, died at 4:30 o'clock yesterday afternoon at the home of her adopted daughter, Dean Mary L. Matthews, of the Purdue school of home economics, 629 Waldron Street, West Lafayette. Death came peacefully after an illness of about three months, of complications which followed a heart attack. Members of her immediate family, who had been constantly at her bedside, were with her.

Throughout her life, Mrs. Meredith had maintained an active interest and participation in public affairs, and despite her advanced years had remained active as a trustee of the university and in civic affairs. She had been on the Purdue board since 1921 and was reappointed by Governor McNutt last July for another term of three years.

LONG PUBLIC CAREER
The public career of Mrs. Meredith began in 1882 upon the death of her husband, Henry Clay Meredith, when she assumed active charge of a 400-acre farm near Cambridge City, and also the management of a famous herd of Shorthorn cattle and flock of Shropshire sheep which he had exhibited at leading fairs and expositions. Although it had been unheard of in those days for a woman to show livestock, Mrs. Meredith set the precedent, winning many state and national prizes. Because of her achievements in this field, she soon became widely known, and in 1889 was invited to speak on crops and livestock production before farmers' institutes, then being started by the Indiana state board of agriculture. She gave her time for two years, because, as she related one time a few years ago, the board decreed that no woman should be paid for their services.

"QUEEN OF AGRICULTURE"

Mrs. Meredith's reputation grew and she was called to many states to speak on farm and home topics. At one time, following an address in Mississippi, she was named by that state as the "Queen of American Agriculture." Her public work continued, although she was still managing her farm and livestock, and in 1893 she was named as Indiana representative on the World's Columbian exposition at Chicago. She became known as "the lady manager" from Indiana, serving as chairman of the committee on awards, in which she was called upon to name more than 100 judges from all over the world. In 1896, she was called to the University of Minnesota to organize the department of home economics. After five years, however, she gave up that post to return to her friends in Indiana and to her Oakland farm in Wayne county.

Since then she had remained in this state, living on her farm with Dean [Mary] Matthews except for trips out of the state to speak at various events, a gift for which she had become more widely known than ever. She had written for many farm publications, and from 1921 to 1931 was woman's editor of the *Breeder's Gazette*, national farm publication.

RECEIVES HONORS

While serving as a member of the board of trustees, Mrs. Meredith had been especially active in the cause of women students and was one of the first supporters of the move for a department of physical education for women and also for the women's residence halls. The Virginia C. Meredith club, an organization of home economics students, was named in her honor, and the Tippecanoe County Federation of Clubs has established a loan fund for women students at Purdue, also bearing her name.

In 1930 she was awarded a gold medal by the state of Wisconsin for "eminent service."

As a speaker, Mrs. Meredith had few equals among women of the nation. Besides her long experience on the farm institute staff, she was called up to speak before all sorts of gatherings. Her last public address took place last May, when she spoke at the tenth anniversary of the Purdue school of home economics.

Besides her interest in agriculture, she was long identified with progressive organizations for women and was one of the organizers of the Indiana Federation of Clubs, of which she was honorary president.

HISTORICAL FAMILY

Mrs. Meredith came from a family prominently identified with history, both in Virginia and in Indiana. She was born on a Fayette county farm November 5,

1848, a daughter of Austin B. and Hannah A. Claypool. She was graduated from Glendale college in 1866 and, after spending a few years at her home, was married to Mr. Meredith, who was active in state affairs, serving on the board of agriculture and also as speaker of the house of representatives. His death, in 1882, left Mrs. Meredith without children to manage the farm, a task she accepted and which helped her to make a prominent mark in the world.

Surviving, besides the adopted daughter, is an adopted son, Meredith Matthews, both of whom she took as small children upon the death of their mother; and a brother, Frank J. Claypool of Muncie, also a member of the Indiana board of agriculture; a sister, Mrs. Morrell Earl, of Muncie, died here in 1931, and a brother, Marcus S. Claypool, died in 1927.

FUNERAL SATURDAY

The funeral will be held at 9:30 o'clock Saturday morning at the home, in charge of the Rev. Dr. W. R. Graham, of the Central Presbyterian church, of which she had been a member for many years. The body will be taken to Cambridge City for burial in the Meredith family lot.

Appendix 7

Complete Text of "Mrs. Virginia Meredith,"
Lafayette (Ind.) Journal and Courier, 12 December 1936

The spirit of Mrs. Virginia Claypool Meredith, her glowing faith, her pioneer personality, her abiding Americanism, her sane and sound wholesomeness, envigored and expressed with the true orator's force and clarity, will continue for many years to influence the lives and careers of her friends and associates left behind.

Mrs. Meredith was remarkable in so many ways it is difficult to appraise her services without appearing to exaggerate. To rhapsodize, or wax fulsome in her praise would be to risk feeling in imagination the frank displeasure of a plain-thinking, plain-speaking spirit, one of whose most charming characteristics was a sense of humor.

Yet something of the greatness, the fine, high quality, the gallant leadership, the keen intelligence, the human heartedness, the clear vision and large achievements of Virginia Meredith ought to be told.

In Mrs. Meredith's own experiences, activities, attainments, performances, writings and constructive record in the field of stock-raising is to be found ample basis for the South's bestowal upon her of the title, "Queen of American Agriculture."

Since 1921 Mrs. Meredith had shone most brightly and had grown most definitely in usefulness as a trustee of Purdue university. Her reappointment to the board last July was a fair tribute to her outstanding devotion and initiative as a representative of woman's interests in our higher education for practical home-making.

Mrs. Meredith gained recognition nationally at the time of the 1893 Columbian exposition. She was honored by many states, including Minnesota, where she pioneered in education for girls; in Wisconsin, where she received a gold medal for "eminent service," and in Mississippi, where her eloquence and intelligence won for her the royal appellation, "Queen of American Agriculture."

Whether as an aggressive, successful stock-raiser, carrying on the large business of a departed husband; as a messenger to farmers' institutes, passing-on her own experiences to men and women; as an orator contacting groups in many other states; as an educator establishing new ideas and modern methods, or as the distinguished trustee of a university, working with extraordinary energy and loyalty for progress and soundness in teaching Americanism and wholesome, common sense doctrines and homely living to the young, Mrs. Meredith was ever a valued contributor to the general good. She had very definite fundamental ideas as to the aims and functions of Purdue university as a sound factor in the education of young womanhood for home-making.

Keen of wit, zestful, humorous, understanding, sympathetic, widely read, quick at repartee, sure in decision as between right and wrong; courageous and frank in support of her convictions, Mrs. Meredith combined in one vibrant and friendly personality those myriad qualities that make for leadership.

Neither titles nor medals of precious worth, nor the applause of thrilled multitudes may express with any measure of adequacy the significance or extent of the great service she rendered to her state, to Purdue university and to those who were fortunate enough to know her as friend and counsellor.

Notes

Introduction

1. Thomas R. Johnston and Helen Hand, "Virginia Meredith—Member of the Board, 1921–1936," *The Trustees and the Officers of Purdue University, 1865–1940* (Lafayette, Ind.: Purdue University, 1940), 308.

CHAPTER 1

A Hoosier Family's Rise to Prominence

1. Edward F. Claypool, letter to W. W. English, 13 October 1888. Indiana Historical Society, Indianapolis, Ind. Attached to this letter is a three-page, typed, unpublished biography (n.d.) of Newton Claypool written by his son, Edward Claypool.

2. Ibid.

3. "Mrs. Virginia C. Meredith, Honorary President I. F. C.," *Indiana Club Woman* 9, no. 4 (May–June 1930): n.p.; "After a New Pattern. How Some Women Succeed," *The Farmer's Wife,* October 1934, 5–6.

4. "Mrs. Virginia C. Meredith, Honorary President I. F. C."

5. "Early Days of Indiana. The Claypools and Conwells—Betty Brazier and Others" (newspaper clipping), *Daily Sentinel* (city unknown), 20 September 1883.

6. Connersville, Ind., Sesquicentennial Book Committee, *The Book of the 150th Year of Connersville, Indiana* (Connersville, Ind.: City of Connersville, 1963); also see Ch. 1, n. 1.

7. Rebecca Shepherd, et al., "Newton Claypool," *A Biographical Directory of the Indiana General Assembly,* vol. 1, 1816–1899 (Select Committee on the Centennial History of the Indiana General Assembly in cooperation with the Indiana Historical Bureau, 1980), 67; "Early Days of Indiana." During this time period, the Indiana Constitution required officeholders in the General Assembly to be elected on an annual basis.

8. "After a New Pattern," 5–6.

9. *Indiana State Board of Agriculture Annual Report,* 1854–1855, xi.

10. See Ch. 1, n. 1.

11. Shepherd et al., 67.

12. H. S. K. Bartholomew, "Virginia C. Meredith," *Indiana Magazine of History* 35 (March 1939): 49.

13. Robert W. Topping, "Austin Bingley Claypool," *The Book of Trustees: Purdue University, 1865–1989* (West Lafayette, Ind.: Purdue University, 1989), 64.

14. *History of Fayette County, Indiana* (Chicago: Warner, Beers, and Co., 1885), 262–63.

15. Topping, 64; *History of Fayette County, Indiana,* 262–63.

16. *History of Fayette County, Indiana,* 262–63.

17. Topping, 64.

18. *Indiana State Board of Agriculture Annual Report,* 1858, 413.

19. *Indiana State Board of Agriculture Annual Report,* 1867, 375–76.

20. *Indiana State Board of Agriculture Annual Report,* 1871, vol. 1, 150.

21. Topping, 64.

22. *Indiana State Board of Agriculture Annual Report,* 1867, 453.

23. *Indiana State Board of Agriculture Annual Report,* 1877, vol. 19, 180.

24. Ibid., 5.

25. *Indiana State Board of Agriculture Annual Report,* 1871, vol. 1, 11.

26. *Indiana State Board of Agriculture Annual Report,* 1877, vol. 19, 5.

27. Ibid., 31.

28. *Indiana State Board of Agriculture Annual Report,* 1879, vol. 15, 8.

29. Purdue University, Board of Trustees meeting minutes, 12 June 1874, vol. 1, 157.

30. Ibid., 140.

31. Ibid., 155; Purdue University Reamer Club, *A University of Tradition: The Spirit of Purdue* (West Lafayette, Ind.: Purdue University Press, 2002), 103.

32. Purdue University Reamer Club, 103.

33. "Mrs. Meredith, Famed Hoosier Leader, Is Dead. Queen of Agriculture and Purdue Trustee for Many Years Expires at 88 and Leaves Valued Heritage," *Lafayette (Ind.) Journal and Courier,* 11 December 1936.

34. "A Woman as a Farmer. The Success of Mrs. Virginia C. Meredith. One of the Best Known Stock Raisers in the State—Her View of the Farming Business," *Indianapolis News,* 3 January 1900.

35. "Virginia Meredith, Queen of Agriculture, Is Dead," *Richmond (Ind.) Palladium and Sun-Telegram,* 11 December 1936.

36. "After a New Pattern," 5–6.

37. Virginia Meredith, "Roads of Remembrance. A Memorial Address" (speech). In program for Purdue University Memorial Day Exercises, West Lafayette, Ind., 13 May 1933.

38. "Honoring Those Who Have Achieved—Virginia C. Meredith," *Purdue Alumnus* 22 (November 1934): 4–5.

39. Glendale (Ohio) Female College, "Tenth Annual Catalogue of Glendale Female College, Glendale, Hamilton County, Ohio, for the Year Ending 24 June 1864" (Cincinnati, Ohio: Moore, Wilstach, and Baldwin, 1864), 13.

40. Ibid., 13.

41. Ibid., 12.

42. Ibid., 15.

43. Ibid.

44. Ibid., 16.

45. Ibid.

46. Bartholomew, 50.

47. U.S. Works Progress Administration, *Indiana and Indianans* (Indianapolis: Indianapolis Public Library, 1939), 1569–70.

CHAPTER 2
An Independent Woman Emerges

1. Martin L. Bundy, "Gen. Sol. Meredith. Sketch of a Remarkable Self-Made Man. His Career from a Wood-Chopper to a Major General," *Indianapolis Times*, 25 February 1882; "General Solomon Meredith Was of Outstanding Character" (newspaper clipping), n.p., n.d. Modified from original biography printed in the *Richmond (Ind.) Palladium*, 30 January 1864.

2. *The History of Wayne County, Indiana, Together with Sketches of Its Cities, Villages, and Towns*, vol. 1 (Chicago: Inter-state Publishing Company, 1884), 664; Bundy.

3. Ibid.

4. Bundy; "Meredith's Legislative Record Marked by Sound Judgment" (newspaper clipping), n.p., n.d. Modified from original biography printed in the *Richmond (Ind.) Palladium*, 30 January 1864; Virginia Meredith, "The Story of Oakland Farm" (booklet), n.p., n.d.

5. "General Solomon Meredith Was of Outstanding Character."

6. Andrew White Young, *History of Wayne County, Indiana, From Its First Settlement to the Present Time; With Numerous Biographical and Family Sketches* (Cincinnati, Ohio: R. Clarke & Co., 1872), 270.

7. "When Lincoln's Funeral Train Passed Through Cambridge City," *Cambridge City (Ind.) Tribune*, 26 April 1928.

8. *Cambridge City, Indiana: One Hundred and Fifty Years, 1836–1986* (Dublin, Ind.: Prinit Press, 1986), 14.

9. Virginia Meredith, "Gen. Sol. Meredith," *Richmond (Ind.) Daily Sun-Telegram*, 12 May 1897.

10. *History of Wayne County, Indiana*, vol. 1, 664.

11. Meredith, "Gen. Sol. Meredith."

12. Meredith, "The Story of Oakland Farm."

13. Ibid.

14. "The Master of Meredith House," *Indianapolis Star Magazine*, n.d.

15. Meredith, "The Story of Oakland Farm."

16. Ibid.

17. R. L. Ulrich, "Oakland Farm: The History of a House" (pamphlet) (Cambridge City, Ind.: The Simplistic Press, 1972).

18. Copies of Solomon Meredith's letterhead were obtained from the Indiana Historical Society, Indianapolis.

19. William Carroll Latta, *Outline History of Indiana Agriculture* (West Lafayette, Ind.: Epsilon Sigma Phi [Alpha Lambda Chapter], Purdue University, and Indiana County Agricultural Agents Association, 1938), 190 and 211.

20. Bundy.

21. "Mrs. Meredith, Famed Hoosier Leader, Is Dead."

22. Ulrich.

23. *Indiana State Board of Agriculture Annual Reports*, 1853–58.

24. "Agricultural Fairs. Cambridge City Indiana. One Hundred Years (1836–1936)" (booklet), September 1936, 47.

25. *Indiana State Board of Agriculture Annual Report,* 1872, vol. 2, 75.

26. Ibid., 104.

27. Purdue University Department of Animal Sciences, "Indiana Livestock Breeder's Association Hall of Fame," November 2007.
<http://www.ansc.purdue.edu/ilba/HallOfFame.htm>

28. Bundy.

29. Ibid.

30. "Lieutenant Samuel Meredith" (obituary), *Richmond (Ind.) Palladium,* 10 February 1864.

31. "David Meredith" (obituary), *Richmond (Ind.) Humming Bird,* 13 April 1867.

32. *The History of Wayne County, Indiana, Together with Sketches of Its Cities, Villages, and Towns,* vol. 2 (Chicago: Inter-state Publishing Company, 1884), 585.

33. Bundy.

34. "After a New Pattern," 5.

35. Ibid.; Shepherd, et al., 269.

36. Shepherd, et al., 269.

37. *History of Wayne County, Indiana,* vol. 2, 585.

38. "After a New Pattern," 5.

39. Untitled, *Richmond (Ind.) Telegram* (newspaper clipping), c. 28 April 1870. This article, located in the private collection of the Robert Miller Family, described the wedding of Virginia Claypool and Henry Meredith.

40. "Matrimonial," *Richmond (Ind.) Palladium,* [1870].

41. Ulrich.

42. "Honoring Those Who Have Achieved," 4.

43. "Virginia Claypool Meredith" (unpublished manuscript), n.p., n.d.

44. *Indiana State Board of Agriculture Annual Report,* 1870, vol. 12, 133.

45. Meredith, "The Story of Oakland Farm."

46. *Indiana State Board of Agriculture Annual Report,* 1873, vol. 15, 100.

47. "At Rest. Obsequies of Gen. Solomon Meredith at Cambridge City, Yesterday," *Indianapolis Journal,* 25 October 1875.

48. Ibid.

49. Ibid.

50. "Gen. Solomon Meredith," *Masonic Advocate* (photocopy), 1875.

51. The location of the grave of Solomon Meredith's daughter, Mary, who preceded him in death, is unknown. Mary's death occurred before Solomon Meredith purchased Oakland Farm, so it seems likely that her gravesite is at Capitol Hill Cemetery in Cambridge City, Indiana.

52. *Indiana State Board of Agriculture Annual Report,* 1876, vol. 18, 58–59 and 63–64.

53. *Indiana State Board of Agriculture Annual Report,* 1882, vol. 24, 18.

54. *History of Wayne County, Indiana,* vol. 2, 586.

55. Untitled, *Cambridge City (Ind.) Tribune,* 13 January 1881.

56. All statistics regarding Henry and Virginia Meredith's production at Oakland Farm were drawn from the U.S. Bureau of the Census, *Indiana, Wayne Township, U.S. Tenth Census of Agriculture,* 1880, Reel 3966 (Washington, D.C., 1880).

57. U.S. Bureau of the Census, *U.S. Census, 1880, Jackson, Wayne, Indiana,* Family History Library Film 1254322, NA film number T9-0322, 165A. <www.ancestry.com>

58. "Mrs. Meredith, Famed Hoosier Leader, Is Dead."

59. "After a New Pattern," 5–6.

60. Antoinette Van Hoesen Wakeman, "Women as Stock Farmers," *The Chautauquan* (weekly news magazine), 15 September 1892, 736.

61. "Obituary—Hon. H. C. Meredith," *Richmond (Ind.) Evening Item,* 6 July 1882.

62. "A Woman as a Farmer."

63. Meredith, "The Story of Oakland Farm."

64. Johnston and Hand, 308.

CHAPTER 3

The Woman Farmer from Cambridge City

1. "A Woman as a Farmer."

2. "Mrs. Virginia C. Meredith, Honorary President I. F. C."

3. U.S. Census Office, "Occupations (Table CIII) from the U.S. Census, 1880," in *Compendium of the Tenth Census* (1 June 1880) (Washington, D.C.: Government Printing Office, 1885), 1368.

4. Dorothea Kahn, "Women Become Full Farmers in Activities of Agriculture. Write Their Names High on Agriculture's Roll of Honor," *Christian Science Monitor,* 18 November 1931.

5. "A Woman as a Farmer."

6. C. M. Ginther, "Representative Woman Agriculturist," *Orange Judd Farmer (Ill.),* 6 April 1901.

7. Information about property purchased and sold by Solomon Meredith, Henry C. Meredith, and Virginia C. Meredith was found in various land abstracts in Jackson Township and Washington Township, Wayne County, Indiana.

8. "Honoring Those Who Have Achieved," 5.

9. "Mrs. Virginia C. Meredith, Honorary President I. F. C."

10. Ginther.

11. "Indiana Short-horns," *Breeder's Gazette* 5 (14 February 1884): n.p.

12. Ibid.

13. "Sale of South Downs at Oakland Farm," *Cambridge City (Ind.) Tribune,* 18 September 1884.

14. Ibid.

15. "A New Bull for the Meredith Herd," *Breeder's Gazette* 8 (24 September 1885): 492.

16. Ibid.

17. "Mrs. Meredith's Sale of Short-Horns," *Cambridge City (Ind.) Tribune,* 26 May 1887.

18. Ibid.

19. Ibid.

20. "Mrs. H. C. Meredith's Offering," *Breeder's Gazette* 40 (26 May 1887): 832.

21. "Mrs. Meredith's Sale of Short-Horns."

22. "The Short-Horn Cattle Sale. Fair Attendance, but Prices Rule Light," *Cambridge City (Ind.) Tribune,* 25 April 1889.

23. Untitled, *Cambridge City (Ind.) Tribune,* 14 May 1891.

24. "Department Notes: Experiment Station," *Purdue Exponent* 8, no. 8 (28 January 1897): 105.

25. "Public Sale of Short-Horns by Mrs. Virginia C. Meredith at Cambridge City, Ind.," *Breeder's Gazette* 19 (May 13, 1891): 376.

26. Untitled, *Breeder's Gazette* 18 (31 December 1890): 515; "Short-Horn Breeders in the Hoosier State," *Breeder's Gazette* 19 (28 January 1891): 65.

27. *Indiana State Board of Agriculture Annual Reports, 1882–1906.*

28. Esther Griffin White, "Virginia Claypool Meredith. Combing the Widest Culture with the Acumen of the Practical Woman of Affairs, She is Known as a Successful Stock-Breeder as Well as a Lecturer and Writer," *Dignam's Magazine,* vol. 3, no. 1, September 1905, 5–6.

29. "Mrs. Meredith's Short-Horns and Southdowns," *Breeder's Gazette* 28 (28 August 1895): 136; "Virginia Meredith, 'Queen of Agriculture' Dies in Lafayette," *Indianapolis News,* 11 December 1936.

30. "A Woman as a Farmer."

31. "Mrs. Virginia C. Meredith, Honorary President I. F. C."

32. "Women Who Run Their Own Farm and Make Them Pay," *Chicago Daily Tribune,* 18 November 1900.

33. Gertrude Edwards, handwritten notes from c. 1970; "They Achieve," *Indianapolis Star,* 14 June 1947.

34. Blanche Foster Boruff, "In Memoriam—Virginia Claypool Meredith," in *Women of Indiana* (Indianapolis: Indiana Women's Biography Association, M. Farson [c. 1941]), 200; Margaret Moore Post, "Mrs. Meredith Served Agriculture," *Indianapolis News,* 28 January 1976; Meredith, "The Story of Oakland Farm"; "One of State's Outstanding Women," *Richmond (Ind.) Item,* 5 January 1936.

35. "Queen of American Agriculture," *International Altrusan* 13, no. 8 (April 1936): 8.

36. "Mrs. Meredith, Famed Hoosier Leader, Is Dead."

37. Mary Matthews, "Biography of Virginia Meredith" (unpublished manuscript), 25 February 1937.

38. Virginia Claypool Meredith, "Quarter Century Reunion Glendale College. 1854–1879. Class of [18]66" (booklet), 1879, 47–48.

39. Ibid., 48.

40. Ibid., 42.

41. Purdue University, personnel records of Mary L. Matthews, 1912–35.

42. Circumstantial evidence regarding the birth of Meredith Matthews was found in the *Indianapolis, Indiana, Directories, 1887–90* (Indianapolis: R. L. Polk and Co., 1897–90).

43. "Queen of American Agriculture," *International Altrusan* 13, no. 8 (April 1936): 8.

44. Purdue University Office of the Registrar, phone conversation with Frederick Whitford, 2007.

45. Information about Meredith Matthews was obtained from the U.S. Census for 1920 and for 1930; California Department of Health Services, Certificate of Death for Meredith Matthews, 2 February 1962.

46. California Department of Health Services, Certificate of Death for Meredith Matthews, 2 February 1962.

47. "Mrs. Meredith's Sale of Short-Horns"; "The Short-Horn Cattle Sale."

48. "Oakland Farm and Its Owners," *Ohio Farmer*, 8 May 1902, 440.

49. "A Woman as a Farmer."

50. "Mrs. Virginia C. Meredith, Honorary President I. F. C."

51. Boruff, 200.

52. Bartholomew, 53.

53. "History of Oakland Farm," *(Richmond, Ind.) Daily Sun-Telegram*, 10 July 1902, 4.

54. Ibid.

55. Bartholomew, 54.

56. "History of Oakland Farm."

57. "Mrs. Virginia Claypool Meredith," *Journal of Home Economics* 29, no 3 (March 1937): 180.

58. White, 5–6.

59. Bartholomew, 53.

60. "Great Herd To Be Sold. The Meredith Short Horns Will Go at Auction," *(Richmond, Ind.) Daily Sun-Telegram*, 2 August 1902; "The Last Oakland Farm Cattle Sale," *Cambridge City (Ind.) Tribune*, 11 September 1902.

61. "Great Herd To Be Sold."

62. "The Last Oakland Farm Cattle Sale."

63. "Great Herd to Be Sold."

64. "History of Oakland Farm"; "The Last Oakland Farm Cattle Sale."

65. White, 5–6.

66. Untitled, *Cambridge City (Ind.) Tribune*, 28 May 1903.

67. White, 5–6.

68. Untitled, *Cambridge City (Ind.) Tribune*, 20 October 1904.

69. Untitled, *Cambridge City (Ind.) Tribune*, 11 June 1903.

70. White, 5–6.

71. Untitled, *Cambridge City (Ind.) Tribune*, 17 September 1903.

72. Luther M. Feeger, "Meredith Monument, Once on Farm, Later Moved to Cemetery," *Richmond (Ind.) Palladium-Item and Sun-Telegram*, 17 March 1965.

73. White, 5–6.

74. Earl E. Robbins, "Memorial from the Indiana Livestock Breeders' Association," in "Virginia C. Meredith—A Trustee of Purdue University. 1921–1936, Purdue University" (memorial service program), 12 January 1937.

75. White, 5–6.

76. William Carroll Latta, letter to Virginia Meredith, 12 January 1904. Letter book, 30 November 1903 to 3 August 1904, 290.

77. Virginia Meredith, letter to United States Senator Charles Warren Fairbanks, 20 February 1904.

78. "The Shorthorn Sale," *Cambridge City (Ind.) Tribune,* 28 September 1905.

79. "Norborough Short-horns," *Breeder's Gazette* 61 (10 April 1912): 900.

80. "The Indiana State Fair," *Breeder's Gazette* 48 (20 September 1905): 522; "The Shorthorn Sale."

81. "The Cattle Department," *Breeder's Gazette* 54 (16 September 1908): 491.

82. Ibid.

83. "$58,000 in Prizes at Indiana State Fair. Silver Cup from Mrs. Meredith," *Indianapolis News,* 14 August 1908.

84. "The Cattle Department."

85. Robbins.

86. "History of Oakland Farm." See also Ch. 2, n. 51.

87. White; George S. Cottman, "John Mahoney: An Indianapolis Sculptor," *Indiana Magazine of History* 25 (1929): 191.

88. "History of Oakland Farm."

89. A note attached to a newspaper clipping (n.p., n.d.) found in the private collection of the Robert Miller Family states, "'Turk' and 'Tom' are buried beside each other west of the Monument"; "After a New Pattern," 5–6; Meredith, "Roads of Remembrance."

90. Meredith, "Roads of Remembrance."

91. From an untitled newspaper clipping (n.p., n.d.) found in the private collection of the Robert Miller Family.

92. Untitled, *Cambridge City (Ind.) Tribune,* 21 September 1905. A note with a picture of the badge that was presented to Virginia Meredith was found in the private collection of the Robert Miller Family attached to this newspaper article.

93. "The Meredith Monument To Be Removed to Riverside Cemetery," *Cambridge City (Ind.) Tribune,* 13 August 1908; Feeger.

94. "The Meredith Monument To Be Removed to Riverside Cemetery."

95. Feeger.

96. "The Meredith Monument To Be Removed to Riverside Cemetery."

97. Argus Ogborn, interview with Allison Feemster, 1 April 1964 (two-page, handwritten note), about moving the Meredith monument.

98. "Library Gets Jeweled Sword of the Late General Meredith," *Cambridge (Ind.) City Tribune,* 7 June 1928.

99. Ibid.

100. Virginia Meredith, "The Need of Special Training for Agricultural Pursuits" (speech), in *Indiana State Board of Agriculture Annual Report,* 1905, vol. 46, 566.

101. "A Woman as a Farmer."

102. Ibid.

103. Ibid.

104. "One Woman to Another," *Breeder's Gazette* 96 (October 1931): 8.

CHAPTER 4
A Voice for Rural People
1. William Carroll Latta, "Report on Farmers' Institutes for the Year 1902," 16, in *Purdue University Farmers' Institutes Annual Reports, 1889–1911* (n.p., [1911]).
2. "Honoring Those Who Have Achieved," 4.
3. Frederick Whitford and Andrew G. Martin, *The Grand Old Man of Purdue University and Indiana Agriculture: A Biography of William Carroll Latta* (West Lafayette, Ind.: Purdue University Press, 2005), 123.
4. William Carroll Latta, Report of the Superintendent, c. 21 December 1900. Letter book, 13 November 1900 to 13 July 1901, 169.
5. William Carroll Latta, "Indiana Farmers' Institutes from Their Origin, in 1882, to 1904," 27, in *Purdue University Farmers' Institutes Annual Reports, 1889–1911* (n.p., [1911]).
6. William Carroll Latta, "Report on Farmers' Institutes for the Years 1889–1893," 7, in *Purdue University Farmers' Institutes Annual Reports, 1889–1911* (n.p., [1911]).
7. Jack Edward Walters, ed., *The Semi-Centennial Alumni Record of Purdue University* (West Lafayette, Ind.: Purdue University, May 1924), 8.
8. William Carroll Latta, "Indiana Farmers' Institutes from Their Origin, in 1882, to 1904," 68, in *Purdue University Farmers' Institutes Annual Reports, 1889–1911* (n.p., [1911]).
9. William Carroll Latta, letter to Virginia Meredith, 23 December 1895. Letter book, 13 November 1895 to 3 August 1896, 289.
10. William Carroll Latta, "Report on Farmers' Institutes for the Years 1889–1893," 7, in *Purdue University Farmers' Institutes Annual Reports, 1889–1911* (n.p., [1911]); William Carroll Latta, "Report on Farmers' Institutes for the Year 1894," 4, in *Purdue University Farmers' Institutes Annual Reports, 1889–1911* (n.p., [1911]).
11. William Carroll Latta, "Indiana Farmers' Institutes from Their Origin, in 1882, to 1904," 28, in *Purdue University Farmers' Institutes Annual Reports, 1889–1911* (n.p., [1911]).
12. Thomas R. Johnston, "Woman Trustee of Purdue Aids in Things Progressive" (newspaper clipping), n.p., n.d.; "Mrs. Meredith, Famed Hoosier Leader, Is Dead."
13. "Indiana Woman Lauded at Ingham Farm Club" (newspaper clipping), n.p., 1934.
14. William Carroll Latta, letter to Virginia Meredith, 22 January 1896. Letter book, 13 November 1895 to 3 August 3, 1896, 504.
15. William Carroll Latta, letter to Virginia Meredith, 21 November 1895. Letter book, 13 November 1895 to 3 August 1896, 71.
16. William Carroll Latta, "Indiana Farmers' Institutes from Their Origin, in 1882, to 1904," 28–29, in *Purdue University Farmers' Institutes Annual Reports, 1889–1911* (n.p., [1911]).
17. Bartholomew, 51; William Carroll Latta, Schedule of Farmers' Institutes for the Season of 1899–1900, c. 25 October 1899. Letter book, 18 July to 2 February 1900, 385–88.
18. "Virginia C. Meredith," *Biographical and Genealogical History of Wayne, Fayette, Union, and Franklin Counties, Indiana, vol. 1* (Chicago: Lewis, 1899), 453.
19. Bartholomew, 51.
20. "Indiana Woman Lauded at Ingham Farm Club"; "Department Notes: Experiment Station," *Purdue Exponent* 8, no. 10 (25 February 1897): 133.

21. Bartholomew, 51.

22. "A Woman as a Farmer."

23. Ibid.

24. Ibid.

25. "Honoring Those Who Have Achieved," 4–5.

26. "After a New Pattern," 5–6.

27. William Carroll Latta, letter to Virginia Meredith, 8 December 1894. Letter book, 23 March 1894 to 5 January 1895, 760.

28. William Carroll Latta, letter to M. M. C. Hobbs, 20 August 1894. Letter book, 23 March 1894 to 5 January 1895, 360.

29. William Carroll Latta, letter to C. B. Harris, 11 April 1894. Letter book, 23 March 1894 to 5 January 1895, 126.

30. William Carroll Latta, letter to Virginia Meredith, 31 March 189[4]. Letter book, 23 March 1894 to 5 January 1895, 61. The letter is dated 31 March 1893, but since it is bound in the March 1894 section of this book, it should likely be dated 1894.

31. William Carroll Latta, letter to Virginia Meredith, c. 14 May 1894. Letter book, 23 March 1894 to 5 January 1895, 208.

32. William Carroll Latta, letter to Virginia Meredith, 7 July 1894. Letter book, 23 March 1894 to 5 January 1895, 265.

33. William Carroll Latta, letter to Virginia Meredith, c. 23 July 1894. Letter book, 23 March 1894 to 5 January 1895, 310.

34. William Carroll Latta, letter to Virginia Meredith, 8 August 1894. Letter book, 23 March 1894 to 5 January 1895, 351.

35. William Carroll Latta, letter to Virginia Meredith, 19 June 1896. Letter book, 13 November 1895 to 3 August 1896, 929.

36. "A Woman as a Farmer."

37. William Carroll Latta, letter to Virginia Meredith, 9 September 1899. Letter book, 18 July 1899 to 2 February 1900, 137.

38. William Carroll Latta, letter to Virginia Meredith, 18 September 1899. Letter book, 18 July 1899 to 2 February 1900, 173.

39. William Carroll Latta, letter to county chairmen for Farmers' Institutes, 29 December 1903. Letter book, 30 November 1903 to 3 August 1904, 202.

40. William Carroll Latta, letter to Virginia Meredith, 21 January 1904. Letter book, 30 November 1903 to 3 August 1904, page 355.

41. William Carroll Latta, letter to Virginia Meredith, 1 August 1904. Letter book, 30 November 1903 to 3 August 1904, 989.

42. William Carroll Latta, letter to Virginia Meredith, 28 July 1904. Letter book, 30 November 1903 to 3 August 1904, 979.

43. "Department Notes. Experiment Station," *Purdue Exponent* 8, no. 8 (28 January 1897): 105.

44. William Carroll Latta, letter to Virginia Meredith, 31 July 1901. Letter book, 23 November 1900 to 13 July 190, 164; William Carroll Latta, "Report on Farmers' Institutes for the Year 1902" 7, in *Purdue University Farmers' Institutes Annual Reports, 1889–1911* (n.p., [1911]).

45. "A Preble Co., O[hio]., Institute," *Ohio Farmer,* 17 March 1906, 315.

46. William Carroll Latta, letter to Virginia Meredith, 18 April 1904. Letter book, 30 November 1903 to 3 August 1904, 752.

47. "Summer Dairy Meeting," *Indiana Farmer's Guide,* 31 July 1920, 13.

48. Untitled, *Cambridge City (Ind.) Tribune,* 21 February 1895.

49. "Farmers' Institute. The Opening Session Last Night—Greetings of Welcome, Eloquent Responses, Etc.," *Vicksburg (Miss.) Evening Post,* 21 February 1895.

50. Ibid.

51. Ibid.

52. "The Farmers' Institute. To Be Held at Vicksburg from February 20 to 22, 1895," *Vicksburg (Miss.) Evening Post,* 20 February 1895.

53. "Farmers' Institute. The Opening Session Last Night."

54. "After a New Pattern," 5–6.

55. Ibid.

56. "Farmers' Institute. The Opening Session Last Night."

57. "Farmers' Institute. Last Night's Session," *Vicksburg (Miss.) Evening Post,* 22 February 1895.

58. Untitled, *Cambridge City (Ind.) Tribune,* 4 March 1895.

59. "After a New Pattern," 5–6.

60. "Farmers' Institute," *Vicksburg (Miss.) Evening Post,* 25 February 1895.

61. Untitled, *Cambridge City (Ind.) Tribune,* 4 March 1895.

62. "Farmers' Institute," *Vicksburg (Miss.) Evening Post,* 25 February 1895.

63. Bartholomew, 55; Virginia Meredith, "Farm Life: Its Privileges and Possibilities," *Indiana State Board of Agriculture Annual Report,* 1892, vol. 33, 540–43.

64. Meredith, "Farm Life: Its Privileges and Possibilities," 541.

65. "A New Contributor," *Breeder's Gazette* 24 (13 December 1893): 390.

66. "Women and the Farm—I," *Breeder's Gazette* 24 (13 December 1893): 391.

67. Ibid.

68. Ibid.

69. Ibid.

70. Ibid.

71. Ibid.

72. Ibid.

73. "Women and the Farm—III," *Breeder's Gazette* 25 (3 January 1894): 3.

74. "Women and the Farm—II," *Breeder's Gazette* 24 (27 December 1893): 432.

75. Ibid.

76. "Women and the Farm—V," *Breeder's Gazette* 25 (17 January 1894): 34.

77. Ibid.

78. "Women and the Farm—VII," *Breeder's Gazette* 25 (31 January 1894): 67.

79. Ibid.

80. "Women and the Farm—V."

81. "Women and the Farm—IV," *Breeder's Gazette* 25 (10 January 1894): 18.

82. "Women and the Farm—VI," *Breeder's Gazette* 25 (24 January 1894): 50.

83. "Women and the Farm—IV."

84. Ibid.

85. "Women and the Farm—VI."

86. "Women and the Farm—VIII," *Breeder's Gazette* 25 (7 February 1894): 83.

87. "Mrs. Virginia C. Meredith, Honorary President I. F. C."

88. Ginther.

89. Untitled, *Southern Planter,* March 1892, 136.

90. "Indiana Woman Lauded at Ingham Farm Club."

91. Meredith, "The Need of Special Training for Agricultural Pursuits," 567.

92. Virginia Meredith, "Why Short-Horns Are the Best Cattle for Indiana Farms" (speech), in *Indiana State Board of Agriculture Annual Report,* 1905, vol. 46, 317–18.

93. Meredith, "The Need of Special Training for Agricultural Pursuits," 567.

94. E. L. D. Seymour, *Farm Knowledge: A Complete Manual of Successful Farming Written by Recognized Authorities in All Parts of the Country; Based on Sound Principles and the Actual Experience of Real Farmers,* vol. 4 of *Farm Life* (Garden City, N.Y.: Doubleday, Page, & Company, 1918), 165.

95. "One of 'The Gazette's' Most-Esteemed Contributors This Week Assumes Editorial Charge of a Page To Be Devoted to the Women and the Boys and Girls of the Stock-Farm Home," *Breeder's Gazette* 79 (12 May 1921): 858.

96. "In and About the Farm Home," *Breeder's Gazette* 81 (26 January 1922): 107; Untitled, *Breeder's Gazette* 81 (23 February 1922): 260; The Home, *Breeder's Gazette* 84 (1 November 1923): 553.

97. "Talks with, by, and about Boys and Girls Who Are Keenly Interested in Clubwork, Which Is Supported by Breeders, Farmers, and Businessmen," *Breeder's Gazette* 79 (19 May 1921): 901.

98. "Likes Mrs. Meredith's Page," *Breeder's Gazette* 80 (15 September 1921): 369.

99. "A New Outlook Changes the Inlook—Reading and Music in Farm Homes— A Farmer's Wife Loves the Tennessee Mountain Country—'Duffy's Whiskey' and Old Age," *Breeder's Gazette* 80 (29 September 1921): 441.

100. Ibid.

101. "The Farm Home," *Breeder's Gazette* 81 (15 June 1922): 806.

102. "An Inspiring Interpretation, with Practical Applications to the Life of Stock-Farm Boys and Girls, of the Old Juvenile Rhymes Beginning 'Mary Had a Little Lamb,'" *Breeder's Gazette* 79 (23 June 1921): 1109.

103. "A New Outlook Changes the Inlook," 441.

104. "Encouraging Students and County Teachers, and the Improvement of Country Schools Are Subjects Worthy of Earnest Thought by America's Womanhood—and Manhood as Well," *Breeder's Gazette* 79 (9 June 1921): 1036.

105. "The Response of Boys and Girls to Modern Methods of Teaching—A Kansas Club Member's Letter—An Indiana Lad Who Grew Watermelons This Year—An Iowa Breeder's Son Who Is Raising Duroc-Jerseys," *Breeder's Gazette* 80 (22 September 1921): 408.

106. "Poultry Projects Interest and Reward Young Folk in California and Illinois, and Dairy Calves Are Appreciated by a Kentucky Girl and a Wyoming Boy Who Care for Them Intelligently," *Breeder's Gazette* 80 (14 July 1921): 52.

107. "'Breakfast Nooks' in Farm Homes—The Social Value of the Morning Meal—The Scarcity and Use of Fine Table Linen—An Eyesore Made Lovely by Flowers," *Breeder's Gazette* 80 (1 September 1921): 284.

108. "How Several Mothers Who Studied Child Management at College Are Making Practical Use of Their Scientific Training in Their Own Homes," *Breeder's Gazette* 80 (4 August 1921): 150.

109. Ibid.

110. "The Farm Home," *Breeder's Gazette* 82 (6 July 1922): 20.

111. "The Motherless Child," *Breeder's Gazette* 82 (7 December 1922): 814.

112. "Two Noted European Visitors, A Woman's Tribute to a Cornbelt Farm Home, and an Experiment in Running a Household According to a Schedule," *Breeder's Gazette* 80 (18 August 1921): 220.

113. "The Farm Home," *Breeder's Gazette* 82 (3 August 1922): 124.

114. "How Several Mothers," 150.

115. "The Farm Home," *Breeder's Gazette* 84 (16 August 1923): 184.

116. "The Farm Home," *Breeder's Gazette* 82 (7 September 1922): 278.

117. "The Farm Home," *Breeder's Gazette* 84 (13 September 1923): 312.

118. Ibid.

119. "The Home," *Breeder's Gazette* 85 (7 February 1924): 170.

120. "Next Christmas," *Breeder's Gazette* 90 (25 November 1926): 594.

121. "One Woman to Another," 8.

122. Ibid.

123. "The Good Promise," *Breeder's Gazette* 97 (April 1932): 3.

124. "Virginia Meredith, Queen of Agriculture, Is Dead."

CHAPTER 5
Empowering Women Through Club Work

1. "Virginia Meredith, Queen of Agriculture, Is Dead."

2. Boruff, 200; Post.

3. The Who-When-What Co., "Mrs. Virginia C. Meredith," in *The Who-When-What Book* (Chicago: The Who-When-What Co., 1900), 32.

4. Arcada Stark Balz, ed., *History Indiana Federation of Clubs* (Fort Wayne, Ind.: Fort Wayne Printing Co., 1939), 61.

5. "Former Prominent County Resident Served on Board for Columbian Exposition," *Richmond (Ind.) Palladium and Sun-Telegram,* 11 October 1933; Bartholomew, 55; Untitled, *The Indiana Club Woman* 6, no. 4 (4 June 1898), n.p.

6. Virginia Meredith, "Supplemental Sketch," in "An Appreciation of the Six Charter Members of the Helen Hunt Club Presented to the Club on Founder's Day, September Six, Nineteen Twenty" (unpublished manuscript), 6 September 1920.

7. Irene Hasket, Untitled (newspaper clipping), n.p., 29 April [c. 1936].

8. Ophelia Shults, "Supplemental Sketch," in "An Appreciation of the Six Charter Members of the Helen Hunt Club Presented to the Club on Founder's Day, September Six, Nineteen Twenty" (unpublished manuscript), 6 September 1920.

9. Women's Clubs of Indiana, "Indiana State Federation of Clubs Year Book. 1907–1908," 74.

10. Shults.

11. Ibid.

12. Women's Clubs of Indiana, "Indiana State Federation of Clubs. Manual. 1906–1907," 20.

13. "Charter Members of Helen Hunt Club at Cambridge" (newspaper clipping), n.p., circa 1935.

14. "History of Cambridge City Library" (unpublished report), November 1939, 1.

15. Meredith, "Supplemental Sketch."

16. "History of Cambridge City Library," 1.

17. Ibid., 2.

18. Ibid.

19. Meredith, "Supplemental Sketch."

20. Indiana Federation of Clubs, "Representatives, Women's Literary Clubs of Indiana" (pamphlet), 1899.

21. Balz, ed., 116; Mrs. Frank J. Sheehan, *The Indiana Club Woman: Historical Edition*, July/August 1927, 4.

22. Balz, ed., 44.

23. Indiana Club Union, "First Convention of the Indiana Club Union" (conference program), 3–4 June 1890; Sheehan, 4.

24. Balz, ed., 45.

25. Indiana Union of Literary Clubs, "The Bulletin" (detailed summary from conference program), 1892, 1; Indiana Union of Literary Clubs, "Minutes and Constitution of the Indiana Union of Literary Clubs," 1902, 5–6.

26. Indiana Union of Literary Clubs, "Minutes and Constitution of the Indiana Union of Literary Clubs," 1902, 6.

27. Ibid., 10.

28. Johnston and Hand, 308; Indiana Union of Literary Clubs, "Minutes and Constitution of the Indiana Union of Literary Clubs," 1894, 15–16.

29. Sheehan, 7.

30. Indiana Union of Literary Clubs, "Programme, Sixth Annual Convention" (conference program), 14–16 May 1895.

31. Balz, ed., 62.

32. Sheehan, 7.

33. Ibid., 44.

34. Indiana Union of Literary Clubs, "Programme, Sixth Annual Convention" (conference program), 14–16 May 1895.

35. Indiana Union of Literary Clubs, "Minutes and Constitution of the Indiana Union of Literary Clubs. Sixth Annual Convention," 1895, 7.

36. Indiana Union of Literary Clubs, "Proceedings of the Sixteen Annual Convention," 1905, 29–30.

37. Indiana Union of Literary Clubs, "The Seventeenth Annual Convention of the Indiana Union of Literary Clubs" (conference program), 9–11 October 1906.

38. Women's Clubs of Indiana, "Indiana State Federation of Clubs Manual, 1906–1907," 8.

39. Indiana Union of Literary Clubs, "The Seventeenth Annual Convention of the Indiana Union of Literary Clubs" (conference program), 9–11 October 1906.

40. Balz, ed., 113.

41. Ibid., 115.

42. Ibid., 114.

43. Sheehan, 2.

44. Balz, ed, 117.

45. Esther H. Billings, "Indiana Federation of Clubs: 1890–1920" (unpublished manuscript), 1.

46. Balz, ed., 116.

47. Ibid., 118.

48. Ibid.

49. Ibid., 119.

50. Women's Clubs of Indiana, "Indiana State Federation of Clubs Manual, 1906–1907," 10.

51. Balz, ed., 120.

52. Ibid., 119.

53. Women's Clubs of Indiana, "Indiana State Federation of Clubs Manual, 1906–1907," 12.

54. Billings, 1.

55. Sheehan, 16.

56. Billings, 1.

57. Women's Clubs of Indiana, "Indiana State Federation of Clubs Manual, 1906–1907," 34.

58. Women's Clubs of Indiana, "Indiana State Federation of Clubs Year Book. 1909–1910."

59. Women's Clubs of Indiana, "Indiana State Federation of Clubs Manual, 1906–1907," 13.

60. Ibid., 48.

61. Ibid., 34.

62. Ibid., 3.

63. Ibid., 5–6.

64. Women's Clubs of Indiana, "Indiana Federation of Clubs Year Book. 1911–1912," 158.

65. Women's Clubs of Indiana, "Minutes of the Trustees: 1912–1925," 30 October 1912, 2.

66. Balz, ed., 60.

67. Women's Clubs of Indiana, "Minutes of the Trustees: 1912–1925," 21 October 1913, 24.

68. Ibid., 17 February 1915, 53.

69. Ibid., 28 October 1915, 56.

70. Ibid., 30 October 1912, 3.

71. Women's Clubs of Indiana, "Indiana Federation of Clubs Year Book. 1912–1913," 74.

72. Women's Clubs of Indiana, "Minutes of the Trustees: 1912–1925," 13 August 1914, 36.

73. Women's Clubs of Indiana, "Minutes of the Trustees: 1912–1925," 28 October 1915, 55.

74. Women's Clubs of Indiana, "Indiana State Federation of Clubs Year Book. 1907–1908," 18.

75. Ibid., 21.

76. Women's Clubs of Indiana, "Indiana Federation of Clubs Year Book. 1910–1911," 23.

77. Women's Clubs of Indiana, "Indiana Federation of Clubs Year Book. 1914–1915," 19–25.

78. Women's Clubs of Indiana, "Indiana Federation of Clubs Year Book. 1912–1913," 78.

79. Women's Clubs of Indiana, "Indiana Federation of Clubs Year Book. 1916–1917," 77.

80. "Queen of American Agriculture," *International Altrusan* 13, no. 8 (April 1936): 8.

81. Women's Clubs of Indiana, "Indiana Federation of Clubs Year Book. 1918–1919," 7.

82. Women's Clubs of Indiana, "Indiana Federation of Clubs Year Book. 1936–1937," 9.

83. Mrs. George W. Jaqua, "From the Indiana Federation of Clubs," in "Virginia C. Meredith—A Trustee of Purdue University. 1921–1936, Purdue University" (memorial service program), 12 January 1937.

84. Women's Clubs of Indiana, "Indiana Federation of Clubs Year Book. 1937–1938," 11.

85. Balz, ed., 431.

86. Ibid.

87. Balz, ed., 432.

88. "Forest Dedicated to Mrs. Meredith," *Indianapolis Star,* 28 May 1938.

89. Indiana Federation of Clubs, "Memorial Forest Dedicated," *The Indiana Club Woman,* June–July 1938, 18.

90. Indiana Federation of Clubs, "Virginia Claypool Meredith Memorial Forest" (unpublished manuscript).

91. Balz, ed., 433.

92. "Shoals Forest in Dedication," *Shoals (Ind.) News,* 3 June 1938.

93. "Forest Dedicated to Mrs. Meredith."

94. "Shoals Forest in Dedication."

95. Balz, ed., 433; "Forest Dedicated to Mrs. Meredith."

96. Balz, ed., 432; "To Dedicate Forest Site Near Shoals."

97. Mrs. George W. Jaqua, "Accepting Our Responsibilities" (speech), n.d., 9.

98. Ibid.

CHAPTER 6

The Lady Manager from Indiana at the Chicago World's Fair

1. Frank Cassell and Marguerite Cassell, "Pride, Profits, and Politics: Indiana and the Columbian Exposition of 1893," *Indiana Magazine of History* 80, no. 2 (June 1984): 93.

2. Reid Badger, *The Great American Fair: The World's Columbian Exposition and American Culture* (Chicago: Nelson Hall, 1979), 49; Moses P. Handy, ed., *The Official Directory of the World's Columbian Exposition, May 1st to October 30th, 1893. A Reference Book of Exhibitors and Exhibits; of the Officers and Members of the World's Commission* (Chicago, W. B. Conkey Company, 1893), 41.

3. Handy, ed., 51.

4. Badger, 51.

5. Handy, ed., 51.

6. Virginia C. Meredith, "Final Report of Mrs. Virginia C. Meredith, Chairman of the Committee on Awards of the Board of Lady Managers" (unpublished manuscript), 27 June 1896, 2.

7. B. F. Havens, "Indiana World's Columbian Exposition, 1893. Final Report of B. F. Havens, Executive Commissioner" (Terre Haute, Ind.: Board of World's Fair Managers, Indiana, April 1894), 2. Located at the Chicago Public Library, Chicago; Handy, ed., 83.

8. Handy, ed., 57.

9. Meredith, "Final Report of Mrs. Virginia C. Meredith," 2.

10. World's Columbian Exposition, Board of Lady Managers Vol. 1, Official Record, 6.

11. Enid Yandell, Jean Loughborough, and Laura Hayes, "To the Board of Lady Managers," in *Three Girls in a Flat* (Chicago: Knight, Leonard, and Co., 1892), 53.

12. Jeanne Madeline Weimann, *The Fair Women: The Story of the Woman's Building, World's Columbian Exposition, Chicago* (Chicago: Academy Chicago, 1981), 42.

13. Handy, ed., 83.

14. "Virginia C. Meredith," in *Biographical and Genealogical History of Wayne, Fayette, Union and Franklin Counties, Indiana, vol. 1* (Chicago: Lewis, 1899), 452.

15. Weimann, 248.

16. Bertha Palmer, letter to Virginia Meredith, 26 February 1892. Vol. 12, 354–55.

17. Bertha Palmer, letter to Virginia Meredith, 24 July 1892. Vol. 13, 914.

18. Bertha Palmer, letter to Virginia Meredith, 21 April 1891. Vol. 11, 35–36.

19. "After a New Pattern," 5–6.

20. World's Columbian Exposition, Board of Lady Managers Vol. 2, Executive Committee Minutes. 8–30 April 1891, 3.

21. Weimann, 45; Handy, ed., 177.

22. World's Columbian Exposition, Board of Lady Managers Vol. 1, Official Record, 7; Handy, ed., 177.

23. Handy, ed., 177–78.

24. Weimann, 48.

25. World's Columbian Exposition, Board of Lady Managers Vol. 1, Official Record, 21.

26. Ibid., 3.

27. Ibid., 80 and 85.

28. Ibid., 95.

29. "Work of the Lady Managers," *Chicago Daily Tribune,* 22 April 1891.

30. World's Columbian Exposition, Board of Lady Managers Vol. 1, Official Record, 73.

31. Ibid., 90.

32. Weimann, 76 and 105.

33. World's Columbian Exposition, Board of Lady Managers Vol. 1, Official Record, 29 and 51.

34. Ibid., 60–61.

35. Meredith, "Final Report of Mrs. Virginia C. Meredith," 3.

36. World's Columbian Exposition, Board of Lady Managers Vol. 1, Official Record, 64–65.

37. Weimann, 51.

38. World's Columbian Exposition, Board of Lady Managers Vol. 1, Official Record, 71–72.

39. Virginia Meredith, "Woman's Department, World's Columbian Exhibition" (speech), in *Indiana State Board of Agriculture Annual Report,* 1892, vol. 33, 116.

40. World's Columbian Exposition, Board of Lady Managers Vol. 1, Official Record, 75.

41. Ibid., 107-8.

42. Ibid., 108.

43. Ibid.

44. Ibid., 109.

45. Ibid.

46. Meredith, "Final Report of Mrs. Virginia C. Meredith," 3.

47. World's Columbian Exposition, Board of Lady Managers Vol. 2, Executive Committee Minutes. 8–30 April 1891, 3.

48. Cassell and Cassell, 96.

49. Handy, ed., 83.

50. Havens, 7.

51. "What Women Have Done: A Report of Their World's Fair Work Prepared and Submitted," *Chicago Daily Tribune,* 28 July 1891.

52. Ibid.

53. Virginia Meredith, "Woman's Department, World's Columbian Exhibition" (speech), in *Indiana State Board of Agriculture Annual Report,* 1892, vol. 33, 117.

54. "Review of the Week in Detail: Work of Columbian Exposition Officials During the Last Seven Days," *Chicago Daily Tribune,* 23 May 1891.

55. Bertha Palmer, letter to Virginia Meredith, 9 June 1891. Vol. 11, 42.

56. "Thinks It May Be Refused," *Chicago Daily Tribune,* 6 August 1892.

57. Virginia Meredith, "Woman's Department, World's Columbian Exhibition" (speech), in *Indiana State Board of Agriculture Annual Report,* 1892, vol. 33, 117–18.

58. Ibid.

59. Havens, 5 and 8.

60. Havens, 9.

61. Havens, 8.

62. Ibid., 31.

63. Cassell and Cassell, 112–13 and 115.

64. Havens, 23.

65. World's Columbian Exposition, Board of Lady Managers Vol. 1, Official Record, 134.

66. Ibid., 135.

67. Ibid., 139.

68. Ibid., 145.

69. Meredith, "Final Report of Mrs. Virginia C. Meredith," 5.

70. World's Columbian Exposition, Board of Lady Managers Vol. 1, Official Record, 145–46.

71. Ibid., 147–48.

72. Ibid., 145–46.

73. Ibid., 150.

74. Ibid., 151.

75. Ibid., 174.

76. Bertha Palmer, letter to Virginia Meredith, 13 July 1891. Vol. 11, 55.

77. Weimann, 92.

78. Bertha Palmer, letter to Virginia Meredith, 4 August 1891. Vol. 11, 34.

79. World's Columbian Exposition, Board of Lady Managers Vol. 1, Official Record, 183.

80. Ibid., 184.

81. Ibid., 192.

82. Ibid., 138.

83. "How By-Laws Can Be Changed. The Board of Lady Managers Has a Debate on the Subject—The Morning Session," *Chicago Daily Tribune,* 8 September 1891.

84. Bertha Palmer, letter to Virginia Meredith, 28 August 1891. Vol. 10, 432–33.

85. "Belva Was Squelched. The Women's Council Sits Down on Mrs. Lockwood," *Chicago Daily Tribune,* 26 February 1891.

86. Virginia Meredith, "The Relation of Women to the Columbian Exposition" (speech), in "The Bulletin" (detailed summary from conference program), 1892, 12.

87. Ibid., 12.

88. Bertha Palmer, letter to Virginia Meredith, 14 January 1892. Vol. 11, 225–26.

89. "Mrs. Meredith's Ambition," *Chicago Daily Tribune,* 16 August 1891.

90. "Principal Events of the Last Seven Days in World's Fair Circles," *Chicago Daily Tribune,* 22 August 1891.

91. Bertha Palmer, letter to Virginia Meredith, 22 August 1891. Vol. 10, 343–44.

92. "After a World's Fair Position," *Chicago Daily Tribune,* 10 September 1891.

93. Ibid.

94. "Exposition Notes," *Chicago Daily Tribune,* 13 October 1891.

95. "Cottrell Made Chief," *Chicago Daily Tribune,* 18 October 1891.

96. Ibid.

97. Meredith, "Final Report of Mrs. Virginia C. Meredith," 91.

98. "To Discuss the Subject of Awards," *Chicago Daily Tribune,* 7 January 1893.

99. Who-When-What Co., 32; Bartholomew, 54.

100. Meredith, "Final Report of Mrs. Virginia C. Meredith," 6–7.

101. Ibid.

102. Ibid., 7.

103. Ibid., 5.

104. Ibid.

105. Ibid., 6.

106. Ibid., 5–6.
107. Ibid., 5.
108. Ibid., 4–5.
109. Ibid., 31–32.
110. Ibid., 25–26.
111. Ibid., 10.
112. Ibid.
113. Ibid.
114. "After a New Pattern," 5–6.
115. Meredith, "Final Report of Mrs. Virginia C. Meredith," 10.
116. Ibid., 11.
117. Ibid.
118. Ibid., 14–15.
119. Ibid., 15.
120. Ibid., 16–17.
121. Ibid., 17.
122. Ibid.
123. Ibid., 18.
124. Ibid., 18–19.
125. Ibid., 19–20.
126. Ibid., 23.
127. Ibid., 26.
128. Ibid.
129. Ibid., 27–28.
130. Ibid., 37.
131. Ibid., 29.
132. Ibid.
133. Ibid., 31.
134. Ibid., 31–32.
135. Ibid., 32.
136. Ibid.
137. Ibid., 33.
138. Ibid., 33–34.
139. Ibid., 33.
140. Ibid., 33–34.
141. Ibid., 34–35.
142. Ibid., 35.
143. Ibid., 36.
144. Ibid., 36–37.
145. Ibid., 37.
146. Ibid., 38.
147. Ibid., 37.
148. Ibid., 39.

149. Ibid., 41–42.

150. Ibid., 42.

151. "They Want 140 Women Judges. Lady Managers Prepare a List and Submit It to Mr. Thacher," *Chicago Daily Tribune,* 29 June 1893.

152. Meredith, "Final Report of Mrs. Virginia C. Meredith," 43.

153. "Mr. Thacher Offers 60, Where 130 Are Requested—Lady Managers Must Meet," *Chicago Daily Tribune,* 30 June 1893.

154. Ibid.

155. Meredith, "Final Report of Mrs. Virginia C. Meredith, " 43.

156. Ibid., 45.

157. Ibid.

158. Ibid., 45–46.

159. Ibid., 71.

160. Ibid., 47.

161. Ibid.

162. Ibid., 48.

163. Ibid.

164. Ibid., 48–49.

165. Weimann, 570.

166. Ibid.

167. "Lady Managers Disagree," *New York Times,* 6 August 1893.

168. "To Censure Mrs. Ball: Board of Lady Managers Rehearses Personal Matters," *Chicago Daily Tribune,* 5 August 1893.

169. Weimann, 573.

170. Ibid., 572.

171. Meredith, "Final Report of Mrs. Virginia C. Meredith," 47.

172. Ibid., 51.

173. Ibid.

174. Ibid.

175. Ibid., 58–59.

176. Ibid., 50.

177. Ibid., 51–52.

178. Ibid., 52.

179. Bertha Palmer, letter to Virginia Meredith, 14 October 1893. Vol. 16, 90.

180. Ibid., 91

181. Bertha Palmer, letter to Virginia Meredith, 25 October 1893. Vol. 16, 166.

182. Meredith, "Final Report of Mrs. Virginia C. Meredith," 51.

183. Ibid., 52.

184. Ibid.

185. Ibid., 53.

186. Ibid.

187. Ibid., 56.

188. Ibid., 56–57.

189. Ibid., 56.

190. Information about the history of the Isabella coin was obtained from the U.S. Department of the Treasury "United States Mint" Web site, last accessed 28 November 2007. <http://www.usmint.gov/>

191. Untitled, *Cambridge City (Ind.) Tribune,* 26 October 1893; Untitled, *Breeder's Gazette* 24 (8 November 1893): 310.

192. Untitled, *Cambridge City (Ind.) Tribune,* 26 October 1893.

193. "Lady Managers Are Emancipated," *Chicago Daily Tribune,* 15 September 1893.

194. Ibid.

195. Who-When-What Co., 32; Meredith, "Final Report of Mrs. Virginia C. Meredith," 92.

196. Meredith, "Final Report of Mrs. Virginia C. Meredith," 74.

197. Ibid., 74.

198. Ibid.

199. Ibid.

200. Ibid., 76.

201. Ibid.

202. "To Give Diplomas. Lady Managers' Plan to Outwit John Boyd Thacher," *Chicago Daily Tribune,* 17 October 1893.

203. Meredith, "Final Report of Mrs. Virginia C. Meredith," 74; "Work of the Women. Some of the Things Accomplished by the Great World's Fair," *Chicago Daily Tribune,* 6 October 1894.

204. "To Give Diplomas."

205. Meredith, "Final Report of Mrs. Virginia C. Meredith," 73.

206. "Will Give Awards to Artisans. President Cleveland Signs the Bill Championed by the Lady Managers," *Chicago Daily Tribune,* 9 December 1893.

207. "Women at a Banquet. Last Social Function of the Board of Lady Managers," *Chicago Daily Tribune,* 4 November 1893.

208. "Will Give Awards to Artisans."

209. Meredith, "Final Report of Mrs. Virginia C. Meredith," 73.

210. Ibid., 79.

211. Ibid., 79; Weimann, 588.

212. "Work of the Women."

213. Meredith, "Final Report of Mrs. Virginia C. Meredith," 81.

214. Ibid.

215. Ibid.

216. Ibid., 84.

217. Ibid.

218. Ibid.

219. White, 5–6.

220. Meredith, "Final Report of Mrs. Virginia C. Meredith," 83.

221. Bertha Palmer, letter to Virginia Meredith, 19 October 1894. Vol. 17, 790.

222. Meredith, "Final Report of Mrs. Virginia C. Meredith," 86.

223. "Reports Are Nearly Complete. Work of Board of Lady Managers of World's Fair about Done," *Chicago Daily Tribune,* 8 November 1895.

224. Virginia C. Meredith, "Final Report of Mrs. Virginia C. Meredith, Chairman of the Committee on Awards of the Board of Lady Managers" (unpublished manuscript), 27 June 1896, 86.

225. "Reports Are Nearly Complete. Work of Board of Lady Managers of World's Fair about Done," *Chicago Daily Tribune,* 8 November 1895.

226. Meredith, "Final Report of Mrs. Virginia C. Meredith," 85 and 91.

227. Weimann, 588.

228. Meredith, "Final Report of Mrs. Virginia C. Meredith," 79.

229. "Costumes To Be Seen at the Ball. Rich Dresses and Expensive Ornaments To Be Worn by Those Present," *Chicago Daily Tribune,* 19 October 1892.

230. Nancy Huston Banks, "World's Fair Women," *Harper's Bazaar,* 21 January 1893, 46.

231. "Salon Day at the Arche Club. Chicago Painters and Sculptors Will Be Discussed by Mrs. Mary Ford," *Chicago Daily Tribune,* 26 March 1895.

232. "For the Love of Art. Arche Club Celebrates Its First Birthday with a Salon," *Chicago Daily Tribune,* 30 March 1895.

233. "A Trio of Notable Women," *The Atlanta Journal,* n.d.

234. "Virginia C. Meredith," in *Biographical and Genealogical History of Wayne, Fayette, Union, and Franklin Counties, Indiana, vol. 1* (Chicago: Lewis, 1899), 452.

235. "Notable Chicagoans Revive World's Fair Memories: Pleas for Art," *Chicago Daily Tribune,* 1 February 1923.

236. "Former Prominent County Resident Served."

237. Ibid.

CHAPTER 7
Advancing the Science of Home Life

1. Meredith, "The Story of Oakland Farm."

2. *Cambridge City, Indiana.*

3. "History of Oakland Farm."

4. Indiana Home Economics Association, "A History of Home Economics in Indiana. Golden Anniversary: 1913–1963" (booklet), 1963, 9.

5. Dave O. Thompson, *A History: Fifty Years of Cooperative Extension Service in Indiana* (n.p., [1962]), 53.

6. Latta, *Outline History,* 346.

7. Indiana Home Demonstration Association, "50 Years Learning and Service: 1913–1963" (booklet), 1963.

8. William Carroll Latta, letter to Virginia Meredith, 17 April 1894. Letter book, 23 March 1894 to 5 January 1895, 144.

9. William Carroll Latta, letter to Mrs. J. Lawrence, 21 December 1894. Letter book, 23 March 1894 to 5 January 1895, 862.

10. William Carroll Latta, letter to Col. L. O. Suman, 5 January 1895. Letter book, 23 March 1894 to 5 January 1895, 984.

11. William Carroll Latta, letter to Mrs. W. W. Stevens, 9 April 1894. Letter book, 23 March 1894 to 5 January 1895, 99.

12. Lou Malcomb, "List of Articles Written by Women, Appearing in the Reports of the Indiana State Board of Agriculture" (presentation given as part of the Indiana Library Federation Conference, Division on Women in Indiana Libraries, Indianapolis, April 2002).

13. William Carroll Latta, letter to Samuel Lucas, 5 December 1895. Letter book, 13 November 1895 to 3 August 1896, 145; William Carroll Latta, letter to J. Sherfick, 12 December 1895. Letter book, 13 November 1895 to 3 August 1896, 224.

14. William Carroll Latta, letter to chairmen of Farmers' Institutes, 13 December 1895. Letter book, 13 November 1895 to 3 August 1896, 226.

15. William Carroll Latta, report of Putnam County Farmers' Institute, 20 November 1895. Letter book, 13 November 1895 to 3 August 1896, 67.

16. "Trains Girls as Farmers. Agricultural School of Minnesota Teaches Them Art of Husbandry. On a Par with Men," *Chicago Daily Tribune,* 15 October 1899; University of Minnesota School of Agriculture, "Come to the School of Agriculture at University Farm, St. Paul," *University of Minnesota Bulletin* 6, no. 8 (10 May 1903).

17. "After a New Pattern," 5–6.

18. "Queen of American Agriculture," *International Altrusan* 13, no. 8 (April 1936): 9.

19. "Trains Girls as Farmers."

20. Untitled, *Farm Students' Review* 1, no. 11 (November 1896): 161.

21. "Mrs. Henry C. Meredith's Short-Horn Sale," *Breeder's Gazette* 7 (25 June 1895): 966–67.

22. Andrew Boss, "A History of the School of Agriculture of the University of Minnesota" (unpublished manuscript), 1941, 104.

23. "Queen of American Agriculture," *International Altrusan* 13, no. 8 (April 1936): 9; "After a New Pattern," 5–6; "Mrs. Virginia C. Meredith, Honorary President I. F. C."; "Mrs. Virginia Claypool Meredith," *Journal of Home Economics* 29, no. 3 (March 1937): 180; "Honoring Those Who Have Achieved," 4.

24. "Queen of American Agriculture," *International Altrusan* 13, no. 8 (April 1936): 9; "After a New Pattern," 5–6.

25. Bartholomew, 53.

26. Untitled, *Farm Students' Review* 4, no. 5 (April 1899): 56; Bartholomew, 53; Untitled, *University of Minnesota Ariel* 22, no. 26 (1 April 1899): 365.

27. Boss, "A History of the School of Agriculture," 104.

28. Untitled, *Breeder's Gazette* 32 (4 August 1897): 65.

29. Johnston, "Woman Trustee of Purdue."

30. Untitled, *Farm Students' Review* 7, no. 1 (January 1902): 9.

31. Boss, "A History of the School of Agriculture," 104.

32. Andrew Boss, "When the Girls Crashed the Gates," in *The Gopher Countryman,* April 1931, 11.

33. Boss, "A History of the School of Agriculture," 104.

34. Adel Thompson Peck, letter to Juniata Shepperd, 23 June 1923.

35. "Trains Girls as Farmers."

36. Virginia C. Meredith, "Historical Sketch of School of Agriculture" (unpublished manu-script), c. 1923.

37. Ibid.

38. Ibid.

39. Boss, "A History of the School of Agriculture," 69.

40. Ibid., 70; Untitled, *University of Minnesota Ariel* 20, no. 33 (3 June 1897): 35; "Waymarks for Women," *Congregationalist*, 14 September 1899, 351; "Trains Girls as Farmers."

41. Boss, "A History of the School of Agriculture," 70.

42. Grace B. Andrews, An account about being one of the first graduates of the School of Agriculture (unpublished manuscript), n.d.

43. University of Minnesota School of Agriculture, Course Catalog, in *University of Minnesota Bulletin* 1, no. 2 (1 April 1898): 22–23.

44. Ibid, 24.

45. Ibid, 25.

46. Ibid.

47. University of Minnesota School of Agriculture, Course Catalog, in *University of Minnesota Bulletin* 1, no. 2 (1 April 1898): 25–26.

48. University of Minnesota School of Agriculture, Course Catalog, in *University of Minnesota Bulletin* 4, no. 9 (1 July 1901): 30.

49. Meredith, "Historical Sketch."

50. Untitled, *Farm Students' Review* 2, no. 12 (December 1897): 377.

51. "Agricultural Girls," *Farm, Stock, and Home* 14 (15 April 1898): 162.

52. "Trains Girls as Farmers."

53. "Women to Aid the Unions," *Chicago Daily Tribune*, 10 May 1900.

54. Note about Virginia C. Meredith becoming godparent to the School of Agriculture Class of 1901, c. 1901.

55. "A Woman as a Farmer."

56. "Second Annual Conference on Home Economics" (proceedings from conference held 3–7 July 1900 at Lake Placid, N.Y.), 11; "Mrs. Virginia Claypool Meredith," *Journal of Home Economics* 29, no. 3 (March 1937): 180.

57. Untitled, *Massachusetts Ploughman and New England Journal of Agriculture*, 21 July 1900, 4.

58. University of Minnesota College of Human Ecology, *Journey Home: A Celebration and Evolution of Home Economics at the University of Minnesota* (St. Paul, Minn.: University of Minnesota College of Human Ecology, 1998), 5.

59. University of Minnesota College of Home Economics, "History of the Division of Home Economics" (unpublished manuscript), 1925, 1.

60. University of Minnesota College of Human Ecology, *Journey Home*, 85; *University of Minnesota Bulletin* 3, no. 10 (1 July 1900): 9.

61. University of Minnesota College of Agriculture, Course description for home economics classes taught by Virginia Meredith, *University of Minnesota Bulletin* 3, no. 10 (1 July 1900): 15.

62. Ginther.

63. Florence M. Albright, "The Home and Family," *Indiana Farmer's Guide*, 17 July 1920, 18.

64. "Chicago Woman Speaks on Way to Bring Up Children," *Chicago Daily Tribune*, 24 October 1902.

65. "Oakland Farm and Its Owners."

66. Boss, "A History of the School of Agriculture," 74.

67. "Principal Tucker Asked to Resign," *Farmer's Guide* 19, no. 12 (15 June 1903): 255.

68. Untitled, *Farm Students' Review* 7, no. 5 (May 1902): 73.

69. University of Minnesota Board of Regents, meeting minutes, 3 June 1903, 560.

70. Ibid., page 21.

71. "The School of Agriculture," *Farm, Stock, and Home* 19, no. 13 (1 July 1903): 270.

72. "Is It A 'School for Scandal'?" *Farm, Stock, and Home* 19, no. 14 (15 July 1903): 286.

73. "A Loss to the State," *Farm, Stock, and Home* 19, no. 16 (15 August 1903): 318.

74. "A Large Man Not Wanted," *Farm, Stock, and Home* 19, no. 17 (1 September 1903): 336.

75. University of Minnesota Board of Regents, executive committee minutes, 13 August 1903.

76. "Virginia C. Meredith," *Biographical and Genealogical History of Wayne, Fayette, Union, and Franklin Counties, Indiana, vol. 1* (Chicago: Lewis, 1899), 452.

77. "One of State's Outstanding Women"; White, 6.

78. White, 6.

79. Untitled, *(Richmond, Ind.) Daily Sun-Telegram,* 12 June 1906.

80. "Official Program, Richmond Chautauqua," *(Richmond, Ind.) Daily Sun-Telegram,* 25 August 1906; "Queen of American Agriculture," *International Altrusan* 13, no. 8 (April 1936): 9.

81. Untitled, *Cambridge City (Ind.) Tribune,* 12 May 1910.

82. Purdue University, Ninth Announcement of the Winter School of Agriculture, 4 January to 19 March 1897.

83. William Carroll Latta, letter to Virginia Meredith, 15 July 1901. Letter book, 15 July 1901 to 9 December 1901, 10.

84. William Carroll Latta, letter to Virginia Meredith, 18 July 1901. Letter book, 15 July 1901 to 9 December 1901, 43.

85. William Carroll Latta, letter to Virginia Meredith, 31 July 1901. Letter book, 15 July 1901 to 9 December 1901, 165.

86. William Carroll Latta, letter to Mrs. Cal Husselman, 24 July 1901. Letter book, 15 July 1901 to 9 December 1901, 101.

87. William Carroll Latta, letter to Virginia Meredith, 12 August 1901. Letter book, 15 July 1901 to 9 December 1901, 279.

88. William Carroll Latta, letter to J. J. Billingsley, 6 October 1902. Letter book, 10 June 1902 to 4 December 1902, 529.

89. "A Mother-Daughter Team," *Purdue University Perspective,* Spring 1997, 4.

90. Purdue University School of Consumer and Family Sciences, "Virginia C. Meredith: The Driving Force," in *Inspiring Families and Building Communities for 75 Years* (calendar and essays), 2001, 9.

91. Meredith, "The Need of Special Training," 566.

92. Purdue University School of Home Economics Faculty, Memorial Resolution for Dean Emeritus Mary Lockwood Matthews (two-page typed document), 18 June 1968; William Murray Hepburn and Louis Martin Sears, *Purdue University: Fifty Years of Progress* (Indianapolis: Hollenbeck Press, 1925), 117; Purdue University, Board of Trustees meeting minutes, 6–7 June 1905, vol. 3, 209; Purdue University, *The Debris* (student yearbook), 1928, 28.

93. Purdue University, Board of Trustees meeting minutes, 31 October 1905, vol. 3, 233.

94. Indiana Home Economics Association, "A History of Home Economics in Indi-ana," 35.

95. Hepburn and Sears, 118.

96. Purdue University School of Consumer and Family Sciences, "Virginia C. Meredith: The Driving Force."

97. Indiana Home Economics Association, "A History of Home Economics in Indiana," 35; Purdue University, Board of Trustees meeting minutes, 12 June 1912, vol. 4, 14.

98. Untitled, *Gopher* 31 (1918): 92.

99. "Dean Matthews an Early Progressive," *Purdue University Perspective,* Spring 1997, 5.

100. Mary Matthews, letter to Miss. J. J. Sheppard, 22 June 1923; Purdue University School of Home Economics Faculty, Memorial Resolution.

101. "School of Home Economics—Biographical Sketch of Dean Mary L. Matthews," *Purdue Alumnus* 17, no. 6 (March 1930): 5.

102. Hepburn and Sears, 118.

103. Purdue University, Board of Trustees meeting minutes, 14 April 1926, vol. 6, 463.

104. Ibid., 482.

105. Purdue University, Board of Trustees meeting minutes, 28 September 1926, vol. 6, 566.

106. Purdue University. Personnel records of Mary L. Matthews, 1912–35

107. Purdue University, Board of Trustees meeting minutes, 14 April 1926, vol. 6, 467.

108. Purdue University, Board of Trustees meeting minutes, 11 April 1926, vol. 6, 188.

109. Purdue University School of Consumer and Family Sciences, "Virginia C. Meredith: The Driving Force."

110. "Trustees Authorize Economics Building," *Purdue Alumnus* 8 (May 1921): 8.

111. Purdue University School of Home Economics Faculty, Memorial Resolution.

112. Purdue University, Board of Trustees meeting minutes, 28 September 1926, vol. 6, 566.

113. Purdue University, "Reports of the President and Other Officers of Purdue University for the Biennium Ending September 30, 1928," *Bulletin of Purdue University,* no. 8, May 1930, 92.

114. Purdue University, Board of Trustees meeting minutes, 4 January 1927, vol. 6, 617.

115. Indiana Home Economics Association, "A History of Home Economics in Indiana," 36.

116. "Memorandum of Needs for Various Departments of the University," Purdue University, Board of Trustees meeting minutes, 21 October 1931, vol. 8 (in appendix).

117. H. E. Young, "25 Years of Extension Work in Indiana: Historical Narrative and Achievement Summary (Purdue University, 1939), 26.

118. Eastside Homemakers Demonstration Club, "History of Home Economics Work in Indiana" (unpublished manuscript), December 1949.

119. Thompson, 60–61.

120. Indiana Extension Homemakers Association, "Indiana Extension 75th Anniversary, 1913–1988" (booklet), 1988, 5.

121. Latta, *Outline History,* 304.

122. Indiana Home Demonstration Association, "50 Years Learning and Service."

123. Latta, *Outline History,* 304.

124. Indiana Home Demonstration Association, "50 Years Learning and Service"; Indiana Extension Homemakers Association, "Indiana Extension 75th Anniversary," 5; Latta, *Outline History,* 304.

125. Indiana Extension Homemakers Association, "Indiana Extension 75th Anniversary," 5.

126. Indiana Home Demonstration Association, "50 Years Learning and Service."

127. Ibid.

128. Indiana Extension Homemakers Association, "Indiana Extension 75th Anniversary," 5.

129. H. E. Young, "25 Years of Extension Work in Indiana," 26.

130. "Death of Lucy Wade Shocks Many Friends," *Purdue Exponent* 36, no. 70 (22 November 1924): 22.

131. "Miss Lucy Wade Dies in Hospital," *Purdue Exponent* 36, no. 44 (23 October 1924): 1.

132. "Miss Wade Will Be Buried This Morning," *Purdue Exponent* 36, no. 46 (25 October 1924): 1.

133. "Faculty Resolution," *Purdue Exponent* 36, no. 74 (27 November 1924): 3.

134. "A Work of Art," *Scrivener* 1, no. 3 (May 1928): 31.

135. "Exhibit of Indiana Art Held in Union Building," *Purdue Exponent* 39, no. 139 (3 March 1928): 1.

136. "Campus Societies Become Hosts at Union Art Exhibit," *Purdue Exponent* 39, no. 49 (15 March 1928): 1.

137. "Local Essay Contest Closes on Saturday," *Purdue Exponent* 39, no. 155 (22 March 1928), 1; "Prize Essays and Poems on Art Exhibit Announced," *Purdue Exponent* 39, no. 163 (31 March 1928): 1.

138. "Hoosier Arts Salon Ends with Banquet," *Purdue Exponent* 39, no. 162 (30 March 1928): 1.

139. Purdue University College of Consumer and Family Sciences, List of monetary gifts to purchase *An Old Red Dress,* n.d.

140. "Prize Winning Picture Donated as Memorial," *Purdue Exponent* 39, no. 181 (21 April 1928): 1.

141. Purdue University, *The Debris* (student yearbook), 1925, 330.

142. Purdue University, *The Debris* (student yearbook), 1927, 306; Purdue University, *The Debris* (student yearbook), 1928, 288.

143. Lillian Murphy, tribute to Virginia C. Meredith, in "Virginia C. Meredith—A Trustee of Purdue University. 1921–1936, Purdue University" (memorial service program), 12 January 1937; Edward C. Elliott, "Foreword," in "Virginia C. Meredith—A Trustee of Purdue University. 1921–1936, Purdue University" (memorial service program), 12 January 1937.

144. Johnston, "Woman Trustee of Purdue."

145. Purdue University, faculty meeting minutes, 25 January 1937. This document contained a write-up by the faculty concerning the death of Virginia Meredith.

146. Purdue University, Board of Trustees meeting minutes, 11 June 1928, vol. 7, 234.

147. Purdue University, Board of Trustees meeting minutes, 10 April 1929, vol. 7, 420; Purdue University, Board of Trustees meeting minutes, 21 October 1931, vol. 8, 262; Purdue University, Board of Trustees meeting minutes, 13 June 1932, vol. 8, 519; Purdue University, Board of Trustees meeting minutes, 19 April 1933, vol. 8, 717; Purdue University, Board of Trustees meeting minutes, 16 January 1935, vol. 9, 530; Purdue University, Board of Trustees meeting minutes, 17 April 1935, vol. 9, 634.

148. "Mrs. Virginia Claypool Meredith," *Journal of Home Economics* 29, no. 3 (March 1937): 180.

149. "Mrs. Virginia C. Meredith, Honorary President I. F. C."

150. Boruff, 200; Johnston and Hand, 307–08; "Mrs. Meredith, Trustee, Awarded Signal Honor," *Purdue Exponent* 41, no. 113 (4 February 1930): 1.

151. "Woman Trustee of Purdue Is Honored. Wisconsin Tribute Paid Mrs. V. C. Meredith," *Muncie Morning Star,* 3 February 1930.

152. "Mrs. Virginia C. Meredith, Honorary President I. F. C."

153. "Dr. Helen E. Clark, 88," *Lafayette (Ind.) Journal and Courier,* 4 January 2001.

154. Purdue University College of Consumer and Family Sciences, "Foods and Nutrition: Avanelle Kirksey" Web site, last accessed 28 November 2007. <http://www.cfs.purdue.edu/fn/alumni/Kirksey2007.shtml>

155. Purdue University, "Presentation To Honor Women Pioneers Through Purdue's History" (press release), 30 August 2006.

156. "Purdue Honors 15 Women Pioneers," *Lafayette (Ind.) Journal and Courier,* 3 September 2006; Purdue University Council on the Status of Women, "Women Pioneers of Purdue University" (booklet), 30 August 2006; "15 To Go First onto List of Pioneers," *Inside Purdue,* 6 September 2006, 4.

157. University of Minnesota College of Human Ecology, "Centennial 100—Presented April 2000," *Kaleidoscope,* Spring 2006, 24.

CHAPTER 8

Purdue University's First Woman Trustee

1. *Lafayette, Indiana, Directory, 1918* (Detroit, Mich.: R. L. Polk and Co., 1918).

2. Purdue University, Personnel records of Mary L. Matthews, 1912–35.

3. Johnston and Hand, 19.

4. Ibid.

5. Purdue University, Board of Trustees meeting minutes, 1 July 1921, vol. 5, 305.

6. Ibid., 305–14.

7. Ibid., 313.

8. Purdue University, Board of Trustees meeting minutes, 8 October 1924, vol. 6, 226.

9. Purdue University, Board of Trustees meeting minutes, 14–15 October 1925, vol. 6, 416; Purdue University, Board of Trustees meeting minutes, 19 April 1933, vol. 8, 754; Purdue University, Board of Trustees meeting minutes, 1 December 1931, vol. 8, 329; Purdue University, Board of Trustees meeting minutes, 18 April 1934, vol. 9, 265; Purdue University, Board of Trustees meeting minutes, 16 October 1935, vol. 10, 2.

10. Purdue University, Board of Trustees meeting minutes, 9 April 1930, vol. 7, 765.

11. Purdue University, Board of Trustees meeting minutes, 16 January 1935, vol. 9, 522.

12. Purdue University, Board of Trustees meeting minutes, 11 October 1922, vol. 5, 576.

13. Purdue University, Board of Trustees meeting minutes, 4 January 1927, vol. 6, 615.

14. Purdue University, Board of Trustees meeting minutes, 1 July 1921, vol. 5, 314.

15. Johnston and Hand, 307–8; Purdue University Reamer Club, 108; A. H. MacCarthy, "First Ascent of Mount Eon and Its Fatalities," *Canadian Alpine Journal* 12 (1921–22): 16.

16. Purdue University, Board of Trustees meeting minutes, 2 September 1921, vol. 5, 364.

17. Purdue University, Board of Trustees meeting minutes, 4 August 1921, vol. 5, 316.

18. Ibid., 324.

19. Ibid., 326.

20. Hepburn and Sears, 124; Purdue University Reamer Club, 94.

21. Purdue University, Board of Trustees meeting minutes, 2 September 1921, vol. 5, 352.

22. Purdue University Reamer Club, 94.

23. Hepburn and Sears, 124.

24. Ibid., 129.

25. Purdue University, Board of Trustees meeting minutes, 21 April 1922, vol. 5, 468.

26. Purdue University, Board of Trustees meeting minutes, 16 May 1922, vol. 5, 469.

27. Ibid., 472.

28. Ibid., 479.

29. Purdue University, Board of Trustees meeting minutes, 13 June 1922, vol. 5, 534.

30. Ibid., 535.

31. Purdue University, Board of Trustees meeting minutes, 8 June 1931, vol. 8, 236.

32. Purdue University, Board of Trustees meeting minutes, 2 September 1922, vol. 5, 560.

33. Purdue University, Board of Trustees meeting minutes, 9 April 1924, vol. 6, 139.

34. Ibid.

35. Purdue University, Board of Trustees meeting minutes, 9 April 1924, vol. 6, 140.

36. Ibid.

37. Purdue University, Board of Trustees meeting minutes, 8 October 1924, vol. 6, 216.

38. Ibid.

39. Ibid., 217.

40. Purdue University, Board of Trustees meeting minutes, 8 May 1925, vol. 6, 317–18.

41. Purdue University, Board of Trustees meeting minutes, 14 April 1926, vol. 6, 486.

42. Purdue University, Board of Trustees meeting minutes, 14 June 1926, vol. 6, 546.

43. Ibid., 546.

44. Purdue University, Board of Trustees meeting minutes, 14 March 1922, vol. 5, 438.

45. Purdue University, Board of Trustees meeting minutes, 21 December 1923, vol. 6, 86.

46. Purdue University, Board of Trustees meeting minutes, 16 November 1923, vol. 6, 63.

47. Ibid.

48. Purdue University, Board of Trustees meeting minutes, 21 December 1923, vol. 6, 87.

49. Ibid.

50. Purdue University, Board of Trustees meeting minutes, 31 December 1923, vol. 6, 92.

51. Purdue University, Board of Trustees meeting minutes, 9 April 1924, vol. 6, 109.

52. Purdue University, Board of Trustees meeting minutes, 5 January 1926, vol. 6, 445; Purdue University, Board of Trustees meeting minutes, 8 May 1925, vol. 6, 320–21.

53. "Portrait Features Palette Club Exhibit," *Richmond (Ind.) Palladium and Sun-Telegram,* 21 May 1929.

54. "Palette Club Exhibit Will Open on May 19. Portrait of Mrs. Meredith by King To Be Feature of Spring Show," *Richmond (Ind.) Palladium and Sun-Telegram,* 18 May 1929.

55. Purdue University, Board of Trustees meeting minutes, 10 June 1929, vol. 7, 526.

56. Purdue University, Board of Trustees meeting minutes, 10 October 1923, vol. 6, 27.

57. Purdue University, Board of Trustees meeting minutes, 9 June 1924, vol. 6, 173.

58. Purdue University, Board of Trustees meeting minutes, 16 January 1925, vol. 6, 262.

59. Purdue University, Board of Trustees meeting minutes, 18 April 1934, vol. 9, 294–95.

60. Ibid.

61. Purdue University, Board of Trustees meeting minutes, 14 January 1931, vol. 8, 88.

62. Ibid.

63. Purdue University, Board of Trustees meeting minutes, 1 August 1933, vol. 9, 8.

64. Purdue University, Board of Trustees meeting minutes, 25 April 1923, vol. 5, 637.

65. Purdue University, Board of Trustees meeting minutes, 1 August 1933, vol. 9, 42.

66. Purdue University, Board of Trustees meeting minutes, 21 October 1933, vol. 9, 42.

67. Purdue University, Board of Trustees meeting minutes, 16 January 1935, vol. 9, 535.

68. Purdue University, Board of Trustees meeting minutes, 1 August 1933, vol. 9, 43; Purdue University, Board of Trustees meeting minutes, 17 April 1935, vol. 9, 658.

69. Purdue University, Board of Trustees meeting minutes, 12 June 1923, vol. 5, 692; Purdue University, Board of Trustees meeting minutes, 5 May 1931, vol. 8, 199; Purdue University, Board of Trustees meeting minutes, 8 June 1931, vol. 8, 241.

70. Ruth W. Freehafer, *R. B. Stewart and Purdue University* (West Lafayette, Ind.: Purdue Research Foundation, 1983), 9.

71. Purdue University, Board of Trustees meeting minutes, 13 October 1926, vol. 6, 606.

72. Purdue University, Board of Trustees meeting minutes, 14–15 October 1925, vol. 6, 417.

73. Purdue University, Board of Trustees meeting minutes, 14 April 1926, vol. 6, 458.

74. Purdue University, Board of Trustees meeting minutes, 10 October 1928, vol. 7, 333.

75. Purdue University, Board of Trustees meeting minutes, 8 October 1930, vol. 8, 47.

76. Purdue University, Board of Trustees meeting minutes, 14 April 1926, vol. 6, 498.

77. Purdue University, Board of Trustees meeting minutes, 14–15 October 1925, vol. 6, 402.

78. Ibid., 417–18.

79. Purdue University, Board of Trustees meeting minutes, 5 January 1926, vol. 6, 431.

80. Purdue University, Board of Trustees meeting minutes, 14 June 1926, vol. 6, 525.

81. Purdue University, Board of Trustees meeting minutes, 14 April 1926, vol. 6, 488.

82. Ibid., 499.

83. Purdue University, Board of Trustees meeting minutes, 14 June 1926, vol. 6, 554.

84. Ibid., 547.

85. Ibid., 554.

86. Purdue University, Board of Trustees meeting minutes, 28 September 1926, vol. 6, 586.

87. Purdue University, Board of Trustees meeting minutes, 11 June 1928, vol. 7, 277.

88. Purdue University, Board of Trustees meeting minutes, 26 July 1928, vol. 7, 286.

89. Ibid.

90. Purdue University, Board of Trustees meeting minutes, 18 April 1934, vol. 9, 297.

CHAPTER 9

A Landmark for Veterans and a Home for Women

1. Purdue University, "Purdue Memorial Union. 75 Years. 1924–1999" (brochure), 1999.

2. Hepburn and Sears, 156; Purdue University, "Purdue Memorial Union. 75 Years."

3. Mary Matthews, "Biography of Virginia Meredith."

4. Purdue University, Board of Trustees meeting minutes, 2 September 1921, vol. 5, 364.

5. Purdue University, Board of Trustees meeting minutes, 12 October 1921, vol. 5, 382.

6. Purdue University, "Purdue Memorial Union. 75 Years."

7. Purdue University, Board of Trustees meeting minutes, 3 February 1922, vol. 5, 419.

8. Purdue University, "Purdue Memorial Union. 75 Years."

9. Purdue University, Board of Trustees meeting minutes, 3 February 1922, vol. 5, 419–20.

10. Ibid.

11. Ibid., 420.

12. Purdue University, Board of Trustees meeting minutes, 4 April 1922, vol. 5, 440.

13. Purdue University, "Purdue Memorial Union. 75 Years."

14. Purdue University, Board of Trustees meeting minutes, 10 October 1923, vol. 6, 19.

15. Ibid., 24.

16. Ibid.

17. Purdue University, Board of Trustees meeting minutes, 21 December 1923, vol. 6, 86.

18. Purdue University, Board of Trustees meeting minutes, 31 December 1923, vol. 6, 93.

19. Ibid., 94.

20. Purdue University, Board of Trustees meeting minutes, 9 April 1924, vol. 6, 108.

21. Purdue University, Board of Trustees meeting minutes, 29 July 1924, vol. 6, 201.

22. Ibid., 202.

23. Purdue University, Board of Trustees meeting minutes, 8 October 1924, vol. 6, 215; Purdue University, "Purdue Memorial Union. 75 Years."

24. Purdue University, "Purdue Memorial Union. 75 Years."

25. Purdue University, Board of Trustees meeting minutes, 21 December 1923, vol. 6, 74.

26. Purdue University, Board of Trustees meeting minutes, 8 October 1924, vol. 6, 215.

27. Ibid.

28. Purdue University, Board of Trustees meeting minutes, 8 April 1925, vol. 6, 227.

29. Purdue University, Board of Trustees meeting minutes, 8 May 1925, vol. 6, 314.

30. Purdue University, Board of Trustees meeting minutes, 8 June 1925, vol. 6, 358.

31. Purdue University, Board of Trustees meeting minutes, 4 January 1927, vol. 6, 650.

32. Edward C. Elliott, letter to Allison E. Stuart, 17 December 1926.

33. Allison E. Stuart, letter to Edward C. Elliott, 21 December 1926.

34. Ibid.

35. Purdue University, Board of Trustees meeting minutes, 13 April 1927, vol. 6, 690.

36. Purdue University, Board of Trustees meeting minutes, 10 April 1929, vol. 7, 439.

37. Purdue University, Board of Trustees meeting minutes, 14 May 1929, vol. 7, 456.

38. Purdue University, Board of Trustees meeting minutes, 10 April 1928, vol. 7, 468.

39. Purdue University, Board of Trustees meeting minutes, 10 June 1929, vol. 7, 528.

40. Purdue University, Board of Trustees meeting minutes, 29 July 1930, vol. 7, 904.

41. Purdue University, Board of Trustees meeting minutes, 9 June 1930, vol. 7, 830.

42. Virginia Meredith, "Union Memories," in Mary Margaret Kern, "The Memorial Union" (pamphlet), 1927.

43. Purdue University, Board of Trustees meeting minutes, 9 April 1924, vol. 6, 138.

44. Purdue University, Board of Trustees meeting minutes, 29 July 1924, vol. 6, 201.

45. Purdue University, Board of Trustees meeting minutes, 8 April 1925, vol. 6, 284–85.

46. Purdue University, Board of Trustees meeting minutes, 10 September 1921, vol. 5, 367.

47. Ibid.

48. Ibid., 368.

49. Ibid., 369.

50. Purdue University, Board of Trustees meeting minutes, 21 November 1921, vol. 5, 387.

51. Purdue University, Board of Trustees meeting minutes, 14 March 1922, vol. 5, 435.

52. Ibid., 435–36.

53. Purdue University, Board of Trustees meeting minutes, 2 September 1922, vol. 5, 549.

54. Purdue University, Board of Trustees meeting minutes, 21 April 1922, vol. 5, 461.

55. Ibid., 461.

56. Purdue University, Board of Trustees meeting minutes, 13 June 1922, vol. 5, 529.

57. Ibid., 529.

58. Ibid., 531.

59. Purdue University, Board of Trustees meeting minutes, 2 September 1922, vol. 5, 544.

60. Ibid., 546.

61. Purdue University, Board of Trustees meeting minutes, 28 September 1926, vol. 6, 613.

62. Purdue University, Board of Trustees meeting minutes, 10 October 1928, vol. 7, 318.

63. Purdue University Reamer Club, 48; Joel A. Buchanan, e-mail to Frederick Whitford, 29 June 2006. This correspondence contained information on the history of the old pump that originally stood near Ladies Hall on the Purdue University campus in West Lafayette, Ind.

64. Purdue University Reamer Club, 49.

65. Purdue University, Board of Trustees meeting minutes, 8 June 1925, vol. 6, 362.

66. Purdue University, Board of Trustees meeting minutes, 3 August 1925, vol. 6, 370.

67. Purdue University, Board of Trustees meeting minutes, 21 September 1927, vol. 7, 23.

68. Purdue University, Board of Trustees meeting minutes, 12 October 1927, vol. 7, 75.

69. Purdue University, Board of Trustees meeting minutes, 13 October 1926, vol. 6, 609; Purdue University, Board of Trustees meeting minutes, 13 June 1927, vol. 6, 814; Purdue University, Board of Trustees meeting minutes, 21 September 1927, vol. 7, 3.

70. Purdue University, Board of Trustees meeting minutes, 4–5 January 1928, vol. 7, 142.

71. Ibid.

72. Ibid.

73. Ibid.

74. Ibid., 144.

75. Ibid., 145.

76. Purdue University, Board of Trustees meeting minutes, 11 June 1928, vol. 7, 171.

77. Purdue University, Board of Trustees meeting minutes, 11 April 1928, vol. 7, 191.

78. Ibid., 216.

79. Purdue University, Board of Trustees meeting minutes, 9 October 1929, vol. 7, 631.

80. Ibid., 632.

81. Purdue University, Board of Trustees meeting minutes, 15 November 1929, vol. 7, 641 and 660.

82. Ibid., 661.

83. Purdue University, Board of Trustees meeting minutes, 8 January 1930, vol. 7, 677.

84. Ibid.

85. Ibid., 678.

86. Ibid., 683.

87. Purdue University, Board of Trustees meeting minutes, 8 October 1930, vol. 8, 47.

88. Purdue University, Board of Trustees meeting minutes, 9 April 1930, vol. 7, 775.

89. Ibid., 786.

90. Purdue University, Board of Trustees meeting minutes, 9 June 1930, vol. 7, 809.

91. Ibid., 810.

92. Ibid., 833.

93. Purdue University, Board of Trustees meeting minutes, 29 July 1930, vol. 7, 888.

94. Ibid., 900.

95. Purdue University, Board of Trustees meeting minutes, 18 October 1933, vol. 9, 103.

96. Purdue University, Board of Trustees meeting minutes, 17 January 1934, vol. 9, 126.

97. Ibid.

98. Ibid., 125.

99. Ibid., 159.

100. Ibid., 158.

101. Purdue University, Board of Trustees meeting minutes, 18 April 1934, vol. 9, 214.

102. Ibid., 267; Purdue University, Board of Trustees meeting minutes, 17 October 1934, vol. 9, 487.

103. Purdue University, Board of Trustees meeting minutes, 18 April 1934, vol. 9, 270; Purdue University, Board of Trustees meeting minutes, 25 April 1934, vol. 9, 309; Purdue University, Board of Trustees meeting minutes, 17 October 1934, vol. 9, 48.

104. Purdue University, Board of Trustees meeting minutes, 25 April 1934, vol. 9, 305.

105. Ibid., 331.

106. Ibid., 307.

107. Ibid., 339.

108. Purdue University, Board of Trustees meeting minutes, 17 October 1934, vol. 9, 452 and 510.

109. "Dedicate New Women's Hall. Co-ed Housing Plan Discussed," *Purdue Exponent* 46, no. 32 (21 October 1934): 1; "150 Persons Attend Exercises," *Purdue Exponent* 46, no. 32 (21 October 1934): 1; "Will Dedicate Residence Hall This Morning. Mrs. Meredith to Preside," *Purdue Exponent* 46, no. 31 (20 October 1934), 5.

110. "Mrs. Meredith Will Officiate at Dedication," *Purdue Exponent* 46, no. 23 (9 October 1934): 1.

111. "Dedicate New Women's Hall," 1.

112. "Women's Hall at Purdue Scene of Dedication Rites," *Lafayette (Ind.) Journal and Courier,* 20 October 1934.

113. "Dedicate New Women's Hall," 1; "Women's Hall at Purdue Scene of Dedication Rites."

114. Purdue University, Board of Trustees meeting minutes, 16 October 1935, vol. 10, 143.

115. Ibid., 143.

116. Ibid., 140.

117. Ibid., 141.

118. Ibid., 143.

119. Purdue University, Board of Trustees meeting minutes, 23 November 1935, vol. 10, 159.

120. Ibid., 160.

121. Ibid., 161.

122. Purdue University, Board of Trustees meeting minutes, 15 April 1936, vol. 10, 297.

123. Ibid.

124. Purdue University, Board of Trustees meeting minutes, 25 September 1936, vol. 10, 398.

125. Ibid., 400 and 404.

126. Ibid., 418.

CHAPTER 10

Farewell to the Grand Lady of Agriculture

1. Purdue University, faculty meeting minutes, 25 January 1937. This document contained a write-up by the faculty concerning the death of Virginia Meredith.

2. "Program Will Pay Tribute to Mrs. Meredith," *Purdue Exponent* 48, no. 71 (13 January 1937): 1.

3. Latta, *Outline History,* 318.

4. Kahn.

5. Ibid.

6. Ibid.

7. Meredith, "Roads of Remembrance."

8. Virginia Meredith, "Introduction," in *Stories and Sketches of Elkhart County,* by Henry Sager Knapp Bartholomew (Nappanee, Ind.: E. V. Publishing House, 1936), vii–viii.

9. "500 Will Hear Aviatrix Talk," *Purdue Exponent* 46, no. 28 (16 October 1934): 1.

10. "Mrs. [Amelia Earhart] Putnam to Lecture at Special Convo," *Purdue Exponent* 47, no. 41 (6 November 1935): 1.

11. "Famous Aviatrix Addresses Capacity Convo Audience," *Purdue Exponent* 47, no. 45 (12 November 1935), 1.

12. "No. 1 Purdue Woman Still Active at 87" (newspaper clipping), n.p., 4 January [1936].

13. "Heart Attack Fatal to University Trustee," *Purdue Exponent* 48, no. 64 (11 December 1936): 1; "Virginia Meredith Dies in Lafayette," *Indianapolis Star,* 11 December 1936.

14. Purdue University Board of Trustees, message of sympathy to Mrs. Meredith, in Purdue University Board of Trustees meeting minutes, 25 September 1936, vol. 10, 418.

15. "Mrs. Meredith, Famed Hoosier Leader, Is Dead."

16. "Meredith Rites Are Impressive," *Lafayette (Ind.) Journal and Courier,* 12 December 1936.

17. "Mrs. H. C. Meredith, Farm Expert, Dead. Indiana Woman, 88, Became a National Figure as an Agriculture Lecturer," *New York Times,* 11 December 1936.

18. "Virginia Claypool Meredith," *Indianapolis Star,* 12 December 1936.

19. "Queen of American Agriculture Completes Career. Purdue Trustee for Many Years Expires; Leaves Valued Heritage," *Purdue Alumnus* 24, no. 3 (December 1936): 4.

20. "Mrs. Virginia Meredith," *Lafayette (Ind.) Journal and Courier,* 12 December 1936.

21. Edward C. Elliott, "Foreword," in "Virginia C. Meredith—A Trustee of Purdue University. 1921–1936, Purdue University" (memorial service program), 12 January 1937.

22. Edward C. Elliott, letter to the deans and heads of schools and departments from the president's office, 11 December 1936. Purdue University Board of Trustees records, Office of the Purdue University Board of Trustees, Hovde Hall, West Lafayette, Ind.

23. "Meredith Rites Are Impressive."

24. Ibid.

25. Ibid.

26. Virginia C. Meredith, handwritten will, 2 May 1927. Meredith's will and a record of the State of Indiana's execution of it on 31 December 1936 are found at the Alameda McCollough Library, Tippecanoe County Historical Association, Lafayette, Ind.

27. "Program Will Pay Tribute to Mrs. Meredith," 1; Purdue University, Board of Trustees meeting minutes, 21 December 1936, vol. 10, 466.

28. "Program Will Pay Tribute to Mrs. Meredith," 1.

29. Purdue University, Board of Trustees meeting minutes, 20 January 1937, vol. 10, 550.

30. Esther Marguerite Hall Albjerg, "Mrs. Virginia Claypool Meredith," in "Virginia C. Meredith—A Trustee of Purdue University. 1921–1936, Purdue University" (memorial service program), 12 January 1937.

Epilogue

1. David E. Ross, "From the University Trustees," in "Virginia C. Meredith—A Trustee of Purdue University. 1921–1936, Purdue University" (memorial service program), 12 January 1937.

2. Meredith, "The Need of Special Training," 567.

Sources

Abbreviations

CC   Cambridge City Public Library History Room, Cambridge City, Ind.

GF   General Federation of Women's Clubs, Indiana Federation of
            Clubs (Collection 29), Indiana State Library, Indianapolis, Ind.

HR   Hicks Repository, John W. Hicks Undergraduate Library,
            Purdue University Libraries, West Lafayette, Ind.

MN   University Archives, University of Minnesota Libraries,
            Minneapolis, Minn.

PU   Archives and Special Collections, Purdue University Libraries,
            West Lafayette, Ind.

WCE   World's Columbian Exposition, Board of Lady Managers Records,
            Chicago History Museum, Chicago, Ill.

"15 To Go First onto List of Pioneers." *Inside Purdue,* 6 September 2006, 4.
"150 Persons Attend Exercises." *Purdue Exponent* 46, no. 32 (21 October 1934): 1.
"500 Will Hear Aviatrix Talk." *Purdue Exponent* 46, no. 28 (16 October 1934): 1.
"$58,000 in Prizes at Indiana State Fair. Silver Cup from Mrs. Meredith." *Indianapolis
    News,* 14 August 1908.
"After a New Pattern. How Some Women Succeed." *The Farmer's Wife,* October 1934, 5–6.
"After a World's Fair Position." *Chicago Daily Tribune,* 10 September 1891.
"Agricultural Fairs. Cambridge City Indiana. One Hundred Years (1836–1936)" (booklet).
    September 1936. CC
"Agricultural Girls." *Farm, Stock, and Home* 14 (15 April 1898): 162. **MN**
Albjerg, Esther Marguerite Hall. "Mrs. Virginia Claypool Meredith." In "Virginia C.
    Meredith—A Trustee of Purdue University. 1921–1936, Purdue University"
    (memorial service program). 12 January 1937. Virginia Meredith Collection. **PU**
Albright, Florence M. "The Home and Family." *Indiana Farmer's Guide,* 17 July 1920, 18.
Andrews, Grace B. An account about being one of the first graduates of the School of
    Agriculture (unpublished manuscript). N.d. In folder marked "Historical Papers
    of the Department of Agriculture of the University of Minnesota," Box 2, School
    of Agriculture Records (Collection 343). **MN**
"At Rest. Obsequies of Gen. Solomon Meredith at Cambridge City, Yesterday." *Indianapolis
    Journal,* 25 October 1875.

Badger, Reid. *The Great American Fair: The World's Columbian Exposition and American Culture.* Chicago: Nelson Hall, 1979.

Balz, Arcada Stark, ed. *History Indiana Federation of Clubs.* Fort Wayne, Ind.: Fort Wayne Printing Co., 1939. **GF**

Banks, Nancy Huston. "World's Fair Women." *Harper's Bazaar,* 21 January 1893, 46.

Bartholomew, H. S. K. "Virginia C. Meredith." *Indiana Magazine of History* 35 (March 1939): 49–57.

"Belva Was Squelched. The Women's Council Sits Down on Mrs. Lockwood." *Chicago Daily Tribune,* 26 February 1891.

Billings, Esther H. "Indiana Federation of Clubs: 1890–1920" (unpublished manuscript). **GF**

Boruff, Blanche Foster. "In Memoriam—Virginia Claypool Meredith." In *Women of Indiana.* Indianapolis: Indiana Women's Biography Association, M. Farson (c. 1941), 200.

Boss, Andrew. "A History of the School of Agriculture of the University of Minnesota" (unpublished manuscript). 1941. In folder marked "A History of the School of Agriculture," Box 9, Ag. Director's Office (Collection 922). **MN**

———. "When the Girls Crashed the Gates." In *The Gopher Countryman,* April 1931, 11. In folder marked "Hist. Home Economics—Virginia Meredith," Box 4, College of Home Economics (Collection 2006-00024). **MN**

" 'Breakfast Nooks' in Farm Homes—The Social Value of the Morning Meal—The Scarcity and Use of Fine Table Linen—An Eyesore Made Lovely by Flowers." *Breeder's Gazette* 80 (1 September 1921): 284.

Buchanan, Joel A. E-mail to Frederick Whitford, 29 June 2006.

Bundy, Martin L. "Gen. Sol. Meredith. Sketch of a Remarkable Self-Made Man. His Career from a Wood-Chopper to a Major General." *Indianapolis Times,* 25 February 1882.

California Department of Health Services. Certificate of Death for Meredith Matthews, 2 February 1962.

Cambridge City, Indiana: One Hundred and Fifty Years, 1836–1986. Dublin, Ind.: Prinit Press, 1986.

"Campus Societies Become Hosts at Union Art Exhibit." *Purdue Exponent* 39, no. 49 (15 March 1928): 1.

Cassell, Frank, and Marguerite Cassell. "Pride, Profits, and Politics: Indiana and the Columbian Exposition of 1893." *Indiana Magazine of History* 80, no. 2 (June 1984): 93.

"The Cattle Department." *Breeder's Gazette* 54 (16 September 1908): 491.

"Charter Members of Helen Hunt Club at Cambridge" (newspaper clipping). N.p., c. 1935. **CC**

"Chicago Woman Speaks on Way to Bring Up Children." *Chicago Daily Tribune,* 24 October 1902.

Claypool, Edward F. Letter to W. W. English, 13 October 1888. Indiana Historical Society, Indianapolis, Ind.

"Congratulations at Dedication: Eloquent Words Uttered by Mrs. Virginia Meredith." *Connersville (Ind.) Evening News,* 13 April 1909.

Connersville, Ind., Sesquicentennial Book Committee. *The Book of the 150th Year of Connersville, Indiana.* Connersville, Ind.: City of Connersville, 1963.

"Costumes To Be Seen at the Ball. Rich Dresses and Expensive Ornaments To Be Worn by Those Present." *Chicago Daily Tribune,* 19 October 1892.

Cottman, George S. "John Mahoney: An Indianapolis Sculptor." *Indiana Magazine of History* 25 (1929): 191.

"Cottrell Made Chief." *Chicago Daily Tribune,* 18 October 1891.

"David Meredith" (obituary). *Richmond (Ind.) Humming Bird,* 13 April 1867. CC

"Dean Matthews an Early Progressive." *Purdue University Perspective,* Spring 1997, 5.

"Death of Lucy Wade Shocks Many Friends." *Purdue Exponent* 36, no. 70 (22 November 1924): 22.

"Dedicate New Women's Hall. Co-ed Housing Plan Discussed." *Purdue Exponent* 46, no. 32 (21 October 1934): 1.

"Department Notes: Experiment Station." *Purdue Exponent* 8, no. 8 (28 January 1897): 105.

"Department Notes: Experiment Station." *Purdue Exponent* 8, no. 10 (25 February 1897): 133.

"Dr. Helen E. Clark, 88." *Lafayette (Ind.) Journal and Courier,* 4 January 2001.

"Early Days of Indiana. The Claypools and Conwells—Betty Brazier and Others" (newspaper clipping). *Daily Sentinel* (city unknown), 20 September 1883. Indiana Historical Society, Indianapolis.

Eastside Homemakers Demonstration Club. "History of Home Economics Work in Indiana" (unpublished manuscript). December 1949. Private collection of Sandy Martin.

Edwards, Gertrude. Handwritten notes from c. 1970. In Meredith File. CC

Elliott, Edward C. "Foreword." In "Virginia C. Meredith—A Trustee of Purdue University. 1921–1936, Purdue University" (memorial service program). 12 January 1937. Virginia Meredith Collection. PU

———. Letter to Allison E. Stuart, 17 December 1926. In folder marked "4 January 1927," Purdue University Board of Trustees records, Office of the Purdue University Board of Trustees, Hovde Hall, West Lafayette, Ind.

———. Letter to the deans and heads of schools and departments from the president's office, 11 December 1936. Purdue University Board of Trustees records, Office of the Purdue University Board of Trustees, Hovde Hall, West Lafayette, Ind.

"Encouraging Students and County Teachers, and the Improvement of Country Schools Are Subjects Worthy of Earnest Thought by America's Womanhood—and Manhood as Well." *Breeder's Gazette* 79 (9 June 1921): 1036.

"Exhibit of Indiana Art Held in Union Building." *Purdue Exponent* 39, no. 139 (3 March 1928): 1.

"Exposition Notes." *Chicago Daily Tribune,* 13 October 1891.

"Faculty Resolution." *Purdue Exponent* 36, no. 74 (27 November 1924): 3.

"Famous Aviatrix Addresses Capacity Convo Audience." *Purdue Exponent* 47, no. 45 (12 November 1935), 1.

"Farmers' Institute. Last Night's Session." *Vicksburg (Miss.) Evening Post,* 22 February 1895.

"Farmers' Institute. The Opening Session Last Night—Greetings of Welcome, Eloquent Responses, Etc." *Vicksburg (Miss.) Evening Post,* 21 February 1895.

"The Farmers' Institute. To Be Held at Vicksburg from February 20 to 22, 1895." *Vicksburg (Miss.) Evening Post,* 20 February 1895.

"Farmers' Institute." *Vicksburg (Miss.) Evening Post,* 25 February 1895.

"The Farm Home." *Breeder's Gazette* 81 (15 June 1922): 806.

"The Farm Home." *Breeder's Gazette* 82 (6 July 1922): 20.

"The Farm Home." *Breeder's Gazette* 82 (3 August 1922): 124.

"The Farm Home." *Breeder's Gazette* 82 (7 September 1922): 278.

"The Farm Home." *Breeder's Gazette* 84 (16 August 1923): 184.

"The Farm Home." *Breeder's Gazette* 84 (13 September 1923): 312.

Feeger, Luther M. "Meredith Monument, Once on Farm, Later Moved to Cemetery." *Richmond (Ind.) Palladium-Item and Sun-Telegram,* 17 March 1965.

"Forest Dedicated to Mrs. Meredith." *Indianapolis Star,* 28 May 1938.

"Former Prominent County Resident Served on Board for Columbian Exposition." *Richmond (Ind.) Palladium and Sun-Telegram,* 11 October 1933.

"For the Love of Art. Arche Club Celebrates Its First Birthday with a Salon." *Chicago Daily Tribune,* 30 March 1895.

Freehafer, Ruth W. *R. B. Stewart and Purdue University.* West Lafayette, Ind.: Purdue Research Foundation, 1983.

"General Solomon Meredith Was of Outstanding Character" (newspaper clipping). N.p., n.d. Modified from original biography printed in the *Richmond (Ind.) Palladium,* 30 January 1864. Wayne County Historical Society, Richmond, Ind.

"Gen. Solomon Meredith." *Masonic Advocate* (photocopy), 1875. Virginia Meredith Collection. **PU**

Ginther, C. M. "Representative Woman Agriculturist." *Orange Judd Farmer (Ill.),* 6 April 1901.

Glendale (Ohio) Female College. "Tenth Annual Catalogue of Glendale Female College, Glendale, Hamilton County, Ohio, for the Year Ending 24 June 1864." Cincinnati, Ohio: Moore, Wilstach, and Baldwin, 1864.

"The Good Promise." *Breeder's Gazette* 97 (April 1932): 3.

"Great Herd To Be Sold. The Meredith Short Horns Will Go at Auction." *(Richmond, Ind.) Daily Sun-Telegram,* 2 August 1902.

Handy, Moses P., ed. *The Official Directory of the World's Columbian Exposition, May 1st to October 30th, 1893. A Reference Book of Exhibitors and Exhibits; of the Officers and Members of the World's Commission.* Chicago: W. B. Conkey Co., 1893.

Hasket, Irene. Untitled (newspaper clipping), n.p., 29 April [c. 1936]. Virginia Meredith Collection. **PU**

Havens, B. F. "Indiana World's Columbian Exposition, 1893. Final Report of B. F. Havens, Executive Commissioner." Terre Haute, Ind.: Board of World's Fair Managers, Indiana, April 1894. Chicago Public Library, Chicago.

"Heart Attack Fatal to University Trustee." *Purdue Exponent* 48, no. 64 (11 December 1936): 1.

Hepburn, William Murray, and Louis Martin Sears. *Purdue University: Fifty Years of Progress.* Indianapolis: Hollenbeck Press, 1925.

"History of Cambridge City Library" (unpublished report). November 1939. **CC**

History of Fayette County, Indiana. Chicago: Warner, Beers, and Co., 1885.

"History of Oakland Farm." *(Richmond, Ind.) Daily Sun-Telegram,* 10 July 1902.

The History of Wayne County, Indiana, Together with Sketches of Its Cities, Villages, and Towns, vols. 1 and 2. Chicago: Inter-state Publishing Company, 1884.

"The Home." *Breeder's Gazette* 84 (1 November 1923): 553.

"The Home." *Breeder's Gazette* 85 (7 February 1924): 170.

"Honoring Those Who Have Achieved—Virginia C. Meredith." *Purdue Alumnus* 22 (November 1934): 4–5.

"Hoosier Arts Salon Ends with Banquet." *Purdue Exponent* 39, no. 162 (30 March 1928): 1.

"How By-Laws Can Be Changed. The Board of Lady Managers Has a Debate on the Subject—The Morning Session." *Chicago Daily Tribune,* 8 September 1891.

"How Several Mothers Who Studied Child Management at College Are Making Practical Use of Their Scientific Training in Their Own Homes." *Breeder's Gazette* 80 (4 August 1921): 150.

"In and About the Farm Home." *Breeder's Gazette* 81 (26 January 1922): 107.

Indiana Club Union. "First Convention of the Indiana Club Union" (conference program). 3– 4 June 1890. **GF**

Indiana Extension Homemakers Association. "Indiana Extension 75th Anniversary, 1913–1988" (booklet). 1988. Kokomo-Howard County Public Library, Kokomo, Ind.

Indiana Federation of Clubs. "Memorial Forest Dedicated." *The Indiana Club Woman,* June–July 1938, 18. **GF**

———. "Representatives, Women's Literary Clubs of Indiana" (pamphlet). 1899. **GF**

———. "Virginia Claypool Meredith Memorial Forest" (unpublished manuscript). In folder marked "C. L. M.—ESO. June 1 1947." **GF**

Indiana Home Demonstration Association. "50 Years Learning and Service: 1913–1963" (booklet). 1963. Virginia Meredith Collection. **PU**

Indiana Home Economics Association. "A History of Home Economics in Indiana. Golden Anniversary: 1913–1963" (booklet). 1963. Virginia Meredith Collection. **PU**

Indianapolis, Indiana, Directory, 1887–90. Indianapolis: R. L. Polk and Co., 1887–90.

"Indiana Short-horns." *Breeder's Gazette* 5 (14 February 1884): n.p.

Indiana State Board of Agriculture Annual Reports. 1853–1906. **HR**

"The Indiana State Fair." *Breeder's Gazette* 48 (20 September 1905): 522.

Indiana Union of Literary Clubs. "The Bulletin" (detailed summary from conference program). 1892. **GF**

———. "Minutes and Constitution of the Indiana Union of Literary Clubs." 1894. **GF**

———. "Minutes and Constitution of the Indiana Union of Literary Clubs. Sixth Annual Convention." 1895. **GF**

———. "Minutes and Constitution of the Indiana Union of Literary Clubs." 1902. **GF**

———. "Proceedings of the Sixteen Annual Convention." 1905. **GF**

———. "Programme, Sixth Annual Convention" (conference program). 14–16 May 1895. **GF**

———. "The Seventeenth Annual Convention of the Indiana Union of Literary Clubs" (conference program). 9–11 October 1906. **GF**

"Indiana Woman Lauded at Ingham Farm Club" (newspaper clipping). N.p., 1934. Virginia Meredith Collection. **PU**

"Indoors and Out." *Breeder's Gazette* 32 (4 August 1897): 68.

"An Inspiring Interpretation, with Practical Applications to the Life of Stock-Farm Boys and Girls, of the Old Juvenile Rhymes Beginning 'Mary Had a Little Lamb.'" *Breeder's Gazette* 79 (23 June 1921): 1109.

"Is It A 'School for Scandal'?" *Farm, Stock, and Home* 19, no. 14 (15 July 1903): 286. **MN**

Jaqua, Mrs. George W. "Accepting Our Responsibilities" (speech). N.d. In folder marked "Latin-American Historical." **GF**

———. "From the Indiana Federation of Clubs." In "Virginia C. Meredith—A Trustee of Purdue University. 1921–1936, Purdue University" (memorial service program). 12 January 1937. Virginia Meredith Collection. **PU**

Johnston, Thomas R., and Helen Hand. "Virginia Meredith—Member of the Board, 1921–1936." In *The Trustees and the Officers of Purdue University, 1865–1940.* West Lafayette, Ind.: Purdue University, 1940.

Johnston, Thomas R. "Woman Trustee of Purdue Aids in Things Progressive" (newspaper clipping). N.p., n.d. Private collection of the Robert Miller Family.

Kahn, Dorothea. "Women Become Full Farmers in Activities of Agriculture. Write Their Names High on Agriculture's Roll of Honor." *Christian Science Monitor,* 18 November 1931.

"Lady Managers Are Emancipated." *Chicago Daily Tribune,* 15 September 1893.

"Lady Managers Disagree." *New York Times,* 6 August 1893.

Lafayette, Indiana, Directory, 1918. Detroit, Mich.: R. L. Polk and Co., 1918.

"A Large Man Not Wanted." *Farm, Stock, and Home* 19, no. 17 (1 September 1903): 336. **MN**

"The Last Oakland Farm Cattle Sale." *Cambridge City (Ind.) Tribune,* 11 September 1902.

Latta, William Carroll. General correspondence and papers. 1894–1904. W. C. Latta Collection. **PU**

———. *Outline History of Indiana Agriculture.* West Lafayette, Ind.: Epsilon Sigma Phi (Alpha Lambda Chapter), Purdue University, and Indiana County Agricultural Agents Association, 1938. W. C. Latta Collection. **PU**

———. *Purdue University Farmers' Institutes Annual Reports, 1889–1911.* N.p., [1911]. W. C. Latta Collection. **PU**

"Library Gets Jeweled Sword of the Late General Meredith." *Cambridge (Ind.) City Tribune,* 7 June 1928.

"Lieutenant Samuel Meredith" (obituary). *Richmond (Ind.) Palladium,* 10 February 1864.

"Likes Mrs. Meredith's Page." *Breeder's Gazette* 80 (15 September 1921): 369.

"Local Essay Contest Closes on Saturday." *Purdue Exponent* 39, no. 155 (22 March 1928), 1.

"A Loss to the State." *Farm, Stock, and Home* 19, no. 16 (15 August 1903): 318. **MN**

MacCarthy, A. H. "First Ascent of Mount Eon and Its Fatalities." *Canadian Alpine Journal* 12 (1921–22): 16.

Malcomb, Lou. "List of Articles Written by Women, Appearing in the Reports of the Indiana State Board of Agriculture." Presentation given as part of the Indiana Library Federation Conference, Division on Women in Indiana Libraries, Indianapolis, April 2002.

"The Master of Meredith House." *Indianapolis Star Magazine.* N.d. Virginia Meredith Collection. **PU**

"Matrimonial." *Richmond (Ind.) Palladium,* [1870]. Private collection of the Robert Miller Family.

Matthews, Mary. "Biography of Virginia Meredith" (unpublished manuscript). 25 February
   1937. In a folder marked "Meredith, Virginia Claypool," Box 8, Ag. Director's Office
   (Collection 922). **MN**
———. Letter to Miss. J. J. Sheppard, 22 June 1923. In folder marked "Historical Papers of
   the Department of Agriculture of the University of Minnesota," School of Agriculture
   Records (Collection 343). **MN**
"The Meredith Monument To Be Removed to Riverside Cemetery." *Cambridge City (Ind.)
   Tribune,* 13 August 1908.
"Meredith Rites Are Impressive." *Lafayette (Ind.) Journal and Courier,* 12 December 1936.
"Meredith's Legislative Record Marked by Sound Judgment" (newspaper clipping).
   N.p., n.d. Modified from original biography printed in the *Richmond (Ind.)
   Palladium,* 30 January 1864. Wayne County Historical Society, Richmond, Ind.
Meredith, Virginia Claypool. "Farm Life: Its Privileges and Possibilities" (speech).
   In *Indiana State Board of Agriculture Annual Report,* 1892, vol. 33, 540–43. **HR**
———. "Final Report of Mrs. Virginia C. Meredith, Chairman of the Committee on Awards
   of the Board of Lady Managers" (unpublished manuscript). 27 June 1896. In vol. 19.
   WCE
———. "Gen. Sol. Meredith." *Richmond (Ind.) Daily Sun-Telegram,* 12 May 1897.
———. Handwritten will. 2 May 1927. Alameda McCollough Library, Tippecanoe County
   Historical Association, Lafayette, Ind.
———. "Historical Sketch of School of Agriculture" (unpublished manuscript). Circa 1923.
   In folder marked "Historical Papers of the Department of Agriculture of the University
   of Minnesota," Box 1, School of Agriculture Records (Collection 343). **MN**
———. "Introduction." In *Stories and Sketches of Elkhart County,* by Henry Sager Knapp
   Bartholomew. Nappanee, Ind.: E. V. Publishing House, 1936.
———. Letter to United States Senator Charles Warren Fairbanks, 20 February 1904.
   Fairbanks Manuscripts Department, The Lilly Library, Indiana University,
   Bloomington, Ind.
———. "The Need of Special Training for Agricultural Pursuits" (speech). In *Indiana State
   Board of Agriculture Annual Report,* 1905, vol. 46, 566–73. **HR**
———. "Quarter Century Reunion Glendale College. 1854–1879. Class of [18]66"
   (booklet). 1879. Glendale Heritage Preservation Archive, Glendale, Ohio.
———. "The Relation of Women to the Columbian Exposition" (speech). In "The Bulletin"
   (detailed summary from conference program), 1892. **GF**
———. "Roads of Remembrance. A Memorial Address" (speech). In program for Purdue
   University Memorial Day Exercises, West Lafayette, Ind., 13 May 1933. **PU**
———. "The Story of Oakland Farm" (booklet). N.p., n.d. **CC**
———. "Supplemental Sketch." In "An Appreciation of the Six Charter Members of the
   Helen Hunt Club Presented to the Club on Founder's Day, September Six, Nineteen
   Twenty" (unpublished manuscript). 6 September 1920. **CC**
———. "Union Memories." In Mary Margaret Kern, "The Memorial Union" (pamphlet).
   1927. **PU**

———. "Why Short-horns Are the Best Cattle for Indiana Farms" (speech). In *Indiana State Board of Agriculture Annual Report*, 1905, vol. 46, 317–18. **HR**

———. "Woman's Department, World's Columbian Exhibition" (speech). In *Indiana State Board of Agriculture Annual Report*, 1892, vol. 33. **HR**

"Miss Lucy Wade Dies in Hospital." *Purdue Exponent* 36, no. 44 (23 October 1924): 1.

"Miss Wade Will Be Buried This Morning." *Purdue Exponent* 36, no. 46 (25 October 1924): 1.

"A Mother-Daughter Team." *Purdue University Perspective*, Spring 1997, 4.

"The Motherless Child." *Breeder's Gazette* 82 (7 December 1922): 814.

"Mrs. [Amelia Earhart] Putnam to Lecture at Special Convo." *Purdue Exponent* 47, no. 41 (6 November 1935): 1. In Scrapbook 20, Amelia Earhart Papers. **PU**

"Mrs. H. C. Meredith, Farm Expert, Dead. Indiana Woman, 88, Became a National Figure as an Agriculture Lecturer." *New York Times*, 11 December 1936.

"Mrs. H. C. Meredith's Offering." *Breeder's Gazette* 40 (26 May 1887): 832.

"Mrs. Henry C. Meredith's Short-Horn Sale." *Breeder's Gazette* 7 (25 June 1895): 966–67.

"Mrs. Meredith, Famed Hoosier Leader, Is Dead. Queen of Agriculture and Purdue Trustee for Many Years Expires at 88 and Leaves Valued Heritage." *Lafayette (Ind.) Journal and Courier*, 11 December 1936.

"Mrs. Meredith's Ambition." *Chicago Daily Tribune*, 16 August 1891.

"Mrs. Meredith's Sale of Short-Horns." *Cambridge City (Ind.) Tribune*, 26 May 1887.

"Mrs. Meredith's Short-Horns and Southdowns." *Breeder's Gazette* 28 (28 August 1895): 136.

"Mrs. Meredith, Trustee, Awarded Signal Honor." *Purdue Exponent* 41, no. 113 (4 February 1930): 1.

"Mrs. Meredith Will Officiate at Dedication." *Purdue Exponent* 46, no. 23 (9 October 1934): 1.

"Mrs. Virginia Claypool Meredith." *Journal of Home Economics* 29, no. 3 (March 1937): 180.

"Mrs. Virginia C. Meredith, Honorary President I. F. C." *Indiana Club Woman* 9, no. 4 (May–June 1930): n.p. **GF**

"Mrs. Virginia Meredith." *Lafayette (Ind.) Journal and Courier*, 12 December 1936.

"Mr. Thacher Offers 60, Where 130 are Requested—Lady Managers Must Meet." *Chicago Daily Tribune*, 30 June 1893.

Murphy, Lillian. Tribute to Virginia C. Meredith. In "Virginia C. Meredith—A Trustee of Purdue University. 1921–1936, Purdue University" (memorial service program). 12 January 1937. Virginia Meredith Collection. **PU**

National Personnel Records Center. Letter to Frederick Whitford, 16 January 2007.

"A New Bull for the Meredith Herd." *Breeder's Gazette* 8 (24 September 1885): 492.

"A New Contributor." *Breeder's Gazette* 24 (13 December 1893): 390.

"A New Outlook Changes the Inlook—Reading and Music in Farm Homes—A Farmer's Wife Loves the Tennessee Mountain Country—'Duffy's Whiskey' and Old Age." *Breeder's Gazette* 80 (29 September 1921): 441.

"Next Christmas." *Breeder's Gazette* 90 (25 November 1926): 594.

"No. 1 Purdue Woman Still Active at 87" (newspaper clipping). N.p., 4 January [1936]. In folder marked "Meredith," Purdue University Board of Trustees files. **PU**

"Norborough Short-horns." *Breeder's Gazette* 61 (10 April 1912): 900.

"Notable Chicagoans Revive World's Fair Memories: Pleas for Art." *Chicago Daily Tribune,*
    1 February 1923.

Note about Virginia C. Meredith becoming godparent to the School of Agriculture Class
    of 1901. Circa 1901. In folder marked "History 1885," Box 1, School of Agriculture
    Records (Collection 343). **MN**

"Oakland Farm and Its Owners." *Ohio Farmer,* 8 May 1902, 440.

"Obituary—Hon. H. C. Meredith." *Richmond (Ind.) Evening Item,* 6 July 1882.

"Official Program, Richmond Chautauqua." *(Richmond, Ind.) Daily Sun-Telegram,*
    25 August 1906.

Ogborn, Argus. Interview with Allison Feemster, 1 April 1964 (two-page, handwritten
    note). **CC**

"One of State's Outstanding Women." *Richmond (Ind.) Item,* 5 January 1936.

"One of 'The Gazette's' Most-Esteemed Contributors This Week Assumes Editorial Charge
    of a Page To Be Devoted to the Women and the Boys and Girls of the Stock-Farm
    Home." *Breeder's Gazette* 79 (12 May 1921): 858.

"One Woman to Another." *Breeder's Gazette* 96 (October 1931): 8.

"Palette Club Exhibit Will Open on May 19. Portrait of Mrs. Meredith by King To Be Feature
    of Spring Show." *Richmond (Ind.) Palladium and Sun-Telegram,* 18 May 1929.

Palmer, Bertha. General correspondence and papers, 1891–94 (vol. 10–17). **WCE**

Peck, Adel Thompson. Letter to Juniata Shepperd, 23 June 1923. In folder marked "History.
    Virginia Meredith," College of Home Economics (Collection 2006-00024). **MN**

"Portrait Features Palette Club Exhibit." *Richmond (Ind.) Palladium and Sun-Telegram,*
    21 May 1929.

Post, Margaret Moore. "Mrs. Meredith Served Agriculture." *Indianapolis News,*
    28 January 1976.

"Poultry Projects Interest and Reward Young Folk in California and Illinois, and Dairy
    Calves Are Appreciated by a Kentucky Girl and a Wyoming Boy Who Care for Them
    Intelligently." *Breeder's Gazette* 80 (14 July 1921): 52.

"A Preble Co., O[hio]., Institute." *Ohio Farmer,* 17 March 1906, 315.

"Principal Events of the Last Seven Days in World's Fair Circles." *Chicago Daily Tribune,*
    22 August 1891.

"Principal Tucker Asked to Resign." *Farmer's Guide* 19, no. 12 (15 June 1903): 255.

"Prize Essays and Poems on Art Exhibit Announced." *Purdue Exponent* 39, no. 163
    (31 March 1928): 1.

"Prize Winning Picture Donated as Memorial." *Purdue Exponent* 39, no. 181 (21 April
    1928): 1.

"Program Will Pay Tribute to Mrs. Meredith." *Purdue Exponent* 48, no. 71 (13 January
    1937): 1.

"Public Sale of Short-Horns by Mrs. Virginia C. Meredith at Cambridge City, Ind."
    Breeder's Gazette 19 (May 13, 1891): 376.

"Purdue Honors 15 Women Pioneers." *Lafayette (Ind.) Journal and Courier,*
    3 September 2006.

Purdue University. Board of Trustees meeting minutes. 12 June 1874–20 January 1937.
    Office of the Purdue University Board of Trustees, Hovde Hall, West Lafayette, Ind.

————. College of Consumer and Family Sciences. "Foods and Nutrition: Avanelle Kirksey" Web site, last accessed 28 November 2007. <http://www.cfs.purdue.edu/fn/alumni/Kirksey2007.shtml>

————. College of Consumer and Family Sciences. List of monetary gifts to purchase *An Old Red Dress*. N.d. Virginia Meredith Collection. **PU**

————. Council on the Status of Women. "Women Pioneers of Purdue University" (booklet). 30 August 2006. Virginia Meredith Collection. **PU**

————. *The Debris* (student yearbook). 1925–28. **PU**

————. Department of Animal Sciences. "Indiana Livestock Breeder's Association Hall of Fame" Web site. Last accessed 28 November 2007. <http://www.ansc.purdue.edu/ilba/HallOfFame.htm>

————. Faculty meeting minutes. 25 January 1937. Office of the Purdue University Board of Trustees, Hovde Hall, West Lafayette, Ind.

————. Ninth Announcement of the Winter School of Agriculture. 4 January to 19 March 1897. **PU**

————. Office of the Registrar. Phone conversation with Frederick Whitford, 2007.

————. Personnel records of Mary L. Matthews, 1912–35. In Purdue University personnel files, Freehafer Hall, West Lafayette, Ind.

————. "Presentation To Honor Women Pioneers Through Purdue's History" (press release). 30 August 2006. Virginia Meredith Collection. **PU**

————. "Purdue Memorial Union. 75 Years. 1924–1999" (brochure). 1999. **PU**

————. *Purdue University Farmers' Institutes Annual Reports, 1889–1911.* N.p., [1911]. W. C. Latta Collection. **PU**

————. Reamer Club. *A University of Tradition: The Spirit of Purdue.* West Lafayette, Ind.: Purdue University Press, 2002.

————. "Reports of the President and Other Officers of Purdue University for the Biennium Ending September 30, 1928." *Bulletin of Purdue University,* no. 8, May 1930. **PU**

————. School of Consumer and Family Sciences. "Virginia C. Meredith: The Driving Force." In *Inspiring Families and Building Communities for 75 Years* (calendar and essays). 2001. Virginia Meredith Collection. **PU**

————. School of Home Economics Faculty. Memorial Resolution for Dean Emeritus Mary Lockwood Matthews (two-page typed document). 18 June 1968. Virginia Meredith Collection. **PU**

"Queen of American Agriculture Completes Career. Purdue Trustee for Many Years Expires; Leaves Valued Heritage." *Purdue Alumnus* 24, no. 3 (December 1936): 4.

"Queen of American Agriculture." *International Altrusan* 13, no. 8 (April 1936): 8–9.

"Reports Are Nearly Complete. Work of Board of Lady Managers of World's Fair about Done." *Chicago Daily Tribune,* 8 November 1895.

"The Response of Boys and Girls to Modern Methods of Teaching—A Kansas Club Member's Letter—An Indiana Lad Who Grew Watermelons This Year—An Iowa Breeder's Son Who Is Raising Duroc-Jerseys." *Breeder's Gazette* 80 (22 September 1921): 408.

"Review of the Week in Detail: Work of Columbian Exposition Officials During the Last
  Seven Days." *Chicago Daily Tribune,* 23 May 1891.

Robbins, Earl E. "Memorial from the Indiana Livestock Breeders' Association." In "Virginia C.
  Meredith—A Trustee of Purdue University. 1921–1936, Purdue University" (memorial
  service program). 12 January 1937. Virginia Meredith Collection. **PU**

Ross, David E. "From the University Trustees." In "Virginia C. Meredith—A Trustee of
  Purdue University. 1921–1936, Purdue University" (memorial service program).
  12 January 1937. Virginia Meredith Collection. **PU**

"Sale of South Downs at Oakland Farm." *Cambridge City (Ind.) Tribune,* 18 September 1884.

"Salon Day at the Arche Club. Chicago Painters and Sculptors Will Be Discussed by Mrs.
  Mary Ford." *Chicago Daily Tribune,* 26 March 1895.

"The School of Agriculture." *Farm, Stock, and Home* 19, no. 13 (1 July 1903): 270. **MN**

"School of Home Economics—Biographical Sketch of Dean Mary L. Matthews."
  Purdue Alumnus 17, no. 6 (March 1930): 5.

"Second Annual Conference on Home Economics." Proceedings from conference held
  3–7 July 1900 at Lake Placid, N.Y. **HR**

Seymour, E. L. D. *Farm Knowledge: A Complete Manual of Successful Farming Written
  by Recognized Authorities in All Parts of the Country; Based on Sound Principles
  and the Actual Experience of Real Farmers.* Vol. 4 of *Farm Life.* Garden City, N.Y.:
  Doubleday, Page, & Company, 1918.

Sheehan, Mrs. Frank J. *The Indiana Club Woman: Historical Edition,* July/August 1927, 4. **GF**

Shepherd, Rebecca, et al. "Newton Claypool." In *A Biographical Directory of the Indiana
  General Assembly,* vol. 1, 1816–1899. Select Committee on the Centennial History of
  the Indiana General Assembly in cooperation with The Indiana Historical Bureau, 1980.

"Shoals Forest in Dedication." *Shoals (Ind.) News,* 3 June 1938.

"Short-Horn Breeders in the Hoosier State." *Breeder's Gazette* 19 (28 January 1891): 65.

"The Short-Horn Cattle Sale. Fair Attendance, but Prices Rule Light." *Cambridge City (Ind.)
  Tribune,* 25 April 1889.

"The Shorthorn Sale." *Cambridge City (Ind.) Tribune,* 28 September 1905.

Shults, Ophelia. "Supplemental Sketch." In "An Appreciation of the Six Charter Members
  of the Helen Hunt Club Presented to the Club on Founder's Day, September Six,
  Nineteen Twenty" (unpublished manuscript). 6 September 1920. **CC**

Smith, William Henry. *The History of the State of Indiana from the Earliest Explorations by
  the French to the Present Time: Containing an Account of the Principal Civil, Political
  and Military Events from 1763 to 1903,* vol. 11. Indianapolis: Western Publishing
  Company, 1903.

Stuart, Allison E. Letter to Edward C. Elliott, 21 December 1926. In folder marked
  "4 January 1927," Purdue University Board of Trustees records, Hovde Hall,
  West Lafayette, Ind.

"Summer Dairy Meeting." *Indiana Farmer's Guide,* 31 July 1920, 13.

"Talks with, by, and about Boys and Girls Who Are Keenly Interested in Clubwork,
  Which Is Supported by Breeders, Farmers, and Businessmen." *Breeder's Gazette* 79
  (19 May 1921): 901.

"They Achieve." *Indianapolis Star,* 14 June 1947.

"They Want 140 Women Judges. Lady Managers Prepare a List and Submit It to Mr. Thacher." *Chicago Daily Tribune,* 29 June 1893.

"Thinks It May Be Refused." *Chicago Daily Tribune,* 6 August 1892.

Thompson, Dave O. *A History: Fifty Years of Cooperative Extension Service in Indiana.* N.p., [1962]. Life Sciences Library, Purdue University, West Lafayette, Ind.

"To Censure Mrs. Ball: Board of Lady Managers Rehearses Personal Matters." *Chicago Daily Tribune,* 5 August 1893.

"To Dedicate Forest Site Near Shoals." *Shoals (Ind.) News,* n.d.

"To Discuss the Subject of Awards." *Chicago Daily Tribune,* 7 January 1893.

"To Give Diplomas. Lady Managers' Plan to Outwit John Boyd Thacher." *Chicago Daily Tribune,* 17 October 1893.

Topping, Robert W. "Austin Bingley Claypool." In *The Book of Trustees: Purdue University, 1865–1989.* West Lafayette, Ind.: Purdue University, 1989.

"Trains Girls as Farmers. Agricultural School of Minnesota Teaches Them Art of Husbandry. On a Par with Men." *Chicago Daily Tribune,* 15 October 1899.

"A Trio of Notable Women." *The Atlanta Journal,* n.d. Virginia Meredith Collection. **PU**

"Trustees Authorize Economics Building." *Purdue Alumnus* 8 (May 1921): 8.

"Two Noted European Visitors, A Woman's Tribute to a Cornbelt Farm Home, and an Experiment in Running a Household According to a Schedule." *Breeder's Gazette* 80 (18 August 1921): 220.

Ulrich, R. L. "Oakland Farm: The History of a House" (pamphlet). Cambridge City, Ind.: The Simplistic Press, 1972. **CC**

University of Minnesota. Board of Regents executive committee minutes, 13 August 1903. In vol. 9, April 1903 to 16 March 1905. **MN**

———. Board of Regents meeting minutes, 3 June 1903. In folder marked "Regents Minutes: 1903–1910," Box 13, Ag. Director's Office (Collection 922). **MN**

———. College of Agriculture. Course description for home economics classes taught by Virginia Meredith. *University of Minnesota Bulletin* 3, no. 10 (1 July 1900): 15. **MN**

———. College of Home Economics. "Hist. Home Economics—Virginia Meredith" (folder). Archives (Collection 2006-00024). **MN**

———. College of Home Economics. "History of the Division of Home Economics" (unpublished manuscript). 1925. In folder marked "HE History," College of Home Economics (Collection 2006-00024). **MN**

———. College of Human Ecology. "Centennial 100—Presented April 2000." *Kaleidoscope,* Spring 2006, 24. Virginia Meredith Collection. **PU**

———. College of Human Ecology. *Journey Home: A Celebration and Evolution of Home Economics at the University of Minnesota.* St. Paul, Minn.: University of Minnesota College of Human Ecology, 1998.

———. School of Agriculture. "Come to the School of Agriculture at University Farm, St. Paul." *University of Minnesota Bulletin* 6, no. 8 (10 May 1903). **MN**

———. School of Agriculture. Course Catalog. In *University of Minnesota Bulletin* 1, no. 2 (1 April 1898): 22–26. **MN**

———. School of Agriculture. Course Catalog. In *University of Minnesota Bulletin* 4, no. 9 (1 July 1901): 30. **MN**

University of Minnesota. *University of Minnesota Bulletin* 3, no. 10 (1 July 1900): 9. **MN**
———. *University of Minnesota Bulletin* 4, no. 9 (1 July 1901): 30. **MN**
Untitled. *Breeder's Gazette* 18 (31 December 1890): 515.
Untitled. *Breeder's Gazette* 24 (8 November 1893): 310.
Untitled. *Breeder's Gazette* 32 (4 August 1897): 65.
Untitled. *Breeder's Gazette* 81 (23 February 1922): 260.
Untitled. *Cambridge City (Ind.) Tribune*, 13 January 1881.
Untitled. *Cambridge City (Ind.) Tribune*, 14 May 1891.
Untitled. *Cambridge City (Ind.) Tribune*, 26 October 1893.
Untitled. *Cambridge City (Ind.) Tribune*, 21 February 1895.
Untitled. *Cambridge City (Ind.) Tribune*, 4 March 1895.
Untitled. *Cambridge City (Ind.) Tribune*, 28 May 1903.
Untitled. *Cambridge City (Ind.) Tribune*, 11 June 1903.
Untitled. *Cambridge City (Ind.) Tribune*, 17 September 1903.
Untitled. *Cambridge City (Ind.) Tribune*, 20 October 1904.
Untitled. *Cambridge City (Ind.) Tribune*, 21 September 1905.
Untitled. *Cambridge City (Ind.) Tribune*, 12 May 1910.
Untitled. *Farm Students' Review* 1, no. 11 (November 1896): 161. **MN**
Untitled. *Farm Students' Review* 2, no. 12 (December 1897): 377. **MN**
Untitled. *Farm Students' Review* 4, no. 5 (April 1899): 56. **MN**
Untitled. *Farm Students' Review* 7, no. 1 (January 1902): 9. **MN**
Untitled. *Farm Students' Review* 7, no. 5 (May 1902): 73. **MN**
Untitled. *Gopher* 31 (1918): 92. In folder marked "Hist. Home Economics—Mary Matthews," College of Home Economics (Collection 2006-00024). **MN**
Untitled. *The Indiana Club Woman* 6, no. 4 (4 June 1898): n.p. **GF**
Untitled. *Massachusetts Ploughman and New England Journal of Agriculture*, 21 July 1900, 4.
Untitled. *(Richmond, Ind.) Daily Sun-Telegram*, 12 June 1906.
Untitled. *Richmond (Ind.) Telegram*, c. 28 April 1870. Private collection of the Robert Miller Family.
Untitled. *Southern Planter*, March 1892, 136.
Untitled. *University of Minnesota Ariel* 20, no. 33 (3 June 1897): 35. **MN**
Untitled. *University of Minnesota Ariel* 22, no. 26 (1 April 1899): 365. **MN**
U.S. Bureau of the Census. *Indiana, Wayne Township, U.S. Tenth Census of Agriculture, 1880.* Reel 3966. Washington, D.C., 1880. Indiana State Archives, Indianapolis.
———. *U.S. Census, 1880, Jackson, Wayne, Indiana.* Family History Library Film 1254322, NA film number T9-0322, 165A. <www.ancestry.com>
U.S. Census Office. "Occupations (Table CIII) from the U.S. Census, 1880." In *Compendium of the Tenth Census* (1 June 1880). Washington, D.C.: Government Printing Office, 1885.
U.S. Department of the Treasury. "United States Mint" Web site. Last accessed 28 November 2007. <http://www.usmint.gov/>
U.S. Works Progress Administration. *Indiana and Indianans.* Indianapolis: Indianapolis Public Library, 1939.
"Virginia Claypool Meredith." *Indianapolis Star*, 12 December 1936.

"Virginia Claypool Meredith" (unpublished manuscript). N.p., n.d. Private collection of Norma Bertsch.

"Virginia C. Meredith." In *Biographical and Genealogical History of Wayne, Fayette, Union, and Franklin Counties, Indiana, vol. 1.* Chicago: Lewis, 1899.

"Virginia Meredith Dies in Lafayette." *Indianapolis Star,* 11 December 1936.

"Virginia Meredith, 'Queen of Agriculture' Dies in Lafayette." *Indianapolis News,* 11 December 1936.

"Virginia Meredith, Queen of Agriculture, Is Dead." *Richmond (Ind.) Palladium and Sun-Telegram,* 11 December 1936.

Wakeman, Antoinette Van Hoesen. "Women as Stock Farmers." *The Chautauquan* (weekly news magazine), 15 September 1892, 736.

Walters, Jack Edward, ed. *The Semi-Centennial Alumni Record of Purdue University.* West Lafayette, Ind.: Purdue University, May 1924.

"Waymarks for Women." *Congregationalist,* 14 September 1899, 351.

Webster, Phyllis. E-mail to Frederick Whitford, 8 January 2007.

————. E-mail to Frederick Whitford, 16 June 2007.

Weimann, Jeanne Madeline. *The Fair Women: The Story of the Woman's Building, World's Columbian Exposition, Chicago.* Chicago: Academy Chicago, 1981.

"What Women Have Done: A Report of Their World's Fair Work Prepared and Submitted." *Chicago Daily Tribune,* 28 July 1891.

"When Lincoln's Funeral Train Passed Through Cambridge City." *Cambridge City (Ind.) Tribune,* 26 April 1928.

White, Esther Griffin. "Virginia Claypool Meredith. Combing the Widest Culture with the Acumen of the Practical Woman of Affairs, She Is Known as a Successful Stock-Breeder as Well as a Lecturer and Writer." *Dignam's Magazine* 3, no. 1 (September 1905): 5–6. Morrison-Reeves Library, Richmond, Ind.

Whitford, Frederick, and Andrew G. Martin. *The Grand Old Man of Purdue University and Indiana Agriculture: A Biography of William Carroll Latta.* West Lafayette, Ind.: Purdue University Press, 2005.

Who-When-What Co., The. "Mrs. Virginia C. Meredith." In *The Who-When-What Book.* Chicago: The Who-When-What Co., 1900. Indiana State Library, Indianapolis.

"Will Dedicate Residence Hall This Morning. Mrs. Meredith to Preside." *Purdue Exponent* 46, no. 31 (20 October 1934): 5.

"Will Give Awards to Artisans. President Cleveland Signs the Bill Championed by the Lady Managers." *Chicago Daily Tribune,* 9 December 1893.

"A Woman as a Farmer. The Success of Mrs. Virginia C. Meredith. One of the Best Known Stock Raisers in the State—Her View of the Farming Business." *Indianapolis News,* 3 January 1900.

"Woman Trustee of Purdue Is Honored. Wisconsin Tribute Paid Mrs. V. C. Meredith." *Muncie Morning Star,* 3 February 1930.

"Women and the Farm—I." *Breeder's Gazette* 24 (13 December 1893): 391.

"Women and the Farm—II." *Breeder's Gazette* 24 (27 December 1893): 432.

"Women and the Farm—III." *Breeder's Gazette* 25 (3 January 1894): 3.

"Women and the Farm—IV." *Breeder's Gazette* 25 (10 January 1894): 18.

"Women and the Farm—V." *Breeder's Gazette* 25 (17 January 1894): 34.

"Women and the Farm—VI." *Breeder's Gazette* 25 (24 January 1894): 50.

"Women and the Farm—VII." *Breeder's Gazette* 25 (31 January 1894): 67.

"Women and the Farm—VIII." *Breeder's Gazette* 25 (7 February 1894): 83.

"Women at a Banquet. Last Social Function of the Board of Lady Managers." *Chicago Daily Tribune,* 4 November 1893.

Women's Clubs of Indiana. "Indiana Federation of Clubs Year Book. 1910–1938." **GF**

———. "Indiana State Federation of Clubs Manual. 1906–1907." **GF**

———. "Indiana State Federation of Clubs Year Book." 1907–1910. **GF**

———. "Minutes of the Trustees: 1912–1925." **GF**

"Women's Hall at Purdue Scene of Dedication Rites." *Lafayette (Ind.) Journal and Courier,* 20 October 1934.

"Women to Aid the Unions." *Chicago Daily Tribune,* 10 May 1900.

"Women Who Run Their Own Farm and Make Them Pay." *Chicago Daily Tribune,* 18 November 1900.

"A Work of Art." *Scrivener* 1, no. 3 (May 1928): 31. **PU**

"Work of the Lady Managers." *Chicago Daily Tribune,* 22 April 1891.

"Work of the Women. Some of the Things Accomplished by the Great World's Fair." *Chicago Daily Tribune,* 6 October 1894.

World's Columbian Exposition. Board of Lady Managers Vol. 1, Official Record. **WCE**

———. Board of Lady Managers Vol. 2, Executive Committee Minutes. 8–30 April 1891. **WCE**

Yandell, Enid, Jean Loughborough, and Laura Hayes. "To the Board of Lady Managers." In *Three Girls in a Flat.* Chicago: Knight, Leonard, and Co., 1892.

Young, Andrew White. *History of Wayne County, Indiana, From Its First Settlement to the Present Time; With Numerous Biographical and Family Sketches.* Cincinnati, Ohio: R. Clarke & Co., 1872.

Young, H. E. "25 Years of Extension Work in Indiana: Historical Narrative and Achievement Summary." West Lafayette, Ind.: Purdue University, 1939.

Index

Page numbers in bold refer to photos.

Purdue University presidents
Elliott, Edward. *See* Elliott, Edward C.
Jischke, Martin, 238
Marshall, Henry. *See* Marshall, Henry W.
Owen, Richard, 6
Potter, Andrey, 253, 307
Shortridge, Abraham, 6
Stone, Winthrop. *See* Stone, Winthrop
Purdue University publications
*A History: Fifty Years of Cooperative
Extension Service in Indiana*
(Thompson), 208
Outline History of Indiana Agriculture
(Latta), 300
*Proceedings of the Semi-Centennial
Observance* (Babcock), 255
Purdue Agriculturist, 241
Purdue Alumnus, 305
Purdue Exponent, 294
Purdue University: Fifty Years of Progress
(Hepburn & Sears), 255

Quakers, 8
"Queen of American Agriculture," 61–62,
101, 360, 361, 363

Railroads
Farmers' Institute travel, 52, 60, 62
lines, 14, 146, 157
Meredith family connection, 14, 16, 20
World's Fair and, 136, 146–47, 157
Rand McNally Building, 160
Randolph County, Indiana, 260
Randolph County, Virginia, 1
Reitz, Wilhelmina, 134, 145
Republican National Convention (1856), 14
Residence halls. *See* Dormitories
Reynolds, Andrews, **321**
Richmond, Indiana, 40, 44, 113, 114, 123
*Richmond (Ind.) Palladium and Sun-
Telegram,* **100,** 187
Richmond National Bank, 27
Richmond Palette Club, 255
Riverside Cemetery, Cambridge City, 44–45,
100, 307
"Roads of Remembrance" speech, 271, 302,
309, 356–59

Robbins, Earl, 42, 307
Robert Dale Owen Memorial fund, 122
Roberts, Ralph E., 264, 266
Roberts (professor), 64
Ross, David E.
memorial for Stone, 244
photo of, **321, 322, 328, 329**
and Purdue Memorial Union
construction, 272–75, 279
as Purdue Trustee, 236, 242, 252, 266
on VCM, 308, 336
and women's dormitory projects, 285, 286,
294, 296
Rushville, Indiana, 58
Russell, Phillip, 288, 290, 291, 293

Salazar, Zampini (Countess of Italy), 179
Schoenholtz, Wilhelmina, 250–51
Scholarships, 121–22. *See also* Education
loans
Scholer, Walter, 287, 288
Schools. *See* Purdue University; Universities;
University of Minnesota
Science behind farming, 70
Scientific advances, 80
Sears, Louis M., 230, 255
Secretary of Board of Lady Managers, 140,
141, 149, 151–53
Sewall, May Wright, 144, 145
Seymour, E. L. D., 72
Shealy, Frances M., 295, 297
Sheep. *See also* Livestock
Southdown sheep, xi, 16–17, 20, 22
VCM as speaker at Interstate Farmers'
Institute, 60–62
Shepard-Towner bill, 78
Shepperd, Juniata L., 214, 230
Shoals, Indiana, 127, **192**
Shoemaker, Carolyn E., 235, 250–51, 284,
286, 288, 292, 294
Shorthorn cattle. *See also* Livestock
bulls, 30, 31, 41, **99**
sales and purchases by VCM, 29–31, 38, 40
Solomon Meredith's, 16–17, 20–21
VCM management of, xi, 22, 30–32
VCM speech on, 343–45
winning heifer, 42